the GirL can't CooK

Cinda Chavich

the Girl can't Cook

275 fabulous no-fail recipes a girl can't be without

illustrations by Kirsten Horel

whitecap

Many thanks to Kirsten for bringing my vision of The Girl to life with her art; to Robert, Robin, Elaine and Roberta at Whitecap for their confidence, support and expertise in making this book a reality; and to all of the cooks, chefs and girlfriends who have inspired me.

Cinda Chavich

Copyright © 2004 by Cinda Chavich
Whitecap Books

Edited by Elaine Jones
Proofread by Lesley Cameron
Design by Roberta Batchelor
Illustrations by Kirsten Horel

Printed and bound in Canada

NATIONAL LIBRARY OF CANADA CATALOGUING IN PUBLICATION

Chavich, Cinda
The girl can't cook : 275 fabulous no-fail recipes a girl can't be without / Cinda Chavich.

Includes index.
ISBN 1-55285-526-0

1. Quick and easy cookery. 2. Cookery. I. Title.

TX833.5.C468 2004   641.5′5   C2004-900368-2

The publisher acknowledges the financial support of the Government of Canada through the Book Publishing Industry Development Program for our publishing activities.

Important: Some of the recipes in this book call for the use of raw eggs. Pregnant women, the elderly, young children and anyone with compromised immune system are advised against the consumption of raw eggs. You may wish to consider the use of pasterized eggs. www.aeb.org/safety provides updated information on eggs and food safety.

Contents

Preface

It's time to come clean. The first cookbook I ever owned was called the *I Hate to Cook Cookbook*, a skinny little paperback I bought in a small-town drugstore when I moved out to the middle of nowhere with a guy one summer way back when.

Both were a mistake — although the book, with it's silly anecdotes and 1001 ways to use mushroom soup (also a small-town staple), probably saved me from alternately starving and going insane out there on the bald open prairie.

The moral of this story is the plain truth that, when I left my comfortable middle-class home at age 18, I could not cook. Sure, I had seen steaks grilled, peeled potatoes and husked corn for the pot but, basically, I had no idea how to cook much of anything.

Now that I'm a professional food writer with several cookbooks to my name and hundreds (if not 1001) articles about food and wine published in newspapers and magazines across the continent, it's hard to imagine that Chicken Rice Roger (don't ask) was once one of my specialties. I also found the perfect husband along the way, even though I served him something quite horrific on our first date.

But, like all cooks, I had to start somewhere. And while I know a lot of people who cook exquisite things all the time, I also have a lot of great friends who simply can't — or don't — cook.

It's not that they don't enjoy good food. It's just that they don't think they are capable of making it themselves.

That's where I was way back when I began learning to cook — I learned to cook in self defense. And it wasn't at Le Cordon Bleu or any other culinary school. I needed to eat, so I learned to cook by cooking.

Luckily, the next dime-store paperback recipe book I bought was *Jeannette's Secrets of Everyday Good Cooking*, a basic grounding in French home cooking that soon became as ragged and well-thumbed as the first book and taught me about cream sauces and vinaigrettes and clafouti (not that roasts of veal or celery root were staples in my world).

This girl could not cook, but she was making headway.

Today I have a new goal. I want to teach my friends to make at least a couple of their favorite foods, a meal or two that they can whip out when the mood strikes or duty calls.

Of course, I plan to prove to them, once and for all, that cooking can be fun. But my motivation is again self-defensive. I want to create some new converts to cooking so that next time someone says "I'll shop (or clean) if you cook" or calls for the perfect recipe for their mother-in-law's birthday brunch, I'll just refer them to this book (which I know all of them will buy). More kitchen goddesses means less work for yours truly.

This is my quest. Spread the gospel of simple, satisfying cooking one girl at a time.

I put out the call to some of the kitchen-challenged and busy women I know, offering to talk them through a few of the dishes they love but would never, ever contemplate cooking. Then I developed some tried and true, easy-to-follow recipes for same.

I coached, they cooked. I wrote down every question they asked and explained it in the text.

And guess what? My time-honored old saw — if you can read, you can cook — is no lie. And there's nothing like making something that looks and tastes incredible to spur you on to the next conquest.

This book is not a how-to book or a cooking course, it's a survival manual to get you through life's cooking dilemmas with style. It's loaded with easy instructions and explanations — if you don't understand an ingredient or technique, flip to the glossary in the back or look it up in the index. You'll likely find a tip that will keep you cooking. There are menus for splashy parties and family dinners, ideas for interesting stuff to eat every day and well-tested recipes for appetizers, salads and desserts that you can take anywhere to impress your friends.

So for Jane, Alison, Carol, Anika, Rosemary, Penny, Kirsten, Paula, Molly, Jennifer, Marlene, Shannon, Deanna, Helen, Sharon, Ellen, Lorraine, Mona, Michelle, Cynthia, Susan, Robin, Dorothea, Lisa, Marianne, Anne, Sigrun, Judy, Laura, Janice, Hannah, Madelaine, Debbie, Joceyln, Sarah, Heather, Joanne, Elaine, Maggie and all of those other great girls in my life, young and old, near and far, here's a news flash: The Girls Can Cook!

Introduction

Why would I bother?

Okay, I can hear you harping already.

That Martha Stewart, domestic goddess schtick just isn't your thing. You're into rock climbing, the zen of motorcycle maintenance and the occasional turn around the tango floor. Cooking is for bored housewives and gay men. Furthermore, you're too busy with your job/kids/life to waste time in the kitchen.

I know. When God created Lean Cuisine™ and Swiss Chalet™, she was thinking of you.

While there is truth in all of the above, I'm sure there are also times when you wish you could whip up something simple, elegant and edible that doesn't begin in a box. There are days when a microwave popcorn dinner just doesn't do it for you, when even the best takeout food falls flat.

The day will come (has it?) when you are invited to a potluck party or a baby shower and someone else already has dibs on the bread. Maybe there's a new love you want to lure to your place. Or you just want to feed your family something healthy that you made from scratch.

That's where this book comes riding to the rescue. Not only are the recipes delicious, they're impressive and easy. You can stop at the supermarket on the way home from work on Wednesday and have a great Thai Chicken Salad in your bowl before the credits roll on your favorite 7 p.m. sitcom.

When duty calls, you will show up at the shower/barbecue/holiday dinner with the kind of salad or dessert that will make your mother proud. And when you want to impress someone — or treat yourself to something really special — you'll be astounded at how you were able to serve that steak with a great Bordeaux, and still stay within your budget.

So fill the freezer with frozen food if you like. But make sure you have at least a couple of drop-dead dining tricks in your back pocket for those inevitable days when eating out is not an option.

Keep a copy of this book in your glove compartment and you'll never arrive home bearing cold pizza again. And remember — a girl can discover her inner cook at any age!

The Raw Materials

The old saying "garbage in, garbage out" is the Girl's mantra when it comes to cooking.

She can't stress this point strongly enough. Start with top-quality, tasty ingredients and you will have an instant advantage — the stuff will taste better no matter what you do.

Whenever possible, buy your food locally, directly from the farmer or rancher who grows it or the baker or butcher who makes it. Eat food that's in season — forget about strawberry shortcake in January, make an apple crisp or a chocolate pudding. Spend the extra money to get an authentic artisan cheese or hand-made baguette from a local producer. Then enjoy the simple pleasure of eating something that's made with personal passion, not manufactured in a factory.

You can't make a silk purse (or anything else for that matter) out of a pig's ear, so don't torture yourself in the kitchen trying to work wonders with substandard materials. You wouldn't put watered-down gas in your car or try to climb a mountain with bargain-basement crampons. Treat your body and your kitchen with as much care and respect.

When you start with meat and potatoes, you'll get meat and potatoes (not that there's anything wrong with that). But if you're aiming for an authentic Thai dish, you need to start with authentic ingredients.

Don't be intimidated by using ingredients you haven't tried before. Take it slow. Many ethnic cuisines have wonderful ingredients and convenience products that easily cross over into all of your cooking. For example, a good-quality Indian curry paste makes speedy lamb or chicken curry, but try adding a dollop to some sour cream and mayo for an instant dip or stirring a spoonful into a potato or cauliflower soup for a flavor boost. Italian basil or sundried tomato pesto is another pantry essential — a squeeze of tomato pesto lifts any tomato sauce or stew, and basil pesto thinned with olive oil and a splash of balsamic equals instant salad dressing. You can use pesto instead of fresh basil in any soup or sauce.

But don't be a slave to a recipe, either. If it says lemon juice — try orange juice or vinegar. Apple juice may stand in for white wine, Camembert for Brie. Experiment, play, be creative.

When it comes to fresh fruits, vegetables, meat and fish, buy what's available locally, and in season, and you'll enjoy the finest flavors. Adjust your diet with the seasons — buy a big bag of peppers when they're fresh and cheap and search for a new way to serve them. You'll find your cooking will become instantly more innovative and fun. And you'll stumble upon some amazing recipes that will become part of your own repertoire of favorites.

Good ingredients and the proper tools make cooking easy. Saving a few pennies per pound is a false economy — spend more and you'll eat better quality food that's tastier, easier to cook and likely healthier for you, the environment, the economy and the livelihood of a local farm family.

The Girl hates to preach but she's on her soap box now and she hopes you're listening up. If you take only one concept away from this book, let it be this: Eat locally!

Pantry 101

The best defense is a good offense or, as every Girl Guide knows, be prepared.

That means stocking your pantry and refrigerator with the kind of products that will make your meals taste great, even if you only have the time and energy for a cheese omelet.

Make sure you have good free-range eggs and some flavorful real Parmesan cheese and your omelet will be delicious (and done faster than you can nuke a frozen entrée).

I know, I know, this list looks daunting. But don't panic. Once you find the good Asian grocery and a decent Italian market in your area, you will make sure you have these convenient products in your kitchen at all times. They're some of the secret weapons that good cooks and chefs use to trick you into thinking they've been slaving all day.

Cheese:

Parmigiano-Reggiano (a grating of good-quality Parmesan will save any pasta dish), creamy logs of goat cheese (it can be frozen), feta cheese (keeps indefinitely), grating cheese for pizza (mozzarella, provolone), sliceable cheeses for sandwiches such as Havarti, Cheddar and Gouda (buy it pre-sliced for convenience).

Fats/Oils:

Olive oil (regular and extra virgin), unsalted butter, canola oil, sesame oil.

Vinegars:

Red and white wine vinegar, Japanese mirin and Chinese rice vinegar, balsamic vinegar, cider vinegar.

Seasonings:

Whole black peppercorns (and a decent pepper mill), sea salt, dried basil, thyme leaves, cinnamon, mustard seeds, whole nutmeg, fennel seed, oregano, granulated garlic, chili powder, Hungarian paprika, cumin (whole seed and ground), juniper berries (pick them off the shrubs in the yard), allspice berries (Jamaican food necessity), whole dried chilies, coriander (seeds and powder), white pepper, turmeric, saffron threads.

Sauces/Condiments:

Dijon mustard, curry paste (Thai and Indian), pesto sauce, low-fat mayonnaise, hot sauce (Tabasco in a bottle and Asian chili sauce in a jar), black bean sauce, hoisin sauce, soy sauce, coriander chutney (an Indian staple), good barbecue sauce, lemon juice, Worcestershire sauce, Thai fish sauce, salsa, one good-quality bottled salad dressing.

Olives:

Hit the olive bar at your Italian grocery for some Kalamatas, some nice big green olives and even some that have been marinated and flavored with spices (all make instant appetizers). Get a few cans of anchovy-stuffed olives, and a jar of air-cured black olives (they last forever and make great additions to pasta sauces like Puttanesca, to scatter on pizzas or to use in your own tapenade [page 328]).

Canned Goods:

Low-sodium chicken and beef broth (re-sealable tetra packs are handy), whole and chopped Roma tomatoes, artichoke hearts (packed in water, not oil), black, red and white beans, vegetarian refried beans, kernel corn, beef broth, tomato paste, cans of plain tomato sauce (check labels for no added fats), chickpeas, chipotle chilies, sweetened condensed milk, light coconut milk, canned salmon, tuna and clams, smoked oysters, anchovy fillets, clam juice.

Frozen Goodies:

Smoked salmon, nuts (toasted hazelnuts, almonds, pecans, walnuts, pine nuts), thick Greek-style pita breads (whole-wheat, for instant pizza crusts), sliced air-dried salami, whole-wheat tortilla shells for wraps, goat cheese, fresh Italian sausages, peas, orange juice concentrate, gourmet ice cream or frozen yogurt, puff pastry.

Fresh Essentials Year-Round:

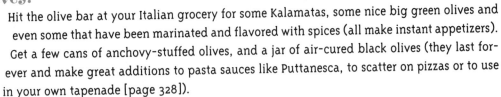

Whole grain bread, large free-range eggs, milk, unsalted butter, cooking onions, green onions, garlic, ginger, tomatoes, English cucumbers, mixed salad greens, romaine lettuce, bell peppers, baking and boiling potatoes (a.k.a white and red), celery, carrots, mushrooms, plain yogurt, sour cream, selection of cheeses, fruits like oranges, lemons, limes, apples, bananas, grapefruit, sturdy herbs like rosemary and thyme.

Dry Goods and Other Stuff:

Maple syrup, good coffee and loose teas, shelf-stable boxes of real orange juice, sundried tomatoes (packed in oil and dried), a variety of long and short dried pasta (fettuccine, rotini, penne, spaghetti), orzo, couscous, egg noodles, Asian rice noodles, tahini (sesame paste), natural peanut butter (no added sugar or hydrogenated fats), honey, real vanilla extract, bittersweet chocolate, raisins, dried apricots and cranberries, red currant jelly, apricot jam, good-quality biscotti, water biscuits/crackers/flatbreads, flour (unbleached, whole-wheat, rye), sugar (granulated, brown and icing sugar), large flake rolled oats, cornmeal, basmati rice, short grain risotto rice (such as Arborio), sushi rice, brown rice, pearl barley, green lentils, popping corn and corn chips (in case all else fails).

Seasonal Fruits and Vegetables:

Buy local and seasonal whenever possible. Farmers' markets, u-pick farms, organic grocers and gourmet shops are all good sources for top-quality local produce. Do your homework and find out who the local growers are, what's in season and stick to it. Some vegetables to try when they're in season locally or look especially fresh in the market include: asparagus, baby artichokes, leeks, wild mushrooms, peas, carrots, green and yellow beans, baby bok choy, corn on the cob, summer squash, new potatoes, beets, kohlrabi, jicama, winter greens like Swiss chard and collard greens, Italian broccoli rabe, cabbage, cauliflower, mung bean sprouts, tomatillos, eggplant, fennel bulbs, sweet and hot peppers, sweet potatoes, rutabagas, parsnips and winter squash. Seasonal fruits include blueberries, peaches, apricots, ox heart plums, pears, rhubarb, strawberries, blood oranges, mangoes, pineapple, quince, clementines, kumquats, watermelon, pomegranates.

Meat/Fish:

Find a great butcher or make friends with an organic farmer. If you frequent the farmers' markets in your town or city in the summer, you'll likely find someone selling their great beef, pastured chicken or amazing lamb. Make an effort to buy locally from good producers and you will always be rewarded with the best meals (and the easiest cooking). Good fresh sausage is another essential — once you find that great local source of fresh Italian sausages, Spanish chorizo and German bratwurst, you will have more essential ingredients in your arsenal. Ditto for a fishmonger. Find someone you trust to provide fresh, high-quality and sustainably caught fish and buy in season.

ROASTED GARLIC

CARAMELIZED ONIONS

REDUCED BALSAMIC VINEGAR

K. HOREL

The Girl's Trilogy
of Trucs

Trucs (tricks for you non-French-speaking girls) are what get most good
cooks through life. The Girl's top three secret weapons are caramelized onions,
roasted garlic and reduced balsamic vinegar. Learn to make these three things,
and everything you make will taste exponentially better. No lie.

1. Caramelized Onions

The Girl is absolutely addicted to onions, and once they've been slowly cooked down into a sweet brown mass (caramelized) you can pile them on or fold them into almost anything with spectacular results. You can make them in advance and keep them in a jar for several days in the refrigerator, or start them an hour before your guests arrive and your house will have that mouthwatering sautéed onion smell that crosses all cultures and age groups on the gotta-have-that scale.

Simply piled on slices of baguette, onions that have been caramelized in good olive oil are an addictive appetizer. Use them on flat bread or scatter them over pizzas, fold them into omelets, add them to simply dressed pastas with black olives and cherry tomatoes, or add them to beef broth and sherry for traditional onion soup. Pile them onto burgers and grilled sausage sandwiches, chop them up for dips and frittatas — a simple caramelized onion is at home at a picnic or a top-drawer cocktail party. Make some now and when you run out, make more.

3 large onions, peeled and thinly sliced
  (white, red and/or yellow)
¼ cup (50 mL) virgin olive oil

1 tsp. (5 mL) sugar
1 tsp. (5 mL) balsamic vinegar

1 Heat the oil in a sauté pan over medium-low heat. Add the onions and stir to coat with the oil. Cover the pan and sweat the onions for 5 minutes. Remove the cover and sauté until the onions begin to turn golden — if they are browning or burning, the heat is too high. Continue to cook on fairly low heat until the onions are very soft and jammy, with a nice color. Stir the sugar and vinegar together and add to the pan, cooking until the liquid is gone. Pile into a bowl and serve warm with bread, or put them in a container and refrigerate until you're ready to use them.

2. Roasted Garlic

This is another item in the Girl's arsenal of great food tricks. So simple yet so effective — after less than an hour in the oven, the aggressive garlic is reduced to a melting mass of sweet, nutty flavor. Make lots of roasted garlic and add it to mashed potatoes, salad dressings, soups and pasta sauces. Or just squeeze it out of the dried roasted skins and slather it on French bread for an easy appetizer. Here's how to do it.

3 heads of garlic
3 tsp. (15 mL) olive oil

1 With a sharp knife, cut off the top $1/2$ inch (1.2 cm) (the pointy part) of each whole head of garlic. You will be able to see the tops of the exposed cloves. Set each head of garlic on a piece of foil, and drizzle with a teaspoon (5 mL) of olive oil. Gather the foil up loosely around the head of garlic to hold the oil around it — the garlic should be wrapped but not sealed. Place the garlic in a preheated 350°F/180°C oven and roast for 45 minutes. Remove the garlic, unwrap and cool slightly. Squeeze the roasted garlic out of the papery husk — it should be reduced to a creamy, sweet, caramel-colored paste. Roasted garlic will keep in a sealed container in the refrigerator for 2 weeks. Have it on hand and ready to use at all times.

3. Reduced Balsamic Vinegar

Well-heeled girls are advised to invest in a bottle of the real *balsamico tradizionale* — that super-expensive, Italian condiment aged for decades in small wooden barrels until it becomes a sweet, syrupy elixir beyond compare. The Girl is still nursing the bottle she brought back from Modena on one of her whirlwind world tours.

But when you're not serving the Queen, you can create a perfectly good syrupy drizzle from a bottle of basic balsamic. The trick is reduction — boiling your balsamic until it's thick and rich. It's up to you how much money you spend on the original bottle of vinegar. The Girl has had success with bottles from the local big box store but be aware that reducing concentrates both fine flavors and faults.

Use this yummy stuff to finish all salads (especially composed salads that cry out for a bit of plate decoration), to drip over grilled fish or veggies, or to brighten any tomato sauce or soup. Try a drop whenever a dish needs a lift.

1 To make it, pour a whole bottle of balsamic vinegar into a stainless steel pot and bring it to a boil. Boil it until it's reduced to $1/4$ of its original volume (if you start with 2 cups/500 mL, boil it down to $1/2$ cup). Do this on a day when you can open the windows as boiling vinegar puts a sharp aroma into the air. Rebottle the vinegar and refrigerate. If you put it into a plastic squeeze bottle with a small tip, you can drip and drizzle it artfully onto plates.

Sustenance

Easy everyday meals that will keep you going
without boring you to death.

Salad Suppers

The Girl is addicted to hearty salad suppers — big bowls of fresh greens and seasonal veggies, topped with grilled meats or cheeses make meals that are not only healthy, they're fast and ultimately satisfying. Creative salads can be a great vehicle for using up leftovers or to showcase fresh, seasonal ingredients.

SALAD

Easy Thai Chicken Salad

This salad is reminiscent of the bowls of noodles and fresh vegetables they serve at Asian noodle houses. Start with a rotisserie chicken, steamed noodles and chopped romaine from the supermarket, and you'll be dining in 30 minutes flat.

If you're feeling really ambitious, and it's a sultry summer evening, grill some fresh chicken instead of going the supermarket rotisserie route. Marinate two boneless breasts in a few tablespoons of the dressing for 15 minutes in a resealable plastic bag while you precook the noodles. Then you can grill the chicken and your salad will have that groovy, smoky, hot/cold thing happening. The Girl has been known to serve this salad on a pretty platter for dinner on the deck — start with the greens, pile the cold noodles in the center, then slice the grilled chicken breasts and fan them artfully on top — too cool!

dressing

1 Tbsp. (15 mL) minced garlic (a garlic press works well)

1 Tbsp. (15 mL) Asian garlic chili paste (a hot condiment called sambal oelek or sambal bajak)

½ cup (125 mL) sweet Indonesian soy sauce (ketjap manis)

6–8 Tbsp. (90–120 mL) fresh lime juice (juice of 1 large lime)

1 Tbsp. (15 mL) sesame oil

salad

½ lb. (250 g) thin Oriental steamed noodles (bagged in the produce department)

6 cups (1.5 L) chopped romaine lettuce or mixed baby greens

½ cup (125 mL) fresh mint leaves, shredded

¼ cup (50 mL) chopped fresh cilantro

1 large carrot, peeled and shredded

½ English cucumber, seeded and cut into matchstick pieces

1 lb. (500 g) barbecued chicken, deboned and slivered (or grill two boneless, skinless chicken breasts)

½ cup (125 mL) finely diced red onion

½ cup (125 mL) dry roasted peanuts, chopped

1 Whirl the dressing ingredients together in a food processor or blender until smooth. The dressing may be made a day in advance and refrigerated.

2 Boil a very large pot of water and add the noodles. Cook them just for a couple of minutes, then drain well in a colander in the sink and rinse under cold water to chill.

3 In a large salad bowl, combine the lettuce, half the mint and half the cilantro, and the shredded carrot. Add just enough dressing to lightly coat the vegetables and toss well. In a separate bowl, toss the cold noodles with some of the remaining dressing (leftover dressing keeps well refrigerated for several days).

4 Divide the salad mixture among four large bowls. Top each salad artfully with a pile of noodles, some cucumber, slivers of cooked chicken, the remaining mint and cilantro, and the onion. Sprinkle with chopped peanuts to garnish. Serves 4.

Girl talk: Ketjap manis, a thick, sweet soy sauce from Indonesia with the consistency of molasses, is the key ingredient in this easy dressing. In a pinch use regular soy sauce, sweetened and thickened with honey or corn syrup (1:1), but make sure to look for the real thing next time you're in the market. It keeps forever.

To "chop" the dry roasted peanuts, simply dump them on the cutting board, place the flat side of your big chef's knife over them and press down — the nuts will crumble into nice small bits, and you won't have them flying around the kitchen.

Girl talk: Don't even think about buying those little cubes of sawdust they sell in boxes at the supermarket and dare to call croutons! Making them is so much better and you can spice them up with whatever you like. Just cut some dense white bread (the Girl likes crusty French or Italian white or sourdough) into 1/2–inch (.5–cm) cubes (it's a great way to use up stale bread and buns). Put the cubes in a large bowl and drizzle with a couple of tablespoons (30 mL) of olive oil. Season with a clove of minced garlic or some garlic powder, some salt and pepper. Get creative if you like — basil and oregano, even cumin, add interesting nuances. Toss to coat the croutons with oil and flavorings, then dump them out on a cookie sheet and toast them in a 400°F (200°C) oven for 10–15 minutes until golden and crisp. Set aside to cool, then store in a covered container or plastic bag at room temperature. Croutons keep indefinitely.

Grilled Chicken Caesar

Top the classic caesar with grilled chicken and it's supper. Some commercial caesar dressings are good, but nothing beats the flavor — and the drama — of creating a perfect caesar from scratch at the table. If you've got strong arms and want to make this at the table, do it by hand. But the Girl prefers the food processor or blender method, for a fast and perfectly emulsified dressing at the touch of a button.

dressing

1 egg yolk

2 anchovies chopped (or 1 tsp./5 mL anchovy paste or Asian fish sauce)

2 Tbsp. (25 mL) fresh lemon juice

1 tsp. (5 mL) Worcestershire sauce

1/4 tsp. (1 mL) salt

dash cayenne pepper or hot sauce

2 cloves garlic, pressed or minced

1/4 cup (50 mL) olive oil

salad

1 chicken breast, skinless and boneless

1/2 head romaine lettuce, washed and torn into bite-sized pieces (about 4–6 cups [1–1.5 L])

1 cup (250 mL) croutons, seasoned with cumin and oregano (see page 22)

1/2 cup (125 mL) freshly grated Parmesan cheese

1 In a large wooden bowl, using a balloon whisk, whisk the egg yolk and anchovies together with the lemon juice until smooth and pale. Add the Worcestershire, salt, cayenne and garlic, and whisk until smooth. Drizzle in the olive oil a few drops at a time, whisking constantly as you add, until the dressing is thick and emulsified. Alternately, put all ingredients except the oil in a food processor, and with the machine running, drizzle the oil in slowly through the feed tube until you have a thick emulsion.

2 Remove 1 Tbsp. (15 mL) of the dressing from the bowl and pour over the chicken breast. Marinate for 5 minutes, then grill the chicken over medium-high heat for 10–12 minutes, brushing with marinade once to glaze after the first 5 minutes of cooking. Discard any leftover marinade. Cook the chicken until it's nicely browned, then slice or chop.

3 When you're ready to eat, add the chopped lettuce to the dressing in the bowl and toss to coat. Add the croutons and grated Parmesan, and toss again. Divide the salad between two plates and top each with half the warm grilled chicken. Serve immediately. Serves 2.

Saganaki on Chopped Tomato, Black Olive and Cucumber Salad

In Greek tavernas, cheeses like kasseri or kefalotyri are often cut in slices, fried in olive oil and served with a squeeze of fresh lemon juice as an appetizer, or meze, with bread and ouzo. The Girl combines the two traditions in this warm salad. Perch a couple of thick slices of golden fried cheese over a traditional Greek salad and voila! — a simple summer supper.

salad

4 large Roma tomatoes, halved, seeds removed and diced

1 green bell pepper, seeded and diced

1 medium or 4 small English cucumbers, quartered lengthwise, seeded and cut into chunks

1/2 cup (125 mL) good-quality Greek olives (like Kalamata)

1 clove garlic, pressed

1 Tbsp. (15 mL) chopped fresh mint

1 Tbsp. (15 mL) chopped fresh oregano

3 Tbsp. (45 mL) virgin olive oil

1 Tbsp. (15 mL) fresh lemon juice

salt and freshly ground black pepper

cheese

1 lb. (500 g) kasseri or kefalotyri cheese, cut into eight slices

2 Tbsp. (25 mL) virgin olive oil

1 Combine the salad ingredients in a large bowl and toss to combine well. Set aside.

2 To fry the cheese, heat the olive oil in a large, nonstick sauté pan over medium-high heat. When the oil is very hot, add the cheese and fry until it is browned on both sides, about a minute per side.

3 Divide the salad among four salad bowls and arrange two slices of fried cheese on top of each. Serve immediately. Serves 2 as a main dish, or 4 as a starter salad.

Japanese Cold Noodle Salad

One of the Girl's favorite summer suppers is a plate of cold noodles and a side of sushi at her local sushi bar. Here is a recipe that approximates that great Japanese classic.

sauce

1/2 cup (125 mL) chicken stock

1/4 cup (50 mL) dark Japanese soy sauce

3 Tbsp. (45 mL) sugar

1/4 cup (50 mL) white vinegar

2 tsp. (10 mL) sesame oil

2 tsp. (10 mL) wasabi or dry mustard powder

salad

2 eggs

1/2 lb. (250 g) steamed Chinese egg noodles
   or ramen

6 dried shiitake mushrooms

1 cup (250 mL) water

2 tsp. (10 mL) sugar

2 tsp. (10 mL) soy sauce

3 green onions, slivered

1/2 English cucumber, seeded and slivered

1 carrot, peeled and slivered or shredded

1 sheet nori (sushi roll seaweed) cut into thin,
   2–inch (5–cm) julienne strips with kitchen shears

1/2 cup (125 mL) slivered barbecued pork or chicken
   (optional)

1 To make the sauce, combine the stock, soy sauce, sugar, vinegar, sesame oil and wasabi and stir well. Chill.

2 Beat the eggs lightly. Heat a 10–inch (25–cm) nonstick pan over medium heat and pour in the eggs. Cook until the omelet is set, then remove from the heat. Turn the omelet out onto a cutting board and chop into thin slivers. Set aside.

3 You'll find the steamed Chinese noodles in bags in the produce department (they need to be kept chilled). Cook the noodles in boiling water until tender, about 8 minutes, then rinse in cold water to chill quickly. Drain well and toss with 1/4 cup (50 mL) of the sauce. Set aside.

4 Soak the dried shiitake mushrooms in hot water for 15 minutes to soften. Place in a small saucepan with the water, sugar and soy sauce. Bring to a boil and simmer until most of the liquid is gone. Remove the mushrooms and cut into slivers.

5 Toss the cold noodles with the slivered mushrooms, omelet, onion, cucumber, carrot and nori, saving some of the cucumber and onion to garnish. Divide the noodles among four serving plates. Pile the slivered pork or chicken, if using, in the center of the noodles and scatter the reserved cucumber and onion around. Pour the remaining sauce over top, dividing evenly. Serves 2–4.

Girl talk: Sometimes noodles (especially the curly steamed Asian variety) seem to stick together in a tangled mop after they're cooked and drained, defying any attempts to toss them with sauces and other additions. If this happens to you, take out your trusty kitchen shears and reach into the mass of noodles, snipping several times in different directions. This will loosen the tangle, but amazingly still leave most of the noodles long and flowing.

Room-temperature Roasted Vegetable Couscous

The Girl loves this hearty fast combination that uses couscous — the Middle Eastern equivalent of Minute Rice. Just roast whatever vegetables you have on hand (feel free to substitute), combine with the stock and couscous and you'll be dining in minutes. It's best served at room temperature. Try it on its own or to round out the Meze Mosh menu, page 141.

1 whole head garlic
2 cups/500 mL cauliflower florets, cut into small
    pieces
1 medium onion, peeled and slivered
1 red bell pepper, seeded and chopped
1 yellow bell pepper, seeded and chopped
1 small zucchini or winter squash, cubed
3 Tbsp. (45 mL) olive oil

1 14-oz. (398-mL) can chickpeas, drained and
    rinsed (1¹/₂ cups/375 mL)
2 cups (500 mL) chicken stock or water
1 tsp. (5 mL) sweet Hungarian paprika
pinch chili flakes
¹/₄ tsp. (1 mL) ground allspice
1¹/₂ cups (375 mL) medium-grain couscous
2 Tbsp. (25 mL) chopped fresh parsley
juice of half a lemon

1 Preheat the oven to 450°F (230°C). Cut the top ¹/₂ inch (1.2 cm) off the head of garlic with a sharp knife to expose the cloves. In a large bowl, combine the garlic, cauliflower, onion, bell peppers and zucchini or squash. Toss with the olive oil to coat and spread the vegetables on a baking sheet. Roast for 25–35 minutes, stirring once or twice, until softened and brown.

2 Place the roasted vegetables in a large saucepan with a lid. Squeeze the roasted garlic out of the head of garlic into the pot, and discard the skin. Stir in the chickpeas, stock or water, paprika, chili flakes and allspice and bring to a rolling boil over high heat.

3 Sprinkle the couscous into the broth and stir to combine. Cover the pot, remove from the heat and let stand 5–10 minutes, until the couscous has absorbed the liquid. Remove the lid, stir again and turn out onto a platter to cool slightly. When it stops steaming but is still warm, sprinkle with parsley and squeeze the lemon juice over top. Serves 2 as a main dish, 4 as a side dish.

Girl talk: Coriander chutney is an East Indian condiment that the Girl always keeps in the fridge. It's essentially like basil pesto, but made with ground cilantro and chilies. Use it when you have no fresh cilantro in the house, but also when your recipe (whether it's Mexican, Southwestern or Southeast Asian) is crying out for the flavor of this unique herb. Find it at Indian groceries and large supermarkets — it's a lifesaver for the gourmet pantry.

Southwestern Chicken and Corn Salad

This makes a fabulous luncheon dish in August, when those first cobs of sweet peaches and cream corn are ready in the garden. Pick them, ferry them directly to your kitchen and make this salad.

dressing

2 green onions, chopped

4 Tbsp. (50 mL) lemon or lime juice

1 tsp. (5 mL) lemon or lime zest

1 tsp. (5 mL) honey

1 tsp. (5 mL) Dijon mustard

3 Tbsp. (45 mL) chopped cilantro leaves
  (or 1 Tbsp./15 mL coriander chutney)

1/4 cup (50 mL) extra virgin olive oil

1 tsp. (5 mL) light soy sauce

1/2 tsp. (2 mL) chili paste or
  (1/4 tsp./1 mL cayenne)

sea salt

salad

4 ears fresh corn

2 boneless, skinless chicken breasts

1 small jicama or young turnip, peeled and
  diced into 1/4–inch (5–mm) pieces

1 red bell pepper, seeded and diced

1 avocado, peeled and diced

2 large ripe tomatoes, seeded and chopped

vegetable oil for frying

6 corn tortillas

sea salt to taste

1 lb. (500 g) mixed salad greens

1 In a blender or food processor, whirl the dressing ingredients together and taste. If you've used lemon instead of lime juice, it might need a touch more honey. Set aside.

2 Remove the leaves and cornsilk from the cobs. Holding the cobs upright on the cutting board, use a sharp knife to remove the kernels, cutting down from the top of the cob to the base. Place the corn kernels in a bowl, along with any of the sweet milky juice that's released.

3 Put the chicken breasts on a plate and drizzle with 1 Tbsp. (15 mL) of the dressing. Rub all over to coat the chicken. Bake the breasts or grill until just cooked (in a 350°F/180°C oven for 30 minutes or about 15 minutes on a hot grill). Set aside to cool and cut into chunks or shreds.

4 Add the chopped jicama (see page 353) or turnip, red pepper, avocado and tomatoes to the corn in the bowl. Add half of the remaining dressing and toss to coat. Set aside.

5 In a nonstick pan, heat about 1/2 inch (1 cm) of canola oil over medium-high heat. Cut the corn tortillas into thin strips. Add them to the hot oil, a few at a time, and deep fry until curled and crisp. Drain on paper towels and sprinkle with a little sea salt.

6 When you're ready to eat, toss the greens with the remaining dressing and divide among four plates. Top each salad with some of the shredded chicken and some of the corn salad. Strew the crispy corn tortilla strips around and serve immediately. Serves 4.

Simple Soups

Soup is a girl's best friend — you can make it in advance, store it in the refrigerator and heat it up whenever the urge to eat hits. Most soups, in fact, actually get better when they have a day or two to let the flavors meld. And once you learn some basic soup techniques, you can create your own soups from the kinds of things we all seem to end up with as leftovers — a portion of cooked rice, a few leftover vegetables, a little pasta sauce or stew. Add some broth, a few vegetables and some spices or fresh herbs, and you'll be eating instantly. Perfect when you're cooking for one.

Solitary Saigon Satay Soup

The Girl is known to hang out in the local Vietnamese noodle house. Bun (cold noodles) in summer and pho (rice noodles in soup in winter) will sustain anyone without ever breaking the bank. One such family-run eatery specializes in Satay Soup — a spicy broth flavored with that yummy coconut and peanut sauce usually reserved for grilled meats. While her favorite Vietnamese chefs make their own satay sauce from scratch, the Girl has found a very passable substitute in a jar at the local Asian grocery store (containing all the good stuff and no MSG). With a can of chicken broth, a packet of instant noodles and some fresh veggies, you'll be slurping this soup in under 10 minutes flat. The perfect dinner for one.

1 tsp. (5 mL) canola oil
1 small onion or large shallot, slivered
2 big cloves garlic, smashed
1–2 Tbsp. (15–25 mL) satay sauce (look for a brand that contains peanuts, coconut, sesame, chilies and maybe even shrimp powder)
2 cups (500 mL) chicken broth
1 cup (250 mL) water

1 Tbsp./15 mL soy sauce
1 package instant noodles (single portion — toss the soup base)
1 green onion, cut into 1–inch (2.5–cm) lengths
1/2 red bell pepper, slivered
12 snow peas slivered
2 tsp. (10 mL) lime juice
cayenne pepper to taste

1 In a saucepan, heat the oil over medium-high heat and add the onion and garlic. Sauté for 1 minute, then add the satay sauce. Stir the sauce for 30 seconds, until fragrant, and pour in the broth, water and soy sauce. Bring to a boil and simmer for 3 minutes.

2 Add the instant noodles, then add the green onion, red pepper and snow peas. Continue to cook a minute or two longer. (Feel free to substitute whatever you have in your fridge — sliced mushrooms, asparagus and bean sprouts are good — and you can add some leftover chicken or barbecued pork or beef strips to your bowl for a heartier meal. Seafood is also good in this soup — raw scallops and shrimps, squid strips or crab can poach along with the veggies.)

3 Before serving, season the soup with lime juice and cayenne pepper. Serve in a big bowl with chopsticks for the noodles and a spoon for the broth. Serves 1 generously.

Girl talk:

Remember those single-serving bags of MSG-loaded noodles and soups that you survived on in college? Well, the Girl has found the noodles (eight instant dried pancakes of egg noodles, sold in a bag without the soup stock) at the local Asian market. They keep indefinitely and are always ready to dump into your own healthy and flavorful broth for instant eating.

Mexican-style Chicken and Tortilla Soup

This is another one-stop supermarket meal that goes together in minutes — pick up some chicken broth, a package of chicken breast fillets, a tomato, a lime and an avocado and you'll be hearing mariachi music before the beer's cold. This recipe serves four if you're serving something else, or makes a light meal for two. Grilled or panfried quesadillas, filled with salsa, cheese and refried beans, make a simple side dish (see page 226).

4 cups (1 L) chicken stock (canned or homemade)
2 plum tomatoes, seeded and finely chopped
juice of 1 lime (about 2 Tbsp./25 mL)
6 drops hot sauce (or more to taste)
1/2 lb. (250 g) boneless, skinless chicken breast
   fillets, cut into bite-sized slivers
freshly ground black pepper

1 cup (250 mL) broken corn chips
   (use a hearty, stone-ground corn chip or a corn
   and bean chip — something substantial that
   won't dissolve in the soup)
1/2 cup (125 mL) shredded Monterey Jack or
   mozzarella cheese
1 firm but ripe avocado, peeled and chopped
2 green onions, chopped
chopped fresh cilantro (optional)

1 In a large saucepan, heat the chicken stock, finely chopped tomato and lime juice over medium-high heat. When the soup beings to boil, reduce the heat to medium-low. Stir in the hot sauce and chicken slivers. Simmer just until the chicken is cooked through, about 2 minutes. Adjust the seasoning to taste with pepper and more hot sauce, and a touch of salt if necessary.

2 Meanwhile, set the table with four wide, shallow soup bowls. In the bottom of each bowl, place a pile of broken tortilla chips. Top with a quarter of the shredded cheese and scatter some of the chopped avocado about. Ladle the hot soup over top, dividing the chicken evenly among the servings. Sprinkle each bowl with some chopped green onion and cilantro and dig in immediately. Serves 4.

Girl talk: If you want to make this soup a little fancier, make your own crisp tortilla chips. Cut fresh corn tortillas into thin strips, and fry in hot oil until crisp. Use them instead of the crumbled tortilla chips for a more dramatic presentation.

Tomato and Lentil Soup

There could be nothing easier than this savory soup — flavored with olive oil and dill, it's like a trip to the Greek islands on a winter afternoon, the classic dish for Lent and other meatless meals. Use the food processor to chop the onions and purée the tomatoes and you'll be eating in 30 minutes flat. A slice of crusty bread, slathered with a piece of creamy, ripe cheese, and a bowl of black olives will finish your meal. Or sprinkle some crumbled feta over each bowl for an added boost of authentic Greek flavor.

1 large onion

1/4 cup (50 mL) flavorful virgin olive oil

2 cloves garlic, minced

1 medium can (about 2 cups/500 mL) Roma tomatoes, puréed (or 1 can plain tomato sauce)

2–3 cups (500–750 mL) chicken broth

1 can (398 mL) brown or green lentils (1 1/2 cups/ 375 mL cooked)

2 Tbsp. (25 mL) chopped fresh dill, divided

1 dried hot chili pepper, crumbled (optional)

1 Tbsp. (15 mL) balsamic vinegar

salt and freshly ground black pepper

crumbled feta cheese (optional)

1 Use the food processor to finely chop the onion. Heat the oil in a soup pot and sauté the onions over medium heat for 10 minutes, until soft.

2 Put the canned tomatoes, juice and all, into the food processor and purée until smooth. Add the purée to the cooked onions in the pot and stir in the broth.

3 Put the lentils in a mesh sieve and run them under cold water. Drain and add the lentils to the soup. Stir in 1 Tbsp. (15 mL) of the dill, the chili pepper if desired, and the balsamic vinegar (if you're stuck with dried dill weed, use 1/3 to half as much). Bring the soup to a boil, then reduce the heat to medium-low and simmer for 30 minutes.

4 Season the soup to taste with salt and pepper. Just before serving, stir in the remaining fresh dill. Ladle into shallow soup bowls and garnish each serving with crumbled feta and more fresh dill, if desired. Serves 4.

Beans and Greens

Fast and healthy — this hearty soup combines simple staples for a speedy weekday meal.

1 medium onion, finely chopped
2 cloves garlic, minced
¼ lb. (120 g) cooked ham, finely chopped
2 Tbsp. (25 mL) olive oil
½ lb. (250 g) winter greens (spinach, mustard greens, chard, etc.)
2 cups (500 mL) chicken broth
2 cups (500 mL) water

½ tsp. (2 mL) thyme
pinch allspice
1 16-oz. can (about 2 cups/ 500 mL) white beans (or substitute other canned beans)
salt and freshly ground black pepper
1 tsp. (5 mL) balsamic vinegar
hot sauce (like Tabasco) to taste

1 In a soup pot, combine the onion, garlic, ham and olive oil and cook over medium heat for 5 minutes.

2 Remove and discard the tough outer leaves and center ribs from the greens, then chop the leaves into small pieces. Add the greens to the pot, along with the broth, water, thyme and allspice. Bring to a boil. Reduce the heat, cover and simmer until the greens are tender, about 20 minutes.

3 Meanwhile, drain and rinse the beans in cold water. Mash half the beans with a fork and stir into the soup, along with the whole beans. Simmer the soup for 10 minutes. Season with salt and pepper and stir in the vinegar. Pass the hot sauce. Serves 2.

BIG
STOCK
OR
SOUP
POT

Killer Clam Chowder

This is the Girl's simplified version of a famous recipe that she wheedled out of one of her chef friends — yes, she does have ways to make them talk. This makes a big pot of soup — enough for a well-attended Christmas Eve soirée or a week of decadent lunches for you. To make fish stock, see page 347.

³/₄ cup (175 mL) butter
¹/₂ cup (125 mL) all-purpose flour
10 cups (2.5 L) fish stock or bottled clam juice
¹/₂ cup (125 mL) chopped carrots
1 cup (250 mL) chopped onions
¹/₂ cup (125 mL) chopped celery
³/₄ tsp. (4 mL) chopped fresh garlic
2 cups (500 mL) peeled and diced potato

1 tsp. (5 mL) chopped fresh thyme
1 tsp. (5 mL) chopped fresh ginger
¹/₈ tsp. (.5 mL) cayenne pepper
salt and white pepper to taste
2 cups (500 mL) half-and-half (cereal) cream
2 cups (500 mL) canned baby clams, juice reserved
minced red pepper and parsley to garnish (optional for everyday but nice for holiday dinners)

1 In a saucepan melt ¹/₂ cup (125 mL) of the butter with the flour and cook, stirring, over medium heat to make a smooth roux. You'll need to stir and cook it together for about 5 minutes.

2 Slowly add the stock to the roux. Whisk the mixture as you gradually add the stock and you won't get any lumps. The resulting thick smooth base is called a fish velouté (la-di-da).

3 In a separate soup pot, melt the remaining ¹/₄ cup (50 mL) of butter over medium-low heat and sauté the carrots, onions, celery and garlic, stirring until the vegetables are soft but not browned. Add the potatoes and the thyme, ginger, cayenne, salt and pepper, and sauté for 5 minutes.

4 Strain the velouté into the pot of sautéed vegetables (straining removes any lumps from the sauce — you can omit this step if you like). Place the chowder over low heat and simmer for 20 minutes, being careful not to burn it.

5 Add the cream and heat through. Adjust the seasoning to taste with salt and white pepper.

6 Stir in the drained clams and heat through. Take care that it doesn't boil — the clams will get tough if you boil them. If your soup is too thick, thin it with some of the reserved clam juice.

7 Ladle the chowder into shallow soup plates and, for a festive touch, sprinkle on a pinch of finely chopped red pepper and parsley. Serve with plenty of French bread. Makes about 12 cups (3 L).

Spicy Mulligatawny

This is one of those soups with both English and Indian roots. It's spicy and exotic, but rather comfortable and familiar, too. Enjoy it as a full meal or to start an Indian feast.

1 cup (250 mL) long grain basmati rice
1 cup (250 mL) coconut milk
1 cup (250 mL) water
$\frac{1}{2}$ tsp. (2 mL) salt
2 Tbsp. (25 mL) olive oil
4 cloves garlic, minced
2 shallots or 1 small onion, minced
3 chicken breast halves, cut into $\frac{1}{2}$–inch
  (1.25–cm) cubes

2 Granny Smith apples, cut into $\frac{1}{2}$–inch
  (1–cm) cubes
1 Tbsp. (15 mL) hot Indian curry paste
  (or more to taste)
6 cups (1.5 L) chicken broth
$\frac{1}{2}$ cup (125 mL) heavy cream
3 green onions, chopped

1   Combine the rice, coconut milk, water and salt and bring to a boil. Cover, reduce the heat to low and simmer until tender. Set aside and keep warm.

2   Heat the olive oil over high heat and sauté the garlic and shallots or onion until just softened. Add the chicken and apples and cook until the chicken is almost cooked through, about 5 minutes.

3   Stir in the curry paste, coating the chicken and apples, and cook together for 1 minute, until the paste is very fragrant. Add the broth, bring to a boil, then reduce the heat to medium-low. Simmer for 15 minutes, until the chicken is cooked but not dried out. Add the cream and heat through.

4   To serve, place about $\frac{1}{3}$ cup (75 mL) of the coconut rice in each individual bowl and ladle hot soup on top. Garnish with chopped green onions. Serves 4–6.

Big Bowl Miso Soup

There's something about miso soup that the Girl craves from time to time. It's always on the menu at her favorite Japanese haunt, but it's so fast to make, it's hardly worth the trip. Add some cooked ramen noodles to each bowl for a more substantial feed.

1 medium carrot, chopped
3 large dried shiitake mushrooms
1/2 cup (125 mL) boiling water
1 tsp. (5 mL) vegetable oil
1/2 small onion, thinly sliced
1 cup (250 mL) bok choy or Chinese cabbage, slivered
4 cups (1 L) vegetable or chicken broth

1/2 lb. (250 g) medium-firm tofu, cut into 1/4–inch (5–mm) cubes (or sliced roasted pork)
1 cup (250 mL) bean sprouts
2 tsp. (10 mL) soy sauce
1/4 cup (50 mL) light miso paste mixed with 1/2 cup (125 mL) boiling water
2 Tbsp. (25 mL) chopped green onion

1 Pre-boil the carrots and mushrooms in the boiling water for 3 minutes. Remove from the heat and drain, reserving the cooking liquid. Slice the mushrooms.

2 In a soup pot or wok, heat the oil over medium-high heat. Add the sliced onion and sauté for 3 minutes. Add the bok choy or cabbage and cook for 3 minutes more.

3 Add the carrots, mushrooms, reserved cooking water and broth to the soup pot. Return to a boil and then reduce the heat to medium. Stir in the tofu cubes (or pork), bean sprouts and soy sauce. Add the miso mixture to the soup and stir. Do not boil. Serve the soup in deep bowls, over some hot cooked ramen noodles if desired. Garnish with green onions. Serves 4.

Soup

Poverty Potage

Here's something to make and eat for that week when you're flat broke — you know, post-Christmas or spring break blues time. This is the Girl's version of Scotch Broth, a great way to stretch a couple of bucks' worth of lamb stew meat, a few root veggies and a handful of barley into a stick-to-your-ribs soup that makes the perfect antidote to winter woes. It's classic fare in every Glaswegian household — how else do you think they afford those pricey single malts?

Ask the butcher at the supermarket for lamb stew meat with bones or lamb shank for this hearty soup. The bones give the broth its special flavor and rich texture. This is the perfect potage to serve in January to celebrate that peasant's poet, Robbie Burns!

½ lb. (250 g) lamb stew meat (shank or
  shoulder), with bones
1 1/2 cups (375 mL) chopped onion
3 stalks celery, chopped
1 tsp. (5 mL) olive oil
4 cups (1 L) chicken broth
5 cups (1.25 L) water
2 cups (500 mL) diced rutabaga

1 cup (250 mL) diced carrots
1 cup (250 mL) pearl barley
1 Tbsp. (15 mL) minced garlic
1 tsp. (5 mL) freshly ground black pepper
1 tsp. (5 mL) chopped fresh thyme (or
  ½ tsp./2 mL dried thyme)
salt to taste

1 Preheat the oven to 450°F/235°C.

2 Using a sharp knife, remove most of the stew meat from the bones. Chop the meat into small cubes and place in a Dutch oven or other large, ovenproof pot. Add the lamb bones, chopped onion, celery and olive oil and stir to combine.

3 Place the pan in the oven for 20–30 minutes, until the bones are browned. (You can also brown the bones on the stove top over medium-high heat, until everything in the pot is beginning to brown.) This browning step adds a lot of flavor to your broth, so don't skip it.

4 Add the broth, water, rutabaga and carrots and bring to a boil. Cover the pot, reduce the heat to low, and simmer for 30 minutes. Remove the lid, add the barley, garlic, pepper and thyme and continue to simmer for 45 minutes, until the barley is tender and the soup is thick.

5 Remove the soup bones from the pot; remove any meat that you can and add it to the soup. Discard the bones. Thin the soup, if necessary, with a little more water. Season with salt and serve. Makes 8 hearty servings (and keeps well in the refrigerator for several days).

Girl talk: Rutabagas are sometimes mislabeled as turnips. They're the big, orange-fleshed root vegetables, while turnips are white with a purple blush on the shoulders. But if you can't find rutabagas, turnips are good in this soup, too.

Thai Hot and Sour soup

Here's the soup for a cold night when the Girl feels something nasty coming on. It's simple and speedy, but it's also good for what ails you and just plain good. Feel free to substitute or add veggies — shredded carrot, celery or fresh bean sprouts are good additions if you have them on hand — or use peeled shrimp instead of chicken. Make it as hot as you like — extra chilies if you're feeling poorly.

3 cups (750 mL) chicken stock (preferably home-made)

1–inch (2.5–cm) piece ginger, sliced

zest of 1 lime, chopped (about 2 tsp./10 mL)

3 Tbsp. (45 mL) fresh lime juice

1/4 lb. (125 g) boneless, skinless chicken, very thinly sliced or shredded

2 fresh tomatoes, seeded and chopped (about 1 cup/250 mL)

1 tsp. (5 mL) Asian chili paste (or 1 fresh jalapeño or serrano chili pepper, sliced)

1/2 cup (125 mL) thinly sliced mushrooms (try some exotic oyster or enoki mushrooms)

1 Tbsp. (15 mL) soy sauce

1/2 tsp. (2 mL) sesame oil

2 green onions, chopped

2 Tbsp. (25 mL) chopped cilantro

1 Combine the stock, ginger, lime zest and juice and bring to a boil over medium heat. Simmer for 2 minutes.

2 Add the chicken and cook for 1–2 minutes, until the chicken has changed color and is barely cooked.

3 Stir in the tomatoes, chili paste (or jalapeño pepper) and sliced mushrooms. Boil for 5 minutes longer, then season with soy sauce and sesame oil. Divide the soup between two deep bowls. Sprinkle with chopped green onions and cilantro and serve immediately, with extra hot sauce on the side. Serves 2.

Between Bread

Burgers, sandwiches, wraps — instant everyday eating often
involves two pieces of bread with something savory in between.

Of course the secret to sandwich success is fresh and delicious bread.
Make the effort to find a good bakery and keep it in business by buying
your bread fresh, several times a week. The Girl has a special soft spot
for good sourdough, olive bread, chewy authentic baguettes and
grainy breads filled with nuts and seeds.

Don't skimp on bread — with a slather of fresh butter, good
hearty bread can sustain you through many a crisis. Bad bread is
a waste of calories and carbs.

Grilled Vegetable Panini

Stack smoky grilled veggies on a chewy Italian roll for a yummy summer lunch or dinner. When the Girl's grilling burgers, she often grills some summer squash, peppers and eggplant, too. You can pile them into a bun on their own, use them as additions to a regular burger or even serve them on the side as an antipasto with bread, chilled and drizzled with a little balsamic vinegar.

1 medium eggplant, unpeeled

3 small to medium zucchini (green or yellow)

1/4 cup (50 mL) olive oil

1 clove garlic, pressed or minced

1 tsp. (5 mL) Italian seasoning (or equal amounts of basil and oregano)

1 large portobello mushroom

1 red bell pepper

1 yellow bell pepper

salt and freshly ground black pepper

4 panini buns, crusty rolls or thick slices of olive bread, toasted

mayonnaise and mustard

olive tapenade (optional; use commercial or homemade, page 328)

1 Cut the eggplant into 1/2–inch (1–cm) rounds. Salt the slices lightly on both sides and place in a colander in the sink to drain for 20 minutes. This will leach out any bitterness in the eggplant. Rinse the slices quickly and pat dry with paper towels.

2 Cut the zucchini lengthwise into slices.

3 Combine the olive oil with the garlic and Italian herbs. Set aside for 10 minutes to meld the flavors.

4 Heat the barbecue to medium-high. Using a pastry brush, brush both sides of the eggplant, squash slices and portobello with the seasoned oil. Grill them until lightly browned. Remove and slice the mushroom into thin ribbons.

5 At the same time, grill the whole bell peppers until blackened. When the peppers are charred on all sides, remove from the heat and cool slightly, then use a paring knife to remove the skin and seeds. Cut the peppers into wide strips and place in a bowl; drizzle with a little of the seasoned oil. (You can also use pre-roasted peppers from a jar to speed things up.)

6 To make the vegetable sandwiches, slather the buns or bread with mayonnaise and mustard. Add a layer of olive tapenade if you have it for a wonderful Mediterranean flavor. Then fill the buns with layers of grilled eggplant, zucchini, grilled mushroom and peppers. Serves 4.

Best Beef Burgers

Nothing beats a good, homemade hamburger, hot off the grill on a summer day. Make your own spicy barbecue sauce (page 328) or find a good-quality commercial sauce to keep on hand. Make sure to cook all ground meats until well done (see page 353).

1½ lbs. (750 g) lean ground beef
1 egg
½ cup (125 mL) dry breadcrumbs or cracker crumbs
freshly ground black pepper
¼ cup (50 mL) spicy barbecue sauce, plus extra
   for basting

1 small onion, finely minced
1 clove garlic, minced
whole-wheat buns, lettuce, tomato, cheese slices,
   white onion slices and other condiments,
   including ketchup, mustard, relish, mayonnaise,
   horseradish, etc.

1 Combine all the ingredients except the buns and condiments, mixing with your hands to incorporate. Add more breadcrumbs if the mixture seems too wet. Form the mixture into 8 large patties. Don't make them too thick as they will shrink in to the middle and thicken as they cook.

2 Grill over medium hot coals or on a gas grill on medium heat for 7 minutes. Turn and brush heavily with barbecue sauce. Cook 7 minutes longer, until they are no longer pink in the center, brushing again with the sauce.

3 Serve the burgers on buns and let everyone help themselves to lettuce, tomato, cheese, onion and condiments (the blue cheese butter on page 136 makes an excellent blue cheese burger). Serves 4–6.

Girl talk: To take a regular beef burger into gourmet territory, try stuffing each patty with a little goat cheese or Stilton. Just cut the cheese into ¾ oz. (20 g) pieces and form the meat mixture around the cheese. You'll get a tasty surprise with every bite. Add some caramelized onions or sautéed wild mushrooms to really gild the lily.

Vegetarian Burgers

No meat — no problem. This is the Girl's version of that mushroom veggie burger from the supermarket freezer. If you wish to grill these burgers, oil the grill well and freeze the burgers before cooking, then put frozen patties directly on the grill and cook until brown and crisp on both sides. Or make them smaller and fry in a little oil in a nonstick pan for falafel-type sandwiches topped with tomatoes and yogurt and stuffed into fresh pita bread — yum, yum, yum.

1 medium potato, peeled and quartered (about 3/4 cup/175 mL mashed)

2 Tbsp. (25 mL) virgin olive oil

1 medium onion, finely chopped (about 1 cup/250 mL)

1 clove garlic, minced

2 carrots, shredded or finely chopped in processor (about 1/2 cup/125 mL)

2 cups (500 mL) finely minced fresh mushrooms (about 1 lb./500 g)

1 can chickpeas (a.k.a. garbanzo beans), rinsed and drained (2 cups/500 mL)

1 Tbsp. (15 mL) soy sauce

salt and freshly ground black pepper

2 tsp. (10 mL) hot sauce or Asian chili paste

3 Tbsp. (45 mL) finely chopped cilantro or parsley

1 1/2 cups (375 mL) cooked brown rice or bulgur

1 egg white

2 Tbsp. (25 mL) dry bread crumbs or flour

1 Cook the potato in boiling water until soft, about 15 minutes. Drain well and mash. Set aside in a large bowl.

2 Heat the olive oil in a nonstick frying pan over medium heat. Add the onion and garlic to the pan, then stir in the carrots. Add the mushrooms to the pan. Stir and sauté until the vegetables are tender and beginning to brown.

3 Meanwhile, place the drained chickpeas in a food processor and process until puréed. Add the chickpea purée to the mashed potato in the bowl. Stir in the sautéed vegetables. Season the mixture with soy sauce, salt, pepper and hot sauce or chili paste. Then add the cilantro or parsley, rice or bulgur and egg white. Stir to combine everything well. Add breadcrumbs or flour if mixture seems too soft.

4 Wet your hands and form the mixture into eight 3–inch (8–cm) patties. Place the patties on a lightly oiled plate and chill for at least 2 hours.

5 Heat 1 1/2 Tbsp. (27 mL) oil in a large, nonstick frying pan. Cook the burgers over medium heat until crusty and golden brown, 3 to 5 minutes per side. Work in two batches, if necessary, to avoid crowding the pan. Add oil only as necessary.

6 Serve the burgers as is or on rolls with sliced tomatoes and lettuce, barbecue sauce and mustard. Makes eight 3–inch (8–cm) burgers.

Girl talk: All vegetarian burgers can be frozen and actually benefit by being grilled straight out of the freezer. After you make your burgers, arrange them on a plate in a single layer, cover with plastic wrap and freeze. Stack them, with a square of parchment paper or waxed paper between each burger, and freeze them in bags or containers.

Tex-Mex Chicken Wraps

This is an easy after-work idea for those ubiquitous boneless chicken breasts or thighs. Remove the skin, coat with a spicy rub and throw them in the oven. Topped with fresh tomato and avocado salsa and wrapped in a whole-wheat tortilla with some brown rice, it's perfect to take along when you're running late for the kid's hockey game or dance class. On a less frantic day, serve the chicken topped with salsa, with the rice on the side.

chicken

1 Tbsp. (15 mL) olive oil
2 Tbsp. (25 mL) fresh lime or lemon juice
1 clove garlic, finely minced
1 tsp. (5 mL) ground cumin
1 tsp. (5 mL) sweet Hungarian paprika
1 tsp. (5 mL) ground oregano

1 tsp (5 mL) chili powder
1/4 tsp. (1 mL) cayenne pepper (omit if your kids hate it hot or increase to taste)
4 boneless, skinless chicken breasts (or about 1 lb./500 g boneless thighs)

salsa

3 Roma tomatoes, seeded and diced (about 1 cup/250 mL)
1 avocado, peeled and chopped
juice of 1/2 lime

1/4 cup (50 mL) chopped fresh cilantro
pinch salt
pinch cumin
1 Tbsp. (15 mL) minced jalapeño pepper

wraps

4 whole-wheat tortillas
2 cups (500 mL) cooked brown rice

1 To make the rub, combine the oil, lemon or lime juice, garlic, spices and cayenne pepper in a small bowl. Slather the rub over the chicken on all sides and set aside in the refrigerator for 10 minutes.

2 Preheat the oven to 375°F (190°C) and arrange the chicken in a single layer on a non-stick baking sheet. Line the sheet with foil or parchment to reduce clean-up time. Bake, uncovered, for 25–35 minutes. The juices should be clear when the chicken is pierced, but don't overcook it — 25 minutes should suffice for a 1/4-lb. (125–g) breast. Remember that breasts can dry out easily and while thighs tend to be more forgiving, they are higher in fat.

3 Meanwhile, combine the chopped tomato, avocado, lime juice, cilantro, salt and cumin in a bowl. Stir in the jalapeño. Set the salsa aside to marinate at room temperature while the chicken cooks.

4 Slice the chicken and roll it up into flour tortillas with the salsa and rice. Serves 4.

Girl talk:

When you're making the brown rice to serve on the side, start with a little sautéed onion and garlic, add 1/2 tsp. (2 mL) each of chili powder, cumin and oregano (per cup of raw rice), and stir in a chopped tomato before you add the two cups (500 mL) of water or broth. Instant Mexi-rice with none of those nasty artificial flavors!

East Meets Western Sandwich

There's something about this easy and old-fashioned Cantonese menu item that's comforting to the Girl — one of those childhood foods that always arrived in perfectly edible condition from the little Chinese take-out joint down the street. Who knows if it's even authentic — but egg foo yong is one Asian dish anyone can make, even without a wok. Slap it between two slices of brown toast and you've got an Asian twist on a classic Western (a.k.a Denver) sandwich. Of course, you can also eat it straight up, or alongside any stir-fry with a bowl of rice.

omelet

1 clove garlic, minced
1 thick slice fresh ginger, minced
3 cups (750 mL) fresh bean sprouts
4 green onions, finely chopped
1 carrot, peeled and grated
6 eggs, beaten

1 tsp. (5 mL) soy sauce
1/2 tsp. (2 mL) salt
1 cup (250 mL) minced cooked ham or 1 can
    (6 oz./184 g) small shrimp, rinsed and drained
canola oil for frying

sauce

1/2 cup (125 mL) chicken broth
1 Tbsp. (15 mL) soy sauce

1/2 tsp. (2 mL) sugar
2 tsp. (10 mL) cornstarch

8 slices grainy bread, toasted and buttered

1 In a large bowl, combine the garlic, ginger, bean sprouts, green onions and carrot. Stir in the beaten eggs, soy sauce and salt to combine well. Fold in the ham or shrimp.

2 Heat a little oil in a large nonstick frying pan over medium-high heat. When the oil is hot, ladle some of the vegetable mixture into the pan, making 3–inch (8–cm) pancakes. If you want one omelet per sandwich, make each as big as your bread (that may mean making them one at a time). If the egg runs out beyond the vegetables, push it back into the omelet with the spatula to keep the edges even.

3 Cook until brown on one side, 3–4 minutes, then flip over to brown the other side. Keep warm on an ovenproof plate in a low oven until all the omelets are finished.

4 Combine the broth, soy sauce, sugar and cornstarch in a bowl and pour into the hot pan. Cook and stir the sauce until it is bubbling, clear and thick, about 3 minutes.

5 Place some egg foo yong on a slice of buttered toast and drizzle with a little sauce. Top with a second piece of toast. Cut each sandwich into four pieces to serve, two standing up in the center and two lying flat on each side, like wings. Serves 4.

Summer Focaccia Grilled Cheese

Get a nice focaccia bread at the local Italian bakery and make this simple sandwich for a summer supper, with a green salad on the side.

2 Tbsp. (25 mL) olive oil
1 clove garlic, crushed
1 8–inch (20–cm) focaccia loaf
(Italian flat bread)

4 oz. (125 g) mozzarella or fontina cheese, thinly sliced
1 large ripe tomato, thinly sliced
¼ cup (50 mL) fresh basil

1 Put the olive oil in a small bowl and add the crushed garlic. Set aside to infuse the oil with the garlic flavor for 10 minutes. Discard the garlic.

2 Using a long, serrated bread knife, cut the foccacia bread horizontally into two rounds, then cut each in half. You will have two moon-shaped sandwiches. Brush the cut sides of the bread with garlic oil. Arrange half of the cheese, tomato and basil leaves on each sandwich half, top with bread and press down lightly.

3 Heat a nonstick sauté pan over medium heat. Brush the top of each sandwich with more oil, and place oiled side down in the pan. Brush the top sides of the sandwiches with oil. Cook until the focaccia is nicely browned on both sides, about 3–4 minutes per side, pressing down with a spatula as you cook so that the melted cheese holds the pieces together. Cut each sandwich in half to serve. Serves 2.

Pita Panini or Pizza

The Girl has discovered that a thick Greek-style pita bread is the perfect vehicle for instant pizzas or folded, cheesy, gooey panini sandwiches.

Pita pizzas make instant snacks or suppers for kids and stylish warm appetizers for parties. Just brush the breads lightly with tomato sauce, olive oil or basil pesto, scatter some of your favorite toppings about (slivered ham or prosciutto, caramelized onions, black olives, minced garlic, dry salami, fresh herbs, fresh sliced tomatoes, etc.) then top with gratings of a great cheese; bake for 5–7 minutes in a 425°F (220°C) oven and voila! — crisp designer pizza for one.

Panini sandwiches are just as easy with Greek pita bread, and they can be made right on top of the stove. Just put your fillings on one side of the bread, top with sliced (not grated) cheese of your choice and fold in half — particularly good when combined with tomatoes, caramelized onions and fresh mozzarella, or olive tapenade (see page 328), goat cheese and fresh basil leaves. Place in a lightly oiled nonstick pan that's been heated on medium-high heat. Press down hard on the sandwich with a spatula as you cook it, or set a heavy cast iron pan on top (this will help to crisp the bread). Turn and crisp the second side the same way. Grab and go.

Chicken Shawarma Sandwich

The Girl has been known to frequent a certain Middle Eastern deli (too frequently, in fact) for their big grilled chicken and pita wraps, oozing with garlicky tahini sauce and piled high with tomatoes, hot peppers and other goodies. Of course, this kind of street food is always best from the source, but you can have yourself a good shawarma feast at home with a little advance preparation.

chicken

2 chicken breasts (about 3/4 lb./350 g)
3 Tbsp. (45 mL) fresh lemon juice
1/4 cup (50 mL) virgin olive oil

pinch of *each* ground allspice, nutmeg, cinnamon,
   freshly ground black pepper, salt, thyme, cayenne
   pepper and coriander

sauce

4 cloves garlic, pressed
salt
2 Tbsp. (15 mL) olive oil
1/4 cup (125 mL) plain yogurt

1/4 cup (50 mL) tahini paste
1/4 cup (50 mL) low-fat mayonnaise
1 Tbsp. (15 mL) fresh lemon juice

sandwiches

4 10–inch (25–cm) pita breads
2 medium tomatoes, chopped
1 small white onion, slivered
2 cups (500 mL) shredded iceberg lettuce

4 radishes, slivered
2 dill pickles, sliced
1/4 cup (50 mL) sliced pickled hot peppers
   (or Asian chili paste)

1 Cut each chicken breast in half, lengthwise, to form two thinner cutlets. Combine the chicken, lemon juice, olive oil and spices. Mix to coat well and marinate for 2–4 hours or overnight in a sealed plastic bag.

2 Whisk together the sauce ingredients and refrigerate.

3 Grill the chicken over medium to high heat for 8–10 minutes, until crispy on the outside and just cooked through. Let rest for 5 minutes. Chop the chicken into chunks.

4 Divide the chopped chicken among the four pita breads, arranging it down the center of each bread round. Top with tomato, onion, lettuce, radish, dill pickle and hot peppers or chili paste.

5 Drizzle each sandwich with 4 Tbsp. (60 mL) of the sauce. Roll the pita tightly around the filling, wrapping the sandwich in a piece of waxed paper or a paper napkin to enclose the bottom and prevent drips. Serve immediately. Makes 4 large sandwiches.

Saigon Satay Chicken Subs

The Girl is smitten with these east-west submarine sandwiches — lovely spicy chicken (or beef), with tons of fresh shredded carrots and cilantro, all tucked into a chewy baguette. A truly exotic sandwich, with roots in Vietnam. Also a great way to get through that leftover turkey breast after Christmas. This is the time to haul out your mandoline if you have one (page 354) to create elegant matchstick carrots and cucumber ribbons. If you like, use a commercial satay sauce in place of this scratch version (see page 29).

sauce

1/4 cup (50 mL) lime juice

1/4 cup (50 mL) fish sauce

2 Tbsp. (25 mL) rice or wine vinegar

1 Tbsp. (15mL) sugar

1/4 cup (50 mL) water

1 tsp. (5 mL) garlic chili paste (or cayenne and garlic powder)

subs

1 large chicken breast (or tender strips of leftover roast or grilled beef), about 6 oz. (175 g)

1 cup (250 mL) shredded carrot or carrot matchsticks (see Girl talk page 47)

1 Tbsp. (15 mL) salt

2 Tbsp. (25 mL) sugar

1/4 cup (50 mL) rice vinegar

2 6–inch/15 cm lengths of fresh baguette, split or 2 crusty sub buns

mayonnaise

thin slices mozzarella cheese

1/2 English cucumber, sliced in thin lengthwise strips

1/2 cup (125 mL) finely sliced white onion (1/2 an onion)

2–3 chopped fresh chilies (serrano are good)

cilantro sprigs

1 Combine the sauce ingredients in a jar or bottle, shake and refrigerate.

2 Poach the chicken in boiling water to cover for about 30 minutes or toss with a little sauce and bake. Cut into chunks. Alternately, start with chunks of boneless leftover cooked chicken or beef.

3 Put the carrots in a colander, sprinkle with the salt and let them drain for an hour to remove moisture. Rinse, pat dry and combine with the sugar, vinegar and about a cup (250 mL) of water. Place in a container and refrigerate for at least an hour (or up to 3 days) to marinate.

4 To assemble the subs, split the baguettes lengthwise and slather each with mayonnaise. Top with chicken and cheese and put on a baking sheet. Slide under a preheated broiler (or into a toaster oven) and broil for 1–2 minutes, just to toast the bread and melt the cheese.

5 Top each sandwich with half of the shredded carrot salad, strips of cucumber, onions, chopped chilies and a handful of cilantro sprigs. Drizzle each with a few tablespoons of the sauce. Press the bread together to enclose the filling and wrap in waxed paper to keep everything inside while you eat. Makes 2 sub sandwiches.

Roti Wraps

A roti is a curry wrapped in a tender flat bread, common in the Caribbean. The Girl, who never met a carbohydrate she didn't like, is particularly smitten with the spicy potato version — straight, or augmented with cauliflower or chickpeas. If you want it really authentic, go to an Indian grocery and buy roti or paratha bread, but an extra-large flour tortilla from the supermarket does the job, too. I know, potatoes wrapped in flatbread may seem excessive, but there are days. Enjoy it on the beach, mon. If you have leftover potatoes in the refrigerator, this is the perfect fast meal.

2 Tbsp. (25 mL) canola oil
1 medium onion, chopped (about 2 cups/500 mL)
2 cloves garlic, minced
1 Tbsp. (15 mL) curry powder
1/2 tsp. (2 mL) ground cumin
1/2 tsp. (2 mL) mustard seed (optional)
1 tsp. (5 mL) hot sauce
1 lb. (500 g) white potatoes, peeled, boiled
   10 minutes, drained and cubed

1/8 tsp. (.5 mL) salt
1 cup (250 mL) canned chickpeas or chopped, cooked
   cauliflower (optional)
squeeze fresh lime juice
2 Tbsp. (25 mL) chopped cilantro
4 extra-large flour tortillas, very fresh (or roti or
   paratha breads)

1 Heat the oil in a large nonstick skillet over medium-high heat. Add the onion and fry for 5–10 minutes, until it is just beginning to brown. Add the garlic, curry powder, cumin and mustard seed, if using, and cook together until fragrant, about 2 minutes. Stir in the hot sauce and salt.

2 Add the cooked potatoes to the pan and stir to coat them well with the spices. Cook together for 5 minutes to heat through. If you're using chickpeas or cauliflower, add them now and heat them up. Squeeze on the lime juice and stir in the cilantro.

3 Divide the filling among the four tortillas, piling it in the center. Fold each roti like a square envelope — bottom up, sides in, top down — then wrap in waxed paper and/or foil for easy eating. Rotis are made for moving and carrying. It's a to-go lunch or dinner. Serves 4.

Girl talk: The Girl once dragged her significant other all over Chinatown in San Francisco to find the ultimate gadget to shred carrots and big daikon radishes. It's a Japanese contraption, with spikes to hold the vegetable above the blades and a crank on top. The shreds come out like long strands of spaghetti, which are perfect to pile onto Vietnamese subs. Also excellent for making perfect shoe string potatoes for deep frying — when you need a fluffy nest of fried potatoes for a spectacular presentation. Not essential, but cool, and safer than a mandoline. If you have neither, use your food processor or the big holes on your box grater and shred carrots lengthwise for the longest strips.

Those Ubiquitous Chicken Breasts

Chicken, chicken, chicken — The Girl sometimes feels like she's living on chicken breasts, they're so quick and easy to cook. But when you're tired of grilled chicken and pan-fried chicken, there are other things you can do with this whitest of white meat. Go crazy with rubs, spices and sauces — it'll still taste like chicken but it may surprise you.

Sesame Ginger Chicken

This sweet and spicy chicken is the Girl's best friend — kids love it, you can chop it up and toss it with a bowl of noodles and stir-fried vegetables, or serve it, chic style, on a bed of summer greens with a soy/sesame vinaigrette. The little black dress of the chicken breast set.

1 Tbsp. (15 mL) sesame oil
½ cup (125 mL) liquid honey
⅓ cup (75 mL) fresh orange juice
2 Tbsp. (25 mL) soy sauce
juice of ½ lemon (about 2 Tbsp./25 mL)

1 Tbsp. (15 mL) minced garlic
1 Tbsp. (15 mL) peeled and minced fresh ginger
1 dried red chili pepper, crushed
2 lbs. (1 kg) boneless, skinless chicken breasts
chopped fresh cilantro to garnish

1 In a microwave-proof bowl, warm the sesame oil, honey, orange juice, soy sauce, lemon juice, garlic, ginger and red chili until the honey is melted. Stir to combine well and set aside to cool.

2 In a resealable plastic bag, combine the chicken pieces and the marinade and place in the refrigerator for 2 hours or overnight.

3 Preheat the oven to 350°F (180°C). Line a baking pan with foil or parchment paper to speed clean-up. Place the chicken in a single layer on the pan, drizzle with the marinade and bake for 45 minutes, basting a couple of times with the pan juices.

4 Remove the chicken from the pan and tent with foil to keep warm. Pour the cooking juices into a small saucepan and boil over medium heat for 10 minutes, until the sauce is reduced to a thick glaze.

5 To serve, slice the chicken breasts and fan on individual plates, then drizzle some of the sauce over top. Sprinkle with chopped cilantro to garnish. Serves 4.

The Dish: The Girl hates to gossip but here's the dish on "seasoned" chicken (and pork and other stuff you'll see at the meat counter). It may sound good to a time-squeezed sort, but beware — "seasoned" is a euphemism for a process used in the meat business to tenderize and plump up inferior cuts with water and salt. The result is meat that's high in sodium, impossible to sear in a pan (it just gets watery) and more expensive, because you're paying for that added H2O weight. Get a quality piece of meat and don't overcook it, and you'll be way ahead on flavor, health and cash.

Kid-Friendly Fingers and Oven Fries

Sure, you can buy frozen chicken fingers but these are so much tastier. Kids will love them with a sweet dipping sauce of apricot jam mixed with a little Dijon mustard. Adults like them, too, with a spicy horseradish dipping sauce made with equal parts of mayo, mustard, sour cream and horseradish. Add a green salad for a complete meal.

fries

6 medium red potatoes

3–4 Tbsp. (45–60 mL) olive oil

salt and freshly ground black pepper

chicken fingers

3 Tbsp. (45 mL) Dijon mustard

1/4 tsp. (1 mL) sweet paprika

1/4 tsp. (1 mL) salt

1/4 tsp. (1 mL) dried thyme leaves

4 boneless, skinless chicken breast halves

1 egg

1/4 cup (50 mL) plain yogurt or buttermilk

2 cups (500 mL) dry breadcrumbs

1/2 cup (125 mL) finely grated Parmesan cheese

1/2 tsp. (2 mL) salt

1/2 tsp. (2mL) freshly ground black pepper

olive oil

dipping sauce

2 Tbsp. (25 mL) apricot jam

1 Tbsp. (15 mL) Dijon mustard

salt and freshly ground black pepper

1 Scrub the potatoes well and cut them into wedges.

2 Arrange on a nonstick baking sheet. Drizzle with olive oil and stir to coat well. Sprinkle with salt and pepper.

3 Meanwhile, combine the mustard, paprika, salt and thyme in a bowl.

4 Using a sharp knife, cut the chicken breasts into long, thin, lengthwise strips. Add the chicken strips to the mustard mixture and toss to coat. Cover and refrigerate for 30 minutes.

5 Whisk the egg and yogurt (or buttermilk) together in another bowl. Combine the breadcrumbs, Parmesan, salt and pepper in a separate bowl.

6 Dip the chicken strips, one at a time, into the egg mixture. Shake off any excess, then roll in the crumbs to coat on all sides. Set the battered chicken on a rack, set over a baking sheet, to allow the coating to set up for about 10 minutes.

7   Preheat the oven to 450°F (230°C). Bake the potatoes for 15 minutes. Lower the heat to 400°F (200°C) and continue to bake for 20–30 minutes, turning the potatoes occasionally, until they are brown and crisp.

8   Coat another baking sheet with olive oil and arrange the chicken fingers on the pan. Bake the chicken fingers alongside the fries, at 400°F (200°C), for 15–20 minutes, until the chicken is crisp and brown.

9   For the dipping sauce, whisk together the jam and mustard and season to taste with salt and pepper. Serve the chicken fingers and fries immediately with dipping sauce or bottled barbecue sauce on the side. Serves 4.

Girl talk: There's a big difference in paprika — some is hot, some is sweet and the cheap stuff can be bitter. It's best to shell out for imported Hungarian or Spanish paprika when you're buying the sweet stuff, as it usually has the best flavor.

Miso Chicken

Another use for that miso paste you have hanging around in the fridge is this great Japanese-style skewered chicken. Serve it as an appetizer or main course augmented with sushi from the deli or a simple bowl of hot basmati rice.

1 lb. (250 g) boneless chicken, breasts or thighs
2 Tbsp. (25 mL) light Japanese soy sauce
3 Tbsp. (45 mL) mirin (Japanese sweetened rice wine)

2 Tbsp. (25 mL) light miso
1 tsp. (2 mL) minced ginger
1 clove garlic, minced
3 green onions, minced

1   Cut the chicken into cubes. In a blender, combine the soy sauce, mirin, miso, ginger, garlic and green onions and blend until smooth. Place the chicken in a resealable plastic bag with the marinade and refrigerate for 1 hour or overnight.

2   Thread the chicken on skewers. Grill over medium-high heat until nicely browned, about 7–8 minutes in total. Serve immediately. Serves 2–4.

Chicken Souvlakia with Tzatziki

From girlfriend Laura, who could pass as a Greek with this easy and delicious combo that's off the grill and on your plate in minutes. Serve it with pita wedges and a Greek salad (page 24) on the side, or pile the grilled chicken and tzatziki in split pita breads with sliced tomatoes for a sandwich. Add both to the Girl's Big Vegetarian Buffet (see page 256) for a party menu.

chicken

2 lbs. (1 kg) chicken (or pork or lamb), trimmed
1/4 cup (50 mL) fresh lemon juice
5 Tbsp. (65 mL) olive oil
1 Tbsp. (15 mL) oregano

1/4 tsp. (1 mL) freshly ground black pepper
1/2 tsp. (2 mL) rosemary
1 large clove garlic, minced
Tzatziki

1 Cut the meat into strips and place on bamboo skewers that have been soaked in water (this will prevent them from burning up on the grill).

2 Combine the remaining ingredients (except for the Tzatziki), pour over the meat and marinate in the refrigerator for 1 hour (or up to 24 hours). Grill the chicken skewers over medium-high heat, just until the juices run clear, about 7–8 minutes. Serve with the Tzatziki on the side. Serves 4–6.

Tzatziki

1/2 English cucumber (about 3/4 cup/175 mL), shredded
2 cups (500 mL) skim milk yogurt
1 cup (250 mL) sour cream

4 garlic cloves, minced
2 Tbsp. (25 mL) chopped fresh dill or mint
salt and freshly ground black pepper
extra virgin olive oil

1 Wash the cucumber well and, using a box grater with large holes, shred it, skin and all, into a colander to drain. Add a little salt to draw out excess moisture. Wrap the drained cucumber in a paper towel and press to remove excess moisture.

2 Whisk together the yogurt and sour cream. Stir in the garlic, fresh dill or mint and reserved cucumber. Season to taste with salt and pepper, and chill. Drizzle with a little olive oil before serving. Makes 3 1/2 cups (875 mL).

Chicken Ribbons with Mustard Sauce

Get yourself a bag of bamboo skewers and you'll impress your family with these speedy and stylish kebabs. Just make sure you soak the skewers in warm water before you thread on the meat — or your skewers may go up in flames!

8 small red potatoes (about 1 lb./500 g)
1/4 cup (50 mL) honey
3 Tbsp. (45 mL) smooth Dijon mustard
1 Tbsp. (15 mL) fresh lemon juice
1 tsp. (5 mL) chopped fresh thyme (or 1/2 tsp./ 2 mL dried)

1/4 tsp. (1 mL) white pepper
4 boneless, skinless chicken breasts (about 1 lb./500 g)
8 medium white mushrooms, halved
16 cherry tomatoes

1 Cut the potatoes in half. Place a steamer basket over a couple of inches of boiling water in a saucepan, add the potatoes and steam until almost tender, about 10 minutes.

2 For the marinade, whisk together the honey, mustard, lemon juice, thyme and white pepper in a small bowl.

3 Cut the chicken breasts into thin lengthwise strips, about eight strips per breast. Place them in a bowl with half of the marinade and toss to coat well. Set aside in the refrigerator for 1 hour.

4 In another bowl, combine the potatoes and mushrooms with the remaining marinade. Toss to coat.

5 Soak about 20 bamboo skewers in water for 30 minutes. Thread the chicken onto the skewers, accordion style. On separate skewers, alternate steamed potatoes, mushrooms and cherry tomatoes.

6 Grill the skewers over medium-high heat for 6–8 minutes, just until the chicken is cooked through and the vegetables begin to brown. Serve each person a few chicken skewers and a couple of vegetable skewers. Serves 4.

Lemon Chicken

Inspired by that popular Cantonese restaurant dish, this is a great way to add instant flavor to everyday chicken breasts. Put on a pot of rice to complete the meal.

chicken

2 lbs. (1 kg) boneless, skinless chicken breasts, cut into strips or large cubes

1/2 cup (125 mL) freshly squeezed lemon juice (2 lemons)

3 cloves garlic, pressed or minced

2 tsp. (10 mL) minced fresh ginger

1/2 cup (125 mL) all-purpose flour

1 tsp. (5 mL) ground ginger

1/2 tsp. (2 mL) salt

pinch cayenne pepper

1/2 cup (125 mL) canola oil

2 cups (500 mL) broccoli florets (optional)

sauce

1/2 cup (125 mL) chicken broth

2 Tbsp. (25 mL) lemon juice

1 Tbsp. (15 mL) brown sugar

1 tsp. (5 mL) cornstarch

1 lemon, sliced paper thin using a mandoline or food processor with a slicing disc (discard seeds)

1 Combine the chicken with the 1/2 cup (125 mL) lemon juice, garlic and fresh ginger. Marinate for 1 hour. Drain the chicken, discarding the marinade.

2 In a bowl or plastic bag, combine the flour, ground ginger, salt and cayenne. Add the marinated chicken and shake around to coat well.

3 In a wok or large nonstick pan, heat the oil over medium-high heat. Cook the chicken in batches until golden and crisp, about 5–6 minutes. Remove the chicken from the oil using a slotted spoon and set aside to drain on paper towels. Meanwhile, if using the broccoli, blanch for 3 minutes in a pot of boiling water, until it's bright green and tender. Drain well.

4 Discard the excess oil in the wok and reheat the pan. In a small bowl, whisk the broth, 2 Tbsp. (25 mL) lemon juice, brown sugar and cornstarch together. Add to the hot wok, along with the sliced lemon, and boil over high heat until the sauce is thick and smooth. Place the chicken on a serving platter, surround with broccoli florets, and drizzle the sauce evenly over top. Serves 4.

Easy Asian

Nothing is faster than tossing up some meat and fresh veggies in
the wok after work. Try any of these speedy stir-fries or curries to put some
exotic Eastern spice into your everyday eats. Rice is always nice alongside.
Add crisp slices of Asian pears, melon or Mandarin oranges for dessert.

Beef and Baby Bok Choy

Beef and broccoli is the usual combination — but the Girl prefers the crunchy fresh flavor of young bok choy in this dish. Steam up some basmati rice and grab your chopsticks.

2 Tbsp. (25 mL) black bean sauce
2 Tbsp. (25 mL) hoisin sauce
2 Tbsp. (25 mL) light soy sauce
1 tsp. (5 mL) sesame oil
1 tsp. (5 mL) Asian chili paste
1 Tbsp. (15 mL) rice vinegar
1/2 lb. (250 g) round or sirloin steak, partially
   frozen

3 Tbsp. (45 mL) peanut or canola oil, divided
1 clove garlic, minced
1 small white onion, slivered
1/2 lb. (250 g) baby bok choy, bases trimmed
   and cut crosswise into shreds
1/3 cup (75 mL) water or broth
1 Tbsp. (15 mL) cornstarch mixed with 1 Tbsp.
   (15 mL) cold water

1 In a small bowl, whisk together the black bean sauce, hoisin sauce, soy sauce, sesame oil, chili paste and rice vinegar. Set aside.

2 Using a very sharp knife, cut the steak into thin strips, across the grain. Place the strips in a bowl and toss with about 1 Tbsp. (15 mL) of the sauce. Set aside to marinate at room temperature for 15 minutes.

3 In a heavy wok, heat 2 Tbsp. (25 mL) of the peanut or canola oil over high heat until the oil is just beginning to smoke. Add half the beef and stir-fry for 2 minutes. Remove with a slotted spoon and set aside. Cook the remaining beef and set aside.

4 Add the remaining oil to the wok and heat over high heat. Add the garlic, onion and bok choy and stir-fry for 2–3 minutes. Add the reserved sauce and water or broth, bring to a boil and cover. Steam for 1 minute.

5 Stir the cornstarch solution into the wok and continue to simmer until the sauce is thickened. Return the beef to the pan and heat through. Serves 2.

Panang Roast Chicken Curry

If you're like most girls, one day you have a hot roasted chicken from the supermarket deli, the next day you have half a cold roasted chicken in the fridge. Add some eggplant, red pepper and exotic spices and in 10 minutes you'll be dining on this amazing Thai curry. Serve it over basmati rice and that's it — dinner's done. Try this dish with leftover turkey, too. Sublime.

1 medium eggplant, peeled and cut into 1/2–inch (1–cm) cubes

½ roasted chicken (about 1 lb./500 g of boneless meat)

1 tsp. (5 mL) vegetable oil

1 clove garlic, minced

1 red bell pepper, seeded and cut into chunks

2–3 tsp. (10–15 mL) Thai red curry paste

1 cup (250 mL) chicken broth

1 2-to 3–inch (5-to 8–cm) piece of lemon grass, finely minced or pulverized in a blender (or 2 tsp./10 mL grated lemon zest)

1 tsp. (5 mL) peanut butter

2 tsp. (10 mL) sugar

1 cup (250 mL) regular or light coconut milk

1 tsp. (5 mL) Thai fish sauce

1 tsp. (5 mL) cooking wine

1 Tbsp. (15 mL) cornstarch mixed with 1 Tbsp. (15 mL) cold water

1 tsp. (5 mL) chopped roasted peanuts

1 tsp. (5 mL) chopped cilantro

1 Bring a pot of water to a boil on the stove and blanch the eggplant for 2 minutes to soften. Drain and set aside. Remove the meat from the chicken and chop into chunks.

2 In a large wok, heat the oil over high heat until the oil is beginning to smoke. Add the garlic and fry for 10 seconds, then stir in the red pepper and curry paste. When the curry paste sizzles, add the broth, lemon grass, peanut butter, sugar, coconut milk, fish sauce and cooking wine, and bring to a rolling boil.

3 Stir in the blanched eggplant and chicken, coating well with the sauce. Bring back to a boil, stir in the cornstarch solution, and simmer until the sauce is thickened and the vegetables are tender, about 3–4 minutes. Serve immediately, sprinkled with chopped peanuts and cilantro. Serves 2–4.

Girl talk: The Girl has recently learned how easy it is to cook authentic-tasting Thai food with a bit of red or green curry paste — they come in resealable tubs and keep in the fridge for months, so she can scoop out some Southeast Asian flavor whenever the mood strikes. Find curry pastes at Asian groceries along with the lemon grass, fish sauce and canned fat-reduced coconut milk you'll need for this fast dish.

Lemon grass looks like tall, pale green onion — but it's tough as nails. Use the bottom few inches of the stalk only, and mince it finely or pulverize it in a blender or food processor. You can also just add a chunk to your sauces for its subtle lemony flavor, then remove it before serving (or substitute a little fresh lemon zest). Leftover lemon grass can be frozen.

Chicken and Red Lentil Curry with Mixed Vegetables

The Girl remembers her trip to Bombay whenever she whips up this simple curry. This is an everyday template for a chicken and vegetable curry that you can change at will — add whatever veggies you have in the fridge, whether it's bell peppers and eggplant, or mixed frozen peas and carrots. Cut firm vegetables like potatoes, carrots, sweet potatoes and rutabagas quite small to ensure they cook through quickly, or use frozen veggies or leftovers. The small red lentils disintegrate into the sauce and thicken it nicely while adding fiber and protein. Put on a pot of basmati rice, and you'll be dining in 30 minutes flat.

1 medium onion
2 cloves garlic, peeled
1 Tbsp. (15 mL) fresh ginger
1 hot chili pepper, seeded
2 Tbsp. (25 mL) vegetable oil
1/2 tsp. (2 mL) whole cumin seeds
1/2 tsp. (2 mL) ground cumin
1/2 tsp. (2 mL) coriander
1/2 tsp. (2 mL) turmeric
1/2 tsp. (2 mL) cayenne
1/2 tsp. (2 mL) garam masala (optional)
8 boneless, skinless chicken thighs, quartered

1 1/2 cups (375 mL) chopped tomatoes, fresh or canned (or plain tomato sauce)
1 1/2 cups (375 mL) water
1/2 cup (125 mL) red lentils
2 cups (500 mL) chopped mixed vegetables (carrots, peas, cauliflower, eggplant, bell peppers and/or potatoes)
salt
1 Tbsp. (15 mL) lemon juice
3 Tbsp. (45 mL) sour cream or plain yogurt (optional)
1 Tbsp. (15 mL) chopped cilantro (or coriander chutney from a jar)

1   In the food processor, combine the onion, garlic, ginger and chili pepper and pulse until minced (or mince by hand). In a deep sauté pan or wok, heat the oil over high heat and cook the cumin seeds until they begin to pop. Be careful that they don't burn. Reduce the heat a little, add the minced vegetables and stir-fry quickly, for about 5 minutes, until the onions are just starting to brown.

2   Stir in the ground cumin, coriander, turmeric, cayenne and garam masala (if using). Cook, stirring, for 1 minute. Add the chicken pieces and stir them around to coat with the spice mixture. Sauté the chicken over medium-high heat for 5 minutes, until it's beginning to brown.

3   Place the tomatoes in the processor (no need to clean it) and process until smooth. Add the tomato purée and water to the sauté pan and bring to a boil.

4   Stir in the lentils and 2 cups (500 mL) mixed vegetables. Bring to a boil, then cover the pan, reduce the heat to medium-low and simmer for 30 minutes.

5   Uncover, stir in the lemon juice, sour cream or yogurt, and cilantro. Serves 4–6.

Almond Chicken

Another favorite dish from the Chinese take-out menu — chicken with mixed vegetables and toasted almonds or cashews. Feel free to substitute other veggies at will, or try this recipe with thinly sliced lean pork. Serve over steamed rice for a meal in a bowl.

2 boneless, skinless chicken breasts

2 tsp. (10 mL) cornstarch

1 Tbsp. (15 mL) cooking sherry or Chinese rice wine

1 Tbsp. (15 mL) light soy sauce

1/2 tsp. (2 mL) salt

1/2 cup (125 mL) sliced fresh mushrooms

1 medium onion, slivered

1 cup (250 mL) chopped celery, cut on the bias

1/2 cup (125 mL) sliced carrots

8 water chestnuts, sliced (or 1/2 cup/125 mL chopped jicama)

1/2 cup (125 mL) frozen peas, thawed

1 cup (250 mL) toasted almonds or cashews

2 Tbsp. (25 mL) canola oil, divided

1/2–inch (1–cm) piece fresh ginger, minced

1 clove garlic, minced

1/2 cup (125 mL) chicken stock

2 tsp. (10 mL) cornstarch dissolved in 1/4 cup (50 mL) stock or water

1 Tbsp. (15 mL) sugar

1 Cut the chicken into 1/2–inch (1–cm) cubes. In a bowl, toss the chicken with the 2 tsp. (10 mL) cornstarch. Add the sherry or rice wine, soy sauce and salt and mix well.

2 Have the mushrooms, onion, celery, carrot, water chestnuts, peas and almonds or cashews measured and ready to go before you start cooking. Heat 1 Tbsp. (15 mL) of the oil in a wok over high heat and add the ginger and garlic. Stir-fry for 10 seconds, then add the chicken and stir-fry just until firm and white, about 2 minutes. Remove the chicken from the pan and set aside.

3 Add the remaining oil to the wok and heat it up for 30 seconds. Add the mushrooms, onion, celery, carrot, water chestnuts and peas. Stir-fry for 2–3 minutes, until the onions are softened. Add the stock and cover the wok. Steam for 2 minutes.

4 Remove the lid and return the chicken to the pan. Add the cornstarch mixture and sugar, and bring to a boil, stirring until the sauce is clear and thick. Stir in the almonds or cashews and serve at once in deep bowls, over lots of hot steamed rice. Serves 4.

Fast Thai Fish Curry

This is one of those meals that you can make with one pit stop at the supermarket. It makes a great one-dish meal on a weeknight, or you can tart it up with some scallops and jumbo shrimp and serve it, with fresh sliced mangoes for dessert, as an instant Friday night dinner for friends.

2 Tbsp. (25 mL) Thai red curry paste

1 can (13 $\frac{1}{2}$ oz./400 mL) fat-reduced coconut milk (usually labeled "lite")

2 tsp. (10 mL) minced ginger

$\frac{1}{2}$ red bell pepper, slivered

2 cups (500 mL) broccoli or cabbage slaw (from the supermarket produce department)

1$\frac{1}{2}$ lbs. (750 g) sole fillets (about 4 small fillets), cut into chunks (or substitute scallops, shrimps and/or mussels)

1 Tbsp. (15 mL) cornstarch dissolved in 1 Tbsp. (15 mL) water (optional)

$\frac{1}{4}$ cup (50 mL) chopped fresh basil

1 Tbsp. (15 mL) lime juice

2 Tbsp. (25 mL) nam pla (fish sauce)

2 green onions, slivered

3 cups (750 mL) cooked basmati rice (or rice noodles)

1 In a wok, heat the curry paste with $\frac{1}{4}$ cup (50 mL) of the coconut milk, mixing it around to form a paste. When the mixture begins to boil, add the remaining coconut milk and ginger. Bring back to a boil and add the red pepper, slaw and sole (frozen is okay). Simmer the mixture for 2–3 minutes, until the fish is cooked through. If a thicker sauce is desired, stir in the cornstarch solution and simmer for 1 minute to thicken. Stir in the fresh basil, lime juice, fish sauce and green onions. Remove from the heat.

2 To serve, press hot cooked rice into a custard cup and unmold in the center of a deep soup plate. Ladle the fish stew around the rice and serve. Serves 4.

Girl talk: Fresh ginger is a staple you should always have on hand. To peel the thin skin from the root, use the edge of a teaspoon. Cut the ginger into $\frac{1}{2}$–inch (1–cm) chunks, then smash it under the flat blade of your chef's knife (like garlic) to make mincing quicker. You can also peel your fresh ginger and freeze it in chunks — use your microplane grater to grate it while it's still frozen for instant fresh ginger flavor.

Pan-Fried Noodles with Oyster Sauce Beef and Snow Peas

The convenient fresh Chinese "steamed" noodles that you find in plastic bags in the produce department need only a few minutes in boiling water to soften, then they're perfect in soups or for pan-frying into crispy noodle cakes. No snow peas? Substitute sliced shiitake or oyster mushrooms or slivered red bell pepper for color.

sauce

1/4 cup (50 mL) oyster sauce

1 Tbsp. (15 mL) soy sauce

1/2 tsp. (2 mL) brown sugar

1/2 tsp. (2 mL) Asian chili paste

1/2 cup (125 mL) chicken stock or water

1–2 tsp. (5–10 mL) cornstarch

stir-fry and noodles

1/2 lb. (250 g) round or sirloin steak, thinly sliced

2 tsp. (10 mL) minced fresh ginger

2 cloves garlic, minced

1 tsp. (5 mL) dark soy sauce

1/2 tsp. (2 mL) cornstarch

1/2 lb. (250 g) steamed Chinese egg noodles (fresh)

1 tsp. (5 mL) sesame oil

canola oil

1 small onion, slivered

1 carrot, cut into thin slices on the diagonal

2 cups (500 mL) fresh snow peas

1 In a small bowl, combine the sauce ingredients. Stir to dissolve the cornstarch. Set aside.

2 In another bowl, combine the meat with the ginger, garlic, soy sauce and cornstarch. Set aside.

3 Heat a large pot of water to a rolling boil and add the noodles, breaking them apart as they cook. Cook for 1 minute, then drain in a colander in the sink. Return them to the pot and toss with the sesame oil.

4 In a wok, heat about 2 Tbsp. (25 mL) of canola oil over high heat until almost smoking. Add half the noodles to the wok, pressing them into a flat mass. When browned on one side, use a wide spatula to lift and flip the noodle cake. Brown the second side lightly, adding more oil if necessary. Set in a serving bowl. Brown the remaining noodles, and place in a separate serving bowl.

5 Add a little more oil to the wok and stir-fry the onion until it is beginning to brown. Add the beef and cook for 1–2 minutes, until brown, then stir in the carrot and snow peas. Stir-fry for 2–3 minutes, then add 2 Tbsp. (25 mL) of water, cover the wok with a lid and steam for 1 minute.

6 Remove the lid and add the sauce mixture. Stir-fry until the sauce boils and thickens. Add a little more cornstarch solution (mix a bit of cornstarch with a touch of water) if it's not thick enough. To serve, spoon the stir-fried beef, vegetables and sauce over the browned noodles. Serves 2.

Japanese curry Chicken

Molly is a young girlfriend with a yen for curry chicken, Japanese-style, which tends to be a lot milder than Indian versions. The Girl asked her Japanese contacts and they came clean — that curry chicken you enjoy with your bento box for lunch is flavored with a commercial mix, a curry powder combo from one of the big brands like Glico or S&B. It's simple — add chicken, veggies and simmer, then dump it all over a bowl of steamed sticky rice. Get your Japanese curry mix at any well-stocked Asian supermarket.

1 lb. (500 g) boneless chicken thighs
1 tsp. (5 mL) curry powder
2 tsp. (10 mL) canola oil
2 large onions, chopped
2 cups (500 mL) water

2 medium potatoes, cubed (about 1½ cups/
  375 mL)
1 package Japanese curry mix for four servings
  (powder or cubes)
1 cup (250 mL) frozen peas, thawed

1 Cut the chicken into bite-sized pieces. Place in a bowl and sprinkle with the curry powder. Set aside.

2 Heat the oil in a sauté pan and cook the onions over medium heat until they begin to brown. Add the chicken and continue to sauté until the chicken is brown. Stir in the water and potatoes, bring to a boil, cover and simmer for 30 minutes. Remove the lid, add the curry mix and simmer 20 minutes longer, until nicely thickened. Stir in the peas and serve immediately. Serves 3–4.

Comforts of Home

After a long day in the trenches, the Girl likes to come home to something familiar and comforting. Chicken or beef stew, meatloaf, baked beans and macaroni all fit the bill — the simple stuff Mom used to make, and food that reheats beautifully. Augment any of these one-dish, family dinners with a simple tossed salad and end with chocolate chip cookies (page 95), apple berry crisp (page 317) or old-fashioned spice cake (page 320).

Chicken and Dumplings

The Girl finds the food of the deep South especially comforting — hearty, homestyle cooking like chicken stew topped with cornmeal dumplings. In this stew, you can have your dumplings soft and steamy, or crisp and golden, depending on how you finish the dish.

stew

2 lbs. (1 kg) boneless, skinless chicken
   (thighs and breasts)
1 Tbsp. (15 mL) vegetable oil
1 onion, chopped
2 cloves garlic, minced
2 large carrots, peeled and chopped
3 stalks celery, chopped

1 small white turnip, peeled and chopped
2 Tbsp. (25 mL) all-purpose flour
1¹/2 cups (375 mL) chicken stock
¹/4 tsp. (1 mL) dried thyme
¹/4 tsp. (1 mL) sage
salt and freshly ground black pepper
3 Tbsp. (45 mL) chopped fresh parsley

dumplings

¹/2 cup (125 mL) cornmeal
¹/2 cup (125 mL) all-purpose flour
2 tsp. (10 mL) baking powder
pinch salt

2 Tbsp. (25 mL) butter
1 egg, beaten
¹/4 cup (50 mL) milk

1 Cut the chicken into 2–inch (5–cm) chunks. In a large Dutch oven, heat the oil over medium-high heat and cook the chicken until it's just beginning to brown, about 5 minutes. Remove the chicken from the pot with a slotted spoon and set aside in a bowl. Add the onion, garlic, carrots, celery and turnip to the same pot. Cook over medium-high heat for 5–10 minutes, until it's beginning to brown. Stir in the flour and slowly add the stock, stirring until the mixture comes to a boil and begins to thicken.

2 Stir in the browned chicken and any juices that have collected in the bowl. Add the thyme and sage, and season with salt and pepper. Cover the pan, reduce the heat to low, and simmer for 30 minutes. Stir in the fresh parsley.

3 Mix up the dumplings. In a bowl, combine the cornmeal, flour, baking powder and salt. In a measuring cup, melt the butter in the microwave for a few seconds, then whisk in the egg and milk. Make a depression in the center of the dry ingredients in the bowl, then add the wet ingredients all at once and stir quickly with a fork, just to moisten everything.

4 When the stew is cooked, spoon the dumplings on top, dotting them over the surface in heaping tablespoons. Cover the pot and steam until the dumplings are tender, about 15 minutes.

5 For a crispy cornmeal topping, transfer the cooked stew to a casserole dish and spoon the dumpling mixture on top. Place the casserole in a preheated 425°F (220°C) oven, and bake for 15–20 minutes, until the top is golden and puffed. Serves 4.

Basic Beef Stew

There's nothing more basic than basic beef stew, but it's a classic to enjoy on a winter evening. Buy a nice loaf of bread to serve alongside or, if you're feeling ambitious, whip up some biscuits (page 338) or cornbread (page 242). Then holler for the hands.

1/4 cup (50 mL) all-purpose flour seasoned with
  salt and freshly ground black pepper
1 1/2 lbs. (750 g) beef stew meat, trimmed
  of fat and cubed
2 Tbsp. (25 mL) canola oil
2 large onions, slivered
2 bay leaves

1 cup (250 mL) diced celery
1 1/2 cups (375 mL) chopped carrots
4 medium potatoes, cubed
1 cup (250 mL) chopped parsnip (optional)
1 1/2 tsp. (7 mL) salt
freshly ground black pepper to taste

1 Put the seasoned flour in a plastic bag. Add the beef cubes, a few at a time, and shake well to coat.

2 In a deep pot or Dutch oven, heat the oil over medium-high heat. Add the beef cubes in batches and brown on all sides in the hot oil. As the meat is browned, remove and set it aside on a plate. If you crowd the pot, the meat won't brown and caramelize like it should, it will simply stew in its own juices, so don't be tempted to rush the process.

3 Add the onions to the pot and cook for 10 minutes, until they are beginning to turn golden brown.

4 Return the meat to the pot and add 3 cups (750 mL) of water. If you're feeling fancy, replace half the water with red wine or dark ale and add a spoonful of brown sugar to balance the flavor. Add the bay leaves. Bring to a boil, then reduce the heat to low, cover the pot, and simmer until the beef is almost tender, 1 1/2–2 hours.

5 Add the celery, carrots, potatoes and parsnips to the pot, and season with salt and pepper. Bring back to a boil and continue to simmer on low heat, covered, until everything is tender, about 20–30 minutes longer. Remove the lid and boil to reduce and thicken the gravy if necessary.

6 Serve the stew immediately or cool and refrigerate overnight (this helps meld the flavors and allows you to skim off any fat that solidifies on the top). Serves 4.

Apple Baked Beans with Chicken Sausage

The Girl has a source of fine fresh sausage from a local shop — a favorite being their chicken and apple sausage. If you can't find a good fresh chicken sausage for this dish, substitute some chunks of boneless, skinless chicken thighs or cook the beans, vegetarian-style, without the meat. A one-dish meal that's perfect winter fare — after you've been out walking, shoveling or building snowmen it makes the house suitably steamy and reheats splendidly.

1½ cups (375 mL) dried navy beans, rinsed

1 Tbsp. (15 mL) molasses

3 slices smoky bacon, chopped

2 Tbsp. (25 mL) olive oil

1½ lbs. (750 g) apple chicken sausage (or skinless, boneless chicken thighs)

2 cups (500 mL) chopped onion

½ cup (125 mL) chopped celery

2 cloves garlic, minced

2 Granny Smith apples, chopped

1 Tbsp. (15 mL) dry mustard

½ tsp. (2 mL) ground sage

pinch ground cloves

2 cups (500 mL) apple cider

1 tsp. (5 mL) sea salt

2 tsp. (10 mL) apple cider vinegar

1 Put the beans and molasses in a pot and cover with plenty of water. Bring to a boil over high heat, boil for 15 minutes, then remove the pot from the heat, cover and let stand 1 hour. Drain the beans and reserve.

2 Meanwhile, in a large Dutch oven, cook the bacon over medium heat until it's beginning to brown. Add the olive oil and sausage and cook until the meat is browned. Remove the sausages from the pan and set aside.

3 Add the onion, celery and garlic to the pan and cook until the onion is soft. Add the apples, dry mustard, sage, cloves, cider and reserved beans to the pot. Bring to a boil and simmer for 30 minutes.

4 Cut the cooked sausage (or chicken) into chunks and stir into the bean mixture with the salt and cider vinegar. Transfer all to an ovenproof casserole dish or bean pot and bake the beans, covered, in a 325°F (160°C) oven, for 2 hours longer. Serves 4.

Filet-O-Fishies

The Girl is always trying to get more healthy fish and seafood into her diet. But since she doesn't live near the sea, it can be a challenge to find fresh and affordable fish. Luckily, decent FAS (frozen at sea) fish fillets that are easy to cook quickly for weekday meals are now available in most supermarkets. Look for bags of individually frozen fillets of halibut, cod, sole and other mild white fish and learn this simple technique to cook them.

frozen fish fillets (halibut, cod, pickerel, snapper, sole, etc.)

salt and freshly ground pepper
all-purpose flour
canola oil

1 Thaw the fish enough to remove the icy coating (they often freeze the fish with a coating of sea water to keep it fresh). Pat dry.

2 Season fillets on both sides with salt and pepper. Put some flour in a shallow bowl and lightly flour the fish on both sides, shaking off any excess flour.

3 Heat a couple of tablespoons of oil in a nonstick frying pan over medium-high heat. When the oil is hot, add the fish to the pan. Pan-fry on both sides until golden brown, about 3–5 minutes per side. You can enjoy your crispy, fried fish as is, with a side of plain rice and steamed veggies, or with oven fries (page 50). Or you can try these easy flavor additions and serving suggestions:

- Using a pastry brush, lightly brush the browned fish with an Asian barbecue sauce, oyster sauce, Indian curry paste or hoisin sauce to add some exotic flavor and serve it atop a Chinese vegetable stir-fry or an Indian biryani (page 127).

- Brush the fish with a little basil or sundried tomato pesto (page 80) and serve it alongside a simple plate of spaghetti with tomato sauce.

- Break the fried fish up into chunks and combine it with some chopped tomatoes, avocado, lettuce, cilantro and salsa, then roll it up in corn tortillas for speedy fish tacos.

- Stack your fried fish in a toasted whole-wheat hamburger bun with lettuce and tartare sauce (or mayo mixed with pickle relish) for a fast fish sandwich. Serves 1 per filet.

Meatball Stew with New Potatoes

With a pound of ground round and a bag of supermarket baby carrots, this makes a hearty family meal. Make this simple stew when you have tiny new potatoes, no bigger than a meatball, or just cube larger spuds.

1 lb. (500 g) lean ground beef
½ cup (125 mL) dry bread or saltine cracker crumbs
1 small onion, minced
1 egg
1 tsp. (5 mL) salt
½ tsp. (2 mL) freshly ground black pepper
½ tsp. (2 mL) thyme
2 cloves garlic, pressed
1 14–ounce (398–mL) can tomato sauce
1½ cups (375 mL) beef broth

1 cup (250 mL) dry red wine
1 cup (250 mL) water
2 cups (500 mL) small cooking onions, peeled, or 2 large onions cut into slivers
2 cups (500 mL) baby carrots or 4 large carrots, cut into chunks
2 cups (500 mL) tiny new potatoes or potato cubes
1 Tbsp. (15 mL) cornstarch mixed with a little cold water
chopped fresh parsley

1 Combine the ground beef, crumbs, onion, egg, salt, pepper and thyme, mixing well with your hands. Shape into 1½–inch (4–cm) meatballs. Arrange the meatballs in a single layer on a baking sheet and bake in a 400°F (200°C) oven for about 12–15 minutes, until nicely browned. Drain the excess fat.

2 Combine the remaining ingredients, except for the parsley and cornstarch solution, in a large ovenproof pot or covered casserole dish and mix well. Gently stir in the browned meatballs, being careful not to break them. Reduce the oven temperature to 350°F (180°C), cover and bake for 1 hour.

3 Check to make sure the potatoes and carrots are tender. Thicken the stew with the cornstarch solution, heating through until the sauce is clear. Serve the stew sprinkled with fresh parsley. Serves 6.

Meatloaf

Nothing like a meatloaf to make a comforting meal. The Girl likes to start with lean ground beef, then spice things up a bit with peppers and barbecue sauce. Make lots and serve extra-thick slices the next day in meatloaf sandwiches. Speed up the prep by using a food processor to mince the veggies, then make the crumbs.

2 lbs. (1 kg) lean ground beef (or 3/4 lean ground beef and 1/4 ground pork)
1 small onion, minced
1/2 red bell pepper (fresh or roasted), minced
2 cloves garlic, minced
1 Tbsp. (15 mL) olive oil
3/4 cup (175 mL) dry bread- or saltine cracker crumbs

1/2 cup (125 mL) barbecue sauce or chili sauce
1 large egg, lightly beaten
1 Tbsp. (15 mL) Worcestershire sauce
1 tsp. (5 mL) Italian seasoning or dried basil
1/2 tsp. (2 mL) salt
freshly ground black pepper
1 cup (250 mL) freshly grated Parmesan cheese (optional but really good in meatballs)

1 Preheat the oven to 350°F (180°C). Crumble the ground meat into a large bowl. Cook the minced onion, red pepper and garlic in the oil over medium-high heat for 5 minutes to soften. Cool slightly and add to the meat in the bowl. Use the processor to make the breadcrumbs, and add to the bowl.

2 Using your hands, mix the meat, vegetables and crumbs. Add the remaining ingredients and continue to knead until everything is evenly mixed. Lightly press the meat mixture into a loaf pan or form into a football-shaped loaf on a rimmed baking sheet. Bake for 45–60 minutes, until the loaf is well-browned on top and the internal temperature reaches 170°F (75°C). (For faster, individual meatloaves, divide the meat mixture into 12 large balls and press them into a muffin pan, then bake at 400°F/200°C for about 25 minutes.)

3 Drain any excess fat and let the meatloaf rest for 10 minutes, then carve into thick slices. Serves 6–8.

Girl talk: Of course this ground meat mixture makes great meatballs, too. Just form it into balls (tiny ones for meatball soup or as big as table tennis balls for spaghetti), then set on a baking sheet and bake at 400°F (200°C) for 20–30 minutes until nicely browned. Precooked meatballs are great to have in the freezer to pop into a meatball stew (page 68) or plain spaghetti sauce.

Cheese and Macaroni

This is a wickedly decadent version of an old favorite that definitely puts the cheese front and center, using three cheeses including a strong-flavored aged Cheddar. For more speed but less intense cheese flavor, use a pre-shredded cheese blend or, for an assertive but creamy sauce, opt for a couple of tubs of potted Old English cheese, a processed but flavorful cheese product you'll find in most supermarkets, in lieu of the grated Cheddar. You can reduce fat marginally by using evaporated milk in place of the cream, but it won't make this high-fat dish much more virtuous. Serve sparingly.

1 lb. (500 g) macaroni or penne
1/4 cup (50 mL) butter
1/3 cup (75 mL) all-purpose flour
2 cups (500 mL) milk
1 cup (250 mL) cream or half-and-half
salt and white pepper

few drops Tabasco sauce
1 lb. (500 g) finely shredded sharp aged
  Cheddar cheese
1/2 lb. (250 g) shredded mozzarella
1/2 cup (125 mL) freshly grated Parmesan cheese

1 Cook the pasta in lots of boiling salted water for about 8 minutes. It should be slightly undercooked. Drain.

2 To make the sauce, melt the butter in a saucepan over medium heat until it's bubbly but not brown. Add the flour and stir for 1 minute to cook the flour. Using a whisk, slowly add the milk, whisking as you go to make sure there are no lumps. Add the cream in the same manner. Bring to a boil, stirring constantly. Continue to whisk until the sauce is smooth and thick, about 5 minutes. Season with salt, pepper and a shot or two of Tabasco sauce.

3 Combine the cheeses. Reduce the heat under the cream sauce to low and add two-thirds of the cheese, reserving the rest for topping. Stir with a spoon just until the cheese is melted. Add the well-drained pasta and stir to combine.

4 Preheat the oven to 350°F (180°C). Pour the macaroni and cheese into a shallow 9- x 13-inch (23- x 33-cm) baking dish. Sprinkle the remaining cheese evenly over top of the baking dish. Place in the oven and bake for about 30 minutes, until nice and bubbly. Serves 6–8.

Girl talk: The Girl rarely indulges in this decadent reminder of her college days but when she does, she likes her mac cheesy and straight up. If you tend to live on this stuff, you might want to throw in something healthy once in awhile — think cooked veggies like spinach, onions and roasted peppers or cooked broccoli, frozen peas and green onions. Some people even like to layer their mac and cheese with fresh sliced tomatoes or tuna fish. Strange but true.

Savory Bread Pudding with Salmon and Dill

This is classic comfort food. Make it the night before and bake it for brunch, or whip it together after work. Use good-quality canned salmon — the Girl goes for sockeye for its amazing wild salmon flavor, healthy Omega 3 oils, and gorgeous color. If you like smoked salmon, use a can of alder-smoked fish from the fish market. This is the perfect place to use up that stale loaf of French bread or any cooked vegetables or cheeses that are hanging around in the refrigerator. Be creative and change the ingredients to suit your mood.

2 Tbsp. (25 mL) olive oil

1 medium onion, chopped or thinly sliced

2 cloves garlic, minced

4 cups (1 L) 2–inch (5–cm) bread cubes (slightly stale French bread is the best)

2–3 Tbsp. (25–45 mL) chopped fresh dill

3 cups (750 mL) chopped fresh spinach

2 cups (500 mL) grated cheese (Gruyère, Gouda, Fontina, etc.)

4 eggs, lightly beaten

1 cup (250 mL) milk

1/2 tsp. (2 mL) salt

1/2 tsp. (2 mL) freshly ground black pepper

1 can (7 1/2 oz./213 mL) sockeye salmon, drained

1 Heat the olive oil in a large nonstick sauté pan over medium heat and slowly cook the onion until soft and caramelized. This will take 20–30 minutes. Add the garlic halfway through cooking.

2 In a large bowl, toss the caramelized onion with the bread cubes, dill and spinach. Mix in 1 1/2 cups (375 mL) of the grated cheese.

3 Whisk together the eggs, milk, salt and pepper. Pour this mixture evenly over the bread cubes and stir until most of the egg mixture has been soaked up by the bread.

4 Preheat the oven to 350°F (180°C). In a deep, 8–inch (20–cm) round or oval casserole dish that has been lightly rubbed with olive oil, layer half of the bread mixture. Break the salmon into chunks and spread evenly on top, then finish with the remaining bread cubes. Press down lightly so that most of the bread is soaked with the egg mixture. Sprinkle with the remaining 1/2 cup (50 mL) of grated cheese.

5 Bake uncovered for 45 minutes, until the pudding is golden brown and crisp on top. Cool 5 minutes before serving. Serves 4.

Basic Risotto

Risotto for everyday? Yesirree girls, risotto is classic comfort food and something you can make when there's nothing in the cupboard but some rice, a can of chicken broth and a moldy chunk of Parmesan in the fridge. And it's fast food, too — cooked in 20 minutes flat. Once you've got the basic risotto down, you can add anything else you have kicking around to spice it up — fresh chopped herbs, a little sausage or prosciutto, fresh or leftover cooked veggies like peas and asparagus, chopped tomatoes or winter squash. Or kick it up for company with wild mushrooms and prawns. Just remember, the broth to rice ratio is four to one. Start with some olive oil and butter, chopped onion, a splash of white wine and finish with a cup or two of grated Parmesan. Use hot broth, add it very slowly, and stir. That's it — really. And eat it immediately. Risotto waits for no one.

4 cups (1 L) broth (vegetable or chicken, home-made if possible)

2 Tbsp. (25 mL) extra virgin olive oil

2 Tbsp. (25 mL) butter

1 cup (250 mL) minced onion

1 clove garlic, minced

1 cup (250 mL) risotto rice (Arborio, Carnaroli or Vialone Nano)

1/2 cup (125 mL) white wine

1 1/2 cups (375 mL) freshly grated Parmesan cheese, divided

1 Put the broth into a saucepan, bring it to a boil over high heat, then reduce the heat to low and keep it warm.

2 Meanwhile, in a wide, nonstick sauté pan, heat the oil and butter together over medium-high heat. Add the onion and garlic and cook for 5 minutes, until softened but not brown. Stir in the rice and cook for about a minute, until the rice is coated and shiny.

3 Add the wine, stirring until it is completely absorbed. Pour yourself a glass, too. You'll be standing here awhile.

4 Now begin adding the hot broth, about 1/2 cup (125 mL) at a time. Stir the risotto with a wooden spoon until the broth is absorbed, then add another ladle of broth. Continue in this manner until the broth is used up and the rice is cooked just *al dente* (toothsome but tender, not mushy). Don't worry about stirring constantly or vigorously — the risotto will be fine even if you almost ignore it, but do stir it and don't add the broth all at once. The more you stir, and the more attention you pay, the creamier the end result. You'll have to start testing the risotto before all of the broth is used up to determine when it's exactly ready. The entire process will take 20–25 minutes.

5 Stir in 1 cup (250 mL) of the cheese and a little more broth, cover the pan and let the risotto rest for 2 minutes before serving in shallow bowls, sprinkled with the remaining cheese. Serves 4.

Risotto Extras

- For wild mushroom risotto, sauté $1/2$ cup (125 mL) fresh or rehydrated dry, sliced wild mushrooms (porcini, morel, chanterelle, portobello) with the onion and garlic.

- If you want to add other vegetables that require some cooking (like fresh asparagus, peas, cubed squash or chopped spinach), add them after about 10 minutes of cooking.

- If you have leftover roasted or grilled vegetables, add them with the cheese at the end. Or you can purée a cup of cooked veggies with a couple of tablespoons of melted butter in the food processor (this works well with anything from steamed asparagus, peas and spinach to carrots, roasted red peppers or pumpkin) and stir the purée into the risotto at the end (the perfect way to add instant color).

- Large peeled and deveined prawns can be added halfway through the cooking time (around the 10-minute mark) or smaller shrimp can be halved lengthwise and stirred in at the end, just before the resting period. They will cook perfectly in the hot rice.

- Minced fresh herbs (basil, thyme, parsley or rosemary) can go in at the end, too.

- Vary the cheese. Try stirring in some aged Friulano, blue cheese or even goat cheese.

Girl talk: Get yourself to an Italian grocery and buy the good stuff — rice and Parmigiano-Reggiano cheese, that is. Risotto rice is a special, short grain rice that's starchy and gets creamy when it's cooked this way. Do not try this at home with long-grain or converted rice or you'll never try to make risotto again.

Arborio is the easiest kind of risotto rice to find (available almost anywhere these days) but you may need a little more broth as it tends to make the stiffest risotto. Being a risotto snob, the Girl prefers Vialone Nano if you can find it — it makes a nice, creamy risotto. Carnaroli is the most expensive risotto rice — tender but firm and unlikely to overcook to mush. Save it for those special dates and really decadent dinners.

The Girl once judged a risotto contest — really — and the winner used some expensive, imported risotto rice from a special region of Italy that cost $16 a pound! But it really did make the difference. His risotto was perfect.

Savory Cheese Pie

This is classic Greek comfort food. Don't panic about making the pastry — it's dead easy to mix up and the olive oil keeps it totally malleable and a breeze to roll (use the same pastry if you want to make spinach pies). You can also use store-bought phyllo pastry. Just line the pan with four to six layers of pastry (each layer brushed very lightly with olive oil), fill with the cheese mixture, then top with more phyllo layers. Roll the edges the same way to seal, brush the top with oil, and score the pastry lightly before baking to make cutting the pie later a little easier. Serve some salad on the side and you've got a vegetarian feast.

pastry

2 cups (500 mL) all-purpose flour

pinch salt

1 egg

$^1/_3$ cup (75 mL) olive oil

$^1/_3$ cup (75 mL) warm water

2 Tbsp. (25 mL) milk, to glaze (optional)

filling

4 oz. (125 g) feta or mizithra cheese, crumbled

4 oz. (125 g) grated kasseri or other aged cheese

1 cup (250 mL) ricotta cheese

2 large eggs

4 green onions, minced

2 Tbsp. (25 mL) minced fresh parsley

freshly ground black pepper

1 tsp. (5 mL) chopped fresh mint

1 To make the pastry, combine the flour and salt in a bowl. Whisk together the egg and oil, then stir into the flour with a fork, until the dough is crumbly. Slowly drizzle in the water, just enough to form a soft dough. Knead until the dough is smooth and elastic, then form into a ball and set in a bowl, covered, to rest for 15 minutes.

2 Preheat the oven to 400°F (200°C). Oil a 9–inch (23–cm) square baking pan or springform pan. Divide the dough into thirds, using two-thirds to line the pan. Roll the dough on a lightly floured surface until it is several inches larger than the pan, then drape it into the pan, overhanging the edges.

3 Combine the remaining ingredients and whisk until smooth. Pour into the crust. Roll the last piece of pastry and lay it over the pie. To seal the edges, fold the bottom crust over the top crust, press and roll to form a rope edge. Brush the pie with milk to glaze if desired.

4 Bake the pie for 45–50 minutes, until it is golden and crisp. Let cool completely before cutting. Serve at room temperature. Serves 4–6.

> **Girl talk:** Mizithra is a kind of Greek sheep's milk cheese — young and salty like feta but with more assertive flavor. Kasseri is a drier, aged sheep or goat's milk cheese, the kind that's sliced and fried in olive oil and flamed with brandy as an appetizer in Greek restaurants. Look for both in specialty cheese sections or Greek delis to make this dish authentic, or substitute similar cheeses like feta, Asiago, Parmesan or aged goat cheese.

Swiss Steak

Not sure where the name comes from, but it's a favorite family-style recipe for tenderizing tougher cuts of beef, like inexpensive round steak. You can use the tenderized minute steaks from the supermarket to speed up the cooking time. Serve it with noodles, polenta (page 165) or baked potatoes. This is the perfect dish to make and eat as leftovers — it's even better the next day.

2 lbs. (1 kg) round steak, cut 1/2 inch
  (1 cm) thick
1/2 cup (125 mL) all-purpose flour seasoned with
  salt and pepper
1/4 cup (50 mL) butter or bacon fat
1/2 cup (250 mL) chopped onions
1 cup (250 mL) chopped green onions
1/3 cup (75 mL) chopped celery
3/4 cup (175 mL) chopped red or yellow bell pepper
1 cup (250 mL) chopped canned tomatoes

1/2 cup (125 mL) water or beef stock
1/2 cup (125 mL) red wine
1 tsp. (5 mL) salt
1/4 tsp. (1 mL) freshly ground black pepper
1/2 tsp. (2 mL) dried thyme
1 bay leaf
1/4 tsp. (1 mL) hot pepper sauce (like Tabasco)
1 Tbsp. (15 mL) Worcestershire sauce
2 Tbsp. (25 mL) chopped fresh parsley

1 Cut the steak into serving size pieces. Place the seasoned flour on the work surface and, using a meat mallet, pound the steaks until they are 1/4 inch (5 mm) thick. Incorporate as much flour as the meat will absorb, reserving the excess.

2 In a Dutch oven, heat the butter or bacon fat over medium-high heat and brown the meat well on both sides. As the meat browns, remove and keep warm.

3 Add any remaining seasoned flour to the fat in the pan and stir to make a paste. Cook, stirring, until it turns brown, like peanut butter, then add the onions, green onions, celery and bell pepper. Cook together for 5 minutes, then stir in the tomatoes, water or stock and wine.

4 Bring to a boil, then return the meat to the pan. Add the salt, pepper, thyme, bay leaf, hot sauce and Worcestershire. Reduce the heat to low, cover and simmer for about 1 1/2 hours (or bake for 2 hours in a 300°F/150°C oven). For the best flavor, make the steak the night before and reheat it. Sprinkle with parsley before serving. Serves 4–6.

Hunter's Chicken

This is a classic dish — chicken pieces cooked low and slow in an Italian-style tomato sauce. It's cheap and cheerful for an everyday family meal and can stand in with fresh pasta for a casual weekend dinner.

1 3–lb. (1.5–kg) chicken, cut up
salt and freshly ground black pepper
3 Tbsp. (45 mL) olive oil, divided
1 onion, sliced
1 large red bell pepper, cored and cut into strips
2 cloves garlic, minced
1/2 cup (125 mL) dry white wine (or red wine)
2 cups (500 mL) canned tomatoes, chopped
  (19–oz./540–mL can)

1 tsp. (5 mL) minced fresh oregano (or 1/2 tsp./
  2 mL dried)
1 tsp. (5 mL) minced fresh thyme (or 1/2 tsp./
  2 mL dried)
1 bay leaf
2 Tbsp. (25 mL) minced fresh basil
1/4 cup (50 mL) finely grated Parmesan cheese

1 Season the chicken with salt and pepper. Heat 2 Tbsp. (25 mL) of the oil in a nonstick pan and sauté the chicken over medium heat for 7–10 minutes, turning occasionally, until nicely browned. Transfer the chicken to a plate.

2 Add the remaining olive oil to the pan and sauté the onion, bell pepper and garlic for 5 minutes. Stir in the wine and simmer for 1 minute, then add the tomatoes, oregano, thyme and bay leaf.

3 Return the chicken to the pan and bring to a boil. Cover and simmer for 45 minutes, or until the chicken is tender. Remove the cover and boil until sauce is reduced and thickened, about 10 minutes longer. Pile the chicken on a platter and sprinkle with fresh basil and freshly grated Parmesan cheese. Serves 4.

Girl talk: For a spicier, more adult dish, stir in some sliced black or green olives, a couple of minced anchovies and a shot of hot sauce just before serving.

Super Fasta Pasta

Pasta meals are perfect for weekdays but you do get into that jar of
sauce and spaghetti rut, don't you? The Girl believes there's a time for a jar
of basic tomato sauce but you'd better be ready to torque it up. Or better yet,
just stick with these simple sauces and tosses — you'll never be stuck
with plain tomato sauce again. Viva Italia!

The Original Fasta Pasta

This is a pasta dish that is created almost completely from jars and cans — when it seems like the cupboard is bare, you can still feast. Add a salad and a tiramisu from the deli and it's an instant casual dinner party.

1/4 cup (50 mL) virgin olive oil

6 oz. (175 g) slivered, cooked ham (or smoked turkey)

3 cloves garlic, minced

3/4 cup (175 mL) sundried tomatoes, in oil, chopped

3/4 cup (175 mL) black olives, pitted and chopped or sliced

1 can (12 oz./398 mL) artichoke hearts, drained and chopped

1–2 crushed red chilies

1 lb. (500 g) short pasta (gemelli, rotini, penne, etc.)

2 Tbsp. (25 mL) basil pesto (or 2 Tbsp./25 mL chopped fresh basil)

1/2 lb. (250 g) goat cheese or feta

salt and freshly ground black pepper

1 In a large sauté pan, heat the oil and cook the ham and garlic together, just until the garlic sizzles. Add the sundried tomatoes, olives, artichokes and chilies, and heat through. Keep warm on low heat.

2 Meanwhile, bring a large pot of salted water to a boil, and cook the pasta until *al dente*, about 8–12 minutes. Drain, then return to the pot and add the contents of the sauté pan. Toss the vegetables with the pasta. Stir in the pesto. Crumble in the cheese and toss. Serve immediately. Serves 4.

Rotini with Tuna Tapenade

The Girl is known for her tapenade (olive paste) that's made with green olives and cut with Italian tuna. Serve it over pasta or on crostini for almost instant appetizers.

1 cup (250 mL) pitted green olives (use the kind that are stuffed with anchovies if you can)

1 Tbsp. (15 mL) minced fresh garlic

2 Tbsp. (25 mL) olive oil

1 3 1/2-oz. (100–mL) tin tuna packed in olive oil

1 tsp. (5 mL) grainy mustard

1/2 tsp. (2 mL) hot pepper sauce

1/2 lemon, juice and minced zest

2 Tbsp. (25 mL) chopped fresh parsley

3/4 lb. (375 g) rotini or other short pasta

1 cup (250 mL) grated Parmesan cheese

1 In a food processor, combine the olives and garlic and pulse until chopped but still chunky. Add the oil, tuna, mustard, hot sauce and lemon juice. Pulse again to combine. The tapenade should be partly pasty and partly coarse. Add the lemon zest and parsley and pulse just to combine. Refrigerate.

2 When ready to serve, cook the pasta until *al dente* and drain well. Toss the hot pasta with the tapenade and grated cheese. Serve immediately. Serves 4.

Penne with Asparagus, Chicken and Roasted Peppers

This is another fast pasta dish to whip up after work. Use your own home-roasted peppers or stop at the supermarket and grab a jar of roasted peppers, along with a rotisserie chicken, some asparagus and Parmesan, and you'll be dining in the 10 minutes it takes to boil the pasta.

2 Tbsp. (25 mL) butter, divided
1/2 lb. (250 g) asparagus, trimmed and
   cut diagonally into 1-inch (2.5-cm) pieces
1 yellow bell pepper, roasted and peeled
1 red bell pepper, roasted and peeled
1 tsp. (5 mL) minced garlic
1 cup (250 mL) chicken stock

1/2 tsp. (2.5 mL) salt
1/2 lb. (250 g) penne pasta
1/2 tsp. (2 mL) dried thyme
1 cup (250 mL) chopped, roasted chicken
1/2 cup (125 mL) freshly grated Parmigiano-Reggiano
freshly ground black pepper

1 In a skillet, heat 1 Tbsp. (15 mL) of the butter and sauté the asparagus for 5 minutes. Dice the roasted peppers and stir into the pan along with the garlic and stock. Bring to a boil, then remove from the heat.

2 Meanwhile, cook the pasta in salted water until just slightly undercooked. Drain.

3 Return the sauce to the heat and stir in the pasta and thyme. Add the chicken, cover, and simmer for 5 minutes longer, until the pasta is *al dente* and the sauce has reduced slightly. Stir in the Parmigiano and the remaining butter and season with pepper. Serves 2–3.

Girl talk: Roasted peppers in a jar are perfectly fine, but you can make your own and save a bundle if you roast and freeze a peck of peppers in the fall. See page 332.

Whole-Wheat Pasta Shells with Spicy Tomato Pesto and Greens

Healthy, healthy, healthy! And fast — especially if you make the tomato pesto in advance and keep some on hand in the fridge. Whole-wheat pasta needs assertive sauce like this spicy tomato pesto. The wilted greens add a healthy jolt of color — arugula and mustard add the most flavor, but you can also use prewashed baby spinach to save time.

tomato pesto

1/2 cup (125 mL) sundried tomatoes

2 cloves garlic, minced

1/4 cup (50 mL) chopped fresh basil

1/4 cup (50 mL) sliced almonds

1/4 cup (50 mL) grated Parmesan cheese

1/2 tsp. (2 mL) salt

1 small dried red chili pepper (or 1/4 tsp./ 1 mL dried red pepper flakes)

2–3 Tbsp. (25–45 mL) extra virgin olive oil

2–4 Tbsp. (25–50 mL) reserved tomato soaking liquid or water

pasta

3/4 lb. (375 g) whole-wheat pasta (small shells, orecchiette or other short pasta)

3 cups (750 mL) fresh greens (Swiss chard, arugula, mustard or baby spinach)

1 Tbsp. (15 mL) olive oil

1 large onion, slivered

1/4 cup (50 mL) stock or water

salt and freshly ground black pepper

extra grated Parmesan cheese to garnish

1 Soak the tomatoes in 1 cup (240 mL) of boiling water for 10 minutes to soften. Drain and reserve the soaking liquid. In a food processor, combine the softened tomatoes, garlic, basil, almonds, Parmesan, salt and chili pepper. Process until smooth, scraping down the sides of the bowl as necessary. Slowly add the 2–3 Tbsp. (25–45 mL) of oil with the machine running. Add the reserved tomato soaking liquid or water, a tablespoon (15 mL) at a time, until you have a smooth pesto. Set aside or refrigerate for up to 1 week.

2 Bring a large pot of salted water to a boil and cook the pasta until *al dente*, about 10–12 minutes.

3 Meanwhile, roll the leafy greens and slice into strips. Chop any stems fine or discard if too woody. Heat the 1 Tbsp. (15 mL) of oil over medium-high heat in a wide sauté pan. Add the onion and cook, stirring, until it is beginning to brown, then reduce the heat to low and continue to cook until the onion is nicely caramelized, about 10 minutes longer.

4 Add the greens to the pan and stir-fry until the leaves turn bright green. Add the stock or water, cover and steam for 2 minutes.

5 Drain the pasta and toss with the tomato pesto and steamed greens. Season with salt and pepper. Pass additional Parmesan cheese at the table. Serves 4.

Farfalle with Salmon and Soybeans

Here's an easy dish for a spring fling when you just want to get something fresh and green back into your life. Simple, clean and healthful, too.

1 boneless salmon fillet, about 6 oz. (175 g)
2 cups (500 mL) fresh spinach
1 1/2 cups (375 mL) farfalle (butterfly) pasta
1 cup (250 mL) shelled soybeans (edamame), from the frozen food section of the Asian grocery
1 Tbsp. (15 mL) chopped fresh dill

3 green onions, minced
1 tsp. (5 mL) finely grated lemon zest (use the microplane grater)
1 Tbsp. (15 mL) fresh lemon juice
2–3 Tbsp. (25–45 mL) fruity extra virgin olive oil
salt and freshly ground black pepper

1 Rub the salmon fillet on both sides with olive oil and season with salt and pepper. Heat a nonstick pan over medium-high heat and sear the salmon until lightly browned on both sides and just cooked through, about 6–8 minutes in total. Set aside.

2 Wash the spinach well to remove any grit and spin to dry. Stack the leaves and roll like cigars, then cut across into thin "chiffonade" strips. Set aside.

3 Meanwhile, bring a big pot of salted water to a boil and add the pasta and soybeans. Boil together for 8–10 minutes, until the pasta is tender but still *al dente*. Drain well and dump into a large serving bowl. Add the spinach strips to the hot pasta and toss until the spinach is wilted. Stir in the dill, green onions, lemon zest, lemon juice and olive oil. Season with salt and pepper. Break the salmon into chunks and toss with the pasta. Serve immediately. Serves 2.

Almost Instant Spinach and Ricotta Lasagna

Nearly all of the ingredients you need for this speedy vegetarian lasagna are available at the supermarket, precooked and ready to combine after work for a fast supper. With a box of oven-ready lasagna noodles (that means you don't even have to boil them), a jar of tomato sauce, some pre-shredded pizza cheese, ricotta and a box of frozen chopped spinach, this is assembly-line cooking at its best. Just chop an onion and pop the cork on your favorite Chianti. You can even make it in a disposable pan. That's *amore!*

1 jar good-quality tomato sauce (about 3 cups/
    700 mL)
1 box oven-ready lasagna noodles (9–12 noodles)
2 Tbsp. (25 mL) olive oil
1 medium onion, chopped
1 clove garlic, minced
1 box (10 oz./300 g) chopped frozen spinach, thawed
    and squeezed to remove all excess moisture

salt and freshly ground black pepper
1 large egg
pinch white pepper
pinch nutmeg
2 cups (500 mL) ricotta cheese
1 1/2 cups (375 mL) shredded Italian cheese
    mixture (mozzarella and Parmesan)

1 Pour 1 cup (250 mL) of the tomato sauce into a lasagna pan to cover the bottom. Place 3 or 4 lasagna noodles side by side, close together but not touching (they will expand as they cook).

2 In a sauté pan, heat the olive oil and sauté the onion and garlic until they are soft and just beginning to brown. Stir in the chopped spinach and heat through. Season with salt and pepper.

3 Layer the cooked spinach mixture evenly over the noodles in the pan. Top with 3 or 4 more noodles and 1 cup (250 mL) of the sauce.

4 In a bowl, beat the egg. Add the white pepper, nutmeg, ricotta cheese and 1/2 cup (125 mL) of the Italian cheese mixture. Mix well and spread evenly over the noodles and sauce.

5 Top with 3 or 4 additional noodles. Pour the remaining sauce over top of the lasagna. Sprinkle evenly with the remaining 1 cup (250 mL) of shredded cheese.

6 Place in a 350°F (180°C) oven for 40–45 minutes, until the noodles are tender and the cheese is lightly browned on top. Let lasagna stand for 10 minutes before cutting. Serves 6.

Girl talk: There are some really good tomato sauces available in jars these days, but you have to read labels to find the best. Look for natural, low-fat versions made with tomatoes and vegetables, with no added fat (or hydrogenated oils), and no excess sugars or preservatives.

Pasta with Roasted Vegetables and Goat Cheese

In the winter, roast the vegetables for this intense sauce in the oven. In the summer, toss them in a grill wok on the gas barbecue for even more smoky character. Crumbled fresh goat cheese adds instant gourmet flavor to this vegetarian pasta dish. It's a great "day after" meal when you've got leftover roasted veggies in the fridge.

1 large eggplant, peeled, salted and rinsed
1 large yellow bell pepper
1 large white onion
1 head garlic, cloves peeled
1/3 cup (75 mL) extra virgin olive oil
1 can (28 oz./796 mL) Roma tomatoes, puréed

1 cup (250 mL) white wine
1 tsp. (5 mL) dried oregano
1 lb. (500 g) short pasta (penne or bow ties)
1 cup (250 mL) soft goat cheese, crumbled
1/4 cup (50 mL) slivered fresh basil
salt and freshly ground black pepper

1 Preheat the oven to 400°F (200°C). Slice the eggplant and cut into 1–inch (2.5–cm) chunks. Cut the bell pepper into cubes and cut the onion into chunks. In a shallow roasting pan, combine the eggplant, pepper and onion with the garlic cloves. Drizzle with the olive oil and toss to coat. Roast in the oven for 45 minutes, until tender, stirring once or twice during the cooking period.

2 Meanwhile, in a large pot, combine the puréed tomatoes, wine and oregano and bring to a boil over medium-high heat. Reduce the heat to medium-low. Simmer, uncovered, for 15 minutes to thicken. Stir in the roasted vegetables and simmer together for 10 minutes longer.

3 Cook the pasta in a large pot of boiling salted water until tender, about 10 minutes. Drain well but don't rinse. Stir the cooked pasta into the sauce and heat through. Add the crumbled cheese and basil, and season to taste with salt and pepper. Serve immediately or turn into a casserole dish and bake at 375°F (190°C) for 10–15 minutes, until the cheese begins to brown. Serves 6.

Girl talk: Goat cheese can be expensive, but the Girl's found a source of the big fat tubes of fresh goat cheese at the local big box store. You can cut the tube into four or six chunks (plastic and all), wrap each tightly in plastic wrap and freeze. When thawed, the cheese isn't as spreadable as the original, but it's perfect to crumble into dishes like this, and when mixed with a little regular cream cheese or sour cream, it's spreadable too.

Greek Pasta Toss with Chickpeas and Feta

Jars, cans and bags — a quick pit stop at the supermarket and you'll have everything you need to whip together this simple and healthy vegetarian supper.

⅓ cup (75 mL) olive oil
1 onion, thinly sliced
3 cloves garlic, minced
1 bunch spinach or chard leaves, washed well and sliced into strips
1 lb. (500 g) fusilli pasta (corkscrew or other short pasta)
¼ cup (50 mL) fresh lemon juice (about 1 lemon)

1 tsp. (5 mL) lemon zest
2 Tbsp. (25 mL) chopped fresh oregano or basil
1½ cups (375 mL) canned or cooked chickpeas, drained
1/4 cup (50 mL) sliced Kalamata or other black olives
salt and freshly ground black pepper
½ cup (125 mL) crumbled feta cheese

1 In a saucepan, heat the olive oil over medium-high heat and sauté the onion and garlic until tender, about 5 minutes. Add the spinach or chard and cook for 5 minutes or until just wilted and bright green.

2 Meanwhile, cook the fusilli according to package directions until *al dente* (tender but still firm). Drain but don't rinse.

3 Scrub the lemon. Use a lemon reamer (page 354) and zester (page 362) to remove the juice and zest from the lemon. Stir the lemon juice, lemon zest, oregano or basil, chickpeas and olives into the sauce and heat through.

4 Add the drained pasta and toss well. Season to taste with salt and pepper and pile into bowls. Top with the crumbled feta cheese. Serves 4.

Girl talk: Buy the prewashed spinach and all you need to do is rinse it. To easily chop leaves into chiffonade (strips), stack them up, roll them like a fat cigar and slice against the grain. Voila!

Penne with Tuna Tomato Sauce

Now is the time to haul out that jar of plain tomato sauce — the Girl has the flavor enhancements to make it marvelous. No tuna on the premises? A can of salmon or baby clams can stand in. Choose a short pasta with lots of nooks to trap the chunky bits in this sauce. A handful of chopped black olives is nice with this combo, too.

3 Tbsp. (45 mL) extra virgin olive oil

2 tsp. (10 mL) chopped garlic (about 2 cloves)

1 cup (250 mL) chopped onion

1/2 cup (125 mL) finely diced red or yellow bell peppers

1 cup (250 mL) diced fresh tomato

1 1/2 cups (375 mL) tomato sauce

healthy pinch cayenne pepper or crushed red chilies (to taste)

1 can (184 g) flaked tuna packed in water, drained and liquid reserved

freshly ground black pepper

3/4 lb. (375 g) penne pasta (or other short, chunky pasta like orecchiette or radiatore)

1/4 cup (50 mL) chopped fresh basil and/or oregano

3/4 cup (175 mL) freshly grated Parmesan cheese, divided

1/4 cup (50 mL) chopped black olives or capers (optional)

1 Heat the olive oil over medium-high heat in a large sauté pan. Sauté the garlic, onion and bell peppers for 5 minutes or until softened.

2 Add the diced fresh tomato and tomato sauce. Stir in the cayenne pepper and the liquid from the can of tuna. Cover the pan and bring the sauce to a boil. Reduce the heat to low and simmer gently for 10–15 minutes, stirring occasionally to make sure the sauce doesn't stick or burn. Taste the sauce and season with black pepper and extra cayenne to taste.

3 While the sauce is simmering, cook the pasta according to the directions on the package until cooked but still firm, about 8–12 minutes. Test it by trying a piece or two. Drain the pasta but don't rinse.

4 Add the cooked pasta to the simmering sauce and cook together for 2–3 minutes. Fold in the tuna, fresh basil and/or oregano, and 1/2 cup (125 mL) of the cheese. Serve in individual pasta bowls, topped with the remaining cheese. Top with chopped black olives or capers, if desired. Serves 3–4.

Fast Food Processor Tomato Sauce

The Girl's Girl Guide training comes to mind when she thinks of those plastic tubs of vegetarian tomato sauce lying in wait in her freezer. It always pays to be prepared, so double this recipe and you'll have something to take to the bank even when you're feeling overdrawn. On the other hand, this staple sauce goes together so quickly, you'll be twirling it through your spaghetti in no time flat.

1 medium onion
3 cloves garlic
1/2 stalk celery
1 medium carrot
3 Tbsp. (45 mL) virgin olive oil
1 red bell pepper, stem and ribs removed (optional)
1 can (28 oz./796 mL) plum tomatoes with juice
1 cup (250 mL) white wine

1/2 cup (125 mL) water
1 tsp. (5 mL) dried oregano
1 tsp. (5 mL) dried basil (or 2 tsp./10 mL basil
    pesto from a jar)
1 bay leaf
1/2 tsp. (2 mL) salt
1/4 tsp. (1 mL) freshly ground black pepper
pinch cayenne

1 Fire up the food processor and pulse the onion, garlic, celery and carrot together until everything is finely minced.

2 In a large saucepan, heat the oil over medium-high heat. Add the minced vegetables and stir. Sauté, stirring occasionally, until they start to change color.

3 Meanwhile, purée the bell pepper, if using, in the food processor (no need to wash it — the food processor, that is), then add the tomatoes and process until smooth. This will pick up any bits of minced vegetables that are left in the machine.

4 When the vegetables are tender and turning golden, pour in the wine and stir up any browned bits (this is known as deglazing the pan, in case you want to impress your friends). Pour the puréed tomatoes into the pan. Add the water to the food processor and whirl again to get the last bits of veggies out and pour into the pan. Stir in the oregano, basil, bay leaf, salt, pepper and cayenne and bring the sauce to a boil. Reduce the heat to low and simmer, uncovered, for 30 minutes.

5 Taste the sauce. Add 1/2 tsp. (2 mL) of sugar if the acidity is too strong, or a touch of vinegar or lemon juice if it seems flat. Makes 4 cups (1 L), enough for 1 lb. (500 g) of dry pasta (6 main course servings).

Girl talk: This kind of simple tomato sauce (a.k.a Marinara) is the basis of almost every Italian dish you will make, whether it's eggplant Parmesan or lasagna. Sure, you can open a jar, but this sauce is fresh, healthy and loaded with veggies — with none of the excess sugar and fat that girls are always trying to avoid.

This is the perfect sauce to:

• Toss with short pasta like penne, and top with lots of grated Parmesan cheese

• Layer with grated mozzarella, Parmesan and ricotta cheese and cooked lasagna noodles for instant lasagna (bake at 350°F/180°C for 45 minutes)

• Spread on top of a precooked or frozen pizza shell or pita bread, then top with shredded pizza cheese (and whatever else is around, from black olives to onions)

• Spread inside a crusty Italian bun or chunk of baguette with some sliced mozzarella and roasted peppers, and grill, for a warm Italian panini sandwich

Here are some other ideas for serving your sauce:

• To stretch a batch of this sauce to feed six elegantly, buy a box of oven-ready cannelloni and stuff them with a filling made with 2 cups (500 mL) of ricotta, 1 package of thawed and well-drained frozen spinach (squeeze it between your fingers to remove all of the water), 2 eggs, 2 cups (500 mL) grated Italian cheese mixture (Parmesan and mozzarella), and a pinch of nutmeg. Pour a bit of the sauce in a large baking dish, arrange the cannelloni in a single layer, pour the rest of the sauce over the pan and sprinkle with another cup of grated Italian cheese. Cover the pan with foil. Bake, covered, at 350°F (180°C) for 1 hour.

• Simmer the sauce and add some precooked meatballs (page 68 or 144), or try the soy burger "meat" balls from the supermarket if you're counting cholesterol. Serve the meatballs and tomato sauce over classic spaghetti or linguine, with a generous topping of freshly grated Parmesan cheese.

• Torque the sauce up to a fiery puttanesca by adding some crushed red chilies, air-dried black olives and capers. Any short pasta works well with this kind of chunky sauce — and don't forget the freshly grated Parmigiano-Reggiano (the REAL stuff!).

• Use the sauce to top a homemade pizza, built on a fresh crust or what-have-you — thick, Greek-style pita breads make a perfect single-serving pie (page 44).

• Got just a little bit of this super sauce left over? Add a cup (250 mL) of it with the 4 cups (1 L) of broth when you're making risotto (with 1½ cups/375 mL of Arborio rice and 1 cup (250 mL) of minced onion), then toss with Parmesan cheese (page 72).

Pasta with Wilted Greens, Italian Sausage and Olives

Here's a great way to get your greens, with a little sausage and olive oil on the side — feel free to substitute any greens for the broccoli rape, an Italian version of the usual supermarket broccoli with smaller heads and more leaves.

1 spicy fresh Italian sausage

1/2 cup (125 mL) minced onion

1 lb. (500 g) broccoli rape (or escarole, Swiss chard, beet greens or spinach)

2 cloves garlic, pressed or minced

4 Tbsp. (50 mL) extra virgin olive oil

salt and freshly ground black pepper

3/4 lb. (375 g) penne or other short pasta

1/4 cup (50 mL) air-cured black olives, pitted and coarsely chopped

2 tsp. (10 mL) finely grated lemon zest

1 cup (250 mL) freshly grated Parmesan cheese

1 Remove the sausage from its casing and crumble into a sauté pan. Cook over medium-high heat until the sausage is beginning to brown. Add the onion and cook 5 minutes longer.

2 Chop the broccoli rape, discarding the lower, tough stems. Add to the pan, along with the garlic and olive oil. Season with salt and pepper. Cover the pan, reduce the heat and cook, stirring occasionally, until the broccoli is just tender, about 5 minutes.

3 Meanwhile, cook the pasta according to package directions until *al dente*. Drain well. Toss the pasta with the broccoli mixture. Add the olives, lemon zest and half the cheese, and mix to combine. Serve immediately, topped with the remaining cheese. Serves 4.

Italian Sausage Sauce

The mamma of all meat sauces. Using real Italian sausage from a reputable Italian grocer will make your spaghetti sauce sing — *O Solo Mio* or maybe even *New York, New York*. The Girl uses Italian sausage meat, pulled out of its casings, like other people use hamburger — it's fresh ground meat that's already spiced, and it's perfect to season your sauce.

1 Tbsp. (15 mL) olive oil
1 onion, minced
1 lb. (500 g) sweet or hot Italian sausage
2 cloves garlic, pressed
splash of red wine

1 28-oz. (796-mL) can Roma tomatoes, crushed
   (or can or jar of meatless spaghetti sauce)
½ tsp. (2 mL) dried basil
½ tsp. (2 mL) oregano

1 In a large sauté pan, heat the oil over medium-high heat and cook the onion until tender and beginning to color, about 5–10 minutes.

2 With a sharp knife, slice the sausage casings lengthwise and crumble the sausage meat into the pan. Discard the casings. Cook the sausage until it's no longer pink and is starting to brown. Stir in the garlic and sauté for 1 minute. Add the wine and stir it around to get any browned bits up off the bottom of the pan.

3 Put the tomatoes into the blender or food processor to purée. Add the tomato purée to the pan, season with basil and oregano, cover, reduce the heat to low and simmer for 15 minutes. That's it. Make this sauce in advance and freeze it for fast weekday suppers. Makes 4 cups/1 L.

Girl talk: I know I told you how you can get your frustrations out by smashing cloves of garlic, but you can also use a garlic press, which is a nifty tool for girls who don't like to get their hands dirty. Peel the clove, put it in the press, close the device and squeeze. Et voila! Perfect garlic purée that's great for smooth sauces and soups, or any time a recipe calls for minced garlic. Your microplane grater (page 351) makes a speedy mince, too.

Breakfasts of Champions

The Girl hates to harp, but what your mother always said is true —
you'll look better and feel better (maybe even make more money)
if you eat your brekkie. Herewith some ideas to get your day revved
up a notch, and start you running on a full tank.

The Grab and Go Egg Burger

Of course, this portable breakfast on a bun has been a signature dish for a certain fast food chain and, truth-be-told, it's the one thing they make that the Girl has been known to grab from the drive-through window enroute to the ski hill. This is really almost as easy and you don't even have to put on your parka.

4 slices back bacon, or sliced deli ham or turkey ham
1 Tbsp. (15 mL) butter
4 large eggs
salt and freshly ground black pepper

4 whole-wheat English muffins, split, toasted and buttered
4 slices mild Cheddar cheese (use processed cheese, if you must, for authenticity)

1 Place the sliced meat on a plate, cover with waxed paper and microwave on high for 2–3 minutes. Set aside.

2 Put a little bit of butter into the bottom of four small soufflé dishes or custard cups (something that's about as big around as your muffin). Break one egg into each dish and beat very lightly, just to break the yolks. Season with salt and pepper. Partially cover each dish with plastic wrap and microwave on medium-high for 1–2 minutes, just until the eggs are set. Let them steam for about 1 minute, to finish cooking, then turn each egg patty out onto a toasted and buttered muffin half. Top with a slice of bacon, ham or turkey and a slice of cheese. Cover with the other toasted muffin half. Grab and go. Makes 4.

Aging Girl's Instant Breakfast, or the Joy of Soy

There comes a time in every girl's life when she knows that the power of PMS is getting the better of her. They say soy will soften the blow, but how's a committed carnivore going to get more of that boring white stuff into her diet? This instant breakfast is just the ticket — good, too, for girls who love to start the day with protein.

½ (1 lb./500 g) package soft tofu
1 cup (250 mL) milk (soy or regular)
2 Tbsp. (25 mL) frozen orange juice concentrate

1 Tbsp. (15 mL) maple syrup or honey
½ tsp. (2 mL) pure vanilla extract
½ frozen banana (optional)

1 Combine all ingredients in blender and blend until smooth. Makes 1 large delicious drink.

Meal in a Muffin

Sometimes there's only time for coffee and a muffin but this is a healthy one — low in fat, high in fiber, and tough enough to toss into your briefcase or backpack. A survival snack. Use the food processor with the grating disc to grate the carrots and apples (or use Girl power and a basic box grater).

1 cup (250 mL) all-purpose flour
1 cup (250 mL) whole-wheat flour
1 cup (250 mL) chopped dates, cut into small
  pieces
³/₄ cup (175 mL) brown sugar
1 Tbsp. (15 mL) ground cinnamon
1 tsp. (5 mL) ground nutmeg
2 tsp. (10 mL) baking soda
¹/₂ tsp. (2 mL) salt

³/₄ cup (175 mL) chopped pecans or
  slivered almonds
2 eggs
1 egg white
²/₃ cup (150 mL) plain, nonfat yogurt
2 tsp. (10 mL) pure vanilla extract
3 cups (750 mL) grated carrots
1 cup (250 mL) grated apple

1 Preheat the oven to 350°F (180°C).

2 In a large bowl, mix together the all-purpose flour, whole-wheat flour, dates, brown sugar, cinnamon, nutmeg, baking soda, salt and pecans or almonds.

3 In another bowl, whisk the eggs, egg white, yogurt and vanilla together until smooth. Pour into the dry ingredients and stir with a fork until just barely combined (a few lumps are okay in muffins). Fold in the grated carrot and apple.

4 Grease a muffin tin or line it with paper cups (this makes removing the muffins extra easy). Spoon the batter into the cups — they should be about ³/₄ full. Bake for 40–45 minutes, until the tops are firm and a skewer inserted into the center of a muffin comes out clean. Makes about 18 muffins.

Girl talk: Dates can be sticky and tough to chop — use your kitchen shears to snip them into usable bits.

The banana is a great fruit until it turns on you — turns black and overripe, that is. The Girl consigns her blackened bananas to the freezer. Peeled and frozen in plastic bags, they're perfect to pull out for a smoothie and they make awesome banana bread (that really dark and delicious kind — see page 310)

Great Granola

So you're a crunchy granola girl, what of it? This great granola makes an instant gourmet breakfast when you're out backpacking and an impressive alternative to the usual boxes of commercial cereal. Bake up a bunch and keep it in the cupboard or freezer, then enjoy it with lots of skim milk, mix it with yogurt, or munch it as a snack straight up. Healthy, too.

8 cups (2L) rolled oats
2 cups (500 mL) wheat germ
2 cups (500 mL) unsweetened shredded coconut
1 cup (250 mL) chopped pecans
1 cup (250 mL) slivered almonds
2 cups (500 mL) shelled, raw sunflower seeds
1/2 cup (125 mL) sesame seeds
1/2 cup (125 mL) flax seeds or milled flax
1 cup (250 mL) canola oil

1 cup (250 mL) honey
1 tsp. (5 mL) salt
2 tsp. (10 mL) cinnamon
1 tsp. (5 mL) freshly grated nutmeg
1 Tbsp. (15 mL) pure vanilla extract
3 oranges, zest only
2 cups (500 mL) raisins, dried cranberries or blueberries
2 cups (500 mL) chopped dried apricots

1 Preheat the oven to 300°F (150°C).

2 In a large bowl, combine the oats, wheat germ, coconut, pecans, almonds, sunflower seeds, sesame seeds and flax.

3 In a small saucepan, heat the oil, honey, salt, cinnamon, nutmeg and vanilla almost to boiling. Drizzle over the dry ingredients, mixing well.

4 Spread the granola in one or two shallow roasting pans or baking sheets. Bake for 30–45 minutes, stirring often to prevent it from burning. Cool.

5 Scrub the oranges. Remove the zest from the oranges using a zesting tool or a microplane grater (the finer the better, but you don't want to grate any of the bitter white pith).

6 Stir the orange zest and dried fruits into the cooled granola mixture. Store in a large jar in a cool place. Serve with milk or yogurt. Makes a bunch.

Girl talk: Substitute any chopped nuts for the pecans in this recipe. If you can't find dried cranberries or blueberries, substitute currants, dried cherries or dried mango bits.

Potato and Spicy Sausage Frittata

A frittata is kind of an all-purpose egg dish, and this is one of those "mother" recipes, a technique you can learn and modify to suit what's in the fridge, especially when there are leftover potatoes around. Always bake or boil an extra potato or two on the weekend, and you'll have the basis for a fast frittata during the week (or substitute a cup or two of frozen hash browns). Use any kind of cheese you like, and add vegetables like sautéed mushrooms or steamed asparagus, or different meats, like ham or prosciutto. Make it in the morning, when you have the time, or enjoy it for a fast supper (and grab a cold piece for breakfast on your way out the door).

4 Tbsp. (50 mL) olive oil, divided
1 large potato, cooked, chilled and thinly sliced or chopped
1/2 cup (125 mL) chopped onion
1 red bell pepper, slivered
1 yellow bell pepper, slivered
2 cloves garlic, minced

1/2 lb. (250 g) fresh spicy Italian or chorizo sausage, removed from the casings and crumbled
8 eggs
4 oz. (125 g) aged Fontina cheese, grated
1 oz. (30 g) grated Parmesan cheese
spicy salsa (see page 331)

1 In a large, nonstick, ovenproof frying pan, heat 2 Tbsp. (25 mL) of the oil over medium-high heat. Add the potato and sauté for 5 minutes, until it begins to brown. Add the remaining oil and the onion and cook for 3–4 minutes more, until it starts to color. Add the slivered peppers, garlic and sausage, cooking until the meat is no longer pink.

2 Beat the eggs in a bowl and pour over the ingredients in the pan. Reduce the heat to medium. Stir the mixture until the eggs begin to set, then reduce the heat to low and let the eggs cook on the bottom, shaking the pan to keep the frittata loosened.

3 Meanwhile, preheat the broiler. When the frittata is nicely browned on the bottom, remove the pan from the heat. Top with the grated cheeses and place the pan under the broiler. Broil for a minute or two, just until the top of the frittata is set and the cheese is melted and beginning to brown.

4 Let the frittata stand for a couple of minutes to cool, then cut into four wedges. Serve with salsa on the side. Serves 4.

Breakfast Bearclaw Cookies

This is the Girl's version of her favorite monster coffee shop cookie. Okay, cookies aren't the best thing for breakfast, but these cookies — as big as a bear claw — are chock-a-block full of good things like rolled oats, nuts and seeds. With a foamy skim milk latte, one will start the day off quite nicely.

2 cups (500 mL) softened butter

2 cups (500 mL) brown sugar

4 large eggs

3/4 cup (175 mL) (1 small tub) plain yogurt
   (or use buttermilk)

2 cups (500 mL) all-purpose flour

2 cups (500 mL) whole-wheat flour

1/2 cup (125 mL) wheat bran

1 Tbsp. (15 mL) baking powder

2 tsp. (10 mL) baking soda

4 cups (1 L) rolled oats

3/4 cup (175 mL) chocolate chips

3/4 cup (175 mL) sunflower seeds

3/4 cup (175 mL) sliced almonds

1 Preheat the oven to 350°F (180°C). In a large bowl, with an electric mixer, cream the butter and sugar for 5 minutes until fluffy. Beat in the eggs, one at a time, and add the yogurt, beating to combine.

2 In another bowl, mix the flours, wheat bran, baking powder, baking soda and rolled oats. Add these dry ingredients to the batter, mixing by hand until well incorporated. Stir in the chocolate chips, sunflower seeds and almonds. The batter will be quite stiff.

3 Rub a heavy baking sheet with butter or oil and line it with parchment paper. Scoop the cookies onto the sheet (about 3–4 Tbsp./50 mL of batter at a time), leaving lots of room between mounds to allow them to spread (about 8–10 cookies per sheet). Flatten the cookies slightly. Bake for 15–18 minutes, until nicely browned. Makes 3 dozen large cookies.

Decadence

The Girl loves to party and what better way to have fun than over food. Here are some memorable menus and dishes to share when you're in the mood to gather around the table with friends, whether it's a special occasion, a themed ethnic dinner party, or just a time to relax and reconnect.

Choose any of the meals or menus in this section, start with an appetizer from the extensive collection (pages 207 to 228), and choose a dessert from the decadent selection at the end of this chapter, or the bake and take desserts (pages 305 to 325). Entertaining is one of life's greatest pleasures. Just do it!

The Impressing Anyone Menu

(or How to Make Your Culinary Reputation with One Meal)

The way to impress anyone important is with a multi-course gourmet meal. This one is outstanding — complete with a subtle, silky soup to start, an easy but very stylish salad with the cachet of a gourmet cheese course, and the always-impressive centerpiece of beef tenderloin in a red wine and wild mushroom sauce.

This is the menu for major celebrations (like New Year's Eve or a significant birthday) or when you need to impress the boss or the country club set. They'll think you slaved, which is the whole point, but it's easier than it looks. Your culinary skills will become instantly legendary, giving you months, if not years, of laurels to rest upon.

Roasted Parsnip Soup

Serve this creamy but light (low-cal) soup to start any fancy dinner, and your guests will be amazed by the rich, subtle and sweet flavor that you've wrested from this humble root. To really gild the lily, top each serving with a swirl of sour cream and a few parsnip chips (sliced off with a vegetable peeler and fried until crisp), or pour the soup around a pile of sautéed wild mushrooms in a wide soup plate (see The Mushroom Thing, page 212). The recipe can easily be doubled.

4 Tbsp. (50 mL) butter, divided
1 Tbsp. (15 mL) honey
6 medium parsnips
salt and white pepper
2 tsp. (10 mL) chopped fresh rosemary or thyme

1 cup (250 mL) chopped onion
6 cups (1.5 L) chicken stock
1/4 cup (50 mL) white rice
3 Tbsp. (45 mL) sour cream
chopped chives and extra sour cream to garnish

1   Preheat the oven to 400°F (200°C).

2   Place 2 Tbsp. (25 mL) of the butter and the honey in a medium-sized bowl and microwave until melted.

3   Peel the parsnips and cut them into thick slices. Add to the bowl and toss to coat with the butter mixture. Season with salt, white pepper and rosemary or thyme, and toss again.

4   Line a baking sheet with foil or parchment paper. Spread the parsnips in a single layer on the baking sheet. Roast for 30 minutes, stirring once, until the parsnips are golden.

5   Meanwhile, heat the remaining 2 Tbsp. (25 mL) of butter in a soup pot and sauté the onion until it's beginning to color. Add the roasted parsnips, stock and rice to the pot and bring to a boil.

6   Cover, reduce the heat to medium-low, and simmer for 25 minutes.

7   Purée the soup in a blender or food processor until smooth. Push it through a strainer or food mill if you want your soup perfectly smooth. (You can make it in advance to this point and chill.)

8   Return the soup to the pot and stir in the sour cream. Heat it through but don't boil it. Think about making it pretty — this is your first chance to impress, so start off right. Garnish each serving with a drizzle of additional sour cream (squiggled out of a plastic squeeze bottle or dolloped and "cut" into heart-shaped swirls) and a few finely chopped chives. Serves 6.

Girl talk: Presentation is power in the culinary world. To decorate with sour cream, dollop five little drops of cream on the soup in a line (easiest if you have it in a squeeze bottle) then draw the tip of a knife through, connecting the dots, to make a chain of pretty heart-shaped swirls.

The Girl once watched a chef get particularly fancy with his mushrooms and creamy soup. He put a 2–inch (5–cm) ring (a cookie cutter or small fish tin with both ends cut out) in the center of each soup bowl, filled it with The Mushroom Thing (page 212) and ladled the cream soup around the outside of the ring. Then he quickly lifted the ring, leaving the mushrooms artfully centered in the bowl and surrounded by soup. Very cool.

Girl talk: Prewashed greens are great — you can use them without washing. But a dip in a sink of ice cold water and a spin in the salad spinner will add crispness to anything green that you plan to serve in a salad. The Girl likes to wash and spin her greens several hours before a special dinner (even the night before), then wrap them loosely in a paper towel, and put them in a plastic bag in the fridge for perfect, crisp results. And they're ready when you are.

Mixed Greens with Gorgonzola Toasts

Don't roll your eyes — it sounds complicated but it's simple and oh-so-stylish, a composed salad course to add pure panache to your dinner party.

dressing

1 Tbsp. (15 mL) balsamic vinegar
1/2 tsp. (2 mL) Dijon mustard
3 Tbsp. (45 mL) extra virgin olive oil

1/2 tsp. (2 mL) salt
freshly ground black pepper

topping

1/2 cup (125 mL) walnuts
1 tsp. (5 mL) minced fresh rosemary (don't use dried rosemary, but you can substitute other fresh herbs like basil or thyme)

6 oz. (175 g) Gorgonzola cheese
1/2 cup (125 mL) cream cheese

salad

1/2 baguette, thinly sliced
8 cups (2 L) mixed baby salad greens

flavorful olive oil for brushing

1   Make the dressing first. In a small bowl, whisk together the vinegar and mustard, then add the oil and whisk until well combined. Season with salt and pepper and set aside.

2   Wash the greens and dry them well with a salad spinner. Place in a large bowl, cover and chill if preparing ahead of time.

3   Make the Gorgonzola topping in the food processor. If your walnuts are whole, put them in the food processor first and pulse until finely ground, adding a touch of olive oil to make a paste. For even more flavor, toast the walnuts for 10 minutes in a 350°F (180°C) oven before grinding.

4   To the walnuts in the food processor, add the rosemary, Gorgonzola and cream cheese and process until well mixed. Set aside in the refrigerator. (Make it the day before if you like.)

5   When you're ready to serve the salad, preheat the broiler and bring the cheese mixture to room temperature. Slice the baguette into 12 1/2–inch (1–cm) slices on the diagonal and brush on one side with olive oil. Set on a baking sheet, oiled side down. Spread a thick layer of Gorgonzola topping on top of each slice. (This can be done an hour in advance.)

6   Place the sheet under the preheated broiler and toast for 5–8 minutes, until the cheese is bubbly and the bread is beginning to brown. Watch carefully as the toasts can burn easily.

7   Just before you're ready to serve the salad, add the vinaigrette to the greens and toss well. Divide the greens among six salad plates. Garnish each salad with two or three warm Gorgonzola toasts, perched architecturally on top. Serves 6.

Peppercorn Beef Tenderloin with Mushroom Wine Sauce

When the Girl needs an ultra elegant, spare-no-expense main course, this is it. And for a dish that's so elegant, it's amazingly easy and fast to cook (the Girl's kitchen-challenged significant other actually pulled this one off perfectly for a Guys Can Cook party). You'll need to take a mortgage out on the tenderloin, though, so PLEASE don't overcook it! The tenderloin should never be cooked beyond medium-rare — it should stay pink and juicy on the inside. Invest in a good meat thermometer and use it. Then head to the local wine shop for a nice bottle of Bordeaux or Shiraz to pour alongside.

tenderloin
1 beef tenderloin roast, about 3 lbs. (1.5 kg)
melted butter or olive oil
Dijon mustard

mixture of black, white, pink and green
   peppercorns, crushed

sauce
1 Tbsp. (15 mL) olive oil
2 shallots, minced
2 cups (500 mL) sliced white or brown mushrooms
1/2 cup (125 mL) dry wild mushrooms, rehydrated
2/3 cups (150 mL) Merlot or other red wine with
  low tannin

1 1/2 cups (375 mL) beef broth
1 Tbsp. (15 mL) water
1 Tbsp. (15 mL) cornstarch
1 Tbsp. (15 mL) Worcestershire

garnish
fresh parsley, watercress or other fresh herbs to garnish platter

1 Ask your butcher for a center cut of tenderloin so that you have a nice, even-sized piece of meat. If you end up with a tail of meat, cut it off and use it for stir-fries, or tuck the end under to make the piece as even as possible and tie it.

2 Rub the beef tenderloin with butter or olive oil and Dijon, then roll it in a mixture of coarsely crushed peppercorns to coat it on all sides. The easiest way to crush the peppercorns is to put them in a sealed plastic bag, and roll over them repeatedly with a rolling pin (or pulse them in an electric spice grinder).

3 Place the tenderloin on a platter, cover with plastic wrap and refrigerate for several hours or overnight. Bring the meat to room temperature 30 minutes before cooking.

4 To cook, preheat the oven to 500°F (260°C). Place the beef on a rack in a roasting pan and roast for 10 minutes, then turn the meat over (use tongs — don't stab it with a fork or you'll lose the precious juices). Insert the meat thermometer and reduce the oven temperature to 400°F (200°C). Continue roasting until the meat thermometer registers 140°F (60°C) for medium rare or 150°F (65°C) for medium (about 35 minutes).

5 Remove the tenderloin from the roasting pan and set aside on a cutting board to rest, tented with a large piece of foil. Let stand 10 minutes before carving to set the juices.

6 Meanwhile, make the sauce. In a sauté pan, heat the olive oil and sauté the shallots and mushrooms until tender. Place the empty roasting pan on top of the stove over medium-high heat and add the wine to deglaze (stir the liquid around to pick up all of the browned bits and flavors left in the roasting pan). Bring to a boil and cook over medium-high heat until the wine has been reduced by half. Add the broth and boil 5 minutes longer. Stir this liquid into the pan with the sautéed mushrooms and bring to a boil.

7 Whisk the water, cornstarch and Worcestershire together in a small bowl. Slowly add to the sauce, whisking to combine. Boil the sauce for 2 minutes, stirring until smooth and nicely thickened. Season with salt and pepper to taste.

8 To serve, carve the tenderloin into thick slices. Arrange on a platter with fresh herbs artfully decorating the edge of the platter (or plate individually with the Garlic Mashed Potatoes, page 104 and Roasted Heirloom Tomatoes, page 105). Drizzle the sauce over the slices of tenderloin to serve, and pass any extra sauce in a bowl with a small ladle. Serves 8–10.

Girl talk: The Girl always keeps a big jar of dried porcini or other wild mushrooms in the cupboard. They last forever and you can rehydrate them in 10 minutes, then use them for anything from pizza and pasta dishes to upscale eats like this. To turn dried mushrooms soft almost instantly, put them into a glass measuring cup with a little water (or white wine). Microwave on high for 2–3 minutes, then let them stand until soft.

Garlic Mashed Potatoes

This is the starch the Girl serves with almost everything — creamy, golden-fleshed potatoes flecked with sweet, nutty roasted garlic. If you don't have roasted garlic in your fridge (shame on you, it's one of the Girl's golden rules), just add four whole peeled cloves to the potatoes while you boil them and mash them into the potato purée (not as good, but passable).

6 medium yellow-fleshed potatoes like Yukon gold (about 3 lbs./1.5 kg)
2 tsp. (10 mL) salt
6 Tbsp. (75 mL) butter

1/2 cup (125 mL) whipping cream (half-and-half or milk if you're more virtuous)
white pepper to taste
1 head garlic, roasted (see page 17)

1 Peel the potatoes and cut each into 6–8 pieces. Put the potatoes in a large pot and cover with cold water. Add the salt and bring to a boil over high heat. Reduce the heat to medium, cover and simmer until just tender, about 10–12 minutes.

2 Drain well and return the pot to the stove, shaking the potatoes to remove excess moisture. Mash the potatoes by hand. Stir in the butter, cream and white pepper. Squeeze the roasted garlic out of the papery skins right into the potatoes and stir well to combine. Serve immediately or place in a bowl, cover with plastic wrap and microwave to heat through just before serving. Serves 6–8.

Girl talk: If the potatoes are young and blemish-free, make a rustic mash of potatoes, skins and all. More fiber, more food value, more texture, more flavor — less work.

Roasted Heirloom Tomatoes

It's always nice to have a few clever things to talk about at a dinner with important near-strangers like your partner's boss or your publisher. After they've oohed and ahhed over the beef, these heirloom tomatoes will give you another scintillating topic to get you through the evening (see page 362 for more on these tasty treats).

½ cup (125 mL) extra virgin olive oil (a flavorful, peppery style)
1 shallot, minced
1 clove garlic, minced
½ cup (125 mL) finely ground breadcrumbs

½ cup (125 mL) grated Parmesan cheese
salt and freshly ground black pepper
12–18 small to medium heirloom tomatoes in a variety of colors (two or three halves per person, depending on size)

1 Heat the oil in a sauté pan over medium heat and cook the shallots and garlic until tender, about 5 minutes. Add the breadcrumbs and stir around for a minute or two to toast. Remove from the heat and cool.

2 Preheat the oven to 400°F (200°C). Stir the grated cheese into the crumbs. Season with salt and pepper. Cut the tomatoes in half and remove any large, obvious cores with a paring knife. Set the tomato halves in a shallow baking dish and season them with salt and pepper. Spread some of the crumbs over each half. Bake until the crumbs are golden, about 5–10 minutes. Serve at once. Serves 6.

Girl talk: You can also do this with oversized cherry tomatoes for a nice addition to any plate. Just cut a cross into the tomatoes, cutting halfway to the base so that they spread apart like flowers, and fill them with the crumb mixture. These tiny tomatoes bake quickly — 5 minutes.

Dining on the Deck

(or The Barbie Party for Girls who Grill)

The backyard barbie is the Girl's favorite kind of casual entertaining, and it's the perfect solution when it's your turn to have friends for dinner. These casual main courses are just the thing for a spontaneous weekday dinner date with that couple you've been meaning to see or to expand into a weekend party. Dining on the deck is easy and unfussy — no formal invitations or advance planning necessary.

Choose an easy appetizer from elsewhere in the book and then put these one-dish entrées together at the last minute while you enjoy a glass of wine and catch up on the latest with your friends. Go Indian or go Greek and pick up the instant accoutrements at the ethnic grocery of your choice. Great girls grill!

Grilled Salmon Skewers on Mixed Greens with Lemon Basil Vinaigrette

The Girl likes to make this kind of main meal salad on a summer evening — it's easy but elegant enough for a casual dinner or luncheon for friends. Compose the salad on individual plates or present it on a gorgeous platter, Niçoise style. A crisp Sauvignon Blanc or a nice Riesling goes perfectly.

½ tsp. (2 mL) salt

3 Tbsp. (45 mL) fresh lemon juice

1 Tbsp. (15 mL) Dijon mustard

2 tsp. (10 mL) honey

2 Tbsp. (25 mL) chopped fresh basil (use pesto in a pinch)

⅓ cup (75 mL) extra virgin olive oil

¾–lb. (350–g) salmon fillet, skinless

1 lb. (500 g) new red baby potatoes, unpeeled and halved, or quartered if large

½ lb. (250 g) fresh green beans

6 cups (1.5 L) mixed salad greens

1 cup (250 mL) cherry tomatoes, halved

1 In a food processor or blender, combine the salt, lemon juice, mustard and honey, and pulse to combine. Add the basil and purée until smooth. With the machine running, slowly drizzle in the olive oil — the vinaigrette should thicken slightly. Set aside.

2 Cut the salmon fillet lengthwise into about 12 thin strips. Lay them in a single layer in a nonreactive dish (glass or ceramic) and pour about ¼ cup (50 mL) of the vinaigrette over top. Cover with plastic and refrigerate for 1 hour.

3 Soak a dozen wooden skewers in water for 15 minutes, then thread the salmon on the skewers accordion-style.

4 Meanwhile, steam the potatoes until barely tender, about 15 minutes. When they are almost done, add the beans to the pot, cover and steam 3 minutes longer, until the beans are just tender-crisp. Drain and chill the beans in a colander under cold running tap water to set the color. Toss the warm potatoes with a third of the vinaigrette. Keep warm.

5 To cook the salmon, heat the barbecue to medium. Brush the grill with oil. Place the salmon skewers on the grill and cook, turning once, until just done, about 4 minutes in total.

6 Toss the greens with a few tablespoons of the vinaigrette, just enough to lightly coat. Pile the greens in the center of four individual dinner plates. Arrange the warm baby potatoes, beans and cherry tomatoes around the edge of the plate, and place three skewers of salmon alongside. Drizzle the beans and tomatoes with the remaining vinaigrette and serve immediately. Serves 4.

Barbecue Pork Tenderloin

The Girl is a big fan of pulled pork sandwiches, but they take all day to cook on the backyard smoker. This version of grilled pork tenderloin has some of that classic pulled pork flavor, but it's lean and ready to eat in half an hour. You can thinly slice the tenderloin and arrange it artfully over greens drizzled with spicy yogurt dressing (see Girl talk), stack it in crusty buns for a pork sandwich with Creamy Coleslaw (page 160) or cut it across the grain into thick slices, like miniature tenderloin steaks, and serve alongside Potato Salad (page 251) and sweet corn on the cob. Also nice served atop Corn and Chili Pepper Pancakes (page 224) as an appetizer.

rub

2 tsp. (10 mL) salt

3 Tbsp. (45 mL) granulated sugar

1 Tbsp. (15 mL) brown sugar

1 Tbsp. (15 mL) ground ginger

1 Tbsp. (15 mL) chili powder

1 Tbsp. (15 mL) granulated garlic

1 tsp. (5 mL) freshly ground black pepper

1 tsp. (5 mL) ground cumin

3 Tbsp. (45 mL) sweet Hungarian or
  Spanish paprika

pork

2 1–lb (500–g) pork tenderloins

2 Tbsp. (25 mL) ballpark mustard (not Dijon)

1 Combine the salt, sugars, ginger, chili powder, garlic, pepper, cumin and paprika. Set the rub aside in a spice jar. Any extra rub keeps indefinitely.

2 Rub the tenderloins all over with mustard. Sprinkle heavily on all sides with the spice rub, massaging into the meat. Set the tenderloins aside for 10 minutes to allow the rub to get tacky — this will help to seal in the juices and form a tasty crust as the pork cooks on the barbecue.

3 Heat the barbecue to high and quickly sear the tenderloins on all sides, about 2–3 minutes in total.

4 Turn off one burner on the grill and shuffle the pork to the cool side. Put the lid down and continue to cook the pork tenderloin over indirect heat until just cooked through, about 30 minutes, or until an instant-read thermometer inserted into the center of the meat registers 155°F (68°C). Pork tenderloin is like a chicken breast — it's lean and becomes dry quickly if overcooked, so don't overdo it. It shouldn't be rare but don't panic if it's a little pink — that's when it's juicy.

5 Set the tenderloins on a cutting board, covered loosely with foil, to rest for 5 minutes. Resting allows the juices to spread throughout the meat — if you slice it immediately all the juice will run out. Slice the pork thinly on the diagonal for sandwiches or salads, or cut it into thick medallions, like small tenderloin steaks, for plating. Serves 4.

Lamb Gyros Wraps

Once, on a cruise ship plying the waters of the Mediterranean Sea, the Girl gorged on tender grilled lamb kebabs called gyros (HEE-ros) created by the expert Greek crew.

These wraps are an easy variation. Marinate the lamb the night before you plan to cook, get some thick, Greek-style pita bread and serve the sandwiches with store-bought tzatziki from the deli counter, or make your own simple sauce (page 52). Summer Sangria (page 112), ouzo or iced sweet mint tea make the perfect quaffers for this casual poolside dinner. Buy some bakeshop baklava and your party is complete.

2 lbs. (1 kg) boneless leg or shoulder of lamb

1/2 cup (125 mL) olive oil

1/4 cup (50 mL) freshly squeezed lemon juice (about 1 large lemon)

1/2 tsp. (2 mL) salt

1/2 tsp. (2 mL) cayenne pepper

3 cloves garlic, pressed in a garlic press or minced

1 bay leaf, crumbled

2 Tbsp. (25 mL) fresh chopped dill (or 2 tsp./10 mL dried)

1 red bell pepper

1 yellow bell pepper

1 medium red onion

12 whole cherry tomatoes

olive oil

salt and freshly ground black pepper

4 thick Greek-style pita breads

tzatziki (commercial or homemade, page 52)

1 If you're using lamb shoulder, make sure you trim off all the excess fat with a sharp knife. Cut the meat into 2-inch (5–cm) cubes and place it in a resealable plastic bag. Combine the olive oil, lemon juice, salt, cayenne pepper, garlic, bay leaf and dill and pour over the meat. Seal and refrigerate for at least 12 hours and up to 24. Cut the peppers and onion into large chunks. Thread the meat on long metal skewers. Thread the vegetables on separate skewers, making one vegetable and one meat skewer per person. Brush the vegetable skewers with olive oil and season with salt and pepper.

2 Grill the meat and vegetable skewers over medium-high heat. Cook the meat for 8 minutes for rare or 10–12 minutes for medium, turning three or four times during cooking. Cook the vegetables until just tender and beginning to char, turning often.

3 Cut the pita breads in half to form pockets. Serve the lamb and grilled vegetables in pita halves with a dollop of tzatziki. Or, for a fancier Greek meal, serve the lamb and vegetable skewers with rice and baked white beans with dill (page 258). Serves 4.

Grilled Sausage Panini with Beer-Braised Onions and Peppers

The Girl would never stoop to serve a hot dog to her stylish set, but designer sausages are perfect for a casual evening with friends. Good sausage is a staple that you should always have on hand. Find a local butcher who makes top quality, fresh pork or chicken sausages — an Italian grocery is probably the best place to start — and stock your freezer.

You can find creative, lean combinations, (everything from chicken and apple to turkey, sage and pine nut sausages), but any decent fresh Italian sausage or well-made bratwurst works with this yummy, onion and pepper topping. Guys love it — dolls, too. Perfect with cold beer and any salad on the side.

2 red and/or yellow bell peppers, slivered
2 large sweet red or white onions, sliced
1/4 cup (50 mL) good-quality virgin olive oil
1 clove garlic, minced
1 Tbsp. (15 mL) sugar

1/2 cup (125 mL) dark beer
salt and freshly ground black pepper
6 lean fresh sausages
6 crusty panini buns

1 Cut the peppers lengthwise, remove the stems and seeds, and slice into long slivers. Cut the onions in half lengthwise and slice thinly. Heat the olive oil in a sauté pan over medium heat. Add the peppers and onions, and cook slowly until they are golden and caramelized. This will take at least 30–45 minutes. Stir in the garlic, sugar and beer, and simmer until most of the liquid is gone and the onions and peppers form a thick, jammy mass. Season with salt and pepper and set aside (this will keep, covered, in the refrigerator for several days. It also makes a great topping for cheese sandwiches or pizzas, so make extra).

2 Grill the sausages over medium heat for 15 minutes, until nicely browned and cooked through. Pile some of the caramelized pepper and onion mixture into each crusty bun along with a hot grilled sausage. Pass the Dijon. Serves 6.

Girl talk: The grill pan or grill wok is one of the best barbecue tools the Girl has ever purchased. With this gadget (a high-sided pan with small holes or small mesh grid), you can stir-fry vegetables for salads, salsas or fajitas right on the barbecue — you get the great smoky flavor and caramelized sugars, and never risk losing those sliced mushrooms or skinny asparagus through the grill. Get one and you'll grill more vegetables.

Warm Grilled Vegetable and Chicken Salad

This Asian-inspired main meal salad is perfect for a Friday night on the deck with friends. Serve it family-style on your prettiest platter after you've started the evening with some nice noshes like take-out sushi or Salad Rolls (page 220) and tall, tropical fruit-based cocktails. Buy the ingredients from the supermarket on the way home from work, and you can be dining in an hour. Or make the dressing the day before and grill your own chicken breasts. Marinate the chicken in a little dressing before grilling.

dressing

¼ cup (50 mL) virgin olive oil

2 Tbsp. (25 mL) toasted sesame oil

2 Tbsp. (25 mL) rice or white wine vinegar

1 Tbsp. (15 mL) soy sauce

2 Tbsp. (25 mL) chopped cilantro

1 green onion, chopped

1 Tbsp. (15 mL) tahini (sesame paste) or
   peanut butter

1 Tbsp. (15 mL) chopped fresh ginger (or 1 tsp./
   5 mL ground ginger)

dash of cayenne

salad

3 Tbsp. (45 mL) olive oil

2 cloves garlic, pressed or minced

¾ lb. (350 g) fresh asparagus, tough bases
   broken off and discarded, tops cut into 3–inch
   (8–cm) lengths

½ lb. (250 g) fresh portobello mushrooms,
   sliced

¾ lb. (375 g) new baby potatoes, halved or
   quartered

½ large red onion, sliced

¾ lb. (375 g) mixed salad greens

1 lb. (500 g) warm barbecued or rotisserie
   chicken breast, slivered

cilantro leaves to garnish

1 Whirl the dressing ingredients together in a food processor until smooth. The dressing may be made a day in advance and refrigerated. Bring to room temperature before using.

2 Combine the olive oil and garlic in a small bowl and let stand to infuse for 10 minutes. Brush the asparagus and mushrooms with the garlic oil and grill in a grill pan (see Girl talk page 110) on the barbecue until lightly browned and tender, about 10 minutes. Set aside.

3 Meanwhile, place the potatoes in a sauté pan with ¼ cup (50 mL) of water, cover and bring to a boil. Steam for 5 minutes. Remove the lid, add the remaining garlic oil and the onion, and continue to cook until the liquid is evaporated and the onions and potatoes are nicely browned, about 10 minutes longer.

4 In a large bowl toss the greens with enough dressing to lightly coat. Arrange the greens in the center of a serving platter, or on four individual plates. Arrange the warm potatoes, grilled asparagus and mushrooms artfully around the edge of the platter or plate. Mound the slivered warm chicken on top of the salad, and drizzle the chicken and vegetables with a little additional dressing. Strew some cilantro leaves over top and pass any remaining dressing. Serve warm. Serves 4.

Summer Sangria

The perfect vessel for putting together a batch of sangria to enjoy on the deck is a large glass jar with a spigot. Use a couple of large pitchers to make this if you haven't got a big enough punch bowl or jar. Serve your sangria in red wine glasses, with a few slices of marinated fruit bobbing around in each glass.

1 lemon, scrubbed
1 orange, scrubbed
2 fresh ripe peaches or nectarines, cut into slivers
½ cup (125 mL) Triple Sec or other orange liqueur

2 bottles light, fruity red or white wine
ice
2–3 cups (500–750 mL) soda water or a
    lemon-lime soda like Sprite or 7-Up

1 Use a food processor or mandoline to thinly slice the lemon and orange. Place the citrus fruit into your vessel, along with the peaches or nectarines and orange liqueur. Add the wine and let the sangria steep for several hours (refrigerate if you have space).

2 When your guests arrive, add ice and soda water (or lemon-lime soda) to chill and dilute to taste. Delicious on the deck! Makes about 12 cups (3 L).

The Fondue Party

Fondue is a cool way for the Girl to cook — or not. Hosting a fondue party has less to do with cooking and more to do with shopping and table setting, which are the Girl's specialties. Fondue is more than a meal. It's interactive dining — an event that's casual, fun and gets friends and strangers talking almost instantly, kind of a party in a pot. All you need to do is get the basics together, set the scene and let your guests dunk, dip and deep-fry their dinner themselves. It's brilliant.

You'll need a few fondue pots — some of the heavy enamel or crockery kind for cheese and chocolate, and a metal pot with a good heat source (even electric) for the oil and broth fondues. Borrow and beg pots from friends and family. Everyone has at least one wedding present languishing in the back of the pantry that they will be glad to bring along.

Then set the table with individual plates and regular cutlery for eating, color-coded fondue forks for keeping everyone's cooking organized, and tiny dishes for sauces (get thee to the Asian market or sushi supply shop for these pretty little gems). Make sure you have lots of wine and then sit down and eat, drink, cook and commiserate.

And don't feel the need to do all of these various fondues — an intimate party may revolve around two or three pots (cheese, oil, chocolate). Or just do the Asian broth fondue — a full meal in a soup pot.

The Big Cheese

What could be better after a day of cross-country or downhill skiing than a chunk of chewy baguette dripping in warm melted cheese. Every fondue party needs at least one cheese thing to start — this is the classic. Feel free to vary the cheeses. A little blue always adds a stylish note. And remember, the better the cheese, the better life gets.

1 cup (250 mL) white wine
1 tsp. (5 mL) lemon juice
1 clove garlic, minced
2 cups (500 mL) grated Gruyère cheese
2 cups (500 mL) grated Emmenthal cheese

2–3 tsp. (10–15 mL) cornstarch
1 Tbsp. (15 mL) Kirsch or brandy
freshly grated nutmeg
1 loaf crusty French or Italian bread cut into
   1–inch (2.5–cm) cubes

1 In a heavy fondue pot, combine the wine and lemon juice and heat to boiling over medium-high heat. Add the garlic. Reduce the heat to low.

2 Toss the grated cheese with the cornstarch, then gradually add it to the pot, a handful at a time, stirring until melted. Continue to heat until the mixture is smooth, stirring frequently.

3 Add the Kirsch or brandy and heat gently for 2–3 minutes longer. Do not allow the mixture to boil. Grate in a touch of fresh nutmeg for true Swiss flavor.

4 Place the fondue pot on its stand over a low flame to keep the cheese mixture hot. Serve with bread cubes for dipping. Serves 4.

Girl talk: If cheese fondue is standing in as a main dish (say with pickles or olives and a green salad), you can make it more substantial by stirring in a can of crab meat. Or, for an easy addition to a casual appetizer buffet, make your fondue with aged Cheddar, stir in a can of chopped green chilies and pass the tortilla chips.

Hot Oil Fondue

This is the way to cook cubes of steak, chicken, scallops and prawns, even tempura shrimp and vegetables. Just spear, dunk and deep-fry — but make sure the oil is hot (at least 375°F/190°C) and don't put those hot forks into your mouth (you might opt for bamboo skewers for cooking to avoid burns). Plan for 2–3 lbs. (1–1.5 kg) of meat and/or seafood for six guests and offer a variety of dipping sauces.

3 cups (750 mL) canola or light olive oil
beef tenderloin or lean, boneless lamb, cut
   into 3/4–inch (2–cm) cubes or thin strips
   pork tenderloin, cubed or sliced

sea scallops, halved crosswise if large
jumbo shrimp, peeled and deveined
dipping sauces (page 117)

1 Heat the oil in a heavy metal or cast iron pot on the stovetop, then carefully move to the table and keep hot on a portable burner. Set the pot on a heatproof stone or wooden slab. The pot should be about one-third full.

2 Dry the meat and fish well with paper towels and arrange on individual platters. Season lightly with salt and freshly ground black pepper.

3 Make sure the oil is at 375–400°F (190–200°C) before you start cooking. Guests spear a piece of meat or seafood and cook for 30–60 seconds, depending on how it is cut. A strip of beef or lamb needs to be threaded, accordion-style, on the skewer for cooking.

4 Don't put too many forks into the pot at once or the oil will cool down and the meat will stew rather than sear. Remove the cooked food from hot forks and place on your plate, then consume with a cold utensil to avoid burns. Each guest should have a selection of tiny bowls filled with an array of dipping sauces.

Asian Broth Fondue

Not technically fondue, this version of a Japanese communal soup, or *shabu shabu*, lets you simmer vegetables and paper-thin pieces of meat or chicken in a flavorful broth for a completely healthy fondue experience. Chopsticks for everyone are a must, along with individual bowls for dipping sauces and a small bowl for rice. This dish can be part of a multi-course fondue party or the centerpiece for an interactive Asian meal.

meat and vegetables

1 lb. (500 g) beef tenderloin or strip loin

1 lb. (500 g) boneless, skinless chicken breast

1 block medium tofu (about 1/2 lb./250 g), cut into 3/4–inch (2–cm) cubes

8 fresh Chinese black mushrooms (or 1 large portobello), sliced

1 bunch asparagus, trimmed

6 green onions, cut in 2–inch (5–cm) pieces

3 baby bok choy or Chinese cabbages, leaves separated and sliced

3 cups (750 mL) fresh bean sprouts

dipping sauce

2 Tbsp. (25 mL) white miso

1/2 cup (125 mL) sesame paste (tahini) or ground sesame seeds

1/4 cup (50 mL) soy sauce

1/4 cup (50 mL) mayonnaise

broth

6 cups (1.5 L) beef or chicken broth, water or a dashi broth mix

2 Tbsp. (25 mL) soy sauce

8 cups (2 L) short-grain steamed rice

1 Trim all of the visible fat from the beef. Put it in the freezer for 30–60 minutes to partially freeze. Using a sharp knife, cut it across the grain into paper-thin strips. Arrange the slices on a platter in an attractive overlapping pattern. Cover with plastic wrap and refrigerate until dinner time.

2 Thinly slice the chicken and arrange on another plate. Cover and refrigerate.

3 Make sure to wash up well (knives and cutting boards) between slicing the beef, chicken and vegetables to prevent any cross contamination. This is important — you don't want to poison your guests!

4 On another platter, arrange the cubed tofu, sliced mushrooms, asparagus, green onions, bok choy and bean sprouts. Cover and refrigerate.

5 To make the dipping sauce, whisk the miso, sesame paste, 1/4 cup (50 mL) soy sauce and mayonnaise together. Divide among tiny bowls, one for each guest.

6 Bring the broth and 2 Tbsp. (30 mL) soy sauce to a boil on the stove, then pour into a large, shallow cast iron or earthenware pot. Set over a heat source (an electric or solid-fuel fondue pot or portable gas burner) at the center of the table. Keep the stock at a low simmer.

7 To cook, guests pick up pieces of meat or chicken with their chopsticks and swish them through the broth for about 10 seconds, until lightly cooked, then dip into the sauce and eat. Vegetables and tofu are cooked the same way, with the meal progressing until all the food has been cooked and consumed. Add more hot broth as necessary to keep the pot topped up. Serve individual bowls of steamed rice on the side, and finish the meal by serving the flavorful broth to your guests — a final clear soup course drunk like tea from small bowls. Serves 6–8.

The Dipping Sauce Stuff

Many people wonder what kind of sauces they should make when planning a fondue party but there are some simple solutions. The easiest is to cheat and buy some prepared sauces — a good bottled chili sauce, barbecue sauce, a seafood sauce with horseradish, a mustard mayonnaise and even a teriyaki sauce can be purchased from the local supermarket. Poured into your stylish little individual sauce dishes, no one will be the wiser. If you look through the shelves at a specialty grocery, you will likely even find some fancier gourmet sauces and condiments to include.

Or you can get creative by combining things like mayonnaise with roasted garlic, pesto or curry paste, or making beef broth and red wine reductions flavored with herbs. Hot mustard or horseradish sauces are always good with beef. Try basil pesto or coriander chutney (an Indian condiment) with seafood.

The Best Chocolate Fondue

The Girl's best advice is to melt a big bar of Toblerone® chocolate (complete with the crunchy bits of nougat) and pass a plate of colorful fresh fruit and chunks of pound cake for dipping. Dead easy and divine.

chocolate
3 3¹/₂–oz. (100–g) bars Toblerone® chocolate
1 cup (250 mL) whipping cream

fruit
chunks of fresh fruit (strawberries, pineapple
  spears, kiwi quarters, melon, banana, sliced
  pears)

1 Chop the chocolate bars. Heat the cream in a saucepan until it begins to boil. Add the chocolate, a little at a time, until the whole thing is melted.

2 Pour into a heavy enamel or ceramic fondue pot and set over a heat source. A candle is usually enough to keep the chocolate moving — too much heat and the chocolate will burn. Serves 4.

Pizza Party

A party where everyone cooks their own food is brilliant for the food-phobic cook — guests are responsible for their own dining disasters and the heat's off you. Pizza is a no-brainer — anyone can build their own delicious pie — and when organized as an interactive group activity, making pizza can be a creative party mixer.

Get everyone chopping, cooking and contributing — a pizza topping potluck always garners great ingredients. Offer to make a couple of batches of pizza dough, then ask each guest to bring a topping, and soon you'll be creating gourmet combinations like fresh figs and Gorgonzola, prosciutto and wild mushrooms with fresh sage, or the best fresh tomato and basil pizzas in town. There is absolutely no recipe — you use what you like.

Then, fire up the oven as hot as it will go, get the pizza stone sizzling and, with a flourish, send those pizzas flying from a pizza paddle into the oven like your favorite TV chef. The Girl guarantees your friends will be impressed.

Whether it's family game night or a party for friends, pizza is something anyone can do. Some of today's hottest chefs have built their careers on crisp, creative pizza, so it can't hurt your reputation to become the pizza queen in your circle. Grab an apron, crack open the Chianti and get cooking!

The Crust

If you ever spend time out in the country, miles from the pizza delivery guy, like I do, knowing how to whip up a pizza from scratch is a lifesaver. But there are easier ways, too.

The fastest way to make a pizza at home is to start with one of the prebaked bread/pizza shells that you'll find at the local supermarket. It's nothing like a scratch crust, but you can dress it up with a slather of pesto (from a jar, of course), some slivered red onions and mushrooms, green pepper and ham, or Italian sausage and black olives. Add the ubiquitous shredded three-cheese mix from the dairy case, and you have an instant after-work dinner that's kid-friendly and cheaper than take-out. A thick, Greek-style pita bread also makes a perfect crisp crust for an instant personal pizza any time.

But if you want authentic, thin-crust Italian pizza (the kind that are becoming extinct as fast food joints replace real pizza with their fat bready pies), take more time and make the dough from scratch. You can do this in your food processor, mixer or even in the bread machine (possibly the only good use for this massive kitchen paperweight). It sounds complicated, but it's dead easy. Really.

This recipe makes enough pizza dough for 3–4 small pizzas — make several batches to feed a crowd for a pizza party, or just make a couple of pizzas on a weeknight instead of ordering out. Excess dough can be frozen. Go nuts at the local Italian deli picking out fancy cheeses and exquisite imported olives, or just open the fridge and see what kind of cheese, sliced sandwich meat and other condiments might work together to get you past dinner time. If you can't face the prospect of making pizza dough, you can usually buy it frozen at the local Italian deli or from any mom-and-pop pizza joint.

3 cups (750 mL) flour (I like to use 2 cups/500 mL
  all-purpose and 1 cup/125 mL cornmeal,
  whole-wheat or barley flour)
2 tsp. (10 mL) instant yeast
1 tsp. (5 mL) salt

1 Tbsp. (15 mL) olive oil
1 cup (250 mL) warm water (about 125°F/50°C)
1 tsp. (5 mL) sugar
cornmeal

1 Place the flour, yeast and salt in the food processor and whirl briefly. Combine the olive oil, warm water and sugar. With the machine running, slowly add the liquid, until the dough comes together in a ball. You can add up to $^1/_4$ cup (50 mL) more warm water if you need to — the dough should be smooth but soft.

2 You can also mix the dough with an electric mixer or with a wooden spoon or your hands. If you mix it by hand, you'll have to knead it for about 10 minutes until it's smooth and elastic, adding more flour if necessary.

3 If you have a bread machine, use the dough cycle and just dump all the ingredients into the machine. It's convenient and easy, because it mixes the dough and gives it a warm place to rise until you're ready to roll out your pizza crusts. You can refrigerate the dough or even freeze it — just bring it back to room temperature before proceeding.

4 When you're ready to cook your pizzas, place a pizza stone (or an inverted heavy baking sheet) on the lowest rack of your oven. The Girl has even successfully used unglazed clay tiles from the hardware store, arranged tightly together on the bottom oven rack, to approximate the clay oven/pizza stone. Preheat the oven to 500°F (260°C) for 30–45 minutes.

5 Divide the dough into 3 or 4 pieces and roll or stretch each into an 8-inch (20-cm) round, the thinner the better.

6 Make your pizza directly on a pizza peel (a long-handled wooden paddle) that has been sprinkled with some cornmeal. The cornmeal will prevent the dough from sticking so you can slide the pizza directly onto the hot stone in the oven. If you don't have a peel, a heavy piece of cardboard covered in foil will work. Dress the pizza lightly with your favorite toppings. Lightly is the operative word here — too much topping makes soggy pizza.

7 Carefully slide the pizza from the peel directly onto the preheated pizza stone and bake for 10–12 minutes, until the bottom is crisp and brown. Repeat with additional pizzas.

8 Let the pizza stand on a cutting board for 2 minutes before cutting into wedges using a chef's knife or a rotary pizza cutter. Serve immediately. Makes 3–4 individual pizzas.

The Toppings

When you're having an interactive pizza party, divide your guests into teams of two (not couples) and let the topping and baking of pies go on all night while you sit in the kitchen, at the bar, or around the dining table, and comment on your cohorts' combinations. Set out the toppings — chopped, cooked, shredded and ready to use — and let the games begin. Anything goes, but here are some tried and true combos.

- Tomato sauce, sautéed mushrooms, sautéed onions, minced garlic, thinly sliced prosciutto and fontina cheese.
- Basil pesto, thinly sliced Roma tomatoes, slivered onions and mozzarella cheese.
- Slivered sundried tomatoes (packed in oil), artichoke hearts (drained well, if canned, and chopped), slivered black olives, slivered fresh basil leaves and grated aged Friulano cheese.
- Tomato sauce, minced fresh basil, black pepper and grated Parmesan cheese.
- Extra virgin olive oil, roasted garlic purée, grilled asparagus, caramelized onions, and grated provolone and Asiago cheese.
- Tomato sauce, fresh mozzarella cheese and anchovies.
- Pesto, Italian sausage (cooked), tomatoes and slivered provolone or Friulano cheese.
- Fruity extra virgin olive oil, quartered fresh ripe figs, crumbled Gorgonzola or Cambozola cheese, minced fresh rosemary, black pepper and chopped chives.
- Tomato sauce, pesto, thinly sliced dry salami, slivered black olives and grated mozzarella cheese.

Passage to India

The Girl loves to travel but her visit to India was truly one of the most memorable of all trips — a country with amazing grace and even more amazing food. You can create your own wonderfully exotic Indian feast at home. Drape the table with pretty silk sari fabric and pass the pappadums. Choose the lamb or chicken for your main course, then augment with as many vegetables dishes as you like.

Feel free to augment your meal with fresh samosas or naan bread from your local Indian restaurant, or farm out the recipes to your friends for an exotic potluck. Then open some jars of mango chutney and find a full-bodied off-dry Gewürztraminer or a fruity Australian Traminer Riesling to serve alongside.

Dal Dip

Start any Indian meal with this spicy split pea spread and crispy pappadums or sliced vegetables for dipping.

2 Tbsp. (25 mL) butter or ghee (clarified butter)
1 tsp. (5 mL) canola oil
1 small onion, finely chopped
1 Tbsp. (15 mL) finely grated or minced fresh ginger
1 clove garlic, finely grated or minced
1 serrano chili pepper, seeded and minced
1/2 tsp. (2 mL) garam masala

1/2 tsp. (2 mL) turmeric
2 cups (500 mL) dried red lentils (the salmon-colored *masoor dal*)
3 cups (750 mL) water
1/2 tsp. (2 mL) salt
1/4 cup (50 mL) plain yogurt or sour cream
2 Tbsp. (25 mL) chopped cilantro

1 Heat the butter and oil in the saucepan over medium-high heat and sauté the onion, ginger, garlic and serrano chili until soft. Stir in the garam masala and turmeric and cook for 1 minute, until the spices are fragrant. Add the lentils and stir them around to coat them with the spices, then pour in the water. Stir in the salt.

2 Cover the pan and bring to a boil. Reduce the heat to medium-low and simmer for 20 minutes, until the lentils completely disintegrate. Check to see that most of the liquid has been absorbed — if not, simmer with the lid off until the dal is thick, then transfer to a bowl.

3 Stir the dal until it is cooled slightly. Whisk in the yogurt or sour cream until the mixture is smooth, then stir in the chopped cilantro. Serve warm or chill. Makes about 2 cups (500 mL).

BOWL OF DIP ☺

Girl talk: Pappadums are wonderful crackers, made from chickpea and lentil flour and dried in the hot Indian sun. They're packaged and sold at Indian grocery stores, usually in flat boxes or stacked like thin, 5–inch (12–cm) wafers in plastic bags. To puff pappadums, fry them in hot oil for a few seconds or cook them in the microwave for about 45 seconds. You can buy large round pappadums or tiny cocktail-sized crackers (which are nice for dipping), plain or spiced. Definitely addictive and good at any party. Try them.

Bharta

The Girl might as well admit it — she's completely addicted to this smoky, spicy eggplant purée from her favorite local curry house. The trick — you must blacken the eggplant on the grill or under the broiler for authentic smoky flavor. This is a great side dish or can be scooped up with naan bread or pappadums for a funky starter. Don't panic if you can't find the fenugreek leaves — they add an authentic edge but you can leave them out and the dish will still be delicious.

1 large eggplant
1 Tbsp. (15 mL) canola oil
1 tsp. (5 mL) whole cumin seed
1 Tbsp. (15 mL) minced garlic
1 Tbsp. (15 mL) minced fresh ginger
1 cup (250 mL) chopped onion
$\frac{1}{2}$ cup (125 mL) chopped tomato
$\frac{1}{2}$ tsp. (2 mL) salt

$1\frac{1}{2}$ Tbsp. (20 mL) curry masala or curry powder (all-purpose MDH brand meat masala is a good product to look for)
1 tsp. (5 mL) sweet Hungarian paprika
$\frac{1}{4}$ tsp. (1 mL) cayenne pepper (or to taste)
$\frac{1}{2}$ tsp. (2 mL) *kasoori methi* (dried fenugreek leaves, found in Indian groceries)
1 Tbsp. (15 mL) chopped fresh cilantro

1 Start by blackening the eggplant. Place the whole eggplant directly over a high flame on your gas stove or directly under the broiler, turning it for 15–20 minutes until it is charred and blackened on all sides. Alternately, heat the barbecue to high and roast the eggplant on the grill. When the eggplant is charred, peel away all of the black skin and rinse away any burnt bits. Remove the stem and mash the flesh in a bowl or whirl in a food processor. Set aside.

2 In a saucepan, heat the oil over medium-high heat and add the cumin seed. Cook for 1 minute, then stir in the garlic and ginger. Fry together for 1 minute and add the onion and tomato. Cook together over medium heat for 5 minutes.

3 Stir in the salt, curry masala, paprika and cayenne. Add the mashed eggplant and stir to combine well. Stir in the *kasoori methi*. Reduce the heat to low and simmer, stirring regularly to prevent burning, for 20–30 minutes. When you see some oil rising to the top of the purée, the bharta is done. Taste the mixture and adjust the salt or cayenne pepper to taste. Place in a small bowl and sprinkle with cilantro. Serves 2–4.

Girl talk: Garam what? Think curry powder — but chocolate brown in color and "dark" in flavor. Like curry spice mixtures, most Indian cooks make their own garam masala from scratch, and grind the whole spices each time they make a dish, but you can find decent mixtures in any Indian grocery. It's a mixture of "hot spices" designed to heat the body — a delicious combination of ground black cardamom, cinnamon, black cumin, cloves, black pepper and nutmeg. Toss some garam masala into your next barbecue marinade or salad dressing for that exotic *je ne sais quoi*.

Saag Lamb

Serve this rich, tender lamb stew over fragrant basmati rice for a simple, one-dish meal. Make it on one of those winter afternoons when you have time to gather together the spices and simmer the stew for a few hours. Or make a speedy lamb curry — replace the spices with a few spoonfuls of jarred Indian curry paste and create this stew in about 20 minutes in the pressure cooker (page 359). The spinach makes this lamb (*gosht*) curry into *saag* (spinach) *gosht* — a good way to get your greens — but the curry is good without it, too.

2 medium onions, chopped

2 Tbsp. (25 mL) grated or minced fresh ginger

3 cloves garlic, chopped

2 dried hot chilies, crumbled

1 Tbsp. (15 mL) ground coriander

1 tsp. (5 mL) ground cumin

1/4 tsp. (1 mL) each: cinnamon, ground cardamom, ground cloves and ground saffron (or substitute 1 tsp./5 mL garam masala if you have it)

2 Tbsp. (25 mL) oil

2 lbs. (1 kg) boneless lamb shoulder or leg, fat removed and cut into 2–inch (5–cm) cubes

2 tsp. (10 mL) salt

3 Tbsp. (45 mL) tomato paste

2 packages (10 oz./350 g) chopped frozen spinach, thawed and squeezed dry

1/2 cup (125 mL) plain, low-fat yogurt

3 Tbsp. (45 mL) chopped cilantro

1 In a blender, combine half the onions with the ginger, garlic and chilies and 1/2 cup (125 mL) water. Blend to purée. Add the coriander, cumin, cinnamon, cardamom, cloves and saffron and mix again.

2 Heat the oil in a heavy saucepan over medium-high heat and fry the remaining onion until golden. Add the mixture from the blender and fry together for 10 minutes more. Add the cubes of lamb and stir to coat completely with the spices. Stir in 1/4 cup (50 mL) of water and the salt, tomato paste and spinach. Simmer, covered, for 1 hour or longer, until the lamb is very tender.

3 Slowly stir in the yogurt and mix well. Heat through but don't boil. Just before serving, stir in the cilantro. Serves 6.

Grilled Tandoori-Style Chicken with Cucumber Raita

The good old summertime is a good time to serve Indian food — any tandoori dish can be cooked on the gas grill with good results. Tandoori and other curry pastes come in jars and make authentic Indian cooking a breeze. Try this spicy marinade on lamb chops or even prawns, skewered for the grill kabob-style. With the cooling raita, serve some fragrant basmati rice or naan bread and crispy pappadums. Cold beer or off-dry white wine is the best match for spicy Indian food. Finish with grilled tropical fruits like mango or pine-apple with coconut ice cream.

2–3 Tbsp. (30–45 mL) tandoori paste
2 cloves garlic, minced
1/2 cup (125 mL) plain yogurt
1 Tbsp. (15 mL) olive oil

1 3 1/2 –lb. (1.8–kg) roasting chicken, cut up
    (or 2 lbs./1 kg boneless, skinless
    chicken thighs)
1 recipe Cucumber Raita

1 Combine the tandoori paste, garlic, yogurt and olive oil. Cut deep slits into the breast and thighs of the chicken pieces. Place the chicken in a resealable plastic bag and pour the marinade over top. Close the bag and refrigerate for 8 hours or overnight. (If using chicken thighs, cut each into four chunks and marinate. To cook, thread loosely on skewers and grill directly over medium heat for about 10–15 minutes in total.)

2 Preheat the barbecue to 500°F (250°C). Grill the chicken over direct medium heat for 10 minutes, turn-ing often, then turn off one burner, and put the chicken on the unlit side. Cook indirectly for 1 hour or until the chicken is just cooked through. Serve with the cucumber raita on the side. Serves 4.

Cucumber Raita

1/2 large English cucumber, shredded
1 Roma tomato, seeded and finely chopped
1/2 tsp. (2 mL) salt
1 cup (250 mL) plain yogurt, strained

2 Tbsp. (25 mL) chopped cilantro
1/4 tsp. (1 mL) ground cumin
1 green onion, minced
freshly ground black pepper

1 Cut the cucumber in half lengthwise, scoop out the seeds and discard. Shred the cucumber using the largest holes on your grater. Cut the tomato in half and squeeze out and discard the seeds, then finely chop the flesh. Place the cucumber and tomato in a colander and toss with the salt — let them drain in the sink for 30 minutes, pressing to remove excess water.

2 To strain the yogurt — for a nice thick raita — line a mesh strainer with cheesecloth or a coffee filter. Set it over a bowl. Spoon the yogurt into the strainer and place it in the refrigerator to drain for 1–2 hours. Mix the drained cucumber, tomato and yogurt with the cilantro, cumin and green onion. Season with pepper to taste and refrigerate. Makes 1 cup (250 mL).

Girl talk: If you can't find a prepared tandoori paste, make your own. You'll need 2 Tbsp. (25 mL) minced fresh ginger; 5 cloves of garlic, pressed; 1 tsp. (5 mL) each of ground coriander, paprika, garam masala, cumin, salt and cayenne pepper. Combine well and mix with the yogurt for the marinade.

Vegetable Biryani

Biryani is an all-in-one rice dish that the Girl likes to make as part of an Indian feast or on its own for a fast weekday supper. Go strictly vegetarian or toss in some cooked meat or seafood. If you can't find biryani paste, fry some ground spices with the onion — about 2 tsp. (10 mL) each of sweet Hungarian paprika, turmeric and garam masala, plus ½ tsp. (2 mL) of cayenne pepper. Feel free to substitute whatever fresh vegetables you have on hand.

2 Tbsp. (25 mL) vegetable oil

1 tsp. (5 mL) salt

1 medium onion, diced

4 Tbsp. (50 mL) biryani paste (or other Indian curry paste)

3–4 cups (750 mL–1 L) chopped mixed fresh or frozen vegetables (carrots, beans, cauliflower, red peppers, mushrooms, peas, etc.)

¾ cup (175 mL) raw basmati rice

¼ cup (50 mL) raw cashews

2–3 Tbsp. (25–45 mL) raisins

1¾ cups (425 mL) water

cooked beef, lamb, chicken or shrimp (optional)

1 In a large saucepan or wok, heat the oil over medium-high heat and sauté the onion until it's beginning to brown. Add the curry paste and cook for 2 minutes. Stir in the vegetables and stir-fry for 2–3 minutes. Add the rice, cashews and raisins and continue to fry for 1–2 minutes.

2 Add the water and salt and mix well. Bring to a boil over high heat, reduce the heat to low, cover and simmer for 30–40 minutes or until the rice is tender and the liquid is absorbed. If you have leftover beef, lamb, chicken or shrimp, add it at this point. Heat through and serve at once. *Serves 4.*

Cabbage Thoran

The Girl fell in love with this yummy combination of cabbage, coconut and spices in southern India. Serve this as a side dish for any Indian-inspired meal and impress your friends with the play of subtle sweet and spicy flavors. To save time, use a bag of preshredded coleslaw to start this simple dish.

1–lb. (500–g) bag precut coleslaw cabbage or
  shredded green cabbage (about 5 cups/1.25L)
1/2 cup (125 mL) dried unsweetened, shredded
  coconut
1 serrano chili, seeds removed, chopped
1 clove garlic
1 cup (250 mL) chopped onion
1/4 tsp. (1 mL) salt

1 tsp. (5 mL) turmeric
1/2 tsp. (2 mL) coriander seeds
1/2 tsp. (2 mL) black mustard seed or *kalonji*
  (black onion seed)
2 Tbsp. (25 mL) canola oil
1/2 cup (125 mL) canned coconut milk
1 tsp. (5 mL) sugar
1/2 lime

1 Place the cabbage in a large bowl. In a food processor, pulse the coconut, chili, garlic and onion together until very finely minced. Add to the bowl with the cabbage, along with the salt, turmeric, coriander and black mustard seed. Mix well.

2 Heat the oil in a wok over medium-high heat. Add the cabbage mixture and stir-fry for 5 minutes. Add the coconut milk and sugar, cover and steam for 5 minutes. Remove the lid and continue to cook just until the cabbage is tender. Squeeze the lime over the dish just before serving. Serves 4.

Intimate Dinner Parties

Whether it's your anniversary, a private New Year's celebration
or just a Saturday night date with a good movie on the tube, the
Girl is a big fan of the romantic meal at home.

These dishes are easy enough that you won't waste quality time in
the kitchen. Start with a simple bistro salad with Goat Cheese Croutons (page
130), a tiny bowl of mushroom bisque or a cool summer soup, and mix and
match with any of these easy entrées. Then end the evening with the
simple berry brûlée (page 139) or the cookies and ice cream (page 140).
Or nibble on a plate of fine cheese or Belgian chocolates.

Crack a bottle of Champagne, light lots of candles and make
yourself comfortable. The night is young, baby!

Mixed Greens with Goat Cheese Croutons

Simple and sublime — a French bistro salad that always reminds the Girl of a romantic trip to Paris starts any dinner for two with style.

balsamic vinaigrette

2 Tbsp. (25 mL) balsamic vinegar

$^1/_2$ tsp. (2 mL) honey

$^1/_4$ tsp. (1 mL) Dijon mustard

$^1/_4$ tsp. (1 mL) salt

1 clove garlic, grated or pressed

$^1/_4$ cup (50 mL) extra virgin olive oil

salad

3 cups (750 mL) mixed salad greens

6 slices French baguette, about 1/2 inch
   (1 cm) thick

olive oil

4 oz. (125 g) creamy goat cheese

freshly ground black pepper

1 Combine the vinaigrette ingredients in a bowl and whisk to combine, or shake together in a small bottle. Set aside.

2 Wash the greens and drain well — a salad spinner is great to get rid of excess moisture. If you wash the greens in advance, wrap them in a paper towel, place in a plastic bag and refrigerate.

3 Preheat the oven to 450°F (230°C). Brush the bread slices lightly with olive oil on both sides and set on a baking sheet. Toast in the oven for 5–10 minutes, until they start to brown around the edges.

4 Slice the goat cheese into six rounds and place a round on each piece of toast. If the cheese crumbles, don't worry, just press it evenly over the toasted bread.

5 Turn the oven to broil and when the broiler is hot, put the toasts back in the oven, about 5 inches (12 cm) below the element. Watch carefully as they can burn easily — the cheese should be melted and bubbly in a minute or two.

6 Meanwhile, toss the greens with just enough of the vinaigrette to coat. It's better to use less dressing than to overdress the greens as you can drizzle more on later. Garnish each salad with three goat cheese croutons, grind some fresh pepper on top and serve warm. Serves 2.

Wild Mushroom and Potato Bisque

This is the Girl's version of that old standby that was once the basis of every creamy, family-style sauce. But with exotic wild mushrooms, a little potato for body and just a touch of fresh cream, it's worlds away from the supermarket staple, and healthier, too. Use the food processor to mince the onion, finely chop the mushrooms and grate the potatoes.

1 Tbsp. (15 mL) olive oil
1 small onion, minced
2 cloves garlic, minced
3/4 lb. (375 g) Yukon Gold potatoes, peeled and grated
1 cup (250 mL) finely chopped wild and domestic mushrooms (brown, oyster, shiitake, portobello, morels, cepes, etc.)

4 cups (1 L) homemade chicken stock or vegetable stock
1 bay leaf
3/4 tsp. (4 mL) minced fresh thyme
1 Tbsp. (15 mL) tomato paste
1/2 cup (125 mL) heavy cream
salt and freshly ground black pepper

1 Heat the oil in a medium-sized pot and sauté the onion and garlic until soft. Add the grated potatoes and mushrooms and continue to cook until the mushrooms begin to give up their moisture, about 5 minutes longer. Add the stock, bay leaf, thyme and tomato paste, and bring to a boil.

2 Cover the pot, reduce the heat to low and simmer the soup for 30 minutes. The potatoes should break down and thicken the soup. Stir in the cream and heat through. For a smoother version, purée half or all of the soup in a blender (or use an immersible hand blender). Season to taste with salt and pepper. Serves 4.

Chilled Tomato Soup with Herbed Tomato Tapenade

Any time the Girl can serve something wonderful without actually cooking, she's thrilled. This refreshing summer soup can even be called gourmet cooking. A cross between gazpacho and classic tomato soup, it's designed to be consumed cold. Serve it as a starter in chilled cappuccino cups for real cachet. The trick to a perfect cold tomato soup is to purée the tomatoes by pressing them through a sieve or using a food mill to separate the skin and seeds from the pulp. Using a food processor or blender creates a thick foam, which is not a good thing.

soup

12 very ripe tomatoes, chopped (the heirloom types have the truest tomato flavor)

1 tsp. (5 mL) salt

freshly ground black pepper

$1/2$ cup (125 mL) tomato juice or water to thin if necessary

dash hot sauce or cayenne pepper

$1/2$–2 tsp. (2–10 mL) granulated sugar

2–3 tsp. (5–15 mL) lime juice

herbed tomato tapenade

1 ripe tomato, seeded and finely chopped

2 shallots, finely chopped

1 Tbsp. (15 mL) extra virgin olive oil

1 tsp. (5 mL) balsamic vinegar

2 Tbsp. (25 mL) chopped chives, basil, rosemary or celery leaves

sprigs of fresh herbs to garnish

1 Chop the tomatoes for the soup, retaining the juices and seeds. Pass the chopped tomatoes and juices through a sieve or food mill, collecting the pulp in a large bowl. Discard the skins and seeds.

2 Add the salt and pepper, tomato juice or water, hot sauce, and the smallest amounts of sugar and lime juice. Because all tomatoes differ in their acidity and sweetness, adjust the flavor of the soup with sugar and lime juice to taste, then chill the soup for 1–2 hours before serving.

3 To make the tapenade, combine the chopped tomato, shallots, olive oil, balsamic vinegar and chopped herbs.

4 Serve the soup cold, in chilled glass cups or small bowls. Garnish each serving with 1–2 Tbsp. (15–25 mL) of the tomato tapenade and a herb sprig. Serves 2 (4 as a small starter).

Oyster and Artichoke Stew

Here's something decadent you can whip up to kick off an evening of romance (these briny bivalves have particular powers, you know). Preshucked oysters are so easy to use — found fresh, in jars, at the seafood counter in almost any decent supermarket. Freshly cooked and sliced artichoke hearts are the best choice for this dish when they're in season — but canned artichokes are almost as good and infinitely easier. Serve this elegant stew with a good baguette or, as they do in the South, over toast points, with a bottle of crisp white wine or Champagne. To turn it into a more casual, one-dish dinner, stir in some cubes of cooked Yukon Gold potatoes right at the end.

2 cups (500 mL) freshly shucked small oysters
1 14-oz. (398-mL) can artichoke hearts, drained
1 lemon (1 tsp./5 mL minced lemon zest)
1 medium leek
$^{1}/_{4}$ cup (50 mL) butter
2 Tbsp. (25 mL) all-purpose flour

1 cup (250 mL) fish, clam or chicken broth
$^{1}/_{2}$ cup (125 mL) white wine or Champagne
$^{1}/_{4}$ cup (50 mL) heavy cream
2 Tbsp. (25 mL) chopped parsley
cayenne pepper

1 Drain the oysters, reserving the liquor. You should have about $^{1}/_{4}$ cup (50 mL) of juice. Halve the oysters if they are large. Set aside.

2 Drain the artichoke hearts. Chop two or three finely, and quarter the rest. Set aside.

3 Wash the lemon well and, using a microplane grater or zester, remove just the yellow part of the peel, leaving the white pith behind. Chop the lemon zest finely — you need 1 tsp./5 mL.

4 Discard the tough green top of the leek or save it for the stock pot (as if!). Cut the white and pale green part of the leek in half lengthwise and rinse it well under running water (leeks can be gritty and this sand can ruin your stew). Slice the leek thinly into half moons and rinse again in a colander. Drain to dry. You should have about 1 cup (250 mL).

5 In a saucepan, heat the butter over medium heat until bubbly. Add the leeks and sauté for 5 minutes. Stir in the flour and cook for 2 minutes, then slowly add the broth, stirring constantly until the sauce is smooth and thick.

6 Stir in the wine and reserved oyster liquor and bring to a boil. Add the cream and simmer until the sauce is thickened nicely. Stir in the reserved artichokes, lemon zest and parsley.

7 Return the sauce to a simmer, then add the oysters. In about 3 minutes, when the oysters are firm and just starting to curl around the edges, and the stew is bubbly, it's ready. Serve the stew in wide, shallow soup bowls, dusted with cayenne pepper. Serves 2 as an entrée, 4 as a starter.

Asparagus Risotto

Risotto is really a technique more than a recipe — and who isn't impressed by the girl who knows her way around a rustic risotto? This version uses asparagus for flavoring and color, but you might just as well add sautéed wild mushrooms, roasted peppers or seafood (or all of the above), and vary the herbs you use, depending on your mood. This makes a simple and comforting main dish or a nice side dish when you're grilling chicken or lamb chops (page 248).

1 lb. (500 g) asparagus
4 cups (1 L) (approximately) canned low-salt chicken broth
2 Tbsp. (25 mL) butter
2 Tbsp. (25 mL) extra virgin olive oil
1 medium onion, finely chopped
1 1/2 cups (375 mL) Arborio rice or medium-grain white rice

1/2 cup (125 mL) dry white wine
2 tsp. (10 mL) finely chopped fresh rosemary
1 1/2 cups (375 mL) freshly grated Parmesan cheese
salt and freshly ground black pepper
fresh rosemary sprigs (optional garnish)

1 Trim the tough ends from the asparagus, discarding the bottom third of each stalk. Cut off the asparagus tips and reserve. Cut the stalks into 1/4– to 1/2–inch-long (.5– to 1–cm) pieces. Set aside. Heat the broth to boiling in a small pot.

2 In a wide sauté pan, melt the butter with the olive oil over medium heat. Add the onion and sauté until tender but not brown, about 8 minutes. Add the rice and stir for 1 minute, until all the grains are coated and shiny.

3 Add the wine and stir until absorbed, about 1 minute. Add a ladle of hot broth (about 1/2 cup/125 mL), along with the chopped rosemary. Simmer until the liquid is absorbed, stirring often. Continue adding broth, 1/2 cup (125 mL) at a time until it's absorbed, and cook, stirring often, for about 10 minutes. Add the asparagus stalk pieces and continue adding the broth until the rice is almost cooked, about 10–15 minutes longer. The rice should be *al dente* (still slightly firm) and the risotto should be loose and creamy, not gummy or dry.

4 Add the asparagus tips and continue cooking until the rice is just tender and the mixture is creamy, adding broth as needed and stirring often, for about 5 minutes longer.

5 Stir in 1 cup (250 mL) of the Parmesan. Season to taste with salt and pepper. Serve in shallow rimmed bowls, topped with the remaining Parmesan and a grinding of pepper. Garnish with a sprig of rosemary if you have it. Some sliced ripe tomatoes on the side make a nice color contrast. Serves 2 heartily as a main dish, or 4 with other courses.

Balsamic Glazed Asparagus

Roasting intensifies the flavor of asparagus, and it's easy to do in the oven or on the grill. And they're so sexy to eat — a vegetable you're allowed to pick up with your fingers. Good alongside steak.

10 medium green asparagus spears
  (about 1 lb./500 g)
1/4 tsp. (1 mL) fine sea salt
1 Tbsp. (15 mL) extra virgin olive oil

1 Tbsp. (15 mL) good-quality balsamic vinegar
freshly ground black pepper
Parmesan shards (optional)

1 Preheat the oven to 400°F (200°C). To clean the asparagus, wash the tops well under running water to remove any grit and snap off the woody ends. The spears will break where the tender stuff begins — don't worry that you're throwing too much away; the ends are tough and unpleasant to eat.

2 Toss the asparagus with the sea salt, olive oil and balsamic vinegar. Place in a single layer on a baking sheet and roast for 12–15 minutes, shaking the pan occasionally to glaze the spears on all sides.

3 Transfer the hot asparagus to serving plates and grind some pepper over each serving. A few shards of Parmesan, peeled off with a vegetable peeler over the hot spears, makes it even better. Serves 2.

Girl talk: For a brilliant green risotto — the perfect spring side dish for grilled salmon — lightly steam half the asparagus stalks (about 1 cup/250 mL) and purée in the food processor or blender with 1–2 Tbsp. (15–25 mL) of softened butter. When the risotto is almost finished, stir in the reserved asparagus purée. If you have no asparagus, try this same technique with fresh or frozen green peas and fresh mint.

Tenderloin for Two

Sometimes the Girl just needs something classic for a special dinner with her significant other. Too much fussing ruins the mood — that's when a simple steak hits the mark. A dollop of the compound blue cheese butter gilds the lily and is also spectacular drizzled over a small baked potato (which you can bake while you're roasting some asparagus to serve alongside — see page 135). Or if you're mashing your spuds, try some of the blue cheese in the mix. If you're off cheese, another simple sauce for steak is horseradish mayo (page 232). Pour your favorite beefy Cabernet Sauvignon or Syrah, start a fire and get ready for romance.

steak

1 tsp. (5 mL) minced garlic
1 Tbsp. (15 mL) olive oil
2 6-oz. (175-g) beef tenderloin steaks, about
   1¹/₂ inches (4 cm) thick

2 tsp. (10 mL) Worchestershire sauce
freshly ground black pepper

blue cheese butter

2 Tbsp. (25 mL) unsalted butter, softened
1 Tbsp. (15 mL) heavy cream or sour cream
3 Tbsp. (45 mL) crumbled Roquefort or
   other blue cheese

2 Tbsp. (25 mL) chopped chives
dash lemon juice
dash cognac

1 Combine the minced garlic with the olive oil and rub over the steaks. Drizzle and rub with Worcestershire, and season with pepper.

2 Beat the butter with the cream or sour cream until soft. Beat in the cheese, chives, lemon juice and cognac. Set aside.

3 Grill the steaks to rare or medium rare — about 5 minutes per side on medium-high heat. Transfer the steaks to individual serving plates and top each with a big dollop of blue cheese butter. Serves 2.

Touchy Feely

Wonder when your steak is done to your liking? Use the steakhouse chef touch test — something the Girl learned from someone used to cranking out dozens of red meat meals at a steakhouse. Call it the steakhouse "rule of thumb." If you know how a steak feels when it's done, you'll never be stuck with over- or undercooked meat again.

Relax your hand and press the triangle of flesh below your thumb. That's how a spongy rare steak feels.

Holding your thumb and index finger together, press the spot again. It's firmer, like a steak cooked medium rare.

When you touch your thumb and middle finger together, the spot gets even firmer, like a steak that's cooked to medium or medium well. Fourth finger — bouncy, tough and well done. If you go any further, that steak is shoe leather!

Mussels in Sundried Tomato and Chipotle Cream Sauce

Spice things up with this saucy combo. Buy the big cultured mussels and you won't have to worry about them being gritty. Serve this with lots of fresh baguette for dipping, or, as a main course, over linguine.

sauce

2 Tbsp. (25 mL) olive oil

$^{1}/_{3}$ cup (75 mL) chopped onion or shallots

1 large clove garlic, minced

$^{1}/_{4}$ cup (50 mL) white wine

$^{1}/_{4}$ cup (50 mL) chopped sundried tomatoes (drained if in oil or softened in hot water and drained, if dry)

1 chipotle pepper in adobo sauce, minced

2 cups (500 mL) heavy cream

1 cup (250 mL) milk

salt, freshly ground black pepper and/or sugar to taste

mussels

2 tsp. (10 mL) olive oil

30–40 large mussels, scrubbed and debearded

$^{1}/_{4}$ cup (50 mL) white wine

chopped Italian parsley

1 Heat the 2 Tbsp. (25 mL) of oil over medium heat in a saucepan and add the onion or shallots and garlic. Cover the pan and let the onion sweat (think of a sauna — it's like sautéing with the lid on) until just translucent, not brown, about 5 minutes.

2 Add the wine and cook over high heat until reduced. Stir in the sundried tomatoes, and add the chipotle, the cream and milk. Simmer the sauce over medium heat until reduced by about one-third; this should take about 15 minutes. The sauce should just simmer, not boil. Cool the sauce and purée using a hand blender, until smooth. Adjust the flavor with a little salt, pepper and/or sugar. The sauce may be made ahead to this point and refrigerated.

3 To cook the mussels, heat the 2 tsp. (10 mL) of olive oil in a large pan or wok over high heat. When the pan is very hot, add the mussels and toss to coat with oil. Add the wine and toss again. Add the prepared sauce to the pan, toss to coat the mussels, then cover the pan.

4 Reduce the heat to medium-low and simmer, covered, just until the mussels pop open, about 2–3 minutes. Serve immediately in deep bowls, sprinkled with parsley. Serves 2 as a main course, 4 as an appetizer.

Girl talk: Impress your friends with this culinary tidbit. The trendy chipotle pepper is just the ubiquitous jalapeño in a different form, one that's been slowly smoked over a wood fire to give it its unique depth of flavor. You'll find chipotles dried or in cans, packed in a rich, dark adobo sauce. The Girl prefers the latter. After you open a can, keep the leftovers in a covered container in the refrigerator. They will keep for several months and are perfect to add smoky spice to stews and sauces of all kinds.

Balsamic Strawberries Brûlée

I know, mixing strawberries and vinegar sounds weird, but try it. A nice, well-aged balsamic (or your home-made balsamic reduction) will bring out the flavor of strawberries and, believe it or not, a good grinding of black pepper adds an intriguing note, too. At least it will give you something to talk about if your date is starting to bottom out.

Serve the strawberries alone, if you're pressed for time, with a little store-bought biscotti on the side. Or save some Champagne for this *sabayon* (a.k.a. *zabaglione*) and whisk it together at the last minute for a grand finale.

the strawberries
1¹/₂ cups (375 mL) sliced fresh strawberries
1 Tbsp. (15 mL) sugar

1 Tbsp. (15 mL) good-quality balsamic vinegar
(or use the balsamic reduction, page 17)

the sabayon
2 Tbsp. (25 mL) sugar
1 egg yolk
3 Tbsp. (45 mL) Champagne

¹/₄ cup (50 mL) whipping cream
1 tsp. (5 mL) sugar

1 Combine the strawberries, 1 Tbsp. (15 mL) sugar and balsamic vinegar in a bowl. Set aside to marinate for about an hour. Divide evenly between two individual, shallow oval ramekins.

2 To make the sabayon, get a big stainless steel bowl, a balloon whisk and a big pot of simmering water. Put the sugar and egg yolk in the bowl, set the bowl over the hot water and start whisking. You can do this in a saucepan over direct heat, but it's riskier and you MUST NOT move from the stove (or your sabayon can cook and curdle and you will have to start all over again).

3 When the mixture is thick and pale yellow, add the Champagne and continue to whisk until light and frothy, about 10 minutes. Remove the bowl from the heat and keep whisking until cool. Meanwhile, get your partner to whip the cream with the 1 tsp. (5 mL) sugar.

4 Using a spatula, carefully fold the whipped cream into the egg mixture. Pile the cream on top and turn it into the custard, using a slicing and scooping motion. This will keep the sabayon from breaking down as quickly.

5 Now preheat the broiler. Spoon the sabayon evenly over the berries. Put the ramekins on a baking sheet and slide them under the broiler, about 2–4 inches (10–20 cm) below the element. Broil, watching constantly, until they just start to turn brown on top. Serve immediately. *Serves 2.*

Nutty Cookies and Cream

If you're not up for the sabayon, this makes a simple but decadent dessert for the noncook — crispy cookies created instantly from a nutty chewy candy bar and gourmet ice cream. Once the Girl learned this cookie trick she vowed never go back to handmade tuiles. She also learned that this is the official bar of the pro rodeo circuit — so make this treat when you've invited a cowboy to dinner.

1 Eat-More® candy bar
1 tub gourmet chocolate or hazelnut ice cream

1 To make the cookies, cut the candy bar into eight equal slices, each about $^3/_4$ inch (2 cm) thick. Line a baking sheet with parchment paper (or use your nifty Silpat, page 360) and set the slices about 3 inches (8 cm) apart on the sheet. Bake in a preheated 350°F (180°C) oven on the middle rack until the bar melts into lacy puddles. Remove from the oven and allow to cool completely, then lift them off the baking sheet with a spatula. Or lift them while still warm and roll them around the handle of a wooden spoon to make cigar shapes. The cookies will keep for a week in a sealed container.

2 To serve, use an ice cream scoop to scoop nice balls of ice cream into your prettiest dishes. Garnish each serving with a couple of cookies. Serves 4.

Exotica:
The Middle Eastern
Meze Mosh

Meze is the new tapas, so plan a party and a dance of the seven veils to chase away those midwinter blues. Lounge around the coffee table on some elegant silk pillows and rugs, pour some sweet mint tea from your samovar and nosh the night away with exotic finger food.

Impress those foodie friends with a themed evening that's exotic and easy at the same time. Make this menu for a big party buffet, or cut it down to a few select courses for a more intimate gathering.

A warm couscous salad (page 26) rounds out the buffet meal or works well with either the meatballs or shrimp as a main course. Other easy additions might include bowls of Kalamata olives and pickled peppers or eggplant from the local deli counter.

Drizzle peeled and sliced oranges with honey, pass the filo pastries and break open some glistening pomegranates for dessert. The Girl never looked better.

Mouhammara

The Girl was down at her favorite Mediterranean café indulging in hummus, pita bread and falafel when she came upon this addictive Syrian red pepper spread. It took a little sleuthing to find a traditional recipe, and a trip to the Iranian shop for pomegranate molasses, but the results were stupendous (the Girl even gave away little jars of her favorite new spread for Christmas). Serve it with sliced baguette or pita bread, along with your own hummus (page 214). You'll be hookah-ed.

3 Tbsp. (45 mL) virgin olive oil
1 small onion, minced
3 cloves garlic, minced
²/₃ cup (150 mL) ground walnuts
4 sweet red peppers, roasted and peeled
    (jarred peppers are fine)

2 hot red peppers, roasted and peeled
2 Tbsp. (25 mL) fresh lemon juice (¹/₂ lemon)
2 Tbsp. (25 mL) pomegranate molasses
    (the secret sauce)

1 In a saucepan, heat the oil over medium-low heat. Add the onion and garlic, cover and sweat for 15 minutes until very tender.

2 Add the walnuts to the pan, increase the heat, and toast for 3 minutes, stirring constantly.

3 Place the roasted peppers, ground walnut and onion mixture, lemon juice and pomegrante molasses into a food processor and purée until smooth.

4 Chill the purée overnight. To serve, spoon into a bowl, drizzle with more virgin olive oil and dust lightly with cumin powder if desired. Serve with pita bread. Makes 2 cups (500 mL).

Girl talk: Pomegranates are one of the Girl's favorite fruits — there's a kind of zen to eating a pomegranate. You can't rush it or you'll just make a mess, and peeling away the thick skin and bitter white pith to reveal the seeds is like opening a beautiful present. Eating a pomegranate, one juicy seed at a time, is like popping bubble wrap — addictive and strangely fun. But keep them away from the white couch and carpet. Pomegranate juice was traditionally used to dye Persian carpets and it will permanently color yours, too.

The pomegranate is also the source for the sweet red syrup called grenadine, which is used in mixed drinks. And Iranian, Arabic, Lebanese and Turkish cuisines often use an unsweetened pomegranate syrup (or pomegranate molasses) for a tart, citrusy flavor.

There's no substitute. Try it brushed over meat for grilling or in a chicken or lamb stew (page 169) — the latter is the perfect main dish to expand this noshing party into a sit-down dinner.

Smoky Eggplant Purée

Here's another spread to smear on those toasts or scoop up with pita chips (page 214). Exotic, easy and low in fat.

1 lb. (500 g) eggplant (about 1 large)
3 Tbsp. (45 mL) olive oil, divided
1 small onion, minced (1/2 cup/125 mL)
2 Tbsp. (25 mL) fresh lemon juice

1 clove garlic, pressed or minced
salt and freshly ground black pepper
1 Tbsp. (15 mL) chopped fresh parsley
1 Roma tomato, seeded and finely chopped

1 Puncture the eggplants with a fork and rub with just enough olive oil to lightly coat. Preheat the broiler or the barbecue and roast the eggplant for 30–40 minutes, until the skin is blackened all over and the center is soft. Peel. Chop the flesh and place it in a colander in the sink to drain the excess liquid.

2 In a sauté pan, heat 2 Tbsp. (25 mL) of the olive oil over medium heat and sauté the onion slowly until golden and caramelized. Cover the pan during the first 10 minutes, then remove the cover and cook until the onion is soft, sweet and nicely colored. Set aside.

3 Meanwhile, in a food processor, combine the remaining olive oil, lemon juice, garlic, salt and pepper. Add the drained eggplant and process to form a smooth purée.

4 Place the purée in a bowl and stir in the caramelized onion, parsley and tomato. Cover and refrigerate for at least 2 hours to meld the flavors. Serve with pita bread triangles or pita chips (page 214) for scooping. Makes 1 1/2 cups (375 mL).

Saffron Meatballs

Garlicky meatballs swimming in golden saffron sauce — the perfect hot nosh for your feast. Serve these meatballs with toothpicks for skewering, or make them tiny and toss with fine egg noodles as a main dish. For an ultra-lean version, substitute ground turkey for the beef. Don't be tempted to omit the saffron threads — they give this dish its distinctive flavor.

meatballs

1/2 lb. (250 g) ground pork
1/2 lb. (250 g) ground beef
2 garlic cloves, minced
1 large egg, lightly beaten
1 slice French bread, crust removed, soaked in milk
  and squeezed dry

1/8 tsp. (.5 mL) cayenne pepper
1 tsp. (5 mL) salt
1/2 tsp. (2 mL) freshly ground black pepper

sauce

1/4 cup (50 mL) extra virgin olive oil
1/3 cup (75 mL) minced onion
1 clove garlic, minced
2/3 tsp. (4 mL) sweet Hungarian paprika
1 cup (250 mL) chicken broth

1/4 cup (50 mL) dry white wine
1/4–1/2 tsp. (1–2 mL) crumbled saffron threads
salt and freshly ground black pepper
4 Tbsp. (50 mL) chopped fresh Italian parsley,
  divided

1 Preheat the oven to 350°F (180°C).

2 Combine the meatball ingredients in a medium bowl, mixing well. Shape the mixture into 1-inch (2.5–cm) balls for appetizers (half as big for noodles). Place meatballs on a shallow baking sheet, and bake for 30–40 minutes, until nicely browned.

3 Meanwhile, make the sauce. In a large sauté pan, heat the oil over medium-high heat and add the onion and garlic. Sauté for 5 minutes, until it's beginning to color, then stir in the paprika and cook 1 minute longer.

4 Combine the broth and wine, then crumble in the saffron. Add the liquid to the pan, along with the cooked meatballs, and bring to a boil. Reduce the heat to low, cover and simmer for 20 minutes.

5 Uncover the pan and simmer until the sauce reduces and thickens slightly. Season to taste with salt and pepper. Stir in 3 Tbsp. (45 mL) of the parsley. To serve, arrange on a deep platter and sprinkle with the remaining parsley (or toss with some freshly cooked fine egg noodles). Makes 32 appetizer-sized meatballs.

Lemon Herb Shrimp Skewers

The Girl loves this clever technique of threading big shrimp on two parallel wooden skewers — it makes them a breeze to flip on the grill and guarantees even cooking every time. These shrimp are perfect for your meze meal, or you can pair them with spinach rice (page 259), tzatziki and pita bread (page 52) for a more traditional Greek meal.

48 large shrimp (about 2 lbs./1 kg)
4 Tbsp. (50 mL) extra virgin olive oil
1 green onion, minced
1 Tbsp. (15 mL) minced fresh Italian parsley
1 Tbsp. (15 mL) fresh or dried mint

1 Tbsp. (15 mL) oregano
1 dried chili pepper, crushed
salt and freshly ground black pepper
1 lemon

1 Peel and devein the shrimp, leaving the tails intact if you like. Combine the olive oil, green onion, herbs and crushed chili pepper in a bowl. Add the shrimp and toss to coat. Cover and refrigerate for 1 hour or overnight.

2 Thread the shrimp on wooden skewers — using two parallel skewers keeps the shrimp nicely uncurled while they cook, and makes it easy to flip them on the grill. Lay the shrimp on your work surface. First push one skewer through all of the "head" ends, then use a second skewer through each of the "tail" ends, doing 6–8 shrimp per skewer. They will lay flat, nested against each other and cook evenly. Season with salt and pepper. Grill over medium heat, just until the shrimp are pink and firm. Don't overcook them.

3 Serve the shrimp on the skewers or remove them from the skewers and pile them on a platter. Squeeze fresh lemon juice over top and serve immediately. Serves 4–6.

Decadent Seafood Dishes

What makes a nicer splash at a dinner party than fresh fish?
Seafood such as shrimp, oysters, scallops or lobster, and lovely pieces of
seared tuna, fresh halibut or salmon always make elegant events.

Choose any of these amazing main dishes as the centerpiece for your
next dinner party. Start with one of the simple salads in the book,
and finish with a drop-dead dessert like any at the end of this section.

Make your seafood menu after you've selected your fish. Take the Girl's
advice and find the best fishmonger in town, then buy whatever they have
that's super fresh. Fish is always fast and fabulous, and it's easy to cook
once you get the hang of it. Learn how to cook fish and you'll succeed
swimmingly on the dinner party circuit.

Roasted Salmon on Braised Baby Bok Choy

This recipe is inspired by the Girl's favorite culinary guru, California chef John Ash. Like her guru, the Girl believes strongly in the concept of fresh, regional, unadulterated food, and this recipe showcases fresh flavors and colors perfectly. Always look for wild Pacific salmon first, fresh in season or flash frozen at sea, or try this method with other fish, like halibut. Find the star-shaped anise (a licorice-flavored spice) at the local Chinese food store.

marinade

¼ cup (50 mL) soy sauce

½ cup (125 mL) Chinese cooking wine

3 Tbsp. (45 mL) honey

2 Tbsp. (25 mL) minced fresh ginger

2 cloves garlic, minced

½ tsp. (2 mL) Asian chili paste

fish

4 6–oz. (175 g) salmon fillets or steaks
(preferably wild)

4 Tbsp. (50 mL) olive oil, divided

1 lb. (500 g) baby bok choy, washed well and
halved lengthwise

4 fresh shiitake mushrooms, sliced

½ cup (125 mL) chicken stock

1 star anise (optional)

1 tsp. (5 mL) sesame oil

salt and freshly ground black pepper

1 In a saucepan, combine the marinade ingredients and bring to a boil. Cool.

2 Place the fish in a single layer in a deep dish, just large enough to hold it. Reserve ¼ cup (50 mL) of the marinade and pour the rest over the fish. Cover with plastic wrap and refrigerate for 1 hour, turning the fish once.

3 Preheat the oven to 450°F (230°C).

4 In a large, nonstick sauté pan that can go into the oven, heat 2 Tbsp. (25 mL) of the olive oil over medium-high heat. When the oil is hot, add the salmon and sauté until the fish is lightly browned, about 3 minutes. Turn each piece of fish over and place the pan quickly into the hot oven. Bake for 4–5 minutes, until the fish is just barely cooked through. This is a restaurant trick for finishing a dish while you devote your stovetop to other tasks, like cooking the bok choy.

5 Heat the remaining 2 Tbsp. (25 mL) oil in another wide sauté pan over high heat. Add the bok choy, cut side down, and mushrooms, and sauté until just beginning to color. Add the reserved ¼ cup (50 mL) of marinade, the chicken stock and star anise. Simmer the bok choy and mushrooms for 6 minutes to reduce slightly.

6 Divide the vegetables and braising liquid among four deep serving bowls. Drizzle with sesame oil and season with salt and pepper. Set a piece of glazed salmon on top and serve immediately. Serves 4.

Bouillabaisse

This is one of the Girl's favorite dishes for entertaining. Make the rich seafood broth in advance, then perfectly poach the fish and seafood just before you sit down to dine. This recipe is endlessly adaptable — use whatever fish is fresh and in season, then add shrimp, mussels, scallops, clams or any combination of shellfish. The secret to this classic stew from the south of France is the subtle licorice flavor of fennel or anise seed in the broth. Don't leave it out. To perfectly present this dish, you'll need some large rimmed soup bowls. Slice a baguette and pass some sweet unsalted butter. *Superbe!*

broth

2 Tbsp. (25 mL) virgin olive oil

2 onions, finely chopped (about 2 cups/500 mL)

3 cloves garlic, minced

1 cup (250 mL) slivered fresh fennel (or 1 cup/ 250 mL slivered celery and 1 tsp./5 mL fennel seed, or a splash of Pernod)

1 tsp. (5 mL) saffron threads, crumbled

2 bay leaves

1 sprig fresh thyme (or $^1/_2$ tsp./2 mL dried)

zest of 1 orange, finely grated

1 red chili pepper, crumbled

8 cups (2 L) fish stock or clam broth

3 Tbsp. (45 mL) tomato paste

1 14–oz. (398–mL) can tomatoes (whirled in a blender until smooth)

2 cups (500 mL) dry white wine

salt and freshly ground black pepper

fish and seafood

2 lbs. (1 kg) white fish (bass, halibut, sablefish, sole)

1 lb. (500 g) large shrimp, peeled and deveined

2 lbs. (1 kg) mussels (or clams), scrubbed

chopped fresh parsley to garnish

1 Make the broth a day in advance. In a large soup pot, heat the olive oil and sauté the onion, garlic and fennel for 10 minutes. Add the saffron, bay leaves, thyme, orange zest, chili pepper, fish stock or broth, tomato paste, tomatoes and white wine. Bring to a boil over high heat, reduce the heat to low, cover and simmer for 30 minutes. Strain, discarding the solids. Season with salt and pepper. You can stop at this point, cover the stock and refrigerate it overnight.

2 Just before you're ready to serve dinner, bring the broth to a boil. Cut the fish into serving pieces and add to the broth. Simmer for 2 minutes. Add the shrimp and mussels. Cover the pot and simmer for 3–4 minutes longer, until the mussels open. Discard any that do not open.

3 Divide the fish and seafood among individual serving bowls (use wide, shallow soup plates) and ladle some of the broth over top. Sprinkle each serving with chopped fresh parsley. Serves 8.

Girl talk: Bouillabaisse is traditionally served with rouille, a spicy red sauce or aïoli, a garlicky mayonnaise. Rouille is made with breadcrumbs, saffron, cayenne, garlic, egg yolks and olive oil, all combined to form a mayonnaise-like emulsion. Aïoli is similar — homemade mayonnaise, combined by hand using a mortar and pestle, with lots of fresh garlic. You can make a speedy version by placing ½ cup (125 mL) of commercial mayonnaise in a blender with 2–3 cloves of chopped garlic. Whirl until smooth, then add ½ tsp. (2 mL) of Dijon mustard and, with the motor running, incorporate about ⅓ cup (75 mL) of tasty extra virgin olive oil into the mayonnaise. Add a large pinch of cayenne pepper or paprika to make it red and spicy. Cover and refrigerate for up to 2 days. Pass the sauce with the bread, so diners can add a dollop to their fish stew.

Buyer Beware: Never ever buy bivalves like mussels or clams if they're packaged (as they do in some supermarkets). Go to a fish market and get fresh seafood that has been stored in the cooler or on ice. Tap the mussels on the counter — if they don't snap shut, they're dead and you should toss them (they can make you sick). After they're cooked, live mussels and clams pop open — any that stay shut should also be discarded.

The Girl prefers mussels to clams for this dish — they're usually cultivated and very clean. Clams tend to be sandy and need to be washed repeatedly before cooking, or they can add an icky grit to your soup. Not worth the risk when you've slaved.

Seared Scallops with Orange Pepper Sauce

Girlfriend Robin asked me to come up with a great dinner party dish that could be whipped up in a few minutes between courses. This is a great one that's been kicking around in the Girl's repertoire for years. Make the sauce in advance, and sear the scallops at the last minute while you cook the fresh pasta. It takes a little fancy footwork at the end, but it's easy, especially if you have a partner to watch the pasta. The whole operation takes about five minutes at this point and your guests will think you're a real chef.

sauce

3 Tbsp. (45 mL) butter, divided
$^1/_2$ cup (125 mL) slivered celery
$^3/_4$ cup (175 mL) slivered leeks, white part only, or slivered white onions
$^1/_2$ cup (125 mL) slivered red bell pepper
1 Tbsp. (15 mL) minced fresh ginger
2 Tbsp. (25 mL) all-purpose flour
$^1/_2$ cup (125 mL) dry white wine
$^1/_2$ cup (125 mL) fish stock (or bottled clam juice)

1 Tbsp. (15 mL) fresh lemon juice
1 bay leaf
$^1/_4$ tsp. (1 mL) sea salt
$^1/_4$ tsp. (1 mL) white pepper
$^1/_8$ tsp. (.5 mL) cayenne pepper
$^1/_2$ cup (125 mL) freshly squeezed orange juice
$^1/_2$ cup (125 mL) whipping cream
2 oranges, sectioned (see page 265)

scallops

1 Tbsp. (15 mL) olive oil
2 lbs. (1 kg) large sea scallops
$1^1/_2$ lbs. (750 g) fresh linguine

3 Tbsp. (45 mL) chopped cilantro (or fresh basil), divided

1 Melt 2 Tbsp. (25 mL) of the butter in a nonstick sauté pan and cook the celery, leeks, red pepper and ginger over medium-high heat for 5 minutes, until the vegetables start to soften. Stir in the flour and cook together for 1 minute. Gradually stir in the wine, stock and lemon juice, then add the bay leaf, salt, pepper and cayenne. Bring to a boil, continuing to stir. The sauce should be smooth and thickened. Cover the pan, reduce the heat to low and simmer for 5 minutes.

2 Add the orange juice to the sauce, increase the heat to medium and boil for 5 minutes. If you are making the sauce in advance, you can chill it at this point and finish it at the last minute.

3 To finish the sauce, heat it to boiling, then stir in the cream and simmer until thick. Stir in the orange sections, adjust the seasonings and keep the sauce warm. Heat a big pot of water over high heat for the pasta.

4 Meanwhile, heat a large nonstick pan over medium-high heat and add the remaining butter and the olive oil. When the fat is very hot, almost smoking, add the scallops, giving them plenty of room in the pan. Sear on one side for about 1 minute, until they look a little brown around the edges. Don't be tempted to lift them too soon or to crowd too many into the pan — they won't get nicely browned and caramelized, which is what you're after. Do the searing in two batches if your pan's not large enough. Turn the scallops and sear on the second side for 1–2 minutes. They should be just barely cooked through. Remove from the heat but keep them warm while you cook the pasta.

5 When the water is boiling, add a teaspoon (5 mL) of salt and the linguine. Cook the pasta until *al dente*, about 3–5 minutes (test it after 3 minutes, and every minute thereafter). It should be cooked through (not white inside) but still a little chewy. If it's mushy, you've overcooked it. Drain the pasta well, but don't rinse, and place in a large bowl.

6 Reserve three scallops to garnish each plate and add the rest to the sauce. Heat through for 30 seconds, then add the hot sauce to the pasta in the bowl. Add 2 Tbsp. (25 mL) of the cilantro and toss to combine.

7 Divide the pasta and sauce between six shallow pasta bowls. Top each serving with three seared scallops and a sprinkling of fresh cilantro. Serves immediately. Serves 6.

Girl talk: This dish only works if you use big, fat scallops, the kind that look like a stack of poker chips. Avoid those tiny Asian scallops — they're salty and unappetizing in anything but chowder.

Individual Lobster Lasagnas with Two Cheeses

This is a wonderful, decadent, make-ahead meal that's perfect for a holiday dinner party — the Girl created it first for a New Year's celebration. Individual oval ramekins make perfect lasagnas for one, but you can also make it in a single pan, then chill, cut and reheat for easy service. Try using no-boil lasagna noodles if fresh sheets are not available.

lobster sauce

1 medium fennel bulb
1 Tbsp. (15 mL) olive oil
1 Tbsp. (15 mL) butter
1 medium white onion, minced
1 medium carrot, finely diced
1 clove garlic, minced
2 Tbsp. (25 mL) cognac
1 cup (250 mL) chopped fresh or canned tomatoes

1 Tbsp. (15 mL) tomato paste
1 cup (250 mL) fish or lobster stock
1/2 cup (125 mL) dry white wine
1/4 tsp. (1 mL) saffron, crushed
1/4 cup (50 mL) heavy cream
2 cups (500 mL) cooked lobster meat, chopped
salt and white pepper to taste

bechamel sauce (optional)

1 1/2 cups (375 mL) milk
1 cup (250 mL) heavy cream
pinch white pepper
big pinch nutmeg

big pinch dried basil
3 Tbsp. (45 mL) butter
1/3 cup (75 mL) all-purpose flour
1/2 cup (125 mL) grated Parmesan cheese

assembly

1 lb. (500 g) fresh lasagna sheets, cut into
   16 3– x 5–inch (8– x 12–cm) rectangles

4 oz. (125 g) shredded dry Friulano cheese
2 oz. (50 g) shredded Parmesan cheese

1 To make the lobster sauce, cut off the long stems and fronds of the fennel and peel the outer layer from the bulb. Finely slice the fennel, reserving some of the fronds for garnish.

2 Heat the oil and butter in a deep skillet and sauté the fennel, onion and carrot for five minutes, until almost tender. Add the garlic and cognac and simmer until most of the liquid has evaporated. Stir in the tomatoes, tomato paste, stock, wine and saffron. Simmer until the sauce has reduced by half.

3 Add the cream and simmer 5 minutes longer, until the sauce is thickened nicely. Stir in the lobster, and season to taste with salt and pepper. Remove the sauce from the heat and keep warm.

4 To make bechamel, heat the milk, cream, pepper, nutmeg and basil to a boil, then remove from the heat and set aside. Heat the butter until foamy, stir in the flour and cook for 2 minutes. Gradually stir in the hot milk mixture, raise the heat and simmer until thick and smooth. Stir in the cheese.

5 Meanwhile, bring a pot of salted water to a boil and cook the pasta until just cooked through but still *al dente*, about 2–3 minutes. Drain and chill in cold water, then drain again. Combine the two cheeses.

6 Preheat the oven to 375°F (190°C). To make individual lasagnas, place a little of the sauce into the bottom of four ovenproof dishes. Top with a sheet of pasta and a layer of the lobster sauce. Add a dollop of bechamel, if using. Sprinkle lightly with the cheeses and add another layer of pasta. Continue layering sauce, cheese and pasta until each individual lasagna has four layers, ending with pasta. Sprinkle the tops with more cheese. Place the individual lasagnas in the oven and bake for 7–8 minutes, just until bubbling and beginning to brown. Garnish each with the reserved fennel fronds and serve immediately.

Serves 4.

Girl talk: The Girl is far too sensitive (and lazy) to boil live lobsters, but if you're not, you'll need about 5 lbs. (2.2 kg) of live lobster to make 2 cups (500 mL) of cooked meat. Steam or boil live lobsters for 12–15 minutes. Crack the shells when cool and reserve the meat (the shells are great for making lobster stock for this dish). Frozen precooked lobster tails or canned, frozen lobster meat is very good and dead easy — the Girl's preference. For a mixed seafood lasagna, substitute some scallops and prawns for the lobster in the sauce.

Halibut Provençal

The Girl's not sure which creative chef first wrapped a piece of fish in prosciutto but it's done in so many restaurants, and she knows exactly why. It makes for an impressive presentation and adds wonderful flavor. Try this technique with other fish, too, even big sea scallops or tiger prawns. The Girl likes to swaddle scallops in strips of prosciutto, skewer them in a series of five and grill. Lovely. This one-dish meal creates an instant South of France feast to set before your guests. Start with some marinated olives (page 213), a creamy soup (like the Gingery Carrot Soup page 285) and finish with the Chocolate Mocha Torte (page 172). Or opt for a simple dish of peeled and sliced oranges drizzled with wildflower honey and Grand Marnier. Don't forget to pop the cork on a pretty pink wine from Provence to set the scene. It's an easy menu with serious wow factor.

the vegetables

3 Tbsp. (45 mL) virgin olive oil
1 onion, halved and slivered
1 lb. (500 g) small new potatoes, cooked, cooled and cut into thick slices
2 cloves garlic, minced
1 red or yellow bell pepper, slivered

1 14-oz. (398-mL) can artichoke hearts, rinsed, drained and quartered
$1/2$ cup (125 mL) chicken broth
1 Tbsp. (15 mL) lemon juice
salt and freshly ground black pepper
$1/4$ cup (50 mL) air-cured black olives

the fish

4 5-oz. (150-g) pieces halibut fillets
salt, freshly ground black pepper and cayenne pepper
8–10 paper-thin slices prosciutto
8 large fresh sage leaves, whole (or use whole basil leaves)

1 Tbsp. (15 mL) butter
1 Tbsp. (15 mL) olive oil
chopped fresh sage leaves (or basil) to garnish

1 In a sauté pan, heat the olive oil over medium heat and sauté the onion until it's beginning to brown. Add the potatoes and continue cooking until they are nicely browned. Add the garlic, bell pepper and artichokes and continue to cook together, until the pepper is tender. Add the broth and lemon juice and simmer for 5 minutes, then stir in the salt and pepper. Arrange the vegetable mixture in a shallow, oven-proof casserole dish (something pretty that you can bring to the table) and scatter the black olives about.

2 Preheat the oven to 400°F (200°C). Season the fish lightly with salt, pepper and cayenne pepper. If you have cut 5-oz. (150-g) pieces from a thick halibut fillet, you should have rectangular fingers, each about 2–3 inches (5–8 cm) across. To wrap the fish pieces, lay two pieces of prosciutto on your work surface, overlapping slightly. Top with two large sage or basil leaves. Set a fish finger on top and wrap the prosciutto tightly around it, enclosing the herbs and the fish inside. If the prosciutto is sliced thinly enough, it will wrap easily and adhere to itself.

3 Heat the butter and oil together in a nonstick sauté pan over medium-high heat. When the pan is nice and hot, add the fish and sauté for about 2 minutes per side, until the prosciutto is nicely browned and crisp and the fish is nearly cooked. Nestle the fish in the vegetables in the casserole dish. Place in the preheated oven and heat for 5 minutes longer, just until everything is heated through.

4 Strew a few chopped sage or basil leaves over top and serve your guests directly from the casserole dish at the table. Serves 4.

  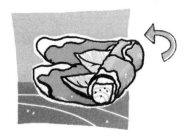

Spicy Thai Seafood Soup

This spicy bouillabaisse makes a fresh, light main dish when you're serving a complete Asian meal. Start with a plate of salad rolls (page 220) or dumplings, and a Thai chicken salad (page 21) or Japanese noodle salad (page 25). This may seem like a long list of ingredients, but if you prep them all in advance, the soup goes together quickly at the last minute.

8 cups (2 L) chicken broth, homemade or canned
5 kaffir lime leaves or zest of one lime (peeled off in wide strips with a vegetable peeler)
1 Tbsp. (15 mL) grated ginger
1 clove garlic, minced
2 Tbsp. (25 mL) soy sauce
2 Tbsp. (25 mL) fish sauce
3 Tbsp. (45 mL) lemon or lime juice
1 hot Thai or serrano chili, chopped
1 tsp. (5 mL) sugar
1 large carrot, shredded or cut into thin matchsticks

1 lb. (500 g) large shrimp, shelled and deveined (21–30 count)
1 lb. (500 g) mussels, scrubbed and debearded
1 lb. (500 g) halibut, sablefish or other white fish fillet, cubed
2 oz. (50 g) rice noodles, soaked in hot water to soften and drained (about 2 cups/500 mL)
2 green onions, cut into 2-inch-long (5-cm) shreds
1/4 cup (50 mL) chopped cilantro
1/4 cup (50 mL) mint or Thai basil, chopped
1 lime, cut into wedges

1 Combine the broth, lime leaves or zest, ginger and garlic and simmer for 15 minutes. Discard the lime leaves or zest. Add the soy sauce, fish sauce, lemon or lime juice, chili and sugar to the broth and simmer for 5 minutes. Add the carrot, shrimp, mussels and fish, cover and simmer for 3 minutes, just until the shrimp turn pink and the mussels open.

2 Heat a pot of water to boiling and add the noodles. Boil for 1 minute to heat through. Drain and divide the noodles between 6 large soup bowls. Top each bowl with some of the seafood and broth. Scatter some of the green onions, cilantro and mint or basil over top. Garnish each bowl with a wedge of lime.
Serves 6.

Girl talk: Kaffir lime leaves come from the wild lime tree. Shiny and aromatic, they're added to soups and sauces to impart their aromatic flavor then removed (like bay leaves). Find them in the frozen food section of most Asian markets.

The Southern Barbecue

Oooo-eee! Go south, young woman, to the land of smoky pulled pork,
chopped slaw and golden fried hush puppies. Make the whole menu and
serve some iced tea and cold beer for a true southern pig pickin'.
Only then will you know the meaning of real barbecue!

Gooey Rack of Ribs with Killer Barbecue Sauce

Baby back ribs are expensive but worth it as a treat — lesser ribs may benefit from a brief blanching to pre-cook, but baby backs just need to be marinated and grilled. Don't forget to peel off the translucent skin on the back of the racks — that helps guarantee that the results are flavorful and tender. The chipotle pepper gives the sauce its secret smoky and spicy flavor. If you must, substitute a minced jalapeño or hot sauce to taste, with a splash of liquid smoke.

barbecue sauce

1 Tbsp. (15 mL) canola oil

1 onion, minced

2 cloves garlic, minced

1 Tbsp. (15 mL) minced fresh ginger

1 14–oz. (398–mL) can tomato sauce

1/2 cup (125 mL) ketchup

2 Tbsp. (25 mL) cider vinegar

1/2 cup (125 mL) strong brewed coffee

1/2 cup (125 mL) maple syrup

2 Tbsp. (25 mL) blackstrap molasses

1 Tbsp. (15 mL) Worcestershire sauce

2 chipotle chilies in adobo sauce, minced

1/4 tsp. (1 mL) cinnamon

salt and freshly ground black pepper

ribs

2–3 sides baby back ribs (close to 2 lbs./
  1 kg a piece)

1 Combine all the sauce ingredients in a saucepan and simmer for 15 minutes on medium-low heat. Cool and purée in a blender or food processor. Pour into a jar and refrigerate.

2 Trim the ribs. Cut off the flap of meat on the inside of the ribs and then turn the rack over. Cut off the rib tips and the pointed end to form a nice rectangular rack (freeze the trimmings to use later in soup stock). Turn the rack over and remove the membrane from the back of the rack of ribs. This membrane, or fell, is tough and your ribs will be tough if you leave it on. Using a knife, free a corner of the membrane, then grasp it tightly with a paper towel or clean cloth and pull the skin away in one piece.

3 Coat the ribs in barbecue sauce and marinate in the refrigerator for 1 hour or up to 8 hours.

4 Heat the barbecue to medium-low (300–325°F/150–160°C). Turn off one burner so you can grill the ribs over indirect heat. Brush the unlit side of the grill with oil and place the ribs on the grill, meaty side down. Cover and grill the ribs for about 1 hour, turning and basting with extra sauce often. Watch to make sure the temperature stays at an even 300–325°F (150–160°C). Stop basting about 15 minutes before the ribs are done. When the ribs are done, the meat will pull away from the ends of the bones. To serve, cut each rack into three or four sections. Serves 4.

Corn Fritters

The Girl loves corn fritters — sometimes called hush puppies in the South. These addictive golden nuggets should keep more than the dog quiet, although they're not for those diet-conscious days. Use fresh corn in season or substitute frozen sweet corn.

3–4 ears fresh corn (1½ cups/375 mL corn kernels)
3 eggs, separated
1 cup (250 mL) all-purpose flour
1 tsp. (5 mL) salt

1 tsp. (5 mL) sugar
2 tsp. (10 mL) baking powder
pinch cayenne pepper
2 cups (500 mL) canola oil for deep frying

1 Remove the husks and silk from the corn and rinse. Cut the stem end flat, then stand the corn on its end in a large bowl. Using a paring knife, cut the corn from the cobs. Scrape the cobs well with the blade of the knife to extract all the juice. Put the corn and juice into the blender or food processor and purée.

2 Put the corn purée in a bowl and mix in the egg yolks, flour, salt, sugar, baking powder and cayenne. In another bowl, beat the egg whites until stiff. Dump the whites on top of the batter and, using a slicing and lifting motion, carefully fold the whites into the batter to lighten it.

3 Heat the oil in a deep fryer or wok to about 375°F (190°C). Use a deep-fat thermometer if you don't have a deep fryer. Be very careful if you do this on the stovetop. Don't walk away from hot oil — it can ignite and cause a fire. Don't let the oil get too hot and scorch or you'll have to start over.

4 Drop the batter by rounded tablespoonfuls into the fat, turning until the fritters are nicely browned on all sides. This should take about 4–5 minutes. Remove the fritters from the oil using a slotted spoon and drain on paper towels. Serves 4–6.

Girl talk: If you want that real southern smoky flavor for your ribs, add some soaked wood chips (wrapped in a punctured foil pouch or in a special smoker box) to the hot side of the grill and keep the lid down while they burn and smoke.

Creamy Coleslaw

This is the slaw to serve with your grilled burgers, fried fish, smoked meat sandwiches — or any time you need a quick, easy salad to accompany a casual meal. The Girl likes to add chopped or grated apples to her coleslaw for extra flavor and crunch.

2–lb. (1–kg) cabbage (1 small head)

2 medium carrots

1 large red apple, unpeeled

4 green onions

⅓ cup (75 mL) low-fat mayonnaise

⅓ cup (75 mL) low-fat sour cream or plain yogurt

1 Tbsp. (15 mL) Dijon mustard

1 tsp. (5 mL) lemon juice

2 tsp. (10 mL) sugar

1 Tbsp. (15 mL) chopped fresh dill (or 1 tsp./ 5 mL dried dillweed)

salt and freshly ground black pepper

1   If you're in a rush, substitute a 2–lb. (1–kg) bag of shredded cabbage and carrot slaw for the shredded cabbage and grated carrots. If you start from scratch, a quick way to slice the cabbage and grate the apple and carrot is with the grating disk on your food processor (you can chop it in the processor, too, but the texture isn't as nice). Make sure you wash the apple well with a food-grade vegetable wash before you grate it, as apples are often treated with wax. If you're grating by hand, use the big holes on your hand-held grater. Chop the onions.

2   In a large bowl, whisk together the mayonnaise, sour cream or yogurt, mustard, lemon juice, sugar and dill. Add the grated carrot, apple, cabbage and green onions, and toss to coat with the dressing. Season with salt and pepper. Serve immediately or chill for several hours. Serves 8.

Peach Cobbler

Real southern barbecue is always served with down-home desserts like this deep dish peach pie. The biscuit topping is flattened into little coins, then pressed over the filling in a cobblestone effect — hence, cobbler!

filling

6 large fresh peaches (or nectarines), peeled
   (about 5–6 cups/1.2–1.5 L)
1/2 cup (125 mL) granulated sugar

1 Tbsp. (15 mL) all-purpose flour
pinch salt
1/4 cup (50 mL) unsalted butter, softened

biscuit topping

2 cups (500 mL) all-purpose flour
pinch salt
5 Tbsp. (65 mL) granulated sugar, divided
1 Tbsp. (15 mL) baking powder

1/3 cup (75 mL) cold shortening, cubed
3 Tbsp. (45 mL) cold butter, cubed
1 egg
1/3 cup (75 mL) milk

vanilla ice cream

1 To peel the peaches, drop them into a pot of boiling water for 20 seconds. Lift them out with a slotted spoon and quickly rinse them under cold tap water. The skins will peel right off (it's not necessary to peel nectarines). Cut the fruit into wedges and place in a bowl, discarding the pits. Toss the peaches with the sugar, flour and salt. Pour them into a 6–cup (1.5–L) shallow baking dish. Dot with butter.

2 Preheat the oven to 400°F (200°C). To make the topping, put the flour, salt, 3 Tbsp. (45 mL) of the sugar and the baking powder into the work bowl of your food processor. Add the shortening and butter and pulse until the mixture is crumbly. You can also do this by hand, using a pastry blender.

3 Beat the egg and milk lightly and add to the dough, stirring quickly to form a smooth stiff dough. Break off little chunks of dough, press them into flattened "cobbles" and cover the entire dish, overlapping the dough as you go. Sprinkle the top with the remaining sugar. Bake for 35–45 minutes, until the cobbler is browned and bubbly. Cool for 20 minutes. Serve warm with ice cream. Serves 6–8.

Wintery Wonders

(or Brawny Bistro Dishes with Style)

Dining in the dead of winter requires hearty stews and divine dishes that speak of cosy fires and snowy sports like skiing and skating. Here are the Girl's favorite foods for warming her guests down to their toes after a day in the woods — or any time that beefy, brawny bistro fare is in order.

Choose any main dish from this section, and augment it with your favorite appetizer or soup and dessert from elsewhere in the book. Serve an appropriate starch — mashed potatoes, egg noodles or polenta — and get out your deep-rimmed pasta dishes. This is bowl food at its best.

Red wine — the big ones like Aussie Shiraz and earthy Syrahs from the Côtes du Rhône — shine with this kind of rich, casual food.

Savory Bread Pudding with Goat Cheese

Slices of olive bread are layered with creamy goat cheese and herbs, then baked in an egg custard in this savory version of a classic bread pudding. It makes a good vegetarian entrée, topped with a hearty roasted vegetable sauce (page 83) or a The Mushroom Thing (page 212), or it can stand in for the starch course with any stew or braised meat. It's also amazing when you're on potluck duty — the kind of dead-easy recipe that impresses all.

1 medium loaf olive bread, sliced ¹/₂–inch (1–cm) thick

6 oz. (200 g) goat cheese, sliced or crumbled

2 large green onions, finely chopped

2 tsp. (10 mL) chopped fresh thyme or parsley

3 large eggs

1¹/₂ cups (375 mL) milk

salt and freshly ground black pepper

1 Cut each slice of bread in halves or quarters, and arrange in overlapping rows in a buttered or oiled shallow baking dish. Tuck the goat cheese between the bread, and strew the green onions and thyme or parsley over top.

2 Beat the eggs with the milk, salt and pepper until well combined. Slowly pour the egg mixture over the bread in the pan, making sure to soak all the slices. Press the bread into the custard to absorb it. Cover and let the dish stand in the refrigerator for 20 minutes.

3 Preheat the oven to 350°F (180°C). Bake the bread pudding for 45–60 minutes, until puffed and golden. Set aside on a rack to cool slightly so the pudding firms up. Cut into pieces to serve. Serves 6–8.

Casserole of Lamb, Rosemary and White Beans with Creamy Polenta

Lamb shoulder chops are economical and shine in this flavorful oven braise. You can also buy a shoulder roast and cut it into serving pieces. This makes a great meal to come home to on a cold night, served with a rustic French Syrah and a pile of creamy polenta or a good loaf of French bread.

beans

1 cup (250 mL) dried flageolet or small white beans, soaked for at least 4 hours

1 small onion, peeled and stuck with 3 whole cloves

1 stalk celery, quartered

1 carrot, quartered

sprigs of fresh thyme, rosemary and parsley, tied in a bundle

lamb

8 lamb shoulder chops or lamb shoulder cut into large pieces (2–3 lbs./1–1.5 kg)

salt and freshly ground black pepper

2 Tbsp. (25 mL) olive oil

8 cups (2 L) thinly sliced Vidalia or other sweet onions

1 Tbsp. (15 mL) chopped garlic

$^1/_2$ cup (125 mL) white wine

2 Tbsp. (25 mL) minced fresh rosemary

2 cups (500 mL) chicken stock

2 Tbsp. (25 mL) tomato paste

1 Start by precooking the beans. In a large pot, place the soaked and drained beans, the whole onion, celery, carrot and herb bundle. Cover with 7 cups of cold water, bring to a boil and simmer for 20–30 minutes. Drain the beans, discarding the vegetables and herbs. If you have a pressure cooker, you can do this in about 10 minutes. Set aside.

2 Season the lamb with salt and pepper. Heat the oil in a nonstick sauté pan and brown the chops in batches over medium-high heat, about 2–3 minutes per side. Brown the meat well — this step adds a lot of flavor to the final dish. Set aside.

3 In the same pan, sauté the sliced onions until golden brown, about 30 minutes on medium-low heat. Add the garlic and white wine and simmer until the wine is gone and the onions are very tender.

4 Preheat the oven to 325°F (160°C). In a wide, oval baking dish (or a heavy casserole with a lid), spread half the onions. Top with the drained beans and the minced fresh rosemary. Arrange the browned lamb chops on top of the beans in a single layer, overlapping slightly if necessary. Spread the remaining onions over top.

5 Whisk the chicken stock and tomato paste together, and pour over the casserole. Cover tightly with foil or a lid, and bake for 2 hours. Remove the cover and bake for 1 hour longer.

6 Remove the baking dish from oven and let stand for 10 minutes. Tilt the pan and skim off the accumulated fat. Take the dish to the table and serve family style in deep soup plates, with creamy polenta. Serves 6–8.

Creamy Polenta

5 cups (1.25 L) water or chicken broth
1 tsp. (5 mL) salt
1 Tbsp. (15 mL) butter
1 cup (250 mL) coarse-ground polenta

3 Tbsp. (45 mL) sour cream
2 oz. (50 g) Parmesan cheese, shredded
1 Tbsp. (15 mL) chopped fresh rosemary or basil

1 Bring the water or broth to a rolling boil and add the salt and butter. Slowly add the polenta to the pot in a steady stream, whisking as you go to prevent lumps from forming. Stir for 5 minutes, then reduce the heat to low and continue to cook for 15 minutes, stirring to make sure the polenta does not stick to the pot.

2 When nicely thickened, remove the polenta from the heat and stir in the sour cream, Parmesan cheese and fresh herbs. Serve immediately. Serves 6.

Girl talk: Like so many soups and stews, this is one dish that actually gets better the longer it cooks. If you have time (or need to hold this dish) just reduce the oven temperature to 250°F (120°C) and cover. It will hold for 1–2 hours. It can also be refrigerated overnight and successfully reheated.

Pork in Apple Cider Sauce

Hard apple cider combines with cream in this mushroom-studded sauce. Serve it over medallions of pork tenderloin — the suave and sophisticated Girl's version of that old out-of-a-soup-can fave (and exponentially better). Serve the creamy sauce over cooked wide egg noodles or with mounds of mashed potatoes (page 104) for a decadent dinner on a cold night.

sauce

2 Tbsp. (25 mL) butter

3 cloves garlic, minced

2 cups (500 mL) minced onion

2 cups (500 mL) sliced mushrooms

2 Tbsp. (25 mL) all-purpose flour

1 Tbsp. (15 mL) Hungarian or Spanish paprika

2 1/2 cups (625 mL) chicken stock

1 cup (250 mL) hard apple cider

1/2 cup (125 mL) whipping cream (or sour cream)

pork

1/4 cup (50 mL) all-purpose flour

1/4 tsp. (1 mL) salt

1/4 tsp. (1 mL) sweet Hungarian paprika

1/4 tsp. (1 mL) freshly ground black pepper

1 1/2 lbs. (750 g) pork tenderloin (2 or 3), cut into 1–inch thick (2.5–cm) rounds

2 Tbsp. (25 mL) olive oil, divided

2 Tbsp. (25 mL) butter, divided

1/4 cup (50 mL) Calvados (apple brandy) or apple cider

to finish

cooked broad egg noodles for 6 (1 1/2 packages)

chopped fresh parsley

1 To make the sauce, heat the butter in a nonstick pan and sauté the garlic and onion over medium heat until tender and beginning to brown, about 15 minutes. Add the mushrooms and continue to cook until the mushrooms are tender and most of the liquid in the pan is gone, about 10 minutes longer.

2 Stir in the flour and paprika, then slowly add the chicken stock and cider. Bring to a boil and simmer for 30 minutes, until the sauce is reduced and nicely thickened. Stir in the cream and simmer 5–10 minutes longer. Keep warm.

3 For the pork, combine the flour with the salt, paprika and pepper in a shallow dish or plate. Put the pork slices between two pieces of waxed paper or plastic wrap and pound lightly with a meat mallet or rolling pin until each piece is about 1/4 inch (5 mm) thick. Set aside on a plate.

4 Heat half the oil and half the butter together in a nonstick pan over medium-high heat. When the oil is hot, dip each pork medallion in the seasoned flour to coat both sides. Shake off any excess flour, and place in the hot pan. (Use tongs to do this and you'll keep your fingers clean.) Sear the medallions in batches adding more oil and butter as required until they are all browned, about 2 minutes per side. Set aside on a plate.

5 Add the brandy or cider to the pan and stir up any browned bits. Pour this into the prepared sauce. Add the meat to the sauce and heat through.

6 To serve, arrange the cooked egg noodles on a large platter. Lay the medallions artfully down the center, overlapping them, then pour the mushroom sauce over all. Sprinkle with parsley and serve family style. Serves 6.

Chicken and Beer Stew

This is a rich and spicy chicken stew with Cajun roots. The Girl has been known to tote a hearty pot of it along on cycling and skiing trips — the stew reheats perfectly and tastes great with rice, fat egg noodles or mashed potatoes on the side. The Maple Sugar Pie (page 176) is an appropriate finale.

spice mixture

2 tsp. (10 mL) salt

2 tsp. (10 mL) garlic powder

1 tsp. (15 mL) cayenne pepper

stew

2 lbs. (1 kg) boneless, skinless chicken thighs

1/2 cup (125 mL) all-purpose flour

2 Tbsp. (25 mL) canola oil

1 medium onion, chopped

1 stalk celery, chopped

2 cloves garlic, minced

1 red or yellow bell pepper, slivered

1 jalapeño pepper, seeded and minced

1 cup (250 mL) canned tomatoes, puréed until smooth (or tomato sauce)

1/2 bottle (12 oz./341 mL) dark beer (the rest is for the cook)

1/4 cup (50 mL) chicken stock

2 tsp. (10 mL) Worcestershire sauce

1 tsp. (5 mL) dried marjoram

1 bay leaf

freshly ground black pepper to taste

1 In a small bowl, combine the salt, garlic powder and cayenne pepper. Rub the chicken all over with 2 tsp. (10 mL) of the spice mixture and let stand at room temperature for 30 minutes.

2 In a plastic bag, combine the flour with 2 tsp. (10 mL) of the spice mixture and shake the chicken pieces in the spiced flour to coat. Reserve any excess spiced flour. In a sauté pan with a lid, heat the oil over medium-high heat. Cook the chicken for 5–10 minutes or until browned on all sides. Remove the chicken from the pan.

3 Reduce the heat to medium. Add the reserved spiced flour to the accumulated fat and oil in the pan. Add an extra teaspoon or two (5–10 mL) of canola oil, if necessary, to create a smooth, creamy paste. Cook, stirring constantly, for 10 minutes, until the paste is dark brown, the color of peanut butter.

4 Add the onion, celery, garlic, bell pepper and jalapeño to the pan, and sauté for 5 minutes. Stir in the tomato purée, beer, chicken stock, Worcestershire, marjoram and bay leaf. Bring to a boil.

5 Return the browned chicken to the pan and reduce the heat to low. Cover and simmer for 45 minutes, or until the chicken is cooked through, adding more stock if the stew seems too thick. Season to taste with pepper. Serves 4–6.

Persian Braised Lamb with Pomegranate

The pomegranate molasses (see page 142) helps to tenderize the lamb and adds an intriguing flavor to the dish. Serve this stew with new potatoes, steamed baby carrots and a fruity Pinot Noir.

1 2–lb. (1–kg) boneless lamb shoulder
1/3 cup (75 mL) unsweetened pomegranate
   molasses (syrup)
salt and freshly ground black pepper
2 Tbsp. (25 mL) olive oil
2 yellow onions, sliced

6 cloves garlic, sliced
1 cup (250 mL) beef broth
1/2 cup (125 mL) red wine
2 Tbsp. (25 mL) tomato paste
fresh pomegranate seeds and chopped mint
   to garnish (optional)

1 Trim the lamb, removing any excess fat and silverskin (the tough membrane surrounding the muscle) and cut into 2–inch (5–cm) chunks. In a nonreactive bowl, toss the lamb with the pomegranate molasses to coat. Season with salt and pepper and set aside to marinate for 1 hour.

2 In a Dutch oven, heat the olive oil over medium-high heat and sauté the onion and garlic until it's beginning to brown. Drain the lamb, reserving the marinade, and add the meat to the pan in batches, frying it until nicely browned on all sides.

3 Preheat the oven to 275°F (140°C). Whisk together the broth, wine, reserved marinade and tomato paste and add it to the pan. Bring to a boil. Cover the pan tightly and place in the oven for 2 hours, until the meat is very tender, stirring occasionally. Serve the lamb garnished with fresh pomegranate seeds and chopped mint. Serves 4–6.

Girl talk: Whenever a recipe for a soup or stew like this calls for chopped tomatoes, you can chop them on a cutting board, whirl them briefly in a food processor or simply squeeze them slowly into the pot through your fingers to break them up (just don't squeeze too fast or you'll be wearing them). Never forget — playing with your food is fun.

Coq au Vin

This is a basic chicken stew with a fancy name — the kind of thing the Girl likes to serve straight out of the oven in her chic French enameled roaster, with the table draped in colorful Provençal linens. Lift the lid at the table and envelop your guests in the steamy aromas of tender chicken braised in red wine. It's traditional to use a cut-up stewing hen but skinless, boneless chicken thighs offer tender, meaty convenience and less fat. Serve this stylish stew over piles of mashed potatoes, with an assertive blush or fruity red wine.

6 slices double-smoked side or
  back bacon, chopped
6 Tbsp. (75 mL) all-purpose flour, divided
1/2 tsp. (2 mL) salt
1/2 tsp. (2 mL) freshly ground black pepper
1/2 tsp. (2 mL) thyme
3–4 Tbsp. (45–50 mL) virgin olive oil, divided
2–3 lbs. (1–1.5 kg) boneless, skinless
  chicken thighs
1 lb. (500 g) carrots, sliced
1 lb. (500 g) small onions, peeled
6 cloves garlic, chopped

1 lb. (500 g) mushrooms (cultivated or exotic),
  sliced or quartered
2 cups (500 mL) chicken broth
2 cups (500 mL) red wine
1/4 cup (50 mL) brandy or cognac
2 Tbsp. (25 mL) tomato paste
1 Tbsp. (15 mL) fresh thyme leaves
1 Tbsp. (15 mL) brown sugar
1 bay leaf
1 tsp. (5 mL) salt
1/2 tsp. (2 mL) freshly ground black pepper
6 Tbsp. (75 mL) chopped fresh parsley or chives

1 In a Dutch oven, cook the bacon until it's starting to brown. Remove the bacon from the pan using a slotted spoon and set aside.

2 In a bowl, combine 4 Tbsp. (50 mL) of the flour with the salt, pepper and thyme. Toss the chicken with the seasoned flour to coat well, shaking off any excess. Add 1 Tbsp. (15 mL) of the oil to the bacon drippings in the pan. Brown the chicken in batches in the hot fat. Remove the browned chicken from the pan and set aside with the bacon.

3 Add the carrots and onions to the pan and sauté in the remaining oil until they begin to brown. Stir in the garlic and the mushrooms and cook a few minutes longer, just until the mushrooms begin to give up their juices. Sprinkle the remaining 2 Tbsp. (25 mL) of flour over the vegetables and stir well, then slowly add the broth, wine and brandy or cognac. Bring to a boil, scraping up any browned bits from the bottom of the pan. Stir in the tomato paste, thyme, sugar, bay leaf, salt and pepper.

4 Preheat the oven to 375°F (190°C). Return the chicken and bacon to the pot. Cover and bake for 30 minutes. Uncover and bake for 30–45 minutes longer, until the stew is thick and the chicken is tender. Sprinkle with parsley or chives and serve from the pot. Serves 8.

Grandes Finales

Party meals should start with some interesting appetizers (page 206) and end with a decadent dessert. These are some of the Girl's favorite finales.

cake

Chocolate Mocha Torte

Like a dense soufflé, this torte will fall as it cools. Make it the night before you serve it to get the right fudgy consistency. Then top it with coffee-spiked mascarpone, and chocolate-covered coffee beans, the ultimate in mocha mojo.

torte

1 cup (250 mL) butter
³/₄ cup (175 mL) sugar, divided
¹/₄ cup (50 mL) very strong coffee (or
   1 Tbsp./15 mL instant espresso powder)

¹/₂ lb. (250 g) bittersweet chocolate, chopped
   (or top-quality chocolate chips)
6 egg yolks
2 Tbsp. (25 mL) all-purpose flour
6 egg whites

topping

¹/₂ lb. (250 g) mascarpone cheese
2 Tbsp. (25 mL) brewed espresso
2 Tbsp. (25 mL) cream

2 Tbsp. (25 mL) sugar
2 Tbsp. (25 mL) brandy
cinnamon and chocolate-covered espresso beans

1 Preheat the oven to 325°F (150°C). Butter a 10-inch (25-cm) springform pan. Line the base with parchment paper. Tightly wrap the outside of the pan with tin foil to seal. Place a baking dish large enough to hold the springform pan into the oven and add 1 inch (2.5 cm) of hot water.

2 Melt the butter in a pot with ¹/₂ cup (125 mL) of the sugar and the coffee. Cook over medium-low heat, stirring, until the sugar dissolves. Add the chocolate and stir until smooth. Remove from the heat and place in a large bowl. Stir in the egg yolks and flour.

3 Beat the egg whites until soft peaks form. Gradually beat in the remaining ¹/₄ cup (50 mL) sugar, beating until the egg whites are shiny and form curled peaks when the beaters are raised. Stir half of the whites into the chocolate mixture. Lightly fold in the remaining whites, just until no white streaks are showing. Spoon the batter into the prepared pan.

4 Place in the water bath and bake for 30 minutes, until the edges puff and crack slightly but the center is not completely set. The cake sets as it cools. Cool in the pan, cover and refrigerate overnight.

5 Loosen the sides of the cake with a sharp knife. Release the sides of the pan and place the cake on a serving platter. Whisk together the topping ingredients. Cut the cake into wedges, wiping the knife clean between each cut. Top each piece with a dollop of mascarpone cream, a dusting of cinnamon and a chocolate-covered coffee bean. Serves 8–10.

Girl talk: Cutting parchment to line a round pan is like making paper dolls. Cut a square of parchment larger than the pan then fold it in half, and then in half in the opposite direction. Hold the central point and continue to fold in half, again and again, to form skinnier and skinnier triangles. Holding the pointy end in the middle of the pan, snip off the other end at the rim. Unfold and you will have a piece of paper that you can drop right into the pan.

 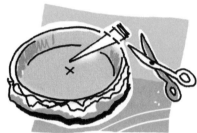 

Iced Coffee

After an Asian meal, a glass of strong, sweet iced coffee makes a satisfying instant dessert. The Girl learned to make this addictive drink at her local Vietnamese noodle house, where they perch an individual stainless steel filter over the ice and sweet milk in your glass, and you can watch the brew drip through. But a shot of espresso from the cappuccino machine works just as well.

double shot espresso or double-strength
  hot coffee (about 1/2 cup/125 mL)

2–3 Tbsp. (25–45 mL) sweetened condensed milk
tall glass filled with ice cubes

1 Put the sweetened condensed milk in the bottom of a tall glass. Fill the glass with ice cubes. Pour the hot coffee over top and serve. Give your guests a long-handled spoon to stir their coffee and ice together. The ice will melt a little and the coffee will mix with the milk to form a sweet rich drink. Serves 1.

Lemon Soufflé Tart

The Girl's brilliant pastry chef girlfriend, Marianne, is the source of many tried and true desserts, including this beautiful and simple lemony tart, a giant step above the traditional lemon meringue. Two-crust pies are so much trickier than tarts, so invest in a two-part 10-inch (25-cm) tart tin and you'll never fear pie again.

crust

2¼ cups (550 mL) all-purpose flour
½ cup (125 mL) sugar
1 cup less 2 Tbsp. (225 mL) butter
1 egg

1 egg yolk
splash lemon juice
splash pure vanilla extract

filling

5 eggs, separated
½ cup (125 mL) granulated sugar
grated rind of 2 lemons

½ cup (125 mL) fresh lemon juice
¼ cup (50 mL) all-purpose flour
2 Tbsp. (25 mL) granulated sugar

garnish

icing sugar and fresh berries

1 For the crust, pulse the flour, sugar and butter in a food processor until finely blended. Add the remaining ingredients and pulse just until a ball forms. Divide the dough in two and press half into a tart pan with a removable bottom. (This makes enough for two 10-inch (25-cm) tarts — the extra dough can be frozen and used for any tart base.) Chill the crust for 30 minutes, then bake at 350°F (180°C) for 15 minutes. Cool.

2 For the filling, whisk together the egg yolks and the ½ cup (125 mL) granulated sugar. Add the lemon rind and juice and whisk to combine, then incorporate the flour. Cook the mixture until slightly thickened, either in a double boiler or in the microwave. If using the microwave, stop and whisk the mixture every 30 seconds to prevent lumps. In a double boiler, cook until thick, stirring constantly. Cool for 15 minutes.

3 Beat the egg whites until soft, then add the 2 Tbsp. (25 mL) of granulated sugar and beat until stiff. Carefully fold the cooled lemon custard into the egg whites to make a lightened, fluffy filling.

4 Pour the lemon soufflé mixture into the prepared crust and bake at 350°F (180°C) for 18–20 minutes, just until the custard is puffed, light brown and firm. Serve at room temperature, dusted with icing sugar and garnished with fresh berries. Serves 8.

Girl talk: For a burst of intense flavor, spread a thin layer of lemon curd (page 288) on the crust before adding the filling.

Tiramisu

Everyone says they love cheesecake. How about this easy and delicious Italian cross between a cheesecake and a trifle? Once very trendy, tiramisu seems to have dropped off the dessert menu, but it's a simple show-stopper and deserves a place in your dessert repertoire.

3 eggs, separated
⅓ cup (75 mL) sugar
1½ cups (375 mL) Italian mascarpone cheese or other double cream cheese
4 Tbsp. (50 mL) orange brandy, divided (or substitute Kahlua for more coffee flavor)

⅓ cup (75 mL) strong coffee or espresso
1 package ladyfinger cookies (about 36)
2 oz. (60 g) grated bittersweet chocolate

1 Beat the egg whites and sugar with an electric mixer until stiff. In another bowl, beat the egg yolks with the cheese and 2 Tbsp. (25 mL) of the brandy. Fold in the egg whites to lighten the mixture.

2 Place the remaining 2 Tbsp. (25 mL) brandy and the coffee in a shallow bowl. Quickly dip each cookie in the coffee mixture and lay side by side in a 9– x 9–inch (23– x 23–cm) glass pan. Cover the bottom of the pan with a layer of cookies.

3 Spread half the cheese mixture over top and sprinkle with half the grated chocolate. Repeat with a second layer of cookies, cheese mixture and chocolate. Cover the pan with plastic wrap and chill the tiramisu overnight. (You can also freeze it for up to 2 weeks. Thaw overnight in the refrigerator before serving.)

4 Cut into squares to serve. Serves 6–8.

Girl talk: Every Italian cook makes tiramisu — and every one is a little different. The Girl recently ran across a homemade version with crumbled amaretti cookies between the layers. A lovely variation, with amaretto liqueur instead of the brandy.

Maple Sugar Pie

A rich sweet pie to enjoy during the midwinter sugaring season — traditionally served when the maple sap starts running in the Great White North and everyone heads to the sugar shack to party. Start with a store-bought frozen pie shell (or even tart shells) to save time.

filling

1 cup (250 mL) brown sugar
2 Tbsp. (25 mL) butter, softened
3 eggs, separated

1 cup (250 mL) maple syrup
1/2 cup (125 mL) half-and-half cream

1 10-inch (25-cm) single crust pie shell

topping

1 cup (250 mL) whipping cream
1/4 cup (50 mL) maple syrup

1 Preheat the oven to 350°F (180°C). In a bowl, combine the brown sugar, butter and egg yolks. Beat with an electric mixer until blended. Beat in the 1 cup (250 mL) maple syrup and the half-and-half cream.

2 In another bowl, with clean beaters, beat the egg whites until stiff. Fold the egg whites into the maple filling to lighten it, using a spatula. Pile the beaten whites on top of the filling and slice through and lift the batter, folding the heavier batter over the lighter egg whites to combine. Don't overmix — the idea of folding in the stiff egg whites is to keep the filling fluffy.

3 Pour the filling into the pie shell and bake for about 1 hour, until the filling is set. Cool the pie completely.

4 To make the maple cream, combine the whipping cream with the 1/4 cup (50 mL) maple syrup and whip, using an electric mixer, until stiff. Serve wedges of sugar pie topped with a dollop of maple cream.
Makes one 10-inch (25-cm) pie.

Girl talk: If a Cajun feast is more to your liking (say, you're celebrating Mardi Gras by serving the Girl's spicy Chicken and Beer Stew, page 168, as an entrée and starting out with a feast of fresh oysters), you can easily morph this sugar pie into southern pecan pie. Simply add a cup of chopped pecans to the filling and top the pie with whole pecans (about another cup), laid out in neat concentric circles over the entire surface, before popping your pie into the oven. Same baking instructions.

Espresso Flan

Like your favorite crème caramel with a shot of Mexican coffee liqueur, this easy and impressive dessert is quite appropriate to end a Southwestern or Latin meal in style. After inverting these individual flans on pretty dessert plates, drizzle each dessert with a little extra Kahlua. Mucho mocha!

1 cup (250 mL) granulated sugar
3 Tbsp. (45 mL) water
2 13–oz. (385–mL) cans evaporated milk
1/3 cup (75 mL) icing (powdered) sugar
1/2 cup (125 mL) espresso or very strong coffee
3 eggs

2 egg yolks
pinch salt
1/4 cup (50 mL) Kahlua
chocolate-covered coffee beans and extra
   Kahlua to garnish

1 Start by caramelizing the sugar. Put the sugar and water in a heavy saucepan over medium heat. The sugar will dissolve as the mixture heats, forming a clear syrup. Swirl the pan a few times at the beginning to help the sugar dissolve. When the syrup is clear, stop swirling the pan and turn the heat up to high. Let the sugar cook until it starts to turn a caramel color. Watch it carefully as it can burn quickly. When it's a nice rich amber color, pour it carefully into eight ovenproof, straight-sided ramekins, swirling each to coat both the bottoms and sides with caramel. Work quickly, as the caramel will set up as it cools, but be careful — the sugar is very hot at this point. Set the ramekins aside.

2 Preheat the oven to 350°F (180°C).

3 In another pan, combine the evaporated milk, icing sugar and coffee. Bring to a boil. Reduce the heat and stir until the sugar dissolves completely. Set aside.

4 In a large bowl, beat the eggs and egg yolks with the salt. Slowly pour in the warm milk mixture, beating constantly. Add the Kahlua, mix well and pour into the prepared molds.

5 Place the ramekins in a large baking pan that has been filled with about an inch (2.5 cm) of hot water. Place the pan in the oven and bake the flans for about 30–35 minutes or until they are nearly set. (They should still be a little jiggly for the most tender final result — overcooking makes a rubbery flan.)

6 Remove the ramekins from the hot water bath, cool for 30 minutes, then cover and refrigerate overnight. To serve, run a knife around the edge of each ramekin to loosen the flan, then invert onto individual dessert plates. Garnish each flan with a chocolate-covered coffee bean and drizzle with a little Kahlua. Serves 8.

Observance

Meals that mark occasions (when you really must cook).

The Big Holiday Dinner

Turkey dinner with all of the traditional trimmings is one meal that everyone must cook — eventually. To avoid the inevitable comparisons with Aunt Martha's bread stuffing or grandma's mincemeat tarts, it's best to forge your own holiday recipe traditions. But what to serve alongside that behemoth of a bird? Start with a pretty seasonal soup and don't look back.

Whisky Squash Soup

A soup course is elegant at any gathering. Make this in advance and serve it while the turkey is resting. Sitting down for soup helps to slow down the pace of the feast, and makes sure that everyone will be at the table when you present the bird.

3 lbs. (1.5 kg) squash (acorn, buttercup, butternut, etc.)
1 Tbsp. (15 mL) butter
1 Tbsp. (15 mL) olive oil
1 large onion, chopped (about 2 cups/500 mL)
1 medium, yellow-fleshed potato, peeled and cubed
6 cups (1.5 L) chicken stock

$^1/_4$ cup (50 mL) rye whiskey
1 bay leaf and 2 sprigs thyme, tied together with string
1 Tbsp. (15 mL) maple syrup
salt and white pepper to taste
$^1/_4$ cup (50 mL) sour cream or whipping cream

1 Cut the squash in half and use a small spoon to scoop out the seeds. Peel the squash and cut the flesh into cubes.

2 In a soup pot, melt the butter with the olive oil over medium heat and cook the onion, covered, until tender, about 5 minutes. Stir in the squash, potato, stock, whiskey, herb bundle and syrup and bring to a boil over high heat.

3 Reduce the heat to low and simmer, uncovered, until the squash is softened, about 30 minutes. Remove the herb bundle and discard. Using a blender, food processor, or hand-held immersion blender, purée the soup until smooth. The blender makes it the silkiest.

4 Return the soup to a simmer over medium heat and cook for 10 minutes. Season to taste with salt and pepper. Whisk in the sour cream or whipping cream, or drizzle a tablespoon or so onto each serving. Serves 8.

The Big Bird

Ten Steps To A Perfect Turkey

1 Buy a turkey. If it's frozen you have to think way ahead — it will take about 4 hours per lb. (10 hours per kg) to thaw the bird in the fridge (that's 2–3 days for a small bird). Don't thaw it at room temperature or cook a partially frozen bird, or you risk salmonella poisoning. To save time, place the turkey, still in its plastic wrap, in a sink and cover completely with cold water. Allow 1 hour per lb. (2 hours per kg) to thaw and keep the water cold.

2 Fresh turkey should be cooked within 2–3 days of purchase. Turkey labeled "previously frozen" must be cooked within 48 hours of purchase.

3 Don't blow calories and fat grams by buying a turkey that's "basted" (injected with saturated fat). It's not necessary for a tender turkey and it just adds calories.

4 Wash your hands with soap and hot water before and after handling raw turkey. Remove the plastic, take the neck and giblets out of the cavity (they should be in a bag), rinse inside and out with cold water and pat dry with paper towels. (Put the neck and giblets in a pot of water with some onion, whole black peppercorns, carrot and parsley and simmer to make a broth for your gravy.) Wash all equipment and surfaces with hot soapy water after handling raw turkey to avoid bacteria transfer and contamination.

5 Place the turkey on a rack in a large roasting pan, breast side up. Brush with oil or melted butter and season inside and out with a little salt and pepper.

6 If stuffing the bird, wait until just before roasting. Do not pack the stuffing — the bird should be filled loosely (or you can cook the stuffing separately in a covered baking dish alongside the bird).

7 Cover the bird loosely with foil. Roast at 325°F (160°C) until the internal temperature reads 180°F (82°C) for a stuffed turkey or 170°F (77°C) for an unstuffed bird. Use an instant-read meat thermometer, inserted in the thickest part of the thigh to test the internal temperature (don't leave it in while the bird is roasting, just during testing). Make sure you take the temperature of the stuffing, too. It should be at least 165°F (73°C) in the center of the stuffing. It doesn't take as long as you think to roast a turkey to perfection — about 3–4 hours for a 12- to 16-lb. (5.5- to 7-kg) stuffed bird. Start checking the temperature early.

8 When the turkey is done, remove the pan from the oven and let the bird rest on the cutting board, covered with a loose piece of foil, for 15–20 minutes. This will allow the juices to set and give you time to make the gravy. Do not leave turkey (cooked or raw) at room temperature for longer than 2 hours. Cooked turkey may be refrigerated up to 4 days or frozen for up to 4 months.

9 Pour the juices in the roasting pan into a heatproof glass measuring cup and set aside. If there is just a small amount of fat/juice in the pan, drain off all but 3 Tbsp. (45 mL). To make gravy, place the roasting pan on top of the stove over medium heat and sprinkle about 3–4 Tbsp. (45–50 mL) of flour over the fat in the pan. Stir with a wooden spoon to moisten the flour and loosen the browned bits. Add the reserved juices and a little water or turkey broth and stir in well — creating a thick paste. Add more water (or leftover liquid from boiling potatoes or peas), a little at a time, stirring as you go to avoid lumps. Let the gravy come back to a boil each time, and add a little more liquid if it's still too thick. Season to taste with salt and pepper. Keep warm in a gravy boat or small pitcher.

10 Using a large spoon, remove all the stuffing from the cavity of the bird and place it in a covered dish in the oven to stay warm. Carve the turkey. Remove the leg and thigh pieces first and slice the meat from the bone, arranging the dark meat at one end of the platter. Slice the breast meat. Start at the base of the breast (where you've removed the legs) and slice vertically, parallel to the breastbone, into thin, even slices. Arrange on a platter, pass the trimmings and the gravy and you're done!

Girl talk: The Girl knows you don't want to hear about this now, but once all that tender turkey is carved off the bones, don't chuck the carcass — save it for soup. Really. Wonderful turkey broth is only a winter afternoon of simmering away. If you can't face cooking anything else for a month, just put the carcass into a heavy plastic bag and freeze it for that day in January when you feel a cold coming on. Then put the carcass in your stock pot (break it into pieces if it's too big), pour in enough cold water to cover the bones by 4 or 5 inches (10 or 12 cm), throw in a couple of carrots, a stalk of celery, a quartered onion, some whole black peppercorns and bay leaves, bring the whole thing to a boil, and let it simmer away on medium-low heat for several hours (four, five, six). Add more cold water after a few hours and continue to simmer. Skim off any gunk that rises to the top of the pot. When it's all steamy and good, strain the stock through a fine mesh sieve into a clean pot, pitch the bones and veggies, and season the broth with salt and pepper. Drink it as is or add some small egg noodles. Or put it into containers and freeze it for soups and sauces later. You'll be glad you did. And now you know how to make chicken soup (same method if you start with a raw chicken, just take it out when the broth is done and save the meat).

Sage Bread Stuffing

The Girl loves stuffing, plain old-fashioned bread stuffing, which is one of those familiar flavors she expects with turkey dinners. But if you're into something more exotic, add some chopped apple or pear, cooked crumbled pork sausage or even nuts to this classic combination. You need about ¾ cup (175 mL) of bread per pound (500 g) of turkey, so adjust the recipe accordingly.

1 loaf day-old French bread, cut into 1/2-inch
　(1–cm) cubes (about 8–10 cups/ 2 L)
¹/₄ cup (50 mL) melted butter
1 cup (250 mL) finely chopped celery
　(including some leaves)
1 large onion, chopped

2 tsp. (10 mL) ground sage
2 tsp. (10 mL) celery salt
2 tsp. (10 mL) dried thyme (or 2 Tbsp./25 mL,
　if you are using fresh thyme)
salt and freshly ground black pepper

1 Place the bread cubes in a large bowl. Heat the butter in a sauté pan over medium heat and cook the chopped celery and onion for 7–10 minutes, until the onions are translucent and tender but not brown.

2 Pour the contents of the sauté pan over the bread cubes and toss to combine. Sprinkle evenly with sage, celery salt, thyme, salt and pepper and toss again to distribute the spices.

3 Stuff the turkey just before you are ready to put it in the oven. If you'd rather cook the stuffing on the side (but who would — it doesn't pick up all of the yummy turkey juices and flavors) you can bake it in a covered casserole dish for about 1 hour, alongside the bird. Just add about 1 cup (250 mL) broth (that turkey broth you made with the giblets or canned broth), to moisten the stuffing while it cooks. Any leftover stuffing that won't fit into the bird can be cooked this way, too.

4 Remove all the stuffing from the turkey before you carve it and keep warm in a covered casserole dish. Don't leave the stuffing inside the turkey after it's cooked — it will spoil. Makes enough stuffing for a 10 to 12–lb. (4.5 to 5.5–kg) turkey.

Honey Roasted Carrots

This is a simple way to dress up the humble carrot. Roasting concentrates its natural sugars. Toss the carrots with honey and herbs in advance, then roast them right before dinner, while the bird's out of the oven and waiting to be carved.

2 Tbsp. (25 mL) butter
1 Tbsp. (15 mL) wildflower honey
12 medium carrots and/or parsnips
   (about 1 lb./500 g total)

salt and white pepper
2 tsp. (10 mL) chopped fresh rosemary or
   thyme leaves

1 Preheat the oven to 375–400°F (190–200°C).

2 Heat the butter and honey in a medium-sized bowl in the microwave until melted.

3 Peel the carrots or parsnips and cut them into thick slices or chunks. To make roll-cut chunks, give the vegetable a half turn after every cut. Add the veggies to the bowl and toss them to coat with the butter and honey mixture. Season with salt, pepper and herbs and toss again.

4 Line a baking sheet with foil or parchment paper. Spread the carrots and parsnips in a single layer on the baking sheet. Roast for 30 minutes, stirring once, until golden. Serves 6–8.

Girl gossip: Last time the Girl found herself in the kitchen of one of the country's top restaurants (yes, she gets around), she noticed that the smart young chefs were boiling their big red and white potatoes whole, peel and all. Dead easy, she thought, but when she asked why these top toques didn't peel, she discovered a secret weapon. When boiled in their jackets, potatoes are tastier and don't get waterlogged. Once the spuds are tender, just drain, cool slightly and slip off the skins with a paring knife. It's speedy and simple at this point, but you have to hold the hot potatoes in a mitt to protect your hand. Then you can mash them (or cool and cube them for salads) and you have dry, delicious spuds, ready to flavor with butter, cream and roasted garlic (page 17). Don't tell anyone I told you.

Braised Fennel Gratin

Your guests will love this unique vegetable, with its hint of licorice, even if they haven't tried it before. You can braise the fennel on the stovetop while the turkey roasts, then arrange it in a baking dish, ready to pop into the oven after you take the turkey out.

4–6 medium fennel bulbs
2 Tbsp. (25 mL) olive oil
1 clove garlic, sliced
1 cup (250 mL) chicken broth

salt and freshly ground black pepper
¾ cup (175 mL) finely grated Parmesan cheese
   (use a rasp grater for the finest cheese)

1 Clean the fennel (see Girl talk), reserving some of the feathery fronds for garnish. Cut each bulb lengthwise into 4–6 wedges. Cut away the core.

2 Heat the olive oil in a large nonstick sauté pan over medium-high heat. Add the garlic and cook for 2 minutes to flavor the oil. Remove the garlic from the pan. Add the fennel wedges to the pan, flat side down, and sauté for 10 minutes or so, just until they begin to brown and caramelize. Add the chicken broth to the pan and bring to a boil.

3 Cover, reduce the heat to low and simmer for 30 minutes, until the fennel is tender. Remove the fennel from the pan and arrange the wedges in a shallow, pretty baking dish that you can take to the table. Turn the heat up to high under the sauté pan and boil the braising liquid until it has reduced down to about 1/3 cup (75 mL), then drizzle it over the fennel.

4 The dish can be made ahead of time up to this point, covered and refrigerated overnight. Before dinner, take the dish out of the refrigerator and bring it to room temperature. Preheat the oven to 375–400°F (190–200°C). Season the fennel with salt and pepper and sprinkle the Parmesan evenly over top. Put the dish into the oven and bake for 10 or 15 minutes, until the cheese is bubbly and browned. Sprinkle with chopped fennel fronds to garnish the dish. Serves 8.

Girl talk:

Fennel looks like a big bunch of celery, white and bulbous at the base and green on top, with feathery, dill-like fronds. Sometimes it's sold whole, sometimes all that you'll find is the truncated white bases — that's okay, since the tops are really not edible (stock pot fodder only). Peel any bruised or damaged outer layers from the bulbs, trim the root, then cut in half through the root end. Fennel can be cut into fine shreds and dressed with vinaigrette for salads or it can be cooked. It makes a great addition to Italian tomato soups and sauces. In fact, on a day when you've got more oven space and you're feeling like a vegetarian dish, oven-braise the fennel wedges with halved canned tomatoes tucked into the spaces between them (you'll only need ½ cup/125 mL broth). Cover the baking dish with foil for the first 30 minutes, then remove and roast for 30 minutes longer before sprinkling on the cheese. Yummy, yummy.

Fresh Cranberry Sauce

Don't forget the cranberry sauce — vital with turkey. Buy a bag of whole fresh or frozen cranberries and follow the directions on the bag to make traditional sauce (boil with some sugar and water until they pop and thicken, then chill). Or, if you forgot to make it, or prefer a tangy fresh relish, get out the food processor and make this last-minute fresh cranberry sauce — the Girl thinks it's actually even better than the cooked stuff. Just don't forget to serve it (it's been done!). Leftovers are great in turkey sandwiches.

1 bag (12 oz./350 g) fresh cranberries
1 small whole orange (a thin-skinned variety),
  unpeeled, scrubbed and quartered

1/2 cup (125 mL) granulated sugar

1 Put the cranberries, orange pieces and sugar into the food processor and process until everything is evenly ground, stopping to scrape down the sides several times. Use the pulsing method (on/off bursts) to make sure everything is getting chopped evenly. This sauce is best if refrigerated for several hours or overnight before serving, but it will also work at the eleventh hour. Makes 3 cups (750 mL).

YUMMY PLATE

Peach Trifle with Sherried Custard Sauce

When the Girl is lucky enough to be invited to somebody else's Christmas dinner, she's always glad to tote along this impressive and easy, no-bake dessert. Get out that crystal punchbowl, girl, or, if you're doing dinner at home, layer the ingredients in pretty individual parfait or stemmed wine glasses. A classic ending to a very Dickensian soirée — and you can do it all a day before your holiday dinner. Merry, merry!

raspberry sauce

1 package (10 oz./300 g) frozen, unsweetened
  raspberries

1/4 cup (50 mL) sugar
2 tsp. (10 mL) cornstarch

custard

3 cups (750 mL) milk or half-and-half cream
4 egg yolks
1/4 cup (50 mL) cornstarch

1/2 cup (125 mL) sugar
3/4 tsp. (4 mL) pure vanilla extract
1/4 cup (50 mL) sherry

assembly

1 pound cake, sliced thinly (or 2 packages [8 oz./250 g]
  soft ladyfingers, halved)
1/2 cup (125 mL) sweet sherry
3 cups (750 mL) canned peaches, drained
  (about 12 peach halves), sliced

1 cup (250 mL) heavy cream
2 Tbsp. (25 mL) sugar
mint leaves to garnish

1 To make the raspberry sauce, place the thawed raspberries in a sieve set over a saucepan and press with a spoon to extract the juice and pulp and remove the seeds. Set the fruit purée over medium heat and stir in the sugar and cornstarch. Cook, stirring constantly, until just boiling and thick. Remove from the heat and cool (may be made 2 days in advance).

2 To make the custard, start with a saucepan that has been rinsed out with hot water but not dried. (This prevents the milk solids from sticking to the bottom of the pan.) Heat the milk or cream until bubbles begin to form around the edges. Do not boil.

3 Beat the egg yolks with the cornstarch and sugar until smooth and slowly whisk in the hot milk. Cook over medium heat, whisking constantly, for 3–5 minutes or until the custard has cooked for about 1 minute and is quite thick. Remove from the heat and place in a bowl. Stir in the vanilla and sherry. Cool slightly, then cover with plastic wrap, placing the wrap directly on the surface of the custard, and refrigerate for up to 2 days.

4 To assemble the trifle, line an 8–cup (12–L) glass trifle bowl with a layer of pound cake or ladyfingers. Sprinkle a little sherry over the cake layer and top with ⅓ of the custard. Reserve a few peach slices for garnish. Arrange about ⅓ of the remaining peaches over the custard, making sure you press some of the pieces close to the glass so they'll show. Drizzle with ⅓ of the raspberry syrup.

5 Repeat the layers of cake, sherry, custard, peaches and syrup, ending with a layer of cake, sherry and custard. Cover the trifle tightly with plastic wrap and refrigerate at least 4 hours or overnight.

6 Before serving, whip the cream with 2 Tbsp. (25 mL) of sugar. Garnish the top of the trifle with the whipped cream, reserved fruit and mint leaves. Bring it to the table in the serving dish so that everyone can ooh and aahh (it doesn't look half as impressive after it's been scooped out, but it tastes divine). Serve in your prettiest dessert dishes. Serves 8.

TRIFLE BOWL

More Holiday Traditions

Meat pies, stollen, nuts and bolts — all Christmas traditions in the Girl's family. Add yours to this list to make the holidays your own.

Christmas Stollen

This is one of those wonderful Christmas breads, shot with fruit and spice, that actually gets better with age. The Girl likes to bake up a double batch and deliver her stollen on Christmas Eve, so her friends have something delicious to nibble while they open their gifts. A fine holiday tradition to start and keep.

1 cup (250 mL) golden raisins
1 cup (250 mL) chopped apricots
1 cup (250 mL) dried currants
$\frac{1}{4}$ cup (50 mL) rum
4 cups (1 L) all-purpose flour
1$\frac{1}{2}$ cups (375 mL) ground almonds
2 Tbsp. (25 mL) baking powder
1$\frac{1}{2}$ cups (375 mL) sugar
1 tsp. (5 mL) salt
$\frac{1}{4}$ tsp. (1 mL) mace

$\frac{1}{4}$ tsp. (1 mL) cardamom
$\frac{1}{4}$ tsp. (1 mL) allspice
pinch each nutmeg and ginger
1 cup (250 mL) cold butter, cubed
2 eggs
2 cups (500 mL) ricotta cheese or quark
$\frac{1}{2}$ tsp. (2 mL) almond extract
1 tsp. (5 mL) rum or rum flavoring
melted butter and granulated sugar

1 Soak the raisins, apricots and currants for several hours or overnight in the $\frac{1}{4}$ cup (50 mL) of rum. In a large mixing bowl, combine the flour, almonds, baking powder, sugar, salt and spices. Using a pastry blender (or your fingertips) blend the butter in until the mixture is crumbly.

2 In the food processor, combine the eggs, ricotta or quark, almond extract and rum and purée until smooth. Add to the flour mixture and mix well. Fold in the raisins, apricots and currants, along with any of the remaining rum they were soaking in.

3 Preheat the oven to 350°F (180°C). Form the dough into a ball and knead until smooth. Divide the dough into two equal pieces. Roll each out on a piece of parchment paper, into an oval about 8 x 10 inches (20 x 25 cm). Crease the dough along its length, slightly off center. Brush with melted butter and, using the parchment paper to lift the dough, fold along the crease like an envelope, folding the larger section first and the small section over it. You will end up with an oval loaf.

4 Place the loaves, on the parchment, onto a baking sheet. Bake for 50 minutes, or until golden. When the stollens are ready, remove them from the oven and set on a rack. Brush with melted butter and sprinkle with sugar. Allow the breads to mellow in airtight containers for 2–3 days before serving. Makes 2 loaves.

Tourtière

This is the Girl's Christmas Eve tradition, a rich, savory meat pie served with a side salad and sweet gherkins, pickled beets or chutney to balance the richness. The filling is enough for three 9-inch (23-cm) pies — exactly the amount of pastry you'll have if you follow the recipe on the box of shortening or lard (lard is actually best for savory pies). Don't give in to your fear of pie crust — the recipe works! The pies can be filled and frozen, unbaked. Thaw in the refrigerator until the pastry is soft, then bake.

filling

1 tsp. (5 mL) olive oil
2 cups (500 mL) finely chopped onion
3 cloves garlic, minced
1 cup (250 mL) minced celery and celery leaves
2 lbs. (1 kg) ground pork
1 lb. (500 g) lean ground beef
1/2 tsp. (2 mL) savory

1/2 tsp. (2 mL) ground sage
pinch each ground cloves and cinnamon
salt and freshly ground black pepper
1 cup (250 mL) water
3 cups (750 mL) hot boiled potatoes, mashed or
  put through a ricer
1/2 cup (125 mL) chopped fresh parsley

pies

pastry for three double-crust pies
1 egg yolk, beaten with 2 Tbsp. (25 mL) milk

1 In a large sauté pan, heat the oil over medium heat and sauté the chopped onion, garlic and celery until soft. Crumble the ground pork and beef into the pan and continue to cook, stirring, until no pink remains in the meat. Drain any accumulated fat from the pan. Add the savory, sage, cloves, cinnamon, salt, pepper and water, cover and simmer for 30 minutes. Stir the mashed potatoes and parsley into the filling and set aside to cool.

2 Make the pastry, following the instructions on the box of shortening or lard. Chill the pastry for 1 hour before rolling.

3 Preheat the oven to 375°F (190°C). Roll the pastry very thin and line three 9–inch (23–cm) pie plates. Fill each with 1/3 of the cooled meat mixture and top with pastry, sealing and fluting the edges with your fingers to form a ruffled border. Cut steam vents in the tops of the pies using a sharp knife. Brush the pies with egg yolk glaze, and bake for 30–40 minutes, until golden brown. Cool for 20 minutes before cutting. Makes 3 meat pies.

Turkey Pot Pie

The perfect solution for leftovers from the big bird. The Girl loves to serve this comfort food in January, too — just freeze that leftover turkey breast or thigh and haul it out when you want to make something special on a wintery night. No one will suspect you're recycling.

turkey filling

2 Tbsp. (25 mL) butter

1 small yellow onion, finely chopped

1 clove garlic, minced

1 Tbsp. (15 mL) all-purpose flour

2 cups (500 mL) winter squash, peeled and cubed (butternut, acorn, etc.)

3 ribs celery, diced

1 cup (250 mL) canned white beans, drained and rinsed

1 tsp. (5 mL) fresh thyme (or 1/2 tsp./2 mL dried thyme)

2 tsp. (10 mL) chopped fresh sage (or 1/2 tsp./2 mL dried sage)

1/4 tsp. (1 mL) freshly ground black pepper

1/2 cup (125 mL) white wine

1/2 cup (125 mL) turkey or chicken stock

3 cups (750 mL) leftover cooked turkey, white or dark meat, cut into 2-inch (5-cm) cubes

dumplings

1/2 cup (125 mL) cornmeal

1/2 cup (125 mL) all-purpose flour

1 1/2 tsp. (7 mL) baking powder

1/2 tsp. (2 mL) salt

2/3 cup (150 mL) finely shredded Parmesan cheese

1 egg, lightly beaten

1/3 cup (75 mL) skim milk

1/2 tsp. (2 mL) Dijon mustard

1 To make the filling, heat the butter in a large pot or Dutch oven over medium heat until melted. Add the onion and garlic to the pan and cook for 5 minutes, just to soften. Stir in the flour and cook for 1 minute. Add the squash, celery, beans, thyme, sage, pepper, wine and stock. Heat to boiling, stirring until thick and smooth. Add the turkey to the pot, cover and simmer for 30 minutes.

2 Preheat the oven to 400°F (200°C).

3 To make the dumplings, combine the cornmeal, flour, baking powder and salt. Stir in the cheese. Whisk together the egg, milk and mustard in a measuring cup. Make a well in the center of the dry ingredients and add the egg mixture, mixing with a fork until the batter is just combined.

4 When the turkey and vegetables are tender, turn the stew into an ovenproof casserole dish. Drop the dumplings over the stew in big spoonfuls. Bake for 20–30 minutes, until the crust is golden brown and the stew is bubbly. Serves 4–6.

Old-Fashioned Gingerbread Girls (or Boys)

At Christmastime, everyone loves gingerbread. Corral some kids and make gingerbread people to hang on the tree or get really ambitious and build a gingerbread mansion. This recipe makes gingerbread suitable for cookies or houses and is great to eat, too. It's a traditional German recipe that needs to mature for several days before baking, so start your gingerbread project a few days before you plan to bake.

gingerbread

$^3/_4$ cup (175 mL) dark brown sugar

$^2/_3$ cup (150 mL) butter

1 egg

3 Tbsp. (45 mL) milk

$^1/_2$ cup (125 mL) molasses

3–4 cups (750 mL–1 L) all-purpose flour

$^1/_4$ tsp. (1 mL) baking powder

2 tsp. (10 mL) ground ginger

1 tsp. (5 mL) cinnamon

$^1/_4$ tsp. (1 mL) allspice

$^1/_4$ tsp. (1 mL) ground cloves

icing

1 egg white

2 cups (500 mL) icing (powdered) sugar

1 tsp. (5 mL) white vinegar or lemon juice

1 In a large bowl, use an electric mixer to cream the brown sugar with the butter until fluffy. Add the egg, milk and molasses and beat until well mixed.

2 In another bowl, combine the flour, baking powder, ginger, cinnamon, allspice and cloves. Add the dry ingredients to the butter mixture, mixing by hand to combine well. The dough should be stiff — if it's sticky, add more flour, 1 Tbsp. (15 mL) at a time. Wrap the dough in plastic wrap or waxed paper and refrigerate overnight or for up to 2 weeks to allow the flavors to meld. This is the secret of great German-style gingerbread. With maturation, the dough gains added depth and flavor.

3 The cold dough will be hard to roll — either let it warm to room temperature before rolling or cut it into thick slices and roll it between pieces of waxed paper. Roll out to the desired thickness, about $^1/_8$–$^1/_4$ inch (3–5 mm) for cookies, and cut into gingerbread people. Use a cookie cutter or make a cardboard stencil (paper-doll style) as a guide. If you want to hang your gingerbread people on the tree, use a drinking straw to punch nice even holes near the top before baking.

4 You can also use this gingerbread for the walls and roof of a gingerbread house. Roll it a little thicker for bigger slabs, measure, and cut carefully using templates.

5 Preheat the oven to 350°F (180°C). Bake the gingerbread on a greased and parchment-lined baking sheet for 8–12 minutes, depending on the thickness. Touch the top — if it springs back, it's done. Cool on wire racks.

6 To make the decorative icing, beat the egg white with an electric mixer and gradually add the icing sugar, beating until the mixture starts to stiffen. Add the vinegar or lemon juice and beat until stiff. Use this icing right away as it hardens fast. It's good for gluing houses together or cementing candy decorations in place. Put the icing in a heavy resealable plastic bag, squeeze out the air and snip off a small corner for a fast and disposable piping bag. Makes 6 dozen gingerbread cookies, four small houses or one large gingerbread house.

Shortbread Cookies

The Girl's mother makes extraordinary Scottish-style shortbread — the same as her mother did and probably her mother before that. Cut into simple, rectangular fingers, these substantial shortbread cookies are even more decadent when dipped or drizzled in melted chocolate.

1 lb. (500 g) unsalted butter at room temperature
1 cup (250 mL) granulated sugar

4–5 cups (1–1.25 L) all-purpose flour, sifted

1 Preheat the oven to 325°F (160°C).

2 Using an electric mixer, cream the butter and sugar together until smooth and fluffy.

3 Gradually add the flour until the mixture just starts to crumble. Mix with a spoon — do not be tempted to use your hands (the heat of your hands will warm the dough too much and make the cookies too hard). The mixture should be very stiff, not sticky and will barely hold together.

4 Dump the dough onto your work surface and, using a wide knife, pat the mixture into a square, about 3/4 inch (2 cm) thick. Cut the shortbread into fingers, about 3/4 x 2 inches (2 x 5 cm).

5 Line your cookie sheet with parchment paper. Using a spatula, lift the cookies onto the cookie sheet, placing the pieces about 1/2 inch (1 cm) apart. Make a simple pattern on the top of each cookie by poking them with the tines of a fork.

6 Bake for 30–40 minutes, or until the edges just barely start to color. The cookies will barely spread, but separate any that are touching while still warm. Cool the cookies on racks. Makes about 4 dozen shortbread cookies.

Chocolate Truffles

Make these on a December afternoon when the shopping is done and you're in the mood to contemplate Christmas. Buy some of those pretty miniature foil cups and some funky boxes (the Girl loves the waxed cardboard Chinese food containers with little wire handles) and make some edible gifts to tote along wherever you visit. Christmas card boxes (with the clear plastic lids) tied with pretty ribbons also make nice containers for these simple homemade bonbons. Thanks to girlfriend Bonnie for years of inspiration like this.

1/4 cup (50 mL) granulated sugar
zest of 1 orange
1 cup (250 mL) shelled hazelnuts, toasted and
  skins removed (see page 287)
12 oz. (350 g) good-quality bittersweet
  chocolate (Valrhona or Callebaut)

1/2 cup (125 mL) unsalted butter
3 Tbsp. (45 mL) orange-flavored liqueur or brandy
  (like Cointreau or Grand Marnier)
1/2 cup (125 mL) Dutch-process cocoa powder

1 In the food processor, combine the sugar and orange zest and process until finely minced. Add the hazelnuts and pulse until the nuts are finely ground.

2 Chop the chocolate and put it in a small glass bowl with the butter. Microwave on medium power for 1 minute, stir, then continue to microwave, a minute at a time, stirring, until the chocolate is melted. Add to the food processor along with the liqueur and whirl to combine. Put the truffle mixture into a bowl, cover and refrigerate until firm.

3 Place the cocoa in a shallow bowl. Scoop out the chocolate mixture and roll into small balls. Use about 2–3 tsp. (10–15 mL) for each truffle. Roll the truffles in cocoa to coat all sides, then set each one in a foil cup. Refrigerate or freeze. Makes 50 or 60 truffles.

Crunchy Almond Bark

The Girl's version of an expensive almond and pecan candy — even more impressive when made by a creative elf at home. Pack it into pretty holiday tins for gourmet gifts.

1 cup (250 mL) butter
1 cup (250 mL) granulated sugar
1 cup (250 mL) blanched almonds, coarsely chopped

6 oz. (175 g) good-quality milk chocolate, grated
3/4 cup (175 mL) pecans, finely ground

1 In a heavy sauté pan, melt the butter and sugar together over medium heat. When the mixture begins to bubble, add the chopped almonds and increase the heat to medium-high.

2 Stirring constantly, cook for 5–7 minutes, until the mixture turns a nice caramel color and the nuts are lightly toasted. Be careful, you can easily overdo it and burn the nuts.

3 Line a baking sheet with parchment paper (or use your Silpat silicon sheet, page 360) and pour the caramelized sugar mixture onto the pan. Use a metal spoon to quickly spread it evenly. While it's still hot, scatter the milk chocolate over top, then evenly sprinkle with the ground pecans. Use the spoon to press the pecans and chocolate down evenly over the entire surface of the hot candy. Cool.

4 When the candy is cold and stiff, break it into chunks and store it in sealed containers.
Makes about 1 lb. (500 g).

Girl talk: Any chocolate you consume should be the real thing — chocolate liquor, cocoa butter, sugar and perhaps a touch of lethicin to make it smooth. Industrial, or what the Girl likes to call "junk chocolate," may contain no chocolate liquor or cocoa butter at all. Much of this fake chocolate contains as little as 5 per cent cocoa, and is loaded with sugar, hydrogenated fat and artificial flavorings. If you read the ingredient list on the label, you'll see what kind of chocolate you're buying.

The best quality dark chocolate has a much higher percentage of cocoa liquor and cocoa butter, 50–70 per cent cocoa solids in dark chocolate, and a little less, 30–35 per cent, in good milk chocolate. You couldn't eat 100 per cent pure chocolate — it would be too bitter. But the trend in gourmet chocolate is toward darker chocolate with far higher percentages of cocoa solids — some as high as 75–85 per cent — and gourmet "single region" chocolate made from beans grown in specific parts of the cocoa world.

Get the good stuff. The latest research says this kind of chocolate may actually be good for your health. Sweet.

Nuts and Bolts

I know, it's so tacky but it's an absolute must in the Girl's Christmas repertoire, just one of those childhood addictions that may only be trotted out once a year. It's the only time the Girl buys a tub of margarine (non-hydrogenated, of course) — or all of that pre-fab cereal, for that matter. But it's essential stuff for real bolts. It's a retro thing.

1 cup (250 mL) non-hydrogenated margarine
3 Tbsp. (45 mL) Worcestershire sauce
12 cups (3 L) Cheerios™
2 cups (500 mL) Shreddies®
3 cups (750 mL) Rice Chex™ or Crispix™ cereal
3 cups (750 mL) roasted peanuts (skinless)

4 cups (1 L) straight pretzels (skinny ones),
   broken into 1–inch (2.5–cm) pieces
1 Tbsp. (15 mL) celery salt
2 tsp. (10 mL) onion salt
1 tsp. (5 mL) garlic powder

1 Get out the biggest roasting pan you have (you might need two).

2 In a small saucepan, melt the margarine and whisk in the Worcestershire. Set aside. Combine the cereals, peanuts and pretzel bits in a pan, and toss. Drizzle the margarine mixture evenly over top, mixing gently with a wooden spoon to coat everything, then sprinkle on the celery salt, onion salt and garlic powder and toss to season everything evenly. Taste — if you think you need more flavoring, add it now.

3 Place the pan(s) in a 200°F (95°C) oven and bake for 1½ hours, stirring occasionally. Cool and store in large plastic containers (or freeze). Then drag it out when you're ready to pass the Sidecars and artichoke dip at the family Christmas party, or whenever you're feeling festive. Weird traditions die hard. Makes tons.

Smoking Bishop

A steaming pudding might just go head to head with a smoking bishop, don't you think? It's all part of that manic holiday emotional roller coaster. But seriously, this is really just another version of mulled wine, culled from the writings of Charles Dickens. The Girl just likes the name for this red wine punch that's infused with winter spices and as purple as a bishop's cloak. And even though you serve it hot, there's nothing better to chill everyone out during the holidays.

1 orange, scrubbed well and sliced

1 lemon, scrubbed well and sliced

2 bottles (1.5 L) dry red wine

½ cup (125 mL) brandy

½ cup (125 mL) port

8 whole cloves

4 cinnamon sticks

4 whole star anise

3 Tbsp. (45 mL) brown sugar

1 In a stainless steel pot or crockpot, combine all the ingredients. Heat together over medium-low heat until almost boiling, but do not boil. Simmer, just below boiling, for 10 minutes, then remove from the heat and let steep for 1 hour.

2 To serve, strain and reheat to just below boiling. Serve hot in mugs. Makes 8 servings.

The Jewish Holiday Dinner

It's always important to accommodate your guests' food preferences, but this meal satisfies whether you're keeping kosher or not. A tender brisket or nice roast chicken (page 234) is a possibility for most high holidays. You can start with homemade chicken soup (page 347) or gefilte fish from the local deli, then finish with an old-fashioned Orange Honey Cake (page 304). Here are some other traditional favorites that will delight your Jewish friends.

Potato Knishes

These addictive little potato packages are just the thing to serve alongside any kind of stewy bits — or as hearty hors d'oeuvres with gefilte fish. Carbs wrapped in carbs — oy!

dough

2 1/4 cups (550 mL) all-purpose flour
1 tsp. (5 mL) baking powder
1/2 tsp. (2 mL) salt

2 eggs
1/2 cup (125 mL) canola oil
1/4 cup (50 mL) water

filling

2 lbs. (1 kg) potatoes
2 cups (500 mL) minced onion
3 Tbsp. (45 mL) butter

1 egg, beaten
salt and freshly ground black pepper

assembly

1 egg beaten with 2 Tbsp. (25 mL) cold water

1   In a large bowl, combine the flour, baking powder and salt. In a small bowl, whisk together the eggs, oil and water. Make a well in the center of the dry ingredients and add the wet ingredients. Combine with your hands to form a smooth dough. Divide the dough into two pieces, wrap in plastic and refrigerate for 1 hour before rolling.

2   Meanwhile, make the filling. Peel the potatoes, cut them into chunks and boil until tender, about 15 minutes. Drain and mash. Sauté the onion in butter until tender, about 10 minutes, then add to the mashed potatoes. Stir in the beaten egg, salt and pepper.

3   Preheat the oven to 350°F (180°C). Remove the dough from the refrigerator and roll it out very thin, cutting it into 10– x 3–inch (25– x 8–cm) strips. Dollop a thick strip of potato filling along the center of each piece of dough. Roll the dough around the filling, pinching to seal the edges. You will have a 10–inch (25–cm) tube, filled with potatoes. Cut the roll into 2–inch (5–cm) pieces, then pinch both ends of each piece to seal the filling inside.

4   Place the knishes, pinched side down, on a parchment-lined baking sheet. Brush the tops with egg wash and bake for 20–25 minutes, until golden. Makes about 30.

Girl talk: Try combining mashed white potatoes and orange sweet potatoes for the filling. Makes a colorful knish.

Best Borscht

This classic beet soup is a meal in itself — a dish with deep roots in Eastern Europe. Make it in the height of summer with tiny new potatoes, green and yellow beans, fresh peas and baby beet tops — then serve it hot or chilled, swirled with cool yogurt and sprinkled with fresh dill. Or start with beef or pork soup bones or spare ribs to make a meat broth base. This version is vegetarian.

3 medium beets, scrubbed but unpeeled
2/3 cup (150 mL) cubed carrots
1 medium onion, finely chopped
2 cloves garlic, minced
2 cups (500 mL) finely shredded green or
   purple cabbage
1 large Yukon Gold potato, peeled and cubed
1 14-oz. (398-mL) can tomatoes, puréed
8 cups (2 L) water or beef broth

1 cup (250 mL) cooked small white beans
3 Tbsp. (45 mL) lemon juice or red wine vinegar
1 Tbsp. (15 mL) sugar
1/2 tsp. (2 mL) sweet Hungarian paprika
2 Tbsp. (25 mL) all-purpose flour
salt and freshly ground black pepper
1/2 cup (125 mL) cream or sour cream
2 Tbsp. (25 mL) chopped fresh dill

1 In a large soup pot, combine the beets, carrots, onion, garlic, cabbage, potato, tomatoes and water or broth. Bring to a boil over high heat, then reduce the heat to low, cover the pot and simmer the soup for 1 hour.

2 Remove the beets from the soup, slip off and discard the skins and chop or grate the beets. Return beets to the soup. Stir in the beans, lemon juice or vinegar, sugar and paprika and return to low heat. Cover and simmer for 15 minutes.

3 Whisk together the flour, salt, pepper and cream or sour cream. In a small bowl, add a few tablespoons of hot broth from the soup and mix well, then whisk the cream mixture into the soup to thicken it. Heat through but do not boil or the soup will curdle. Stir in the fresh dill and serve immediately. Serves 6–8.

Pot-Roasted Beef with Pan Gravy and Kasha Pilaf

Baba coming for dinner? Impress her with this old country pot roast and toothsome pilaf, or serve it when you're entertaining Russian style (very nouveau-Klezmer). It's also the perfect menu for a Sabbath soiree or when you're buttonholed for bar mitzvah duty.

½ cup (125 mL) all-purpose flour
salt and freshly ground black pepper
   (about 1/2 tsp./2 mL each)
3–lb. (1.5–kg) beef brisket or inside round roast
¼ cup (50 mL) canola oil

3 large carrots, cubed
1 large onion, chopped
2 stalks celery, chopped
1 small rutabaga, cubed
2 cups (500 mL) beef broth

1 Combine the flour, salt and pepper. Coat the meat heavily with the spiced flour on all sides.

2 In a Dutch oven (a really heavy cast iron pot is best), heat the oil over medium-high heat. Brown the roast well on all sides, turning constantly. The meat should be dark brown and evenly crusted. Remove the meat from the pan and reduce the heat. Preheat the oven to 275°F (140°C).

3 Add the carrots, onion, celery and rutabaga to the hot oil in the pan and sauté until tender and beginning to caramelize, about 10–15 minutes. Set the browned beef on top of the vegetables, pour the broth over top and tightly cover the pan (a layer of foil beneath the lid gives the necessary seal).

4 Place the covered pan in the oven and roast until the meat is very tender, about 3 hours. Remove the beef from the pan, place on a warm platter and cover with foil to keep warm. Skim the excess fat from the cooking liquid. Strain, pressing the solids through the strainer into the sauce (a food mill is a handy tool for this process), or use an immersible blender to purée everything together. Bring the gravy back to a boil and cook to reduce (use a little flour and butter paste to thicken it if necessary). Slice the beef and serve with the pan gravy. Serves 4–6.

Girl talk: As a sauce cools, the fat rises to the top, making it easier to degrease. You can pour any braising liquid into a heatproof glass measuring cup to let this separation occur naturally, then use a big spoon to scoop off most of the clear fat layer to lighten your sauce. If you have time, many soups and stews benefit from a day in the refrigerator before reheating to mingle flavors. The fat on a chilled soup or stew turns solid and is easy to scoop away.

Fluffy Kasha Pilaf

An Eastern European staple, buckwheat groats, or kasha, have a unique smoky flavor and a warm place in the Girl's heart. This is a traditional recipe — the method of sautéing the grain quickly with an egg keeps the unique conical kernels separate and fluffy when cooked. Eclectic, yes. But addictive.

1 cup (250 mL) buckwheat groats (kasha)
1 egg, lightly beaten
1 Tbsp. (15 mL) olive oil
3 Tbsp. (45 mL) butter, divided
1 medium onion, finely chopped

2 cups (500 mL) chicken or vegetable stock
1/4 tsp. (1 mL) salt
2 cups (500 mL) chopped mushrooms
1 Tbsp. (15 mL) chopped fresh dill

1 Combine the buckwheat groats and beaten egg in a bowl, stirring to coat the grains well. Set aside.

2 In a saucepan with a tight-fitting lid heat the olive oil and 1 Tbsp. (15 mL) of the butter over medium-high heat. Add the onion and cook until soft, about 5 minutes. Add the buckwheat and stir-fry quickly, until the egg is cooked and the grains are separated. Add the stock and salt and bring to a boil. Cover the pan, reduce the heat to low and simmer the buckwheat for 15 minutes.

3 Meanwhile, heat the remaining butter in a nonstick pan and fry the mushrooms until they release their liquid and begin to brown. When the kasha is cooked, fluff with a fork and stir in the mushrooms and fresh dill. Serves 4.

Hamantaschen

Hamantaschen can be stuffed with various fillings, from ground poppy seeds and nuts to sweetened cream cheese and prunes. Here's an old-fashioned recipe — the kind with a rich center oozing raisins, walnuts and prunes — for these addictive three-cornered pastries that the Girl scooped from a real Jewish grandmother.

dough

3 cups (750 mL) all-purpose flour
1/2 cup (125 mL) sugar
1 tsp. (5 mL) baking powder
1/4 tsp. (1 mL) salt

2 eggs, beaten
juice and finely grated rind of 1 orange
1 cup (250 mL) canola oil
1/4 cup (50 mL) liquid honey

filling

1 lb. (500 g) pitted prunes
1 cup (250 mL) sultana (light) raisins
1/2 cup (125 mL) ground walnuts or almonds
rind of 1/2 lemon, grated

rind of 1/2 orange, grated
bit of lemon juice
2 Tbsp. (25 mL) honey, to taste

egg wash

1 egg white beaten with a little water

1 For the dough, combine the flour, sugar, baking powder and salt in a large bowl. Beat the eggs with the orange juice and rind, oil and honey. Combine with the dry ingredients to form a soft dough. Chill.

2 Combine all the filling ingredients in a food processor and purée until smooth.

3 Preheat the oven to 350°F (180°C). Divide the dough in half. Roll each piece out on a floured board and cut out 3-inch (8–cm) circles. Reroll the excess pastry and cut more circles.

4 Place about 1 tsp. (5 mL) of filling in the center of each circle. Bring the dough up from three sides and pinch it together, forming a triangle. The filling should be covered but still visible in the center.

5 Set the pastries on a baking sheet that has been lined with parchment paper. Brush with a little egg wash to give them a nice gloss. Bake for 15 minutes or until lightly browned. Makes a bunch.

Can You Bring an Appetizer?

(or The Obligatory Holiday Cocktail Party)

The Girl loves parties but she's not fond of hosting them — those little cocktail noshes are never enough bang for the time investment buck. But sometimes you just have to schmooze. And if you can't afford to shell out for a good caterer, you might as well DIY because there's nothing tackier than a badly catered party (think of those sad souls who get all of their party food from the freezer section of the local big box store — don't go there).

This collection of appetizers will save you from such mortifying post-party gossip. There are many almost instant appetizers (page 208 to 215). These are the noshes you can pull together anytime. Fine on their own with drinks before heading out to dinner or the backbone of an appetizer buffet that includes a couple of items from the next group, those that require a little more work but are worth the effort. When you're having a real, grown-up party, it's nice to have a couple of noshes that you can pass among your guests on trays. Put the bite on someone to help with the passing — teenagers are usually willing.

Most are perfect to take to someone else's party when they ask you to bring an appetizer, too. All are impressive and easy. Many can be done in advance.

Party Pointers

When you're doing the whole party yourself, choose five or six different noshes from this collection (max.) and calculate two to three pieces of each item per guest.

If your party's really huge, get a few friends to help, or augment the menu with a few good-quality take-out trays from your favorite restaurant. (Think sushi rolls or samosas, antipasto platters from the Italian deli, potstickers and shrimp dumplings from the local dim sum house.) Avoid supermarket freezers!

Don't forget the easy elegance of the cheese course — find the best cheesemonger in town and ask for help. A few small wheels of Brie or Camembert, and some blocks of blue or Asiago, artfully arranged with some baskets of good breads and crackers, can be a focal point of your party buffet. You will also impress even the most finicky foodie if you include some local artisan cheeses and make the occasional, casual pronouncement about their provenance.

Do yourself a huge favor and hire (or designate) a bartender. Keep the choices simple — red and white wine, beer, soda water and lime. Martinis and mixed drinks are fun at a dinner party but a killer for a big crowd. Ask your local wine merchant for suggestions to stock the bar, and consider renting the glassware and dishes if you're hosting a lot of people (the rental company will pick them up the next day and you won't even have to wash them, which is brilliant).

Make sure you let your guests know that the invitation is for cocktails, not dinner, and put a time limit on the party (say 5 p.m. to 8 p.m. or 8 p.m. to 11 p.m.)

Plan, make lists, get organized. Freeze whatever you can and arrange hot hors d'oeuvres on baking sheets so that they can go right into the oven. Stick notes on your platters so that you know what goes where in advance, and find some polite teens or cooking school students to help with plating and passing.

Get the lighting right (gobs of candles), scape the buffet with big bowls of bread, lovely linens and lots of seasonal greenery or flowers, and you're set.

Dip Schtick

Is there a cup of low-fat sour cream in the fridge? Can you add a spoon or two of mayo? This is your dip baseline (or start with strained plain yogurt, page 53). Then add some herbs and other flavorings — for dunking veggies, crackers, chips, breadsticks, etc.

Experiment with these easy add-ins:

- pesto

- curry paste (Indian or Thai)

- puréed salsa and chopped cilantro

- puréed sundried tomatoes, basil, oregano and garlic

- caramelized onions and or roasted garlic and black pepper

- sockeye salmon, chopped dill and a drop of liquid smoke

- fresh basil, fresh rosemary, minced lemon zest, chives, thyme leaves, paprika

Qda (quick and dirty Artichoke Dip)

Purists may consider this tried and true combination a bit dated (even outdated) but the Girl likes to think of QDA as pure retro decadence. People like it. It's easy. Get over it.

2 cloves garlic, pressed
1 cup (250 mL) good-quality bottled mayonnaise
1/4 tsp. (1 mL) cayenne pepper
1 cup (250 mL) freshly grated Parmesan cheese

1 14-oz. (398-mL) can artichoke hearts, rinsed, drained well and chopped
sweet Hungarian paprika or cayenne
sliced baguette or pita chips (page 214)

1 Preheat the oven to 350°F (180°C). Combine the garlic, mayonnaise, cayenne and cheese. Stir in the artichokes. Pile it into a small, ovenproof dish and sprinkle with paprika or extra cayenne. Bake for 15–20 minutes until it's bubbly and starting to brown on top. Place the hot dip on a platter, surrounded by sliced bread or pita chips and watch it disappear. Makes 2 cups (500 mL).

White Bean Slather with Caramelized Onions and Goat Cheese

The Girl often falls back on dips and spreads for parties. They can be whirled up almost instantly in a food processor and they can be made in advance. Like this one, dips can be served at room temperature or successfully reheated at the last minute. This is the mother of all spreads — the kind of chunky concoction to slather thickly on toasted baguette or slices of dense ciabatta bread.

beans

1/2 cup (125 mL) chopped fresh herbs (rosemary, sage, thyme)

2 cloves garlic, minced

1 tsp. (5 mL) balsamic vinegar

dash hot pepper sauce

1 large can (19-oz./540 mL) white beans, drained and rinsed

3 Tbsp. (45 mL) extra virgin olive oil

salt and freshly ground black pepper

onions

2 cups (500 mL) slivered red or white onions

1/4 cup (50 mL) olive oil

to finish

4 oz. (125 g) goat soft cheese, crumbled

1 In a food processor, combine the herbs, garlic, vinegar and hot sauce and pulse to chop. Add half the beans and half the 3 Tbsp. (45 mL) olive oil, and process until smooth. Add the remaining beans and olive oil and process in short bursts until all the ingredients are combined but still chunky.

2 Meanwhile, caramelize the onions. (To sliver the onions, halve them lengthwise, then cut them into slivers across the grain. Chop the slivers coarsely if the onion is large.) Heat the 1/4 cup (50 mL) of olive oil over medium-low heat and cook the onions slowly, stirring often, until they are soft and golden brown. This should take at least 30–40 minutes.

3 Add the bean purée to the onions in the pan and stir to heat through. Sprinkle in the goat cheese, toss together lightly and remove from the heat. The cheese should be melting but still visible in small pieces. Serve warm or at room temperature. Makes 2 cups (500 mL).

The Sundried Tomato thing

This is a no-brainer, but your friends will be impressed. These quick appetizers are colorful and easy to eat in one bite — which is another cocktail food rule. The trick is to use a firm but very young, fresh cheese, one that will suck up the marinade. Don't try this with supermarket mozzarella — it's too firm — you're looking for something that will stay together in cubes but which is unripened.

1 lb. (500 g) fresh mozzarella (bocconcini), pressed
   ricotta, or feta cheese
peppery extra virgin olive oil
dried herbs, like basil, oregano, chili flakes,
   thyme, etc.

freshly ground black pepper
1 jar (8 oz./240 mL) sundried tomatoes in oil
1–2 bunches very fresh, perfect basil leaves

1 Cut the cheese into 1/2– to 3/4–inch (1– to 2–cm) cubes. Place the cubes in a single layer in a dish and drizzle with olive oil, then sprinkle with dried herbs and pepper. Let sit in the fridge for awhile to meld the flavors. Cut the sundried tomatoes into small, bite-sized pieces and use a little of their oil to drizzle over the cheese if you like.

2 When you're ready to serve, make little skewers of the ingredients on round toothpicks or short bamboo skewers — first a basil leaf, then a piece of sundried tomato, then a cube of marinated cheese. This way the green leaf will be on top and the cheese cube will form a base so the skewers will stand upright. Arrange them on a plate, and pass to your guests for an easy-to-eat mouthful of Mediterranean flavor! Makes 2 dozen.

The Prosciutto and Melon thing

For noshes like this, you can buy beautiful small silver skewers (handmade and topped with beads or semi-precious stones) for intimate parties. If the party is large, make a zillion on disposable bamboo skewers and keep passing them.

basil oil

1/4 cup (50 mL) olive oil

1/4 cup (50 mL) (packed) fresh basil leaves

1 small shallot, quartered

skewers

6 oz. (175 g) fresh mozzarella (water-packed balls), drained and cut into 3/4–inch (2–cm) cubes

1 lb. (500 g) cantaloupe or honeydew melon, peeled and cut into 12 cubes

4 thin slices lean prosciutto, cut in 3/4–inch (2–cm) strips

12 small whole basil leaves

1 In a blender or food processor whirl together the olive oil, 1/4 cup (50 mL) basil and shallot to make a smooth emulsion. Marinate the cheese cubes in the mixture. Wrap the melon cubes in the prosciutto.

2 To make the skewers, stab a basil leaf at the base. Follow with a cube of prosciutto-wrapped melon, making sure to secure the prosciutto with the skewer. Follow with a cube of marinated mozzarella. The skewers should stand upright on your platter — ready to be consumed in a mouthful. Makes 12.

The Mushroom thing

This is the thing you can pile on toasts for a simple appetizer, use to garnish a creamy soup, dump over your barbecued steak, or serve with savory bread pudding (page 163) for a vegetarian meal. Sautéed and seasoned mushrooms are always delicious.

2 Tbsp. (25 mL) olive oil
3 cloves garlic, minced
1/2 cup (125 mL) minced onion
1 lb. (500 g) fresh wild and/or domestic mushrooms, sliced (chanterelles, portobellos, morels, porcini, etc.)

salt and freshly ground black pepper
1/4 cup (50 mL) white wine
1/4 cup (50 mL) whipping cream (optional)
1 Tbsp. (15 mL) minced fresh rosemary
1 tsp. (5 mL) minced fresh sage

1 In a nonstick pan, heat the oil over medium-high heat. Add the garlic and sauté for 1 minute, until the garlic just begins to color lightly (not brown). Add the onion and cook a minute longer, then stir in the mushrooms and season with salt and pepper.

2 If you are using any dried mushrooms in the mixture, cover them with cold water or white wine and microwave for 1 minute, then let them sit in the hot liquid until they're rehydrated. Drain and combine with the fresh sliced mushrooms in the pan. Cook until the mushrooms give up their liquid and begin to color, about 5–10 minutes, then stir in the white wine. Cook until most of the liquid is gone.

3 If using cream, stir it in now and continue cooking until the sauce is reduced and thickened. Season with the fresh herbs and serve with toasts or crusty bread. Makes 2 cups (500 mL).

Spicy Marinated Olives

What could be easier? Open a can or jar of olives (black ones, big green ones, anchovy-stuffed ones, dry-cured ones) and toss them with some spicy stuff to crank up the volume. Chic with wine and cheese.

2 cups (500 mL) olives (Kalamata, air-cured black, tiny picholine or queen-sized green)

2 cloves garlic, minced or pressed

zest of lemon, finely grated or minced

2 small dried red chilies, crushed (or 1 tsp./5 mL crushed chilies)

1/4 cup (50 mL) extra virgin olive oil

1 tsp. (5 mL) dried oregano

2 tsp. (10 mL) minced fresh rosemary (no dried, please)

1 Tbsp. (15 mL) balsamic or wine vinegar

1 Drain the olives and combine with the remaining ingredients in a jar. Use the microplane grater to make nice fine bits of lemon zest that will stick to the olives.

2 Shake well to coat the olives with the flavorings and oil. Marinate for a few hours at room temperature before serving, or refrigerate for up to 1 month. Makes 2 cups (500 mL).

Girl talk: If you're serving whole, unpitted olives, make sure to set out a small bowl for the pits. Toss any leftover marinated olives into your favorite pasta dish for a blast of flavor or whirl them up (only pitted varieties, of course) in the food processor for instant tapenade to smear on toasts.

Hummus

This is a good, basic recipe for hummus. When you want a change in flavor and color, try adding a roasted red bell pepper (out of a jar) before puréeing the mixture.

1 19-oz. (540-mL) can chickpeas, drained and rinsed

1 tsp. (5 mL) ground cumin

1/4 cup (50 mL) extra virgin olive oil

1/4 cup (50 mL) tahini paste (sesame seed paste)

2 tsp. (10 mL) sesame oil

juice of one large lemon (about 5–6 Tbsp./ 70–90 mL)

3 cloves garlic, minced

1 tsp. (5 mL) salt

1/4 cup (50 mL) water

1/2 cup (125 mL) chopped parsley (optional)

1 Drain the chickpeas in a sieve over the sink, rinsing them well under running water to remove excess salt. Place the chickpeas, cumin, olive oil, tahini, sesame oil, lemon juice, garlic and salt in a food processor. Process until the hummus is smooth. Add a little water if necessary, if the mixture seems too dry.

2 Add the parsley and pulse just to combine. Serve the hummus immediately with warm pita bread or chips (see below), or cover and refrigerate for up to one week. Makes 3 cups (750 mL).

The Pita Chip

These are so much better than the commercial chips. Low in fat, too. Make sure the pita breads are fairly fresh to begin with — if they're stale, they're harder to separate into rounds.

1/2 cup (125 mL) virgin olive oil

3 cloves garlic, crushed

2 packages pita breads (about 12–16, a white and a whole wheat make a nice contrast)

variety of dried herbs and spices (basil, oregano, thyme, cayenne, paprika, celery salt or spice blends like Cajun spice, Herbes de Provence, Chinese 5-Spice, etc.)

1 Combine the olive oil and crushed garlic in a bowl and let steep 15 minutes to flavor the oil. Using kitchen scissors, cut each pita into two rounds (cut around the edge and separate). Then cut the rounds into wedges (or tear into chips for a more rustic look).

2 Preheat the oven to 400°F (200°C). Using a pastry brush, brush the rough inner side of each piece VERY lightly with olive oil (several chips can be done with one brushful of oil) and lay them rough side up on a cookie sheet.

3 Sprinkle with your choice of herbs and spices. (I like to change my combinations with every pan of chips that I make, so guests get a surprise, but try to stick to traditional combinations like Italian: basil, oregano and pepper; Mexican: cumin, coriander and chili powder, etc.) A light dusting of cayenne adds sparkle to any combination.

4 When the sheet is full (a single but crowded layer), pop it into the oven for 3–4 minutes. Set the timer and watch carefully, as the chips can burn quickly. While one batch is baking, starting working on a second tray and you'll have them all done in less than half an hour. They keep well in a sealed bag, so make them in advance. Makes a huge basket of chips.

The Addictive Rosemary Pecans

The Girl can't get enough of these sweet and spicy nuts, flavored with fresh rosemary and zippy hot pepper. You'll be hooked, too.

3 cups (750 mL) whole pecans
2 Tbsp. (25 mL) olive oil
1/4 tsp. (1 mL) cayenne pepper

1 tsp. (5 mL) salt
2 Tbsp. (25 mL) brown sugar
2 Tbsp. (25 mL) minced fresh rosemary

1 Preheat the oven to 400°F (200°C). Place the pecans on a rimmed baking sheet in a single layer and toast for 5–10 minutes. The nuts should be hot and fragrant, but watch them carefully so they don't burn.

2 Meanwhile, in a large bowl, combine the olive oil, cayenne pepper, salt and brown sugar, mixing it well to form a slurry. Stir in the rosemary. Pour the hot, toasted pecans into the bowl and toss with the seasoning mix for several minutes, until all the nuts are coated and cooled. Makes 2 cups (500 mL).

Killer Crostini

Any time you toast your own bread and top it with great cheese and other flavorful stuff, you've got a wonderful appetizer to pass at a party. Chefs top their crostini with everything from fromage frais (a subtle creamy fresh cheese akin to fresh ricotta) to assertive tapenade. Here is the secret of a simple toasted crouton and a couple of killer toppings.

⅓ cup (75 mL) virgin olive oil
1 clove garlic, smashed

1 baguette (or ½ loaf sourdough or olive bread), sliced on the diagonal

1 Combine the olive oil and garlic in a small bowl and leave at room temperature to infuse the flavor for 15 minutes. Discard the garlic. Cut the bread into slices about ¼–½ inch (.5–1 cm) thick. If using sourdough, cut each slice in halves or quarters to make smaller pieces. Brush the bread slices lightly with the garlic-infused oil on both sides and arrange on a baking sheet. Preheat the oven to 450°F (230°C) and bake the toasts until golden brown, about 8–10 minutes. Crostini may be made ahead and stored, covered, at room temperature.

Gratinéed Tomato topping

⅓ cup (75 mL) pine nuts
¼ cup (50 mL) basil pesto
24 crostini toasts

8 ripe tomatoes, thinly sliced (a variety of heirloom tomatoes make a pretty presentation)
½ lb. (250 g) freshly grated Parmesan or Asiago cheese (or a combination)

1 Toast the pine nuts in a hot dry pan until fragrant and beginning to color. Grind them in the food processor.

2 To assemble, spread a little pesto over each toast and arrange them on a baking sheet. Preheat the broiler. Overlap 2–3 tomato slices over the pesto on each toast, and top with some of the grated cheese. Sprinkle some ground pine nuts over each.

3 Place the crostini under the preheated broiler, about 4–5 inches (10–13 cm) away from the element, and broil just until the cheese melts. Watch carefully to make sure the bread doesn't burn. Remove the crostini from the oven and serve warm. Makes 24.

Blue Cheese and Fig topping

½ cup (125 mL) cream cheese

4 oz. (125 g) blue cheese

1/2 cup (125 mL) balsamic vinegar

½ cup (125 mL) red wine

1 Tbsp. (15 mL) honey

6 firm fresh figs, thinly sliced crosswise

12 sourdough crostini toasts

1 In a small bowl, beat the cream cheese and blue cheese to combine well. Set aside.

2 In a small saucepan, combine the balsamic vinegar, wine and honey and bring to a boil over medium heat. Simmer for 30 minutes, until reduced by three-quarters. Adjust the flavor with a little more honey if you find the mixture too acidic. Add the fig slices and cook together for 1 minute. Remove from the heat and let stand 10 minutes.

3 Slather each crostini toast with a little of the blue cheese spread, then lay three fig slices, overlapping, on top. Serve warm or at room temperature. Makes 12.

Girl talk: If you've taken the Girl's advice and made fig preserves (page 330) you can create these fig and blue cheese crostini almost instantly. Or try a dollop of the blue cheese mixture and a bit of fig preserves perched on a leaf of red endive for another pretty nosh to pass.

Shrimp Cocktail from Scratch

Growing up, the Girl always waited greedily for the holidays, when her father would come home with the annual family treat of fresh jumbo shrimp. Freshly cooked, hand-peeled and dunked in homemade horse-radish sauce, this was perfection. Those frozen trays of waterlogged substandard shrimp masquerading as shrimp cocktail are NOT — this is the only way to do it. Start with the best and biggest shrimp you can afford. Buy them from a good fish market and you won't be disappointed.

cocktail sauce

½ cup (125 mL) bottled chili sauce or ketchup
2 Tbsp. (25 mL) prepared horseradish

2 tsp. (10 mL) freshly squeezed lemon juice

shrimp

2 lbs. (1 kg) good-quality jumbo shrimp
  (16 per lb./500 g or larger), unpeeled
pinch salt

1 To make the cocktail sauce, combine the chili sauce or ketchup, horseradish and lemon juice in a small bowl, cover and refrigerate.

2 Peel the shrimp, leaving the tails intact. With a sharp paring knife, slice a shallow, ⅛-inch (3-mm) groove along the back of the shrimp, and rinse out the black vein. (Or buy peeled and deveined shrimp.)

3 Arrange the shrimp in a single layer in a collapsible metal steamer basket. Fill a large bowl with ice cubes and water. Heat 1 inch (2.5 cm) of water to the boiling point in a sauté pan or Dutch oven that will hold the basket. When the water is boiling, set the basket into the pan and cover. Steam for about 6 minutes, until the shrimp are just cooked through. Check one to make sure it's opaque right through — if not, remove the pan from the heat and let stand, covered, for 2 minutes longer.

4 Dump the shrimp into ice water to chill them quickly, then drain well and refrigerate. Serve the shrimp cold with cocktail sauce for dipping.

Girl talk: Get your shrimp from a good fishmonger and get the goods on the shrimp they're selling. Farm-raised tiger prawns sometimes taste muddy (depending where they're from). Prepare a brine of 2 cups (500 mL) boiling water, 1 cup (250 mL) salt and 2/3 cup (150 mL) sugar and let it cool. Soak the shrimp in the brine for 20 minutes before you peel them. Some shrimp are treated with sodium bisulphite to keep them white — soak them in cold water for 30 minutes before peeling.

Cheese, Onion and Olive Biscuits

Make these biscuits tiny, about an inch (2.5 cm) across, and freeze them, if you like. To serve, split them and spread with a dab of herb cheese (like Boursin) or blue cheese, and warm them in the oven. Or make them bigger, and serve alongside your Bouillabaisse (page 148). Try to find the tiny, slightly wrinkled air-cured olives from southern France.

1 Tbsp. (15 mL) olive oil	freshly ground black pepper
1 medium onion, minced	2 Tbsp. (25 mL) butter, cubed
1^1/$_4$ cups (300 mL) all-purpose flour	10 air-cured black olives, pitted and finely chopped
1^1/$_2$ tsp. (7 mL) baking powder	2 oz. (60 g) grated Parmesan cheese
^{1}/$_2$ tsp. (2 mL) salt	2 oz. (60 g) grated aged Cheddar cheese
1 tsp. (5 mL) mustard powder	2 Tbsp. (25 mL) milk
^{1}/$_2$ tsp. (2 mL) cayenne pepper	1 egg

1 Heat the olive oil over medium-high heat and fry the onion until it starts to brown and caramelize, about 10 minutes. Set aside to cool. Preheat the oven to 350°F (180°C). In a bowl, combine the flour, baking powder, salt, mustard, cayenne and black pepper. Cut in the butter with a fork to form coarse crumbs, then stir in the onion, olives and two-thirds of the cheeses.

2 Beat the milk with the egg, adding just enough to the flour mixture to make a soft dough. Turn the dough out onto a floured surface and knead gently until smooth. Roll to about ^{3}/$_4$ inch (2 cm) thick and cut into tiny, 1–inch (2.5–cm) round or square biscuits.

3 Set the biscuits slightly apart on a greased baking sheet. Brush the tops with milk and sprinkle with the remaining cheese. Bake for 10–12 minutes, until golden, then cool on a wire rack. Makes 30.

Salad Rolls

People are so impressed when the Girl totes along these Vietnamese-inspired appetizers — they're fresh, light and completely guilt-free, and especially nice for a summer party. You can make a batch up early in the day, arrange them on a plate, cover them with a moist paper towel and seal them with plastic wrap. They'll keep in the refrigerator for several hours this way. Just remember to get all the fillings ready before soaking the rice paper.

salad rolls

2 oz. (60 g) rice vermicelli noodles
2 large carrots
1 small English cucumber
4 green onions
16 rice paper wrappers, about 8 or 9 inches
   (20 to 23 cm) in diameter

2 cups (500 mL) shredded romaine or butter lettuce
1/2 lb. (250 g) cooked medium shrimp or
   crab meat

peanut sauce

1/4 cup (50 mL) natural peanut butter
1/2 tsp. (2 mL) Asian hot chili paste

2 Tbsp. (25 mL) soy sauce
2 Tbsp. (25 mL) coconut milk or water

1 Cook the rice vermicelli in a pot of boiling water for 3–5 minutes until tender, then drain and rinse in cold water to chill. Drain well and cut the noodles into 3–inch (8–cm) lengths with kitchen shears. Set aside.

2 Cut the carrots into 2–inch (5–cm) chunks, then cut thin slices from each side, discarding the core. Stack the slices and cut into thin matchstick pieces. This is known as julienne. If you have a mandoline, use it to make the finest strips (see page 354).

3 Cut the cucumber the same way, discarding the seeds in the center. Wash the green onions well, cut off the root ends, and cut the green tops and bases lengthwise into strips before chopping them into 2–inch (5–cm) long slivers.

4 To assemble the salad rolls, quickly dip a piece of rice paper into a bowl of hot water to soften (work with one piece at a time). Set the rice paper on a cutting board or clean kitchen towel. Layer some of the cooked rice noodles, green onions, carrots, cucumber, lettuce and shrimp or crabmeat along the bottom edge of the rice paper. Fold the sides in over the filling, and roll up tightly. The rice paper will stick to itself to seal the roll. Set aside on a plate and cover with a clean damp towel to prevent the rice paper from drying out and getting too chewy. Continue soaking and rolling until all of the rice paper and filling is used up.

5 To make the peanut sauce, whisk the sauce ingredients together until smooth.

6 To serve, use a sharp knife to cut each roll into two pieces on a sharp diagonal. Arrange the rolls, standing or overlapping on a platter, with a bowl of peanut sauce on the side for dipping. Makes 32 pieces.

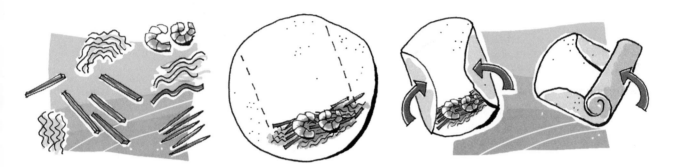

Girl talk: Rice paper is not something you can write on! When you go to the Asian market, look for rice paper in the dried noodle section. It comes in a plastic package, dried and stacked like delicate milky white wafers, usually embossed with a basket weave pattern. Just slide a sheet into a bowl of warm water to moisten for a few seconds then lay it on a clean kitchen towel to soften — in a few minutes it will become soft, pliable and easy to roll.

If you use large cooked shrimp they will make your salad rolls look impressive. Cut each peeled shrimp in half lengthwise and put two or three halves down first, before you start layering the other fillings. They will show prettily through the translucent rice paper once it's rolled up.

Onion Tart

Warm, rich puff pastry is topped with creamy cheese and sweet caramelized onions. Pour a fresh young Riesling or Alsatian Gewürztraminer and enjoy this Black Forest snack.

2 Tbsp. (25 mL) butter
2 large white onions, slivered into thin strips
3 cloves garlic, minced
1 Tbsp. (15 mL) chopped fresh thyme
1 cup (250 mL) white wine
salt and white pepper to taste

1 package (397 g) puff pastry (find it frozen in the supermarket), thawed
4 oz. (125 g) fresh goat cheese, crumbled
4 oz. (125 g) cream cheese
$^1/_2$ cup (125 mL) sour cream

1 Preheat the oven to 350°F (180°C). Melt the butter in a large skillet over medium-low heat. Add the onion and garlic and sauté slowly until golden. Add the thyme, wine, salt and pepper. Simmer until the liquid has evaporated. Set aside.

2 Roll the puff pastry into a thin sheet, large enough to cover an 8– x 14–inch (20– x 35–cm) baking sheet. Place the pastry on a greased baking sheet and set aside.

3 In the food processor, combine the goat cheese, cream cheese and sour cream and whirl until smooth, scraping down the sides as necessary. Spread the cheese mixture evenly over the pastry with a spatula. Scatter the caramelized onions evenly over top, pressing down lightly into the cheese.

4 Bake the tart until golden, about 30–40 minutes. Cut into squares and pass while warm.
Makes 24 pieces.

One-bite Potato Frittatas

The Girl loves these little bites at a tapas party — all you need is a mini muffin pan (the kind you use for those one-bite brownies) and a few basic supermarket ingredients. Make them ahead, if you like, then pop them out into bags and freeze. Reheat on a cookie sheet before serving.

3 cups (750 mL) shredded frozen hash browns, thawed
½ cup (125 mL) crumbled and cooked Italian sausage or chopped cooked ham or prosciutto
1 roasted red bell pepper, finely chopped

3 green onions, finely chopped
6 eggs
3 Tbsp. (45 mL) milk or cream
salt and freshly ground black pepper

1 Preheat the oven to 400°F (200°C). In a large bowl, combine the hash browns with the meat, roasted red pepper and green onions. Whisk the eggs, milk, salt and pepper together and add to the bowl. Stir to combine. Place about 2 Tbsp. (25 mL) of the filling into each greased mini muffin cups. Bake for 12–15 minutes, until set and browned. Makes 2 dozen.

Corn and Chili Pepper Pancakes with Smoked Salmon and Horseradish Cream

This appetizer looks complicated, but it's really done in two easy steps. Whirl the pancake batter stuff together in the food processor, then make the tiny pancakes. (It's a little time consuming, but who can't cook a pancake?) You can make them in advance (even freeze them) and reheat them on a cookie sheet just before serving. You can also whisk together the horseradish cream the day before to save time. If you're short of time, use a base of whole-grain flatbread or crackers instead of the pancakes. Norwegian crispbread crackers (like extra-thin rye crispbreads with onion) can be cut into 2-inch (5-cm) squares using a heavy knife. Assemble them just before you serve to keep the crackers crisp.

horseradish cream

1/3 cup (75 mL) spreadable cream cheese
1 Tbsp. (15 mL) prepared horseradish, drained

1 tsp. (5 mL) wasabi powder (optional)
freshly ground black pepper

pancakes

3 ears fresh corn (or about 2 cups/500 mL
   canned or frozen corn kernels)
2 fresh jalapeño chilies, seeded and minced
1 chipotle chili, chopped
2 cloves garlic, minced
1 red bell pepper, finely chopped
6 green onions, chopped
2 eggs
1 cup (250 mL) all-purpose flour

1/2 cup (125 mL) cornmeal
1 tsp. (5 mL) baking powder
1 tsp. (5 mL) salt
1 cup (250 mL) milk
1/4 cup (50 mL) plain low-fat yogurt
freshly ground black pepper
3 Tbsp. (45 mL) minced cilantro
2 Tbsp. (25 mL) canola oil

to assemble

6 oz. (375 g) cold-smoked salmon or trout,
   sliced paper thin
1 green onion, minced

1 To make the horseradish cream, whisk the cream cheese and horseradish together until smooth. Add the wasabi (if using) and mix to combine well. Season with a little black pepper and chill.

2 Bring a pot of water to a boil and add the corn. Cover and remove from the heat. Let stand 5 minutes. Cool the corn and cut the kernels from the cobs. Place the corn kernels in a bowl with the jalapeño, chipotle, garlic, red pepper and green onions.

3 In a food processor, combine the eggs, flour, cornmeal, baking powder, salt, milk, yogurt and pepper, and whirl until smooth. Add the vegetables and pulse just to mix. Stir in the cilantro. Let stand at room temperature for 30 minutes.

4 Heat the oil in a nonstick frying pan over medium heat. Working in batches, cook the pancakes (make them about 1–2 inches/2.5–5 cm in diameter for cocktails, larger if serving as a side dish). Cook, turning once, until golden on both sides. Drain on paper towels and keep warm. Repeat with the remaining batter.

5 To serve, place a dollop of horseradish cream on each pancake. Separate the thin slices of smoked fish and cut each in half. Roll each piece of smoked fish into a trumpet-shaped coronet and set one on each hors d'oeuvre. Sprinkle with a few pieces of minced green onion and serve. Serves 6.

Girl talk: These corn pancakes are so delicious — make them larger and serve them as a side dish, in a vegetarian menu or even alongside sausages for breakfast.

Bbq Duck Quesadillas

Make a quick trip to the Asian grocer/barbecue house for some lean barbecue duck breast and a jar of hoisin sauce, and these creative quesadillas go together in minutes. Serve them with the salad rolls for a perfect start to any Asian-inspired dinner party.

8 flour tortillas
1 Tbsp. (15 mL) vegetable oil
4 Tbsp. (50 mL) hoisin sauce
1 cup (250 mL) slivered Chinese barbecued duck
  (breast meat)

1/2 lb. (250 g) mozzarella cheese, thinly sliced or
  shredded
1/2 cup (125 mL) cilantro leaves, stems removed
4 green onions, slivered

1   Using a pastry brush, lightly coat one side of each tortilla with oil. Set four tortillas, oil side down, on your work surface. Spread the four tortillas lightly with hoisin sauce. Scatter the slivered duck on top, then top with the cheese. Distribute the cilantro leaves and slivered onions evenly over each tortilla. Top each with a second tortilla, oiled side up, and press lightly to seal.

2   Heat a nonstick sauté or grill pan over medium-high heat. When the pan is hot, use a large spatula to carefully lift one of the filled tortillas into the pan. Cook, pressing lightly as the cheese melts, for about 3–4 minutes. When browned on one side, carefully flip the quesadilla over and brown the second side. Set on a cutting board to cool slightly while you cook the remaining quesadillas (this will allow the filling to set).

3   Cut each quesadilla into 8 wedges and arrange on a platter. Pass while warm. Makes four whole quesadillas, 32 pieces.

Girl talk: By the way, this is the universal method for making quesadillas of all kinds, the perfect hot appetizer. You can either fry them in a pan as described, or grill until lightly browned and crisp on the gas grill (the Girl's favored cooking method, weather permitting).

The Girl's favorite classic quesadilla filling is a light slather of spicy homemade salsa, some slivered ham or cooked chicken, a bit of chopped cilantro and some grated jalapeño-laced Monterey Jack or mozzarella. Paper-thin slices of fresh peaches or mangoes add an exotic touch. But make sure you're judicious about the fillings — for a good crisp quesadilla, less is more.

Mussels Vinaigrette

This is a version of an appetizer the Girl's girlfriend Peg created on the beach during a kayaking trip. If she can do it there, you can do it anywhere. But if you're really pressed for time, just combine the cooked mussels with some fresh supermarket bruschetta, scoop into the reserved shells and serve.

mussels

1 Tbsp. (15 mL) olive oil

1/4 cup (50 mL) minced onion

1 cup (250 mL) white wine

3 lbs. (1.5 kg) mussels in the shell

tomato vinaigrette

1 very ripe tomato, seeded and chopped

2 cloves garlic, pressed or minced

2 green onions, finely chopped

1/4 cup (50 mL) extra virgin olive oil

2 Tbsp. (25 mL) balsamic vinegar

2 Tbsp. (25 mL) minced fresh herbs (basil and/or rosemary, oregano, thyme)

1 tsp. (5 mL) granulated sugar

1 tsp. (5 mL) Dijon mustard

1 Heat the oil in a large pot and fry the onion for 5 minutes. Add the wine and mussels. Bring to a boil over high heat, cover the pot and steam for 5 minutes or until the mussels open. Discard any mussels that don't open. Cool (freeze the broth for your next chowder). Take the mussels out of their shells and save a few dozen of the nicer shells for serving.

2 To make the vinaigrette, whirl the tomato, garlic, green onions, olive oil, balsamic vinegar, herbs, sugar and Dijon together in a blender or food processor.

3 Mix the vinaigrette with the mussels, cover and marinate for a few hours or refrigerate overnight.

4 Spoon the mussel mixture into the reserved shells, making sure you have one or two mussels in each shell. Makes 24 appetizer servings.

Rosemary Citrus Chicken Skewers

Grill or broil these chicken skewers and pass them while warm.

marinade

3 cloves garlic, pressed or minced

⅓ cup (75 mL) olive oil

⅓ cup (75 mL) fresh lime juice

⅓ cup (75 mL) fresh lemon juice

¾ cup (175 mL) orange juice

1 large sprig rosemary, leaves chopped and
  woody stem discarded

⅓ cup (75 mL) white wine

skewers

4 boneless, skinless chicken breasts

1 Tbsp. (15 mL) honey

2 tsp. (10 mL) Dijon mustard

1–2 tsp. (5–10 mL) cornstarch

1 Combine the garlic, oil, lime juice, lemon juice, orange juice, rosemary and white wine, and whisk well to combine.

2 Cut the chicken into 1– to 2–inch (2.5– to 5–cm) cubes and place in a stainless steel or glass bowl, or a heavy, resealable plastic bag. Add half the marinade to the chicken, cover and refrigerate for 4 hours or overnight.

3 Heat the remaining marinade in a small pot until it begins to boil. Whisk the honey and mustard into the marinade. Place the cornstarch in a small bowl, and add a few tablespoons of the marinade, mixing to form a slurry. Slowly whisk the slurry into the boiling sauce and continue to simmer, stirring, until it is nicely thickened. Set aside and keep warm.

4 Soak two dozen 6–inch (15–cm) bamboo skewers in warm water for at least 30 minutes before cooking the chicken. Thread a few pieces of marinated chicken on each skewer and grill or broil over medium-high heat for 7–8 minutes, just until the chicken is cooked through. Brush the skewers with the sauce to glaze just before you remove them from the grill. Serve the skewers with extra sauce for dipping. Makes 24.

The Sunday Roast

(or For The Love of Leftovers)

There is nothing quite so traditional as the Sunday joint — a fat roast of
something or other that you can carve majestically at the table for the family,
with lots of leftovers to squirrel away for fast meals during the week.

While you're roasting your protein, think about popping some side
dishes in the oven, too. A whole head of garlic for your mashed potatoes
(see page 104) or a colorful scallop of potatoes (page 292), some roasted root
vegetables (page 83), a savory bread pudding (page 163), or just a few tiny
Golden Nugget squash, halved, seeded, brushed with tasty olive oil,
and dinner's done!

Roast Beef

A roast of beef makes a lovely meal for almost any occasion — nice medium-rare slices of top-quality, tender beef with rich brown gravy — do it right and everyone will be suitably impressed. Once you get the hang of classic roast beef, you can vary the herbs and spices in your rubs. Try an Italian rub flavored with oregano, basil and garlic, or an Asian rub with hoisin or soy sauce instead of Worcestershire, a bit of ground ginger, chilies and five-spice powder. The cooking method and timing stay exactly the same.

roast

1 Tbsp. (15 mL) black peppercorns

1 tsp. (5 mL) brown sugar

1/2 tsp. (2 mL) salt

1 Tbsp. (15 mL) minced garlic

3 Tbsp. (45 mL) chopped fresh thyme or rosemary (optional)

1 Tbsp. (15 mL) Dijon mustard

1 tsp. (5 mL) Worcestershire sauce

4–to 6–lb. (2–to 3–kg) premium oven roast (prime rib, top sirloin, rib eye, strip loin, tenderloin)

gravy

2 Tbsp. (25 mL) all-purpose flour

1 cup (250 mL) beef stock

1 cup (250 mL) red wine

1 Place the peppercorns in a heavy plastic bag and crush, using a rolling pin or meat mallet.

2 In a small bowl, combine the peppercorns, sugar, salt, garlic, herbs, mustard and Worcestershire. Rub this mixture over the meat and let stand at room temperature for 30 minutes. The roast should not go into the oven straight out of the refrigerator.

3 Preheat the oven to 500°F (260°C). Place the meat in a shallow roasting pan, fat side up, and roast for 15 minutes. Reduce the heat to 325°F (160°C) and continue to roast until the internal temperature is 135–150° F (57–65°C) for rare to medium rare, or 160°F (77°C) for well done. It's up to you but I'd take it out when the temperature reaches 138–140°F (50–60°C) — perfect, juicy, medium-rare roast beef. Use a meat thermometer to test the roast, but as a general rule, brown the roast in a very hot oven to start, then cook about 15 minutes per lb. (500 g) for medium-rare. Don't overcook it — the longer you cook a lean roast, the tougher it gets.

4 Remove the roast from the oven, set it on a platter and tent with foil to keep warm while it rests for at least 10–15 minutes. This is an important step. If you carve the roast too soon the juices will run out and the meat won't be juicy. Once it rests, and the juices settle into the meat, the roast will appear less rare and it will be firmer and easier to carve.

5 This also gives you tons of time to mash some potatoes and make the gravy. Set the roasting pan over medium-high heat on top of the stove and blend the flour into the drippings, stirring until you have a smooth paste that incorporates all the fat in the pan. Slowly add the beef stock and red wine (or some of the water from cooking the potatoes or vegetables) to the pan, stirring constantly with a whisk to eliminate any lumps. Bring the gravy to a boil, stirring until it is smooth and thickened to your liking. Thin with additional stock or water if necessary. Season the gravy with salt to taste. Strain if you want it completely smooth.

6 To carve a prime rib roast, lay it on its side on a cutting board and slice along the ribs to separate the meat from the bone. Then slice the meat toward the bone — the slices will come away from the bone as you carve. To carve a boneless roast, like a rib eye or strip loin, simply slice across the grain.
Serves 8–12.

Girl talk: Two things you need for a proper roast are a roasting pan with a rack, and a meat thermometer. Any shallow, ovenproof pan will do, as long as it's large enough to allow the dry heat to circulate around the roast. A pan that's too small or deep will steam the roast and you won't get the proper searing and browning you need for best results.

Use an instant-read meat thermometer, inserted in the center of the roast near the end of cooking, to guarantee it's done. Leave the thermometer in the meat for 30 seconds and make sure it isn't touching any bone.

Beef Buying Basics

There are many roasts in the supermarket meat case, but only a few of the more expensive cuts will do for a classic Sunday roast. You'll have to make a bit of an investment to end up with the Norman Rockwell result.

If you see something labeled "premium oven roast" you can be sure it's safe to simply season it and fire it into the oven to roast. If the label says "pot roast" or "braising roast," you'll have to use a completely different cooking method — cooking the meat for a much longer time, in a covered roasting pan, with liquid like wine, broth or tomato sauce (see Pot-Roasted Beef, page 203). Pot roast is delicious, but you won't be seeing those slices of medium-rare meat on your plate — expect it to be tender and falling off the bone, more like beef stew than steak.

For dry roasting, choose one of the premium cuts — top sirloin, tenderloin, strip loin, prime rib, rib eye. Other cuts (like sirloin tip, eye of round, outside and inside round, rump and bottom sirloin) can be roasted to medium rare, but benefit from marinating for 12–24 hours, and roasting with a little liquid or some vegetables in the bottom of the pan. Good, but better for casual company.

So buy the right roast and buy enough meat — about 2 lbs. (1 kg) of boneless beef roast for every 6 servings.

Luxe Leftovers

Whenever you have lovely leftover beef roast or steak, Day Two is a golden opportunity to indulge in a big, stylish steak sandwich. Pick up a really good baguette (a good one, mind you) and cut it diagonally into three or four chunks (each should be about 4 to 5 inches/12 cm long). Halve them lengthwise and put them under the broiler to toast for 5 minutes. Butter with garlic butter. Pile on the thinly sliced roast beef and top with some horseradish mayonnaise ($^1/_2$ cup/125 mL of good quality mayo flavored with 2 Tbsp./ 25 mL bottled horseradish, a minced green onion and a $^1/_2$ tsp./2mL of Dijon) or blue cheese butter (page 136). With a pile of caramelized onions on top (page 16) and a tossed romaine salad on the side, this is a sublime supper (and will impress a carnivorous mate).

Sunday Roast Pork

The Girl loves pork. It's lean, easy to cook and a roast pork dinner makes an impressive family meal on Sunday. Start with a roast from the butcher that's been boned and tied, or enclosed in one of the new string mesh sleeves, and pick one that's evenly shaped (not too skinny at one end). Then make a complete roast pork dinner for four in a single pan in just over an hour.

3–lb. (1.5–kg) boned and rolled pork leg roast

2–3 cloves garlic, smashed and roughly chopped

6 fresh sage leaves, sliced, or 2 tsp. (10 mL) chopped fresh rosemary

2 Tbsp. (25 mL) olive oil, divided

salt and freshly ground black pepper

2 cups (500 mL) small baby carrots

8–12 baby or fingerling potatoes, halved (or larger potatoes cut into 1– to 2–inch (3– to 5 cm) chunks

6 cloves garlic, peeled

2 medium onions, peeled and cut into wedges

whole baby yellow beets (optional)

1 cup (250 mL) white wine

extra sprigs fresh sage or rosemary to garnish

1 Preheat the oven to 500°F (260°C).

2 Reach under the string tying the roast to find the cuts where the roast has been deboned. Insert the chopped garlic and sage or rosemary as far inside the roast as you can. If the roast is held in a mesh sleeve, work some of the garlic and herbs under the sleeve to hold it against the meat as it cooks. Rub the roast with about 1 tsp. (5 mL) of the olive oil and season it on all sides with salt and pepper.

3 Find a roasting pan large enough to hold the meat and vegetables in a single layer. Place the carrots, potatoes, garlic cloves, onion wedges and beets, if using, in the roasting pan and drizzle with the remaining olive oil. Toss to coat the vegetables with oil. Season with salt and pepper and toss again. Push the vegetables to the outside of the pan and set the roast in the middle.

4 Place the pan in the preheated oven and immediately reduce the oven temperature to 350°F (180°C). Roast for about 1 hour, stirring the vegetables every 20 minutes and brushing the roast with the fat it releases as it cooks. After 1 hour, test the internal temperature using an instant-read thermometer. The interior should be 145–150°F (63–66°C). You may need to return the roast to the oven for 15 minutes if it has not reached the desired temperature.

5 Remove the roast from the pan and set on a cutting board to rest for 10 minutes. Remove the vegetables from the pan with a slotted spoon and arrange them around the edge of a serving platter. Drain any excess fat from the pan and discard. Place the pan over high heat on the stovetop, add the wine and simmer, scraping up any brown bits. Boil until the liquid has been reduced by half. Season with salt and pepper and strain into a small pitcher.

6 Remove the string or netting from the roast and carve into slices 1/4 to 1/2–inch (.5 to 1 cm) thick. Arrange the pork in the center of the platter and drizzle with the sauce. Tuck some fresh herbs in among the vegetables to garnish the platter. Voila! Sunday dinner for four.

Roast Chicken 101

Roasting a chicken is perhaps the most important thing a Girl should learn — it's homey, smells wonderful in the oven, everyone loves it and it's idiot proof. Think of this as training camp for the big bird day (Thanksgiving or Christmas), and you'll be confident cooking and carving a turkey later on. The only trick to a perfect roast chicken is the chicken itself — shell out for a nice free-range bird and you'll never go back to supermarket fryers. With mashed potatoes and your favorite veg. on the side, this could become your favorite Sunday supper.

1 free-range roasting chicken
  (about 5 lbs./2.5 kg)
salt and freshly ground black pepper
1 Tbsp. (15 mL) minced garlic
2 Tbsp. (25 mL) minced fresh rosemary or
  basil (don't substitute dried)

2 Tbsp. (25 mL) olive oil, divided
1 lemon, cut into quarters
2–3 Tbsp. (25–45 mL) all-purpose flour
2–3 cups (500–750 mL) stock and/or
  vegetable water

1 Rinse the bird inside and out and pat it dry. Season the cavity with salt and pepper. Combine the garlic, rosemary or basil and 1 Tbsp. (15 mL) of the olive oil to form a chunky paste.

2 Now, here's the tricky part. Using your fingers, and starting around the neck cavity, carefully loosen the skin from the breast (that's the plump, meaty side) by inching your fingers between the skin and the meat, right down to where the legs are attached. Go slowly and you won't tear the skin. Push half the garlic/rosemary paste under the skin and slather it around on the meat so it gets into every corner, even over the leg meat. Rub the rest of it inside the cavity of the bird. (You can skip this step the first time and just toss all the garlic and rosemary paste inside the bird, but it won't be the same.) Place half of the lemon wedges inside the cavity of the bird and tie the legs together with string.

3 You'll see that there's a flap of skin over the neck cavity. Tuck this under the bird and twist the wing tips back behind the bird to secure the skin (sort of like clasping your hands behind your neck). Learning this technique will come in handy when you want to stuff a bird as you can fill the neck area with stuffing and hold it in place this way with the taut skin.

4 Set the bird, breast side up, in a roasting pan, on a rack if you have one. It will roast best if the pan isn't too deep. Rub the rest of the olive oil over the bird and squeeze the juice from the remaining lemon quarters over top. If you like, you can cut up some parsnips and carrots to roast alongside the bird.

5 Place the bird in a preheated 450°F (230°C) oven and roast for 20 minutes. Reduce the heat to 400°F (200°C) and continue roasting for about 1 hour, basting occasionally with the fat that will accumulate in the pan. The chicken is done when the skin is brown and crispy, the juices run clear and the leg moves easily in the socket.

6 Place the roasted bird on a cutting board and cover loosely with foil to rest for 15 minutes. It's easier to carve if the meat has cooled slightly.

7 Meanwhile, make the gravy. Remove the rack from the roasting pan and set aside the roasted vegetables (if you've included them) in a covered bowl. Set the roasting pan over medium heat on top of the stove. Discard all but about 2–3 Tbsp. (15–45 mL) of fat from the pan (although you shouldn't have much more than this). Sprinkle some of the flour lightly over the surface of the pan, and stir it into the fat with a wooden spoon, incorporating all the browned bits that are there until you have a paste in the pan. Stirring, slowly add the stock, a little bit at a time. As long as you add the liquid slowly, and whisk or stir to incorporate it with the flour paste as you go, you will never have lumpy gravy. (If you do, don't worry, you can always strain it at the end.) Bring the mixture to a boil, stirring, until it's thick, adding more liquid until your gravy is the consistency that you like. If you've boiled peas or potatoes, save the cooking liquid (a.k.a vegetable water) to add to your gravy for extra flavor.

8 When you're ready to carve your chicken, untie the legs and remove and discard the lemon pieces inside. Serves 4–6.

Leg of Lamb

A leg of lamb is a decadent treat. Find a good butcher and buy locally raised, young lamb for best results. A boneless roast makes for easy carving. Serve it drizzled with this rosemary pesto sauce or some black olive tapenade (page 328), puréed in the food processor and thinned to a saucy consistency with olive oil. Roast some Mini Potato Puffs (page 248) and braise some fennel (page 186) to serve on the side, for a Mediterranean feast.

lamb
1 Tbsp. (15 mL) olive oil
1 Tbsp. (15 mL) lemon juice
1 Tbsp. (15 mL) minced fresh rosemary
1/2 tsp. (2 mL) salt

1/2 tsp. (2 mL) freshly ground black pepper
1 boned, rolled and tied leg of lamb,
   3–4 lbs. (1.5–2 kg)

rosemary pesto sauce
2 anchovy fillets
1 Tbsp. (15 mL) minced garlic
4 Tbsp. (50 mL) minced fresh rosemary
4 Tbsp. (50 mL) Italian parsley

4 Tbsp. (50 mL) toasted hazelnuts or pine nuts
1/2 cup (125 mL) olive oil
freshly ground black pepper

1 Heat the oven to 425°F (220°C). Combine the olive oil, lemon juice, rosemary, salt and pepper in a blender or mini chopper and purée. Rub this mixture over the roast, using your fingers to press it into the spaces where the bone has been removed to season the meat inside and out.

2 Place the roast in a roasting pan just large enough to fit the lamb. Roast for 15 minutes, then turn the roast in the pan and reduce the heat to 375°F (190°C). Continue to roast for 35–45 minutes longer, until the lamb is medium-rare in the center (about 12 minutes per lb./500 g in total).

3 Use an instant-read thermometer to check the internal temperature — 130°F (54°C) for medium-rare (pink), 140°F (60°C) for medium. Remove the roast from the oven and let it rest on a carving board for 20 minutes to allow the juices to set.

4 Meanwhile, make the rosemary pesto sauce. In a blender or food processor, combine all the ingredients and purée to form a smooth sauce. If the mixture is too dense, thin with a tablespoon or two of water.

5 To serve, slice the lamb and arrange on a platter. Pour some pan juices on top and drizzle with pesto. Pass the remaining pesto sauce separately. Serves 6.

The Football Finals – Feeding the Fans

There comes a time in every Girl's life when she must feed the Boys (or at least those friends who are addicted to non-girly pursuits like major football, hockey and other annual sporting finales). This is the time to pull out the nachos, wings, chili and beer. If you've got the whole gang around the TV, feel free to pull out the paper plates, too.

Black Bean Dip

This warm bean dip is addictive with taco chips. Looks nice, too.

1 can (19 oz./540 mL) black beans, drained and rinsed
$\frac{1}{2}$ cup (125 mL) salsa
1 clove garlic, chopped
1 jalapeño chili, chopped
1 small onion, chopped
1 Tbsp. (15 mL) olive oil

$\frac{1}{2}$ tsp. (2 mL) cumin
1 cup (250 mL) grated Cheddar or Monterey Jack cheese
Asian chili paste or hot sauce
chopped black olives, Roma tomatoes and green onions for garnish
tortilla chips

1 Combine the beans and salsa in the food processor and purée.

2 Sauté the garlic, jalapeño and onion in the oil until tender. Add the bean purée and cumin to the sauté pan and cook for 10 minutes, until creamy. Add the grated cheese and stir until melted. Adjust the spice level to your taste with chili paste or hot sauce.

3 Transfer the dip to a plate or small platter and smooth into a 1–inch (2.5–cm) layer. Serve warm, topped with concentric circles of chopped olives, tomatoes and and green onions. Pass the tortilla chips for scooping. Makes 3 cups (750 mL).

Nacho Cheese Dip

If you're going to dip corn chips in cheese, the only kind that really melts is Velveeta®, introduced by Kraft way back in 1928 and marketed for its special, velvety texture when melted. Really, it's trendy..

$\frac{1}{4}$ cup (50 mL) dark beer
1 tsp. (5 mL) ground cumin
$\frac{1}{2}$ tsp. (2 mL) dried oregano
2 cloves garlic, minced
$\frac{1}{2}$ cup (125 mL) purchased or homemade chunky hot salsa (page 331)

1 1–lb. (500–g) package Velveeta® cheese, cut into 1/2–inch (1–cm) cubes
$\frac{1}{4}$ cup (50 mL) chopped fresh cilantro
good-quality tortilla chips (try some of the organic, black bean and stone-ground corn varieties for extra flavor and crunch)

1 In a medium saucepan, combine the beer, cumin, oregano and garlic. Heat over medium-high heat until it begins to boil. Reduce the heat to medium-low and stir in the salsa and cheese, stirring until the cheese is melted and hot. Stir in the cilantro. Transfer to a bowl or cheese fondue dish. Serve warm with tortilla chips for dunking. Makes about 3 cups (750 mL).

Suicide Wings

Look for smoky chipotle chilies in adobo sauce in the Hispanic section or find dried chipotle chilies in the fresh produce section with other dried chili peppers. If you're stumped, just doctor up this wing marinade with some hot sauce (like Asian chili and garlic paste or Tabasco) and a few drops of liquid smoke to mimic the chipotle flavor. And taste the marinade before you add the chicken so that you can make it hotter if you like — what's suicidal for some girls is too tame for others.

3 lbs. (1.5 kg) chicken wings or drumettes
(wings with the tips removed)

4 chipotle chilies in adobo sauce or
4 dried chipotle chilies, rehydrated in warm water

3 cloves garlic, crushed

2 Tbsp. (25 mL) fresh lime juice

1/3 cup (75 mL) tomato sauce or ketchup

3 Tbsp. (45 mL) honey

1 If you want to make your own drumettes, remove the tips and first joint of the wings and save them in the freezer for making broth (see page 347).

2 Combine the chipotles, garlic, lime juice, tomato sauce or ketchup and honey in a food processor and whirl until smooth. Transfer to a nonreactive bowl. Toss the chicken wings with the sauce, cover and marinate in the refrigerator for 30 minutes. Preheat the oven to 375°F (190°C).

3 Line a shallow baking pan with foil. Place the wings in a single layer in the pan and bake for 45 minutes, turning occasionally, until nicely browned and glazed. Serves 4–6.

Girl talk: The Girl likes to serve hot wings with cilantro mayonnaise or creamy avocado dipping sauce to tame some of the heat. An easy way to make cilantro mayonnaise is to combine some commercial mayo with a few tablespoons of coriander chutney. (It comes in jars in Indian groceries and is a staple that the Girl always has on hand in the fridge to add that cilantro kick to tomato or fruit salsas or marinades.)

Or do the creamy guacamole thing — smash up a ripe avocado in a bowl with 1 Tbsp. (15 mL) of lemon juice and add a dollop of mayo and a little cilantro. Both sauces are also great for dipping carrot sticks and other healthy veggies while you watch the game.

Vegetarian Chili

The Girl cajoled this wonderful recipe out of a now-defunct restaurant that specialized in all things healthy, from soup and bread to nuts. This is a great way to get your veggies — you'll never miss the meat — or take on the carnivores at the local chili cook-off.

⅓ cup (75 mL) olive oil

1 lb. (500 g) zucchini cut in 1/2–inch
    (1–cm) dice

1 large onion cut in 1/2–inch (1–cm) dice

4 cloves garlic, minced

1 large red bell pepper, diced

2 28-oz.(796–mL) cans tomatoes with juice

3 large ripe fresh tomatoes cut in 1–inch
    (2.5–cm) dice

1 1/2 Tbsp. (22 mL) chili powder

1 Tbsp. (15 mL) cumin

1 Tbsp. (15 mL) basil

1 Tbsp. (15 mL) oregano

1½ tsp. (7 mL) black pepper

1 tsp. (5 mL) salt

1 tsp. (5 mL) fennel seeds

2 Tbsp. (25 mL) dried parsley

1 19–oz. (540–mL) can red kidney beans, drained
    and rinsed (about 2 cups/500 mL)

1 14–oz. (398–mL) can cooked chickpeas, drained
    and rinsed (about 11/2 cups/375 mL)

2 Tbsp. (25 mL) chopped fresh dill

1 Tbsp. (15 mL) lemon juice

¾ tsp. (4 mL) granulated sugar

hot sauce (optional)

1 In a large Dutch oven, heat the oil over medium-high heat. Add the zucchini, onion, garlic and red pepper and stir-fry until they all begin to soften.

2 Add the canned tomatoes to the pot, squeezing each tomato carefully through your fingers to break it apart (it's faster than chopping). Stir in the fresh tomatoes, chili, cumin, basil, oregano, pepper, salt, fennel and parsley. Simmer, uncovered, stirring often, for 30 minutes. This is one place where dried herbs work well. Don't cut back on the herbs or oil — it seems like a lot but without the meat, this chili needs a lot of seasoning.

3 Stir in the beans, chickpeas, dill, lemon juice and sugar, and cook 15 minutes longer. Spice up the chili to taste with hot sauce, if desired. Serves 6–8.

Meat Lover's Chili

The Girl has been making this chunky chili for years to rave reviews. Her secret ingredient? Ancho chilies. These big dried peppers, available from Latin groceries or in the produce section of well-stocked supermarkets, add a depth of sweet heat like no other chili powder you'll find. Don't forget to roast the chilies on a hot pan (see below) to release the flavor and aroma.

2 dried ancho chilies

3 Tbsp. (45 mL) canola oil

2 lbs. (1 kg) beef round steak and/or pork
   shoulder, cut into 1/4-inch (5-mm) cubes

2 cups (500 mL) chopped onion

4 cloves garlic, chopped

1 Tbsp. (15 mL) ground cumin

2 tsp. (10 mL) crushed hot chili pepper

2 19-oz. (540-mL) cans tomatoes, chopped

1/4 cup (50 mL) rye whiskey

1 Tbsp. (15 mL) oregano

1/4 cup (50 mL) tomato paste

2 cups (500 mL) cooked black or pinto beans
   (rinsed well if canned)

salt and freshly ground black pepper

1 Heat a heavy cast iron pan or griddle over medium-high heat. When the pan is hot, place the dried ancho chilies in the pan. Press down with a spatula for 5–10 seconds, until the chilies soften and release their aromas. Be careful not to scorch the chilies, but don't eliminate this step — it releases wonderful layers of flavor. Place the toasted chilies in a bowl and cover with very hot water. Let them soak for about 20 minutes. When soft, drain and chop, discarding the stems and seeds.

2 In a Dutch oven, heat the oil over medium-high heat and brown the meat in batches, removing it with a slotted spoon and setting it aside in a bowl as it's cooked. Don't overcrowd the pan. If you do, the meat won't caramelize and brown, it will stew in its own juice (not a disaster, but not as much flavor).

3 When the meat is all browned, reduce the heat to medium-low and add the onion and garlic. Sauté for 5 minutes, then stir in the chopped ancho chilies, cumin and crushed hot chili. Cook together for 5 minutes more.

4 Return the browned meat to the pan, and stir in the tomatoes, whiskey and oregano. Bring the chili to a boil, then cover the pot, reduce the heat to low and simmer for 1–2 hours, until the meat is very tender.

5 Stir in the tomato paste and beans. Remove the lid and continue to cook for another 15–30 minutes, until the chili is thickened nicely. Season to taste with salt and pepper. Serves 6–8.

Cornbread

The Girl has a great cast iron baking pan that makes cornbread into cob-shaped sticks — very funky alongside a big bowl of red (page 241). You can use a heavy muffin pan instead or even bake this bread in an 8–inch (20–cm) square pan, but a preheated cast iron pan creates cornbread with a lovely golden crust.

1 cup (250 mL) cornmeal
1/2 cup (125 mL) all-purpose flour
1 tsp. (5 mL) granulated sugar
2 tsp. (10 mL) baking powder
1/4 tsp. (1 mL) baking soda
1/2 tsp. (2 mL) salt
1/4 cup (50 mL) melted butter

1 egg, beaten
3/4 cup (175 mL) buttermilk
1/2 cup (125 mL) heavy cream
1/4 cup (50 mL) cooked corn kernels, whirled in the food processor to chop
1 jalapeño chili, seeded and minced

1 Preheat the oven to 450°F (230°C) and brush a heavy muffin pan with oil. If you have a cast iron pan, preheat it in the oven for 10 minutes.

2 In a large bowl, combine the cornmeal, flour, sugar, baking powder, baking soda and salt. In another bowl, combine the melted butter, egg, buttermilk and cream. Whisk to combine well. Stir the wet ingredients quickly into the dry, then fold in the corn and jalapeño. Don't overmix.

3 Remove the hot pan from the oven and spoon in the batter, filling each cup 3/4 full. Bake for 15 minutes, until golden and firm. Turn the cornbread out of the pan immediately and serve warm. Makes 1 dozen.

Valentine's Day

The day the card manufacturers designated as the most romantic day of the year has lived up to its crass commercial roots, as far as the Girl is concerned. Not only do you have to fight for a seat in a decent restaurant on Valentine's Day, you might just be rushed along and turned out early to accommodate the second seating.

It's far more romantic to plan a quiet evening together at home, shell out for a nice bottle of Champagne and snuggle up by the fire, feeding each other the kind of foods that make the perfect prelude to love.

There are several ideas here for romantic foods to include in a Valentine's Day menu, from starters like fresh oysters to side dishes like crispy potato puffs. Pick your favorites and enjoy the time together. You may choose to cook, or just indulge.

Romance on the Half Shell

If she could convince her significant other to shuck them, the Girl could live on oysters. Sweet, briny and low in calories, an oyster slurped fresh from the shell is one of life's true pleasures. A good, fresh oyster needs no cooking, no sauce, no preparation at all — just open and eat. And once you get the hang of shucking — popping the top shell off without leaving any gritty shell behind — serving fresh oysters at home is both impressive and as easy as a trip to the fish shop. Just follow these tips.

1 First, find a good fishmonger who imports and sells a lot of oysters. Ask where they came from, what variety they are, and ask to see the tag that shows when they were harvested. Properly stored — cups down to prevent the liquor from leaking out — a live oyster can live at least 10 days out of the ocean. When you pick them up, they should be heavy for their size, and will snap tightly shut if they're alive. Discard any that are not alive.

2 Remember, East Coast oysters are smoother, with deeper cups, and are easier to hold and shuck. West Coast oysters have the thinner, ruffled shells. Try different oysters from different waters — it's the microscopic wild food the oyster eats that gives it its unique flavors, from sweet cucumber to briny and flinty undertones.

3 To shuck an oyster properly, set it cup side down on a folded towel, insert a short-bladed shucking knife into the hinge at the pointy end, and twist to pop off the top, cutting the muscle away from the shell. Then loosen the meat from the bottom shell, being careful not to lose any of the liquor, and slurp it down. Don't just swallow an oyster, chew it to get all of the wonderful flavor.

4 The Girl likes her oysters naked, with no sauces or other embellishments. Some people like to add a drop of lemon juice or a drop of hot sauce – the citrus juice actually helps the oyster match better with a crisp wine – or even a mignonette sauce, which is just a little minced shallot, wine vinegar and pepper. French Champagne, Chablis or Sauvignon Blanc is a classic match with oysters, although some people also like fresh oysters with stout or cold saki.

5 Shuck your oysters just before serving and arrange them on a bed of crushed ice or rock salt (to prevent them from tipping over), garnished with lemon wedges. And don't feel guilty when you're eating oysters for Valentine's day — unlike chocolate, they are healthy and low in calories. An oyster contains only 7 calories, so feel free to indulge in a dozen or two.

Moules Marinière

Can you say Riviera? Buy a baguette (a real one) and some crisp white wine and dream about that romantic patio in Monte Carlo. A big bowl of mussels steamed in white wine can be ready to eat in five minutes, if you've got them prepped and ready. Use a crisp Sancerre or New Zealand Sauvignon Blanc in the recipe, and chill another one for sipping, then crank up Edith Piaf on the stereo and indulge. Works as a main dish or as an appetizer for a French bistro meal — pass the *pommes frites* with mayonnaise and fill a bowl with fresh figs for dessert.

2 lbs. (1 kg) large fresh mussels
3 Roma tomatoes, seeded and finely chopped
2 Tbsp. (25 mL) butter
1 Tbsp. (15 mL) extra virgin olive oil
2 shallots, minced

2 cloves garlic, minced
3 green onions, chopped
1 cup (250 mL) white wine
salt and freshly ground black pepper
2 Tbsp. (25 mL) chopped Italian parsley

1 Scrub the mussels well to remove sand and barnacles, and pull off the beards that are hanging outside the shells. If you buy cultured mussels, you can eliminate this step. Make sure the mussels are alive — if you rap them on the counter they should close. Any that don't are dead and should be pitched.

2 To seed the tomatoes, cut them in half across the middle and squeeze gently to remove the seeds. Chop the tomatoes into small cubes.

3 In a large pot or wok, heat the butter and olive oil over medium-high heat. Sauté the shallots and garlic for 5 minutes until soft. Add the green onion and tomato to the pan and sauté for 2 minutes. Add the wine and bring to a boil, then cook together for 2 minutes.

4 Add the mussels and cover the pan. Steam for 5 minutes, shaking the pan, until the mussels have opened. Discard any that don't open.

5 Season with salt and pepper and stir in the parsley. Divide the mussels and cooking liquid between two deep soup bowls. Serves 2 as a main dish with bread (or 4 as an appetizer).

Girl talk: Italian parsley is a lot more flavorful than the usual curly parsley you find in most supermarkets. It has a dark green, flat, jagged leaf — make sure it's parsley and not cilantro you're buying as these herbs look fairly similar. One whiff should tip you off. If you can't find the Italian kind, the curly kind is fine, just milder. When you buy a bunch of parsley, wash it in cold water, shake or spin it dry, and seal in a plastic bag with a paper towel. Your parsley (or other leafy herbs and greens) will stay fresh and crisp longer.

Seared Scallops in Champagne Sauce

Since you've probably already popped the cork, save some Champagne for this simple sauce. Steam some baby vegetables to serve on the side or make a nest of fresh angel hair pasta. Love at first bite and a complete meal for two.

sauce

3/4 cup (175 mL) brut (dry) Champagne

2 shallots, minced

2 Tbsp. (25 mL) whipping cream

1/4 cup (50 mL) cold butter, cut into small cubes

to finish

fresh angel hair pasta and/or steamed baby
  vegetables for two

1 tsp. (5 mL) butter

1 tsp. (5 mL) olive oil

3/4 lb. (375 g) large sea scallops

salt and white pepper

2 Tbsp. (25 mL) chopped chives

1 In a small saucepan, combine the Champagne and shallots and bring to a boil over high heat. Cook for 15–20 minutes, until the liquid has been reduced to only a tablespoon or two (15–30 mL). Remove from the heat, whisk in the whipping cream and the cubed 1/4 cup (50 mL) butter, a few cubes at a time. Return the pan to low heat and continue whisking until all the butter has been added. The sauce should emulsify — if it breaks (if melted butter separates from the sauce) remove from the heat and whisk in a little more cold butter.

2 Meanwhile, cook the pasta in plenty of boiling, salted water until *al dente*. Drain and keep warm.

3 Heat the teaspoon (5 mL) of butter and the olive oil in a heavy, nonstick pan over fairly high heat. Swirl it around and when the fat is really hot and bubbly, add the scallops. They should sizzle when they hit the pan. Sear until golden, about 2–3 minutes on each side, but don't overcook them. The scallops should be nearly rare inside and caramelized outside. Season with salt and pepper.

4 On two warm plates, arrange the seared scallops on a nest of hot pasta. Drizzle with the sauce and sprinkle with the chopped chives. Serves 2.

Baked Halibut with Tapenade Crust and Caponata

If you've taken the Girl's advice and put up some caponata in the freezer, you can be dining on this very chic black and white fish dish, with Mediterranean cachet, in less than 30 minutes. She helped a top chef prepare fish this way for a food and wine pairing event in Napa — just right with a crisp Sauvignon Blanc or unoaked Chardonnay. Nice with roasted potatoes (page 248) alongside or some creamy polenta (page 165).

¾ lb. (150 g) halibut fillet

⅓ cup (75 mL) pitted kalamata olives

1 Tbsp. (15 mL) extra virgin olive oil

1 cup (250 mL) caponata (page 274)

1 Preheat the oven to 325°F (160°C). Trim the edges of the halibut fillet to create an even piece, about 1 inch (2.5 cm) thick. Cut the fillet into two equal squares. Set the fish aside on a baking sheet lined with parchment.

2 In a blender, purée the olives with the olive oil to form a very smooth paste. Press through a fine sieve if necessary to remove any bigger bits.

3 Using a spatula or flexible knife, frost the top of each piece of fish with olive paste, keeping it even and clean on the edges.

4 Bake the fish for 10 minutes, until just barely cooked through. Meanwhile, heat the caponata. To serve, place some caponata in the center of each plate and balance a piece of fish on top. Serves 2.

Lamb Chops with Mustard Rub

Simple and really romantic (especially if he's in charge of the cooking). Find a good butcher and buy some fresh local lamb chops — two or three per person — and make sure they're cut about an inch (2.5 cm) thick. Serve with Mini Potato Puffs (below) and Balsamic Glazed Asparagus (page 135) or Asparagus Risotto (page 134). She'll swoon.

1 Tbsp. (15 mL) olive oil

1/4 tsp. (1 mL) sweet Spanish or Hungarian paprika

1 tsp. (5 mL) minced fresh rosemary

1 clove garlic, pressed or minced

1/4 cup (50 mL) Dijon or grainy mustard

4–6 lamb chops (about 1 lb./500 g in total)

1 Combine the oil, paprika, rosemary, garlic and mustard, and whisk well. Slather onto both sides of the lamb chops and let marinate at room temperature for 15 minutes.

2 Preheat the grill to medium-high or preheat the broiler. Grill or broil the chops for 2–3 minutes per side until nicely brown — they should be cooked rare to medium rare for the juiciest results. Serves 2.

Mini Potato Puffs

The Girl loves this simple technique for making crisp little potatoes. They're perfect alongside your lamb, or eat them as warm appetizers, topped with a dab of sour cream and a tiny spoonful of caviar. Just set out the cream and caviar and feed to your beloved, one precious mouthful at a time.

8–10 tiny new red potatoes

olive oil

sea salt

1 Scrub the potatoes and cut them in half (lengthwise if oval-shaped). Dry the potatoes on paper towels. Rub with olive oil all over, then sprinkle the cut sides generously with sea salt.

2 Preheat the oven to 475°F (250°C). Set the oven rack in the middle of the oven.

3 Put the potatoes on a rack, set on a baking sheet, and bake for 20 minutes. Raise the heat to 500°F (260°C) and bake for 5 minutes longer. The potatoes should brown and puff up. Serve immediately. Serves 2.

Just Bring a Salad

How often does the Girl hear those four fateful words?

If it's Saturday and summer, it must be time to make another salad.

Whether it's the office party, the family reunion or just a friendly potluck,
more often than not the host will say, "just bring a salad." Herewith,
some tried and true portable combinations that will win you the
title of head salad girl.

Potluck Pasta Salad

This simple pasta salad with Mediterranean overtones is pure potluck — the kind of salad to take to the office picnic. In fact, The Girl has done it often. Use any short pasta, but keep a lookout for *fusilli corti bucati* — a cool corkscrew pasta reminiscent of a telephone cord.

dressing

2 Tbsp. (25 mL) red wine vinegar
1 Tbsp. (15 mL) fresh lemon juice
1 Tbsp. (15 mL) Dijon mustard
2 tsp. (10 mL) Worcestershire sauce
1 tsp. (5 mL) granulated sugar
1/2 tsp. (2 mL) salt

1/4 tsp. (1 mL) freshly ground black pepper
2 cloves garlic, chopped
1/2 cup (125 mL) extra virgin olive oil
2 Tbsp. (25 mL) minced parsley
2 Tbsp. (25 mL) basil pesto or minced fresh basil

salad

3 cups (750 mL) short Italian pasta (fusilli,
   small shells, rotini or radiatore)
1 1/2 cups (375 mL) cooked kidney beans
1 1/2 cups (375 mL) cooked chickpeas
1 cup diced (250 mL) yellow bell pepper

1/2 cup (125 mL) sliced black olives
3 large plum tomatoes, seeded and chopped
1/2 red onion, diced
salt and freshly ground black pepper

1 In the food processor, combine the vinegar, lemon juice, mustard, Worcestershire sauce, sugar, salt, pepper and garlic. Process until well combined. With the machine running, slowly pour in the olive oil through the feed tube. Add the parsley and pesto or basil and process until smooth. Set the dressing aside.

2 Cook the pasta in a large pot of boiling salted water until *al dente*, about 8–10 minutes. Rinse under cold running water and drain well, shaking to remove any excess water. In a large bowl, toss the pasta, kidney beans, chickpeas and dressing. Add the yellow peppers, olives, tomatoes and red onion. Chill well. Season with salt and pepper to taste. Serves 8.

SaLaD

The Girl's Perfect Potato Salad

This salad works all year round but not like it does when the first summer veggies appear at the market. With baby new potatoes, fresh peas, radishes and dill, this potato salad is sublime, and simple. A keeper.

2 lbs. (1 kg) small new potatoes, scrubbed

¼ cup (50 mL) reduced-fat mayonnaise

¼ cup (50 mL) low-fat sour cream or plain yogurt

2 tsp. (10 mL) Dijon mustard

1 Tbsp. (15 mL) chopped fresh dill (or
   1 tsp./5 mL dried dill, in a pinch)

1 Tbsp. (15 mL) fresh lemon juice

salt and freshly ground black pepper

½ cup (125 mL) finely chopped celery

2–3 green onions, chopped

6 radishes, sliced

½ cup (125 mL) freshly shelled green peas,
   in season

1 Put a steamer basket in a large saucepan and add about 2 inches (5 cm) of water. Put the potatoes in the steamer basket and steam until tender, about 15–20 minutes. Cool and cut into large cubes.

2 In a bowl, whisk together the mayonnaise, sour cream or yogurt, mustard, dill, lemon juice, salt and pepper. Add the warm chunks of potato to the bowl, and toss with the dressing to coat. Add the celery, green onions, radishes and peas and fold gently to combine, being careful not to break up the potatoes (the Girl hates mushy potato salads).

3 Serve immediately as a warm potato salad or chill for several hours. For a more substantial salad, add a few hard-boiled eggs, chopped. Instead of the shelled peas, you can use chopped edible pod peas or lightly-steamed green beans, cut into small pieces. Makes 6 servings.

In Praise of Sturdy Salads

If you've been out on the potluck summer barbecue circuit lately, you'll know that eight out of every ten salads plunked on the picnic table will be potato.

The reason people bring potato salads is that they are sturdy. Sturdy salads can be made in advance, they travel well and they look good for hours on the buffet. But eight potato salads and a token tabouli do not a potluck make, so get creative when you bring a salad.

For potluck buffets, think about salads based on pasta, rice, grains and the kind of stand-up veggies you find on vegetable trays (things like carrots, cauliflower, broccoli, green onions, cucumbers, zucchini, radishes, etc.). Don't even contemplate a tossed salad unless you're doing the salad course and can toss and compose your salad right before it's served.

For other portable salad ideas see the black bean and brown rice salad (page 277), the Japanese Cold Noodle Salad (page 25) or the couscous salad (page 26).

The Big Green

When fresh lettuces are available at the market (or from the garden) the Girl likes to combine as many as possible for this fresh bowl of summer flavor. Leaf lettuce, baby turnip greens and romaine all complement each other nicely, offering both flavor and texture contrasts and taking a plain green salad into serious gourmet territory. If you can get some watercress or arugula it will give your salad a nice peppery bite, or pick some nasturtium leaves from the flower bed for a similar zing. While you can add anything to a green salad (or nothing at all), it's easy to tote with some chopped green onions, pea shoots and pine nuts balanced on top. Add the sliced pears and avocados with the dressing at the last minute and toss. This salad is comfortable among others on a buffet or individually plated for a fancier dinner.

dressing

1/4 cup (50 mL) orange juice
1 tsp. (5 mL) lemon juice

salt and freshly ground black pepper
4 Tbsp. (50 mL) extra virgin olive oil

salad

8 cups (2 L) mixed salad greens
1 ripe pear (regular or Asian)
1 avocado
1 tsp. (5 mL) lemon juice

2 cups (500 mL) pea shoots (optional but often found at Asian markets)
3 green onions, finely chopped
1/3 cup (75 mL) toasted pine nuts

1 Whirl the dressing ingredients together in a blender to emulsify or combine in a small jar and shake like crazy. Set aside.

2 Wash the greens well in a sink full of cold water and spin dry in a salad spinner. If not using right away, pack loosely in a plastic bag with a piece of paper towel, seal and refrigerate for several hours or overnight. This will insure your salad is crisp.

3 If you're serving immediately, core the pear and slice it very thin, leaving the skin on, and then cut into flat batons or 1–inch (2–cm) squares. Peel the avocado, and cut into thin slices or slivers. Toss the avocado with the lemon juice to prevent it from discoloring. (If you're transporting this salad, don't slice the pear and avocado in advance – do it when you're ready to serve.)

4 Pick out a large, pretty salad bowl and fill with the mixed greens. Toss to combine well. Top with pea shoots, green onions and pine nuts. If you're taking it somewhere, stop at this point. When you're ready to serve, add the pear and avocado, drizzle with the dressing and toss. Serves 6.

Girl talk: There are a couple of decent — but rare — commercial salad dressings out there. The Girl has a standby, from a small local producer, that she keeps in the fridge. But learn to make your own salad dressing and you'll never go back to over-processed supermarket salad dressing. See pages 333–335 for some instant inspiration.

Green Goddess Caesar Salad

You'll be a goddess with this piquant version of traditional green goddess salad dressing. Serve it over a big bowl of romaine, or try it with shredded cabbage and carrot coleslaw. This is the one to serve when beefy burgers are on the menu. Toss it together just before serving.

dressing

1 bunch cilantro, washed and stems removed
   (about 1 cup/250 mL)
2 Tbsp. (25 mL) chopped garlic
2 Tbsp. (25 mL) jalapeño pepper
2 Tbsp. (25 mL) white wine vinegar or lemon juice

2 Tbsp. (25 mL) Dijon mustard
1/2 tsp. (2 mL) salt
1 1/2 cups (375 mL) commercial mayonnaise,
   regular or low fat
1/2 cup (125 mL) plain yogurt or sour cream

salad

1 bunch romaine lettuce, washed and torn into
   bite-sized pieces
1 cup (250 mL) homemade croutons (see below)

1/2 cup (125 mL) freshly grated aged white Cheddar
   or Parmesan cheese

1 For the dressing, combine all the ingredients in a food processor and purée until smooth. Transfer to a clean jar or covered container and refrigerate. It makes 2 cups (500 mL), more than you'll need for one salad, but it keeps for a week in the refrigerator.

2 To assemble the salad, place the lettuce in a large bowl. Toss with just enough of the dressing to coat. Add the croutons and grated cheese and toss again. Serve immediately. Serves 6.

Girl talk: To make spicy homemade croutons for this salad, cut day-old French or sourdough bread into 3/4–inch (2–cm) cubes. Place about 2 cups (500 mL) of the bread cubes in a large bowl and drizzle with 2–3 Tbsp. (25–45 mL) olive oil. Season with 1/2 tsp. (2 mL) each of ground cumin and oregano, and 1 tsp. (5 mL) of minced garlic (or a little garlic powder). Toss to coat the bread cubes with oil and seasonings, then place the croutons on a cookie sheet and toast in a 400°F (200°C) oven for 10–15 minutes, until golden and crisp. Season with a little salt and set aside to cool. Croutons keep well in a plastic bag at room temperature.

East West Shrimp and Rice Salad

This salad — another standout for the summer potluck circuit — is reminiscent of the bowls of noodles and fresh vegetables served at Asian noodle houses. A very stylish salad to make and take.

dressing

4 Tbsp. (50 mL) canola oil
1 Tbsp. (15 mL) toasted sesame oil
2 cloves garlic, minced
2 Tbsp. (25 mL) lime juice
1 Tbsp. (15 mL) soy sauce

1 Tbsp. (15 mL) Asian fish sauce
$^1/_3$ cup (75 mL) chopped fresh cilantro (or 2 Tbsp./
  25 mL corinander chutney)
1 Tbsp. (15 mL) Thai red curry paste
1 Tbsp. (15 mL) brown sugar

salad

$^3/_4$ lb. (375 g) fresh asparagus, cut into
  1–inch (2.5–cm) lengths
1 Tbsp. (15 mL) canola oil
1/2 lb. (250 g) fresh shiitake or portabello
  mushrooms, sliced and slivered
3–4 cups (750 mL–1 L) cooked and chilled basmati
  rice or long grain white rice

4 green onions, chopped
1 cup (250 mL) salad shrimp (cooked)
1 cup (250 mL) fresh bean sprouts
1 cup (250 mL) shredded red bell peppers
$^1/_4$ cup (50 mL) chopped roasted peanuts

1 Whirl the dressing ingredients together in a food processor until smooth. The dressing may be made a day in advance and refrigerated.

2 For the salad, place the asparagus in a bowl with 3 Tbsp. (45 mL) of water. Cover with plastic wrap and microwave on high for 2 minutes, until just lightly steamed. Rinse under cold water to chill. Drain well and place in a salad bowl.

3 Heat the oil in a nonstick skillet and sauté the mushrooms until brown and tender, about 2–3 minutes. Set the mushrooms aside to cool, then add to the salad bowl. Add the rice to the bowl. Stir in the onions (reserving a few for garnish), shrimp, bean sprouts and peppers. Toss the salad with the dressing. Sprinkle with chopped peanuts and reserved green onions just before serving. Serves 8–10.

Israeli Couscous Salad

Couscous is the Girl's best friend — the small-grain couscous practically cooks itself. The larger, Israeli couscous requires a little more prep — but your foodie friends will love the cachet of this artisan, hand-rolled semolina pasta that boils up into toothsome pearls that stand up well in cold salads. Here's one to take when you want to show up with a salad and a story.

2¹⁄₂ cups (625 mL) chicken broth
1 cup (250 mL) Israeli couscous (the large,
    pea-sized dried pasta available at Middle Eastern
    markets and health food stores)
2 Tbsp. (25 mL) extra virgin olive oil
3 green onions, chopped

1 whole roasted red bell pepper, chopped
    (freshly roasted and peeled or from a jar)
1 cup (250 mL) chickpeas (optional)
1 Tbsp. (15 mL) fresh lemon juice
freshly ground black pepper

1 Bring the broth to a boil, add the couscous, cover and reduce the heat to medium-low. Simmer for 15–20 minutes, until the couscous is *al dente* — tender but still firm. Remove from the heat and let stand, covered, for 20 minutes to steam.

2 Place the couscous in a salad bowl. Stir in 1 Tbsp. (15 mL) of the olive oil, and toss until cool. Add the remaining olive oil, green onion, roasted pepper and chickpeas, if using, and stir gently to combine. Season with lemon juice and black pepper. Serve at room temperature. Serves 4–6.

GARDEN
FRESH

seasonal

K. HOREL

The Duty Dinner
(Big Vegetarian Buffet)

Duty calls — a buffet dinner for the local do-gooders.

Expected to cook for the zoo docents or the volunteers from the community
association and want to go animal-neutral, just to be safe? Try this Greek-style
feast — the kind of delicious vegetarian foods they eat in Athens during their many
fast days. You'll never miss the meat, and you can even pass out these easy
homestyle recipes to create a themed potluck buffet.

Add a cheese pie (page 74) to stretch this supper and feed more friends. Finish with
a plate of baklava from the local bakery or the orange honey cake (page 304).

Spicy Whipped Feta

This is a simple spread to serve as an appetizer with crackers or pita bread. Try it to start a Greek meal or whenever you want something fast and flavorful, or use it as a topping for baked potatoes.

½ lb. (250 g) feta cheese
2–3 long green chili peppers (Anaheim or
  Hungarian), seeded and chopped

⅓ cup (75 mL) extra virgin Greek olive oil
3–4 Tbsp. (45–50 mL) fresh lemon juice

1 Crumble the feta and combine with the remaining ingredients in a food processor. Pulse until blended. Refrigerate at least 1 hour before serving with toasts or pita chips (page 214).

Zucchini Fritters

In Greece, these addictive crisp fritters are passed with drinks. No, they're not low in fat, but the Girl was smitten on first bite. You will be, too.

1½ lbs. (750 g) zucchini or other summer squash,
  unpeeled and shredded
1 tsp. (5 mL) salt
½ cup (125 mL) extra virgin olive oil, divided
1 large onion, minced
1 clove garlic, minced

2 large eggs, lightly beaten
½ cup (125 mL) breadcrumbs
½ lb. (250 g) feta cheese, crumbled
3 Tbsp. (45 mL) chopped fresh dill
½ cup (125 mL) all-purpose flour
salt and freshly ground black pepper

1 In a colander, toss the shredded zucchini and salt. Set aside to drain in the sink for 1 hour, then place the zucchini in a clean dishtowel and squeeze to remove excess moisture.

2 Heat 2 Tbsp. (25 mL) of the oil over medium heat in a nonstick frying pan. Sauté the onion and garlic for 10 minutes, until soft.

3 Combine the zucchini and onion in a bowl. Add the eggs, breadcrumbs, feta, dill and flour. Season with salt and pepper. You should have a thick batter — add more flour or breadcrumbs if necessary.

4 Heat the remaining oil in a nonstick pan over medium-high heat. Drop the batter into the hot oil, 1 Tbsp. (15 mL) at a time, and fry in batches until the fritters are brown and crisp on both sides. Drain on paper towels and serve warm. (The fritters may be made in advance, cooled and crisped on a cookie sheet in a 400°F/200°C oven.) Makes about 30 fritters.

My Big Fat Greek Beans

This is the Girl's version of a vegetarian dish found in little tavernas all over Athens. You can buy the huge, white "gigante" beans — as big as your thumb — in Greek groceries. They're worth searching for as they're lovely and meaty when cooked, but you can make this dish with extra large dried lima or butter beans, too. Try to use the fresh dill — it makes a difference — and don't stint on the olive oil. It's healthy and gives this dish the richness it needs.

$^3/_4$ lb. (375 g) large gigante beans or
   extra large dried lima or butter beans
2 Tbsp. (25 mL) chopped flat-leaf parsley
1 Tbsp. (15 mL) chopped fresh dill (or
   1$^1/_2$ tsp./7 mL dried dill weed)
1 large onion
1 stalk celery
2 carrots, peeled

2 cloves garlic
$^1/_3$–$^1/_2$ cup (75–125 mL) virgin olive oil
1 14-oz. (398–mL) can tomatoes, puréed
   in the blender
1 tsp. (5 mL) dried oregano
$^1/_2$ tsp. (2 mL) honey
salt and freshly ground black pepper

1 Soak the beans in water overnight. Drain and rinse. Place the beans in a saucepan and cover with plenty of fresh cold water. Bring to a boil and simmer for 30–40 minutes, until the beans are barely tender but still firm. Drain and toss with the parsley and dill. Arrange the beans in a shallow baking dish. Preheat the oven to 325°F (160°C).

2 If you have a food processor, use it to finely chop the onion, celery, carrots and garlic. Cut everything into chunks and pulse until it's all nicely minced. Or mince by hand.

3 Heat the olive oil in a large skillet and sauté the onion, celery, carrot and garlic over medium heat for 10 minutes. Stir in the puréed tomatoes and oregano and simmer for 10 minutes. Stir in the honey and season with salt and pepper.

4 Pour the vegetable sauce over the beans and stir gently to combine. Bake for 60 to 90 minutes, until the beans are glazed with the sauce and tender. Serves 4.

Wilted Spinach with Rice

This is a popular Lenten dish in Greece but it's a great way to "get your greens" all year round. In spring, when young bitter greens like dandelions, mustard and sorrel are available, substitute them for some, or all, of the spinach, as they do in the Greek countryside.

2 lbs. (500 g) fresh spinach
½ cup (125 mL) extra virgin Greek olive oil
2 onions, minced
3 cloves garlic, minced
1 cup (250 mL) basmati or other long grain rice
1 cup (250 mL) water or vegetable broth

¼ cup (50 mL) minced fresh dill or
 fennel fronds, divided
juice of 1 lemon
salt and freshly ground black pepper
pinch crushed red chili peppers
lemon slices, olives and crumbled feta to garnish

1 Wash the spinach well and remove any tough stems. Shred the spinach and set it aside.

2 Heat the olive oil in a heavy, deep pot and cook the onions over medium heat until translucent. Add the garlic and cook for 1 minute longer, being careful not to burn the garlic.

3 Add the rice and stir to coat the grains with oil. Cook for 2 minutes. Add the spinach and stir to combine. When the spinach is starting to wilt and cook down, add the water or broth and half the dill or fennel. Bring to a boil, reduce the heat to low and cover. Steam until all the liquid is absorbed, about 20 minutes, adding a little more water if necessary. Stir in the lemon juice and remaining dill or fennel. Season with salt, pepper and crushed chilies to taste. Drizzle with a little more olive oil before serving, and garnish with lemon slices, olives and crumbled feta, if desired. Serves 4–6.

Artichokes and Potatoes Braised in Olive Oil

Artichokes appear in the spring in Greece. If fresh baby artichokes aren't available, use canned artichoke hearts in this rich and satisfying vegetarian stew. If you start with large, fresh artichokes, you'll have to be more ruthless about removing the tough outer leaves.

2 cups (500 mL) cold water
1 lemon, halved
12 small artichokes
1/3 cup (75 mL) virgin Greek olive oil
1 small onion, thinly sliced
2 medium carrots, peeled and chopped
2 Tbsp. (25 mL) fresh lemon juice
2 cups (500 mL) water or broth

1 lb. (500 g) small new potatoes, cut into
   chunks
1 lb. (500 g) fresh peas (or frozen, thawed)
1/4 cup (50 mL) chopped fresh dill
3 green onions, chopped
3 Tbsp. (45 mL) chopped fresh mint
salt and freshly ground black pepper

1 Place the water in a bowl and squeeze the lemon into it. Using kitchen shears, trim the points from the tough outer leaves of the artichokes. Slice off the tough part of the stem. Cut the artichokes into quarters, lengthwise, and remove the fuzzy choke (the fuzzy stuff and some of the tiny interior leaves). Place the artichokes in the acidified water to prevent browning.

2 Heat the olive oil in a large sauté pan and sauté the onion for 5 minutes. Add the carrot and sauté for 2 minutes, then stir in the lemon juice and water or broth. Bring to a boil. Drain the artichokes and add them to the pan, along with the potatoes. Cover and simmer over medium-low heat for 45 minutes, until the artichokes are tender. Add the peas and continue to simmer for 5 minutes longer. Stir in the fresh dill, green onions and mint, and season with salt and pepper. Serves 6.

 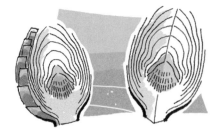 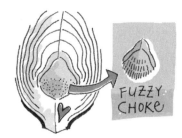

FUZZY CHOKE

Mother's Day and Other Biggie Brekkies.

There are some days of the year when a piece of toast and a bowl of cereal just won't cut it for breakfast. Special mornings (think Christmas morning, Mother's Day, etc.) require special efforts. Sometimes breakfast in bed is the way to go — other times it's a full-on brunch party for 10 with Champagne and orange juice and all of the trimmings. There are lots of breakfast items to mix and match here. Go big or stay simple. You decide.

Blueberry and Cornmeal Flapjacks

These simple corncakes filled with fresh berries are not only gorgeous with their golden color, they're addictive. If you don't have blueberries, try raspberries, and don't forget to pass the maple syrup.

½ cup (125 mL) stone-ground cornmeal
½ cup (125 mL) boiling water
½ cup (125 mL) all-purpose flour
1 Tbsp. (15 mL) baking powder
1 Tbsp. (15 mL) brown sugar

pinch salt
1 egg
¼ cup (50 mL) melted butter
¼ cup (50 mL) milk
1 cup (250 mL) fresh or frozen blueberries

1   Combine the cornmeal and boiling water and stir well. Cool.

2   In another bowl, combine the flour, baking powder, sugar and salt. Whisk together the egg, melted butter and milk and add to the cornmeal, alternately with the dry ingredients. Stir well.

3   Heat a nonstick pan over medium-high heat and brush with a little canola oil. Reduce the heat to medium and spoon the batter into the pan, forming several 3–inch (8–cm) pancakes. Scatter a handful of berries over the top of each flapjack, pressing lightly into the batter.

4   When the pancakes start to brown around the edges and bubbles break on the surface, they're ready to flip. Turn and cook the second side until golden, about 1 minute longer. Makes about 10 pancakes.

Late Summer Garlic and Greens Pie

This crustless quiche is colorful and healthy — perfect for breakfast with friends when you've gathered at the lake for that last long weekend of summer, and the garden is producing its bounty of greens, herbs and zucchini. Vegetarian heaven.

1 lb. (500 g) Swiss chard
1/2 lb. (250 g) arugula or mustard greens
1/4 cup (50 mL) virgin olive oil, divided
1 medium zucchini, shredded
2 cloves garlic, minced
2 cups (500 mL) sliced leeks or chopped yellow
   onion
1 cup (250 mL) minced celery
1/2 yellow bell pepper, chopped

salt and freshly ground black pepper
1/2 cup (125 mL) chopped fresh herbs (basil,
   parsley, thyme, etc.)
4 large eggs
1/2 cup (125 mL) heavy cream
1/2 cup (125 mL) grated Parmesan, divided
1/4 cup (50 mL) grated Swiss cheese
1/4 cup (50 mL) fresh breadcrumbs
2 tsp. (10 mL) olive oil

1 Remove the stems from the chard. Chop the stems and set aside. Roll the chard leaves tightly and slice into thin shreds. Repeat with the remaining greens.

2 Heat 2 Tbsp. (25 mL) of the oil in a large nonstick sauté pan. Cook the shredded greens and zucchini over medium-high heat until tender and most of the liquid is gone, about 10 minutes. Remove from the pan and set aside in a strainer to drain. Place in a large bowl.

3 Add the remaining oil to the pan and cook the chard stems, garlic, leek or onion, celery and bell pepper until tender, about 10–15 minutes. Season with salt and pepper and transfer to the bowl with the greens. Stir in the chopped fresh herbs. Preheat the oven to 350°F (180°C).

4 In another bowl, whisk the eggs with the cream and half the Parmesan. When the vegetables have cooled slightly, stir in the egg mixture.

5 Pour the mixture into an oiled, shallow 10–inch (25–cm) round gratin pan. Combine the remaining Parmesan, Swiss cheese, breadcrumbs and the 2 tsp. (10 mL) of olive oil in a bowl. Sprinkle over top. Bake for 45 minutes, or until the pie is set and browned. Let stand 10 minutes before cutting into wedges. Serves 6.

GRATIN DISH

Mother's Day Apple Cinnamon Strata

This strata is like an upside-down bread pudding, and the fruit, eggs, bread and milk make it a perfect dish to serve for breakfast. It's easy to make the night before a special morning like Mother's Day or any time you want an impressive and easy brunch dish. It also makes a fine home-style dessert, with a dollop of vanilla yogurt or ice cream and a dusting of cinnamon.

4 Tbsp. (50 mL) butter

2 large baking apples, peeled, cored and sliced

$1/2$ cup (125 mL) dark brown sugar, packed

2 Tbsp. (25 mL) maple syrup

1 tsp. (5 mL) cinnamon

8 slices rich egg bread or brioche

3 large eggs

1 cup (250 mL) milk

1 tsp. (5 mL) pure vanilla extract

$1/4$ cup (50 mL) chopped walnuts, toasted

1 Grease a shallow, pretty, 10–inch (25–cm) round tart dish or cake pan. Melt the butter in a sauté pan over medium heat and cook the apples until almost tender. Add the brown sugar, maple syrup and cinnamon and continue to cook until the sugar dissolves and the apples are beginning to caramelize. Pour into the baking pan, overlapping the apple slices artfully in a single layer.

2 Arrange the bread slices over the apples, overlapping them in concentric circles to cover the dish completely. Beat the eggs with the milk and vanilla and drizzle over the bread, soaking each piece. Cover the pan with plastic wrap. Find a plate that just fits inside the dish and invert it over top. Place the strata in the refrigerator overnight, topped with a weight (a can of soup or beans will do). This insures the strata is evenly compressed and all the bread is submerged in the milk mixture.

3 The next morning, preheat the oven to 400°F (200°C).

4 Remove the plastic wrap from the baking pan. Bake the strata for 30 minutes, or until the bread layer is firm and golden. Let cool for 10 minutes. Place a large serving platter over the baking pan and flip so the apple layer is on top. Remove the baking pan to reveal the apple layer. Sprinkle liberally with toasted walnuts. Cut into wedges to serve. Serves 6.

Healthy Breakfast Parfait

Layers of fruit, yogurt and granola make perfect parfaits for a holiday breakfast or brunch. Layer the ingredients in tall champagne glasses and make sure to include long-handled parfait spoons on the table. Très chic!

2 cups (500 mL) lemon yogurt
2 cups (500 mL) diced fresh fruit
  (strawberries, kiwi, cranberries, pears, etc.)

2 cups (500 mL) granola (homemade, page 93, or
  store-bought)

1 Starting from the bottom of a parfait or tall champagne glass, layer the yogurt, diced fruit and granola yogurt. Repeat twice. Garnish with a sprig of fresh mint. Makes 4–6 parfaits.

Fresh Fruit Salad

Choose whatever fruits are in season for your fruit salad. A little sugar and a splash of brandy always add a shot of flavor. Look for a good-quality lemon yogurt (a full-fat Mediterranean style made with lemon curd is best) and serve the fruit salad in pretty glass dishes, for breakfast or even dessert.

3–4 cups (750 mL–1 L) mixed chopped fresh fruit
  (peaches, orange segments, strawberries,
  blueberries, melon cubes, pears, etc.)

2 Tbsp. (25 mL) granulated sugar
1 Tbsp. (15 mL) Grand Marnier or apple brandy
  lemon yogurt and mint leaves for garnish

1 Combine the fresh fruit, sugar and brandy in a large bowl and set aside for 30 minutes. Stir to combine well. Serve in individual dessert dishes, topped with a little lemon yogurt and a sprig of fresh mint. Serves 4–6.

Girl talk: To section an orange, start by cutting a slice off the top and bottom of a large orange. Set the orange on the cutting board and slice away the peel, cutting through to expose the flesh. Then, holding the orange in one hand over a bowl, use a paring knife to cut the sections from the orange, slicing between the membranes to release the flesh only. Place the sections in the bowl with any accumulated juice and discard the peel and membrane. This is the best way to create orange or grapefruit sections for fruit salads or other dishes.

ORANGE

Gingerbread Waffles with Cinnamon Apples

Drizzled with maple syrup or topped with caramelized cinnamon apples, these rich waffles are perfect Christmas morning fare. Or make the waffles for "dessert" at your next summer brunch, topped with fresh fruit and lemon yogurt.

cinnamon apples

3 Tbsp. (45 mL) butter

3 apples, peeled and cut into wedges

1/4 cup (50 mL) dark brown sugar

1/4 tsp. (1 mL) ground cinnamon

1 Tbsp. (15 mL) brandy

waffles

2 cups (500 mL) all-purpose flour

1/2 tsp. (2 mL) salt

1 tsp. (5 mL) ground ginger

1 tsp. (5 mL) ground cinnamon

3 Tbsp. (45 mL) brown sugar

pinch nutmeg

1/2 cup (125 mL) canola oil (or
   melted butter for richer-tasting waffles)

1/4 cup (50 mL) molasses

1 Tbsp. (15 mL) baking powder

1 1/2 cups (375 mL) buttermilk or low-fat yogurt

2 eggs, separated

1 To make the cinnamon apples, heat the butter in a nonstick pan and sauté the apples over medium-high heat until they begin to soften. Add the sugar, cinnamon and brandy and cook until the apples are glazed and the sauce is thickened. Set aside and keep warm.

2 For the waffles, combine the flour, salt, ginger, cinnamon, sugar and nutmeg in a bowl. Set aside.

3 Whisk the oil (or melted butter) and molasses together in a larger bowl. Stir in the baking powder, and whisk in the buttermilk and egg yolks. Stir in the dry ingredients, a little at a time, and blend well. Beat the egg whites until stiff and gently fold into the batter (you can skip this step, but it really helps make the waffles light and crisp).

4 Preheat the waffle iron and brush with a little melted butter or canola oil. Cook the waffles until puffed and crisp. Serve with the cinnamon apples. Serves 4.

Four-Grain Flapjacks

Oats, corn, barley and wheat are combined in these hearty breakfast pancakes, perfect to top with fresh fruit or maple syrup. This is the pancake to make when you want to impress a crowd at your next backyard brunch or if your athletic gang needs some serious complex carbs to hold them until lunchtime. While you're flipping these flapjacks, get your sous-chef to grill some good breakfast sausages and pour the orange juice.

1 cup (250 mL) barley flour	pinch salt
1/2 cup (125 mL) whole-wheat flour	3 large eggs, separated
1/2 cup (125 mL) rolled oats	1/4 cup (50 mL) maple syrup (plus more for serving)
1/2 cup (125 mL) cornmeal	2 1/2 cups (625 mL) buttermilk or plain yogurt
1 1/2 tsp. (7 mL) baking soda	1/4 cup (50 mL) melted butter
1 tsp. (5 mL) baking powder	fresh blueberries or raspberries (optional)

1 In a large bowl, combine the barley flour, whole wheat flour, oats and cornmeal with the baking soda, baking powder and salt. In another bowl, whisk together the egg yolks, maple syrup, buttermilk or yogurt and melted butter. Beat the egg whites until stiff.

2 Stir the wet ingredients into the flour mixture, stirring to combine. Fold in the egg whites to lighten the batter.

3 Coat a nonstick pan or griddle lightly with vegetable oil spray and heat over medium heat. Ladle the batter onto the hot pan, making 5–inch (12–cm) flapjacks. For fresh berry flapjacks, scatter some blueberries or raspberries over the batter right after you ladle it into the skillet.

4 When big bubbles begin to break on the top of the flapjacks, turn them and quickly brown the second side. Serve them immediately with more maple syrup. Makes about 18–20 filling flapjacks.

Girl talk: If barley flour isn't available, try grinding a cup (250 mL) of barley flakes in the blender or food processor. Beating the egg whites separately results in super fluffy flapjacks — you should try it, you'll be amazed — but you can eliminate this step to save time and still have decent, if heavier, pancakes on the plate in 10 minutes.

The Perfect Omelet

Every Girl worth her stilettos should be able to whip up an omelet (for breakfast or whenever she decides to get out of bed). Fill it with leftovers and it's dinner.

3 eggs
1 tsp. (5 mL) cold water
salt and freshly ground black pepper

minced fresh herbs (optional)
1 Tbsp. (15 mL) butter (or tasty olive oil)
grated cheese (optional)

1 In a small bowl, beat the eggs with water using a fork or a whisk. Season with salt and pepper. Add finely chopped herbs if you're having a herb omelet.

2 Heat an 8–inch (20–cm) nonstick pan over medium heat and add the butter. Melt it quickly, but don't let it brown. Pour in the eggs. The egg mixture should sizzle and start to cook as soon as it hits the pan. Use a fork to scramble up the center a bit, and push the cooked bits away from the edges of the pan slightly, just enough to let the runny stuff fill up the space. You can do this again if you like, or poke the center a few times to let the uncooked egg run underneath.

3 When the eggs are set on the bottom, shake the pan or lift the edges carefully to loosen the omelet. The eggs should be almost set on top but not quite — the runny stuff will finish cooking when you fold it over.

4 If you're filling your omelet, add some cheese (or bits of cooked ham, mushrooms and chopped tomato, green onions or leftover curry — whatever you like) along the middle axis, at right angles to the handle. Then slide the omelet away from you onto the plate, flipping the handle up to fold the omelet over onto itself as it exits the pan. That's it. Omelet for one.

Spicy Breakfast Sausage

How to win friends and influence carnivores? Fry up some eggs and potatoes for a hungry man breakfast, with your own breakfast sausage on the side, spiced with the unique flavors of cumin and fennel. Add a hefty dash of cayenne pepper or Asian hot sauce if you prefer your breakfast with a little kick. Make small patties for breakfast, or use this ground meat mixture to make pork burgers for the barbie.

1 lb. (500 g) ground pork
1/2 lb. (250 g) ground beef
2 cloves garlic, minced
1/2 cup (125 mL) minced green onions
1 small sweet red pepper, minced

1 tsp. (5 mL) ground cumin
1/2 tsp. (2 mL) dried thyme
1/2 tsp. (2 mL) fennel seed
pinch cayenne
salt and freshly ground black pepper

1 Combine all the ingredients and mix well. Fry a small sample to taste and adjust the seasonings.

2 Form into small patties and fry in butter until well-browned on both sides. Serves 6.

Pan-Fried Potatoes

The night before a big breakfast, bake or boil a few extra potatoes and refrigerate them. They're perfect for frying up with eggs and sausage.

3 large potatoes, boiled or baked and chilled
2 Tbsp. (25 mL) butter
1 Tbsp. (15 mL) olive oil or bacon fat (from cooking your breakfast bacon)

1 small yellow onion, chopped
2 green onions, chopped
salt and freshly ground black pepper

1 Peel the cold potatoes or leave the skins on if they're thin. Cut the potatoes into quarters, then slice.

2 In a large, nonstick frying pan, heat the butter and oil over medium-high heat. Add the potatoes and yellow onion and fry until the potatoes are browned on one side. Turn and brown the second side. Continue to cook until the potatoes are nicely crisped. Just before serving, stir in the green onions and season with salt and pepper. Serves 4.

Breakfast Hash

This is the perfect hearty, one-dish, morning meal for the gang or the family. It has all of the Girl's favorite flavors — a mess of crispy roasted potatoes scrambled up with eggs and blanketed with gooey Cheddar cheese, and even some healthy veggies thrown in. Get someone to make the toast and you're done. Breakfast of champions.

3 lbs. (1.5 kg) new potatoes (small if possible)
3 Tbsp. (45 mL) olive oil, divided
1/2 tsp (2 mL) sweet Hungarian paprika
1/2 tsp. (2 mL) salt
1/2 tsp. (2 mL) dried thyme
1/2 tsp. (2 mL) oregano
pinch cayenne
1 large onion, chopped

2 cups (500 mL) sliced mushrooms
8 eggs, lightly beaten
salt and freshly ground black pepper
1 large tomato, seeded and chopped
4 green onions, chopped
1/2 lb. (250 g) fresh spinach, washed and shredded
1 cup (250 mL) grated aged Cheddar cheese

1 Cut the potatoes into 1–inch (2.5–cm) chunks. Boil in salted water for 5 to 7 minutes, just to partially cook them. Drain the potatoes and rinse with cold water.

2 Preheat the oven to 400°F (200°C). Return the potatoes to the pot, drizzle them with 2 Tbsp. (25 mL) of the olive oil and sprinkle with the paprika, salt, thyme, oregano and cayenne. Put the lid on the pot and shake — you don't want to break the potatoes but you want to rough up the edges a bit so they get nice and crispy in the oven.

3 Spread the potatoes on a baking sheet in a single layer and bake for 30–45 minutes, until golden. Spread the potatoes in a shallow, oven-proof casserole dish.

4 In a nonstick frying pan, heat the remaining olive oil over medium-high heat and sauté the onion until it begins to brown. Add the mushrooms and cook until soft. Spread the mushrooms and onion evenly over the potatoes.

5 In the same frying pan, over medium heat, scramble the eggs until they are partially cooked and just starting to set. Season the eggs with salt and pepper and spread in a layer over the casserole. Top with the tomato, green onions, spinach and grated cheddar. Bake for 10–15 minutes, until browned and bubbly. Serve immediately, straight from the oven, with toast. Serves 6.

Cinnamon Maple Monkey Bread

The Girl discovered frozen bread dough in the freezer section many years ago. It's the convenient way to have fresh-baked bread at home, create easy bread sticks and calzones (page 273) or make these almost instant sticky cinnamon buns for breakfast. Serve the monkey bread warm, and let your guests pull it apart into portions at the table.

2 loaves frozen bread dough (white)
1/3 cup (75 mL) butter
1/2 cup (125 mL) dark brown sugar
2 tsp. (10 mL) ground cinnamon

1/2 cup (125 mL) maple syrup, divided
1/2 cup (125 mL) chopped walnuts
1/2 cup (125 mL) raisins

1 Thaw the bread dough and cut each loaf into 16 pieces. Preheat the oven to 375°F (190°C).

2 In a small saucepan, melt the butter and stir in the brown sugar and cinnamon. Remove from the heat and set aside.

3 Butter a large, nonstick bundt pan and drizzle in 2 Tbsp. (25 mL) of the maple syrup. Roll the dough pieces into balls about the size of a walnut. Roll each ball in the cinnamon/sugar mixture and arrange in a layer over the syrup. Sprinkle with half of the walnuts, and half of the raisins, then drizzle with a little more syrup. Repeat until you've used up all of the dough, sugar mixture and syrup. Cover the pan with plastic and set in a warm place to rise for 40 minutes, until the bread is almost doubled in size.

4 Bake the bread for 45–55 minutes, or until the loaf has shrunk away from the sides of the pan. Cover it loosely with foil if the top seems to be browning too quickly. Turn out of the pan to cool slightly before serving. Serve warm. Makes 1 loaf.

Girl talk: You can also use this method to create a savory pull-apart bread that's lovely to serve with soups or stews. Just roll the balls of dough in melted butter or olive oil before layering with minced garlic, finely grated lemon zest and fresh minced herbs like rosemary, thyme or oregano.

Day Trippin':
Picnic and Trail Food

Lolling by a stream, noshing on elegant eats, blush wine chilling nearby — a recipe for romance or just a wonderful way to enjoy the summer season with family and friends.

When everyone's keen for a field trip, take along some fresh fruit like watermelon or strawberries, some cheese and crackers, and some cool portable dishes like these.

Take your pick from this collection — one dish for a small group, or more for a big family picnic in the park. Some of these dishes also work well in your backpack, when your picnic is part of a day hike or bike ride.

Don't forget the blanket, the corkscrew and the bug spray!

Calzones

Ahh, Napoli. Even when the Girl isn't on a Roman holiday, she likes to indulge in one of their famous pizza pockets, quite possibly the most perfect portable picnic food known to womankind. But these pockets are nothing like the deep-fried, gooey pastries from the supermarket freezer — the Girl's calzones are simple to make and healthy, filled with her favorite gourmet goodies. Carnivores can augment these vegetarian pies with cooked chicken, slivered prosciutto, Italian sausage or cold cuts.

1 Tbsp. (15 mL) olive oil
1 large onion, halved lengthwise and thinly sliced
1 large red bell pepper, seeded and slivered
1 small chili pepper, minced
3 cloves garlic, minced
2 Tbsp. (25 mL) chopped fresh basil
1 tsp. (5 mL) oregano
salt and freshly ground black pepper
6 sundried tomatoes, soaked in warm water to
   rehydrate, then drained and chopped

2 oz. (60 g) crumbled feta or shredded Parmesan
1 cup (250 mL) 1% cottage cheese or ricotta
1 14-oz. (398-mL) can artichokes, drained and
   chopped
⅓ cup (75 mL) chopped black olives
2 loaves frozen bread dough, thawed
   (whole-wheat)

1 Heat the olive oil in a nonstick pan over medium-low heat and slowly cook the onion until caramelized and golden, about 30 minutes.

2 Add the red pepper and chili pepper and cook for about 5 minutes or until tender. Stir in the garlic and cook 3 minutes longer. Remove the sautéed vegetables from the heat and stir in the basil, oregano, salt, pepper and sundried tomatoes. Set aside the filling to cool slightly, then stir in the feta or Parmesan, cottage cheese or ricotta, artichokes and olives.

3 Preheat the oven to 400°F (200°C). Cut each loaf of bread dough into 6 equal pieces. On a floured board, roll each piece into a 5-inch (12-cm) circle. Wet the edges. Fill with 3 Tbsp. (45 mL) of filling, fold the dough over top and press well to seal. Brush the calzones with milk and poke them with a fork to allow steam to escape during baking.

4 Set the calzones on a baking sheet that has been sprayed with cooking spray and sprinkled with cornmeal. Bake for 20 minutes, until brown. Cool on a rack. These freeze well. Makes 1 dozen.

Girl talk: These pockets of Italian flavor make great lunches — bake a bunch, freeze, then grab and go. They'll be thawed by noon and you can eat them cold or heat them in the microwave. Vary the filling according to what you like, adding chopped cooked Italian sausage, prosciutto or salami for meat lovers. They make great portable lunches for hiking or cycling because they don't get squished in your pack.

Caponata

Here's an addictive chunky condiment with roots in spicy Sicily to serve antipasto style. Pack it along with a loaf of crusty bread, like ciabatta, for a hearty snack on the trail, or toss it with hot pasta and shredded Parmesan cheese for an exquisite vegetarian entrée at the campsite. It's also wonderful spooned over a piece of grilled halibut or stirred into rice. The Girl likes to make caponata when eggplants, peppers and squash are available at the market in August — put it in jars or containers and freeze it for instant eating any time. Equally delicious hot or at room temperature.

2 lbs. (1 kg) eggplant, skin on, cut into cubes
1 lb. (500 g) zucchini or other summer
   squash, cubed
2 tsp. (10 mL) salt
1/2 cup (125 mL) extra virgin olive oil
1 large onion, chopped (about 2 cups/500 mL)
4 large cloves garlic, minced
1 red bell pepper, chopped
1 yellow bell pepper, chopped
1 14-oz. (398-mL) can Roma tomatoes,
   chopped or puréed

1 Tbsp. (15 mL) brown sugar
1/4 cup (50 mL) tomato paste
3 Tbsp. (45 mL) balsamic vinegar
1/2 cup (125 mL) black olives, pitted and chopped
2–3 Tbsp. (25–45 mL) chopped fresh basil or
   rosemary
salt and freshly ground black pepper
hot sauce (optional)

1 Put the eggplant and zucchini cubes in a colander. Toss with the salt and set in the sink to drain for half an hour. Rinse quickly and pat dry.

2 Heat the oil in a large sauté pan or Dutch oven over medium heat. Add the onion, garlic and peppers and sauté for 5 minutes. Add the eggplant and zucchini cubes and sauté for 5–10 minutes longer, until the mixture is beginning to soften. Stir in the tomatoes, cover the pan and cook together for 10 minutes. Remove the lid and continue to simmer until the vegetables are very soft and the liquid in the pan has been reduced, about 5 minutes longer.

3 Whisk the brown sugar, tomato paste and vinegar together. Add to the pan and mix well. Stir in the olives. Remove from the heat and add the fresh herbs. Season with salt and pepper (and a little hot sauce if you like it spicy).

4 Cool to room temperature and serve. Refrigerated in a covered container, caponata will keep for a week, or it may be frozen. Makes 6 cups (1.5 L).

Picnic Deviled eggs

Any girl can boil water and if you've got some eggs in there when it boils, you're halfway to deviled eggs. Everyone loves them and they're classic picnic finger food.

6 large eggs (a few days old are better than super fresh)
3 Tbsp. (45 mL) fat-reduced mayonnaise
1 Tbsp. (15 mL) fat-free sour cream
1/2 tsp. (2 mL) salt

1/4 tsp. (1 mL) freshly ground black pepper
1/2 tsp. (2 mL) dry mustard
1 Tbsp. (15 mL) minced fresh parsley
1 Tbsp. (15 mL) minced fresh chives

1 Place the eggs in a large pot where they will fit in a single layer. Cover them with cold water, deep enough to be about an inch (2.5–cm) above the eggs. Place the pot over medium-high heat and bring to a boil. Just as the water hits a full, rolling boil, remove the pot from the heat, cover and let stand 15 minutes. Drain the hot water and add cold tap water to cover the eggs. Throw in a few ice cubes to make sure the water gets really cold. Tap each egg on the wide end to crack the shell and put it back into the water to cool. Don't forget this step — the water will seep in under the shell and make the eggs infinitely easier to peel.

2 Peel the eggs and slice them in half lengthwise. Remove the yolks carefully and mash with the remaining ingredients, reserving a little parsley or chives for garnish.

3 Heap or pipe the filling back into the egg whites. If you want to take your deviled eggs on a picnic, transport the whites and filling separately. Put the halved eggs in a flat container and fill a resealable plastic bag with the yolk mixture. When you're ready to fill them, cut the corner off the plastic bag and pipe the filling back into the hard-cooked eggs. Makes 12.

Girl talk: Deviled eggs also make great party food. The Girl has a sleek white deviled egg dish to hold these simple creations for home parties — top each egg with a bit of chopped smoked salmon or caviar and a sprig of fresh dill and you're into the big leagues. Or set them atop a green salad drizzled with buttermilk dressing (mayonnaise thinned with a little buttermilk) and invite a couple of girlfriends to lunch. Buy free-range eggs from chickens fed only vegetable feed — the taste and color are far superior.

Speedy Smoked Salmon Rolls

This is the best way to parlay that inexpensive hot smoked salmon from the supermarket fish counter into a tasty and pretty pink spread. You can just tote the spread along with zucchini spears, water crackers or other veggies for dipping, or wrap it up in these colorful and portable tortilla rolls. Cut them after you've found the perfect picnic spot.

4 oz. (125 g) hot smoked salmon pieces
1/2 lb. (250 g) low-fat cream cheese
1/4 cup (50 mL) low-fat sour cream
2 chopped green onions
1/4 cup (50 mL) chopped parsley or
   other fresh herbs

salt and freshly ground pepper
4 large flour tortillas (plain, whole-wheat or
   spinach)
2 cups (450 mL) chopped watercress leaves,
   arugula or romaine lettuce

1 Process the salmon, cream cheese and sour cream in a food processor until you have a smooth spread. Add the green onions, parsley, salt and pepper and pulse to chop and combine (but don't purée). Chill.

2 Lay the tortillas on the counter and spread with a thick layer of salmon spread. Sprinkle 1/2 cup (125 mL) of chopped greens over the bottom two-thirds of each tortilla. The watercress and arugula have a nice peppery flavor that are especially nice with salmon, but you can use regular lettuce, too. Roll the tortillas up tightly (the spread at the top edge should help seal the roll). Wrap each roll tightly in plastic wrap and refrigerate for several hours or overnight.

3 When you're ready to serve, use a serrated knife to cut the rolls into 1–inch (2.5–cm) pieces. Serves 4–6.

Roasted Chicken, Black Bean and Brown Rice Salad

This is a hearty southwestern-inspired salad that you can make with leftover chicken or roasted chicken from the supermarket deli. It stands up well to transporting, and makes a great cold main dish straight from the cooler. Or you can skip the chicken and serve it as a tasty side to any grilled meat or fish.

2 cups (500 mL) water

1 cup (250 mL) long-grain brown rice (or a brown and wild rice mixture)

1 Tbsp. (15 mL) extra virgin olive oil

1 tsp. (5 mL) salt

1/2 cup (125 mL) light mayonnaise

2 cloves garlic, minced

1/2 cup (125 mL) salsa

1 pound (500 g) boneless, skinless roasted chicken, chopped

1/4 cup (50 mL) chopped fresh cilantro

2 cups (500 mL) cooked black beans or 1 19–oz. (540–mL) can black beans, rinsed and drained

6 green onions, chopped

1 cup (250 mL) corn kernels (cut freshly from the cob or canned)

mixed salad greens (optional)

1 Bring the water to a boil. Add the rice, oil and salt. Cover tightly and simmer on low heat for 30 minutes. Remove from the heat and let stand, covered, for 10 minutes. Fluff the rice with a fork and cool, then chill.

2 Combine the mayonnaise, garlic and salsa in a blender or food processor and purée until smooth. Stir the dressing into the rice to combine well. Add the chicken, cilantro, black beans, green onions and corn to the salad mixture and toss gently. Chill the salad until serving time.

3 To serve, line a bowl or platter with greens, if desired, and pile the salad on top. Serves 4–6.

Southwestern Polenta Torte

This is not the kind of dish you're going to haul in your backpack up to a mountain stream, but it's perfect if you're just heading out to the park with the cooler in the trunk or setting up on a blanket in the back yard. It also makes a lovely addition to a brunch buffet and works equally well with other savory fillings. Try roasted vegetables (page 83) and crumbled goat cheese between the layers of polenta, or use a filling of caponata (page 274) and sliced Friulano cheese. Be creative and make this savory "cake" with your favorite flavors. One of the Girl's truly impressive tricks.

polenta layer

4 cups (1 L) vegetable or chicken broth

2 cups (500 mL) water

1 1/2 cups (375 mL) cornmeal

2 Tbsp. (25 mL) butter

1 Tbsp. (15 mL) minced garlic

3/4 tsp. (4 mL) salt

1/4 tsp. (1 mL) freshly ground black pepper

1 Tbsp. (15 mL) chopped fresh oregano

filling layer

2 Tbsp. (25 mL) good-quality olive oil

1 white onion, chopped

1 tsp. (5 mL) granulated sugar

1 red and/or yellow bell pepper, chopped

1 jalapeño pepper, seeded and chopped

3 Roma (plum) tomatoes, seeded and chopped

1/2 tsp. (2 mL) chili powder

1/2 tsp. (2 mL) dried oregano

1/2 tsp. (2 mL) cumin

2 cups (500 mL) shredded cooked chicken (leftover rotisserie or barbecued)

1/2 cup (125 mL) corn kernels

1/2 cup (125 mL) sliced black olives

1 lb. (500 g) grated or thinly sliced Monterey Jack cheese

1 In a large saucepan, bring the broth and water to a boil. Slowly add the cornmeal, whisking constantly to prevent lumps. Reduce the heat to medium-low and add the butter, garlic, salt and pepper. Cook over low heat for 30 minutes, stirring, until the mixture comes away from the sides of the pan. Stir in the oregano and keep warm.

2 Meanwhile, make the filling layer. Heat the oil over medium heat in a large sauté pan and cook the onion with the sugar for 15 minutes or until golden. Add the bell and jalapeño peppers and chopped tomatoes, and cook until most of the liquid is gone and the tomatoes have broken down, about 10 minutes. Stir in the chili powder, oregano and cumin and cook for 1 minute longer. Remove from the heat and stir in the chicken, corn and olives.

3 Preheat the oven to 350°F (180°C). Butter a 10-inch (25-cm) springform pan. Place one-third of the hot polenta in the pan and press to form a smooth layer. Top with half the filling mixture and one-third of the cheese. Repeat the layers once, topping with the remaining polenta and finishing with the cheese.

4 Bake for 30 minutes, until brown and bubbly. Cool slightly or chill before removing the sides from the pan. Serve warm or at room temperature, cut into wedges. Serves 6–8.

Cranberry Oat Jumbles

These are the kind of big, soft cookies that you can carry in your backpack or stuff in your briefcase for breakfast on the road.

1¾ cups (425 mL) rolled oats, divided
1 cup (250 mL) fresh cranberries (or
⅜ cup/175 mL dried)
½ cup (125 mL) butter
1 cup (250 mL) brown sugar
2 eggs
1 tsp. (5 mL) pure vanilla extract

1 cup (250 mL) all-purpose flour
¼ tsp. (2 mL) baking powder
¼ tsp. (1 mL) baking soda
2 tsp. (10 mL) ground ginger
1 tsp. (5 mL) cinnamon
¼ tsp. (1 mL) salt
¾ cup (175 mL) chopped pecans or walnuts

1 Preheat the oven to 375°F (190°C). Place ¾ cup (175 mL) of the oats in a food processor and process for 1 minute to form a fine oat flour. Use the food processor to coarsely chop the fresh cranberries.

2 In a large mixing bowl, cream the butter with the sugar until fluffy. Beat in the eggs and vanilla. In another medium bowl, combine the processed oat flour with the all-purpose flour, baking powder, baking soda, ginger, cinnamon and salt.

3 Slowly add the dry ingredients to the butter mixture and mix well to combine. Fold in the remaining 1 cup (250 mL) of oats. Stir in the cranberries and nuts.

4 Lightly oil a baking sheet and line it with parchment paper. Using an ice cream scoop, scoop the batter into mounds on the baking sheet. Press lightly with a spatula to flatten them slightly, as the cookies won't spread much while baking.

5 Bake for 12–15 minutes or until the cookies are lightly browned and hold their shape. They should be sturdy but soft in the center. Cool on wire racks. Makes 18 cookies.

Survival Bars

The power bar to take you rock climbing or mountain biking in the woods — with natural sugars from honey and lots of complex carbs to stick with you and keep you pumping. The Girl has been known to use these yummy squares for instant breakfasts when she's battling in the concrete jungle, too. You can survive on them — at least for awhile.

½ cup (125 mL) pitted prunes
½ cup (125 mL) dried apricots
½ cup (125 mL) dried cranberries (or raisins)
2 cups (500 mL) quick-cooking rolled oats
1½ cups (375 mL) all-purpose flour
1 tsp. (5 mL) baking powder
1 tsp. (5 mL) ground cinnamon
1 tsp. (5 mL) ground ginger
¼ tsp. (1 mL) salt

1 cup (250 mL) butter, softened
1 cup (250 mL) packed brown sugar
¼ cup (50 mL) honey
2 eggs
2 tsp. (10 mL) pure vanilla extract
¼ cup (125 mL) raw sunflower seeds
¼ cup (125 mL) chopped almonds (or pecans)
3 Tbsp. (45 mL) sesame seeds
½ cup (125 mL) unsweetened coconut

1 Cut the prunes and apricots into small dice, about ¼-inch (5-mm) pieces. Combine with the cranberries or raisins. In a large bowl, combine the rolled oats, flour, baking powder, cinnamon, ginger and salt.

2 In another large bowl, cream the butter and brown sugar with an electric mixer until light and fluffy. Heat the honey for 30 seconds in the microwave to liquefy it. Add the honey, eggs and vanilla to the butter mixture and beat until blended. Gradually add the dry ingredients, stirring by hand until thoroughly mixed. Add the fruit mixture, sunflower seeds, nuts, sesame seeds and coconut. Stir to combine.

3 Preheat the oven to 350°F (180°C). Lightly butter a 13- x 9-inch (32- x 23-cm) baking pan and line it with parchment paper, leaving the paper hanging over the two long sides (this will help you pull the bars out later). Press the mixture into the pan, smoothing it evenly.

4 Bake for 30–35 minutes, until golden and firm. Cool on wire rack before cutting into bars (divide the pan into four equal sections, then cut six bars from each section). Wrap the bars individually in plastic wrap or foil for longer storage and convenience. The bars will actually mellow and improve while wrapped. Makes 24 bars.

Chewy Chocolate Brownies

This is your classic home-style brownie — chewy, nutty and addictive. If you have a miniature muffin pan, tiny two-bite brownies will bake in about half the time. And remember, the better the chocolate, the better the world.

1 cup (250 mL) butter	1 tsp. (5 mL) pure vanilla extract
4 oz. (125 g) unsweetened chocolate, chopped	1 cup (250 mL) all-purpose flour
2 cups (500 mL) sugar	1/2 tsp. (2 mL) salt
4 eggs	1 cup (250 mL) coarsely chopped walnuts or pecans

1 Preheat the oven to 350°F (180°C). Lightly grease a 9– x 13–inch (23– x 32–cm) baking pan. In a saucepan, heat the butter over low heat until half melted. Add the chocolate and stir until both are completely melted. Remove from the heat and stir in the sugar.

2 Beat in the eggs, one at a time, until the mixture is shiny. Stir in the vanilla and add the flour and salt. Stir in the chopped nuts.

3 Pour the batter into the prepared pan and bake for 30 minutes or until firm. A cake tester inserted in the middle of the pan should come out clean. Let cool completely in the pan before cutting into squares. Makes 2–3 dozen.

STIR IN sauce pan

Real Lemonade

Sure, you can buy lemonade in a bottle, but this is the real thing. Tote it along in a picnic jug or thermos with plenty of ice. Add a handful of fresh mint to the hot sugar syrup for a herbaceous touch.

6 cups (1.5 L) water
³/₄ cup (175 mL) sugar
2–3 large lemons

1 Heat the water and sugar on the stove until it's boiling, stirring until the sugar is completely dissolved. Boil for 2 minutes. Remove from the heat and cool.

2 To squeeze the lemons, press and roll them under your palm on the counter to release the juices. (Or stab your lemon with a fork and microwave for 20 seconds to get the juices flowing.) Cut the lemons in half, crosswise, and holding a half lemon over a bowl, use a lemon reamer to press into the center of the fruit and twist out the juice. You will need about ¹/₂ cup (125 mL).

3 Strain the juice through a coarse sieve to remove the seeds. Add the lemon juice and pulp to the sweetened water and chill. Adjust the flavor with more sugar if necessary. The mixture should be strong and lemony, as you'll want to serve it over ice. Makes 6 cups (1.5 L).

Girl talk: The Girl's latest indulgence is the mojito — a frosty summer cocktail created with fresh lime juice, fresh mint and rum. Make this homemade lemonade with lime juice for mojitos. Fill tall glasses with ice and lots of fresh mint leaves, add a shot of white rum and top up with the fresh limeade. Bueno!

The Ladies' Lunch

(A Baby or Wedding Shower Buffet)

Whether it's a baby shower, a wedding or a date with your bridge
club, sometimes the ladies just need to lunch. Smart, sophisticated
food that's light, can be made ahead and works well on a room-
temperature buffet is just the ticket.

Fresh Tomato Tart on Cornmeal Crust

This contemporary tart is inspired by those served in the south of France. Use a variety of colorful heirloom tomatoes and try a sprinkling of herbes de Provence (or some fresh chopped rosemary, lavender and thyme) for added authenticity. To speed up the process, roll out a package of frozen puff pastry for the base, bake according to the directions on the box and top as follows.

tart shell

1¹/2 cups (375 mL) all-purpose flour
2 tsp. (10 mL) active dry yeast
³/4 cup (175 mL) warm water
³/4 cup (175 mL) cornmeal

1 Tbsp. (15 mL) honey
1 Tbsp. (15 mL) olive oil
¹/2 tsp. (2 mL) salt
olive oil for rubbing

topping

8 medium to large fresh tomatoes, sliced
   (a variety of colors is best)
salt and freshly ground black pepper
3 Tbsp. (45 mL) extra virgin olive oil
3 cloves garlic, minced
¹/4 cup (50 mL) chopped fresh basil

2 Tbsp. (25 mL) chopped fresh parsley
3 Tbsp. (45 mL) olive tapenade (page 328) or
   chopped, air-cured black olives
³/4 cup (175 mL) finely grated Parmesan, Asiago
   and/or other strong cheese

1 For the tart shell, combine half the flour with the yeast and water. Let stand 5 minutes to proof. Add the remaining flour, cornmeal, honey, olive oil and salt. Knead with enough extra flour to make a smooth, elastic dough. Form the dough into a ball, rub with olive oil, cover and set aside for 1 hour to rise.

2 Preheat the oven to 450°F (230°C). Punch the dough down and roll into a rectangle. Sprinkle an oblong baking sheet with cornmeal and fit the dough into the pan, rolling and crimping the edges. Prick the surface all over with a fork and bake for 10 minutes. Reduce the heat to 350°F (180°C) and bake for 10 minutes more, until golden.

3 To make the topping, overlap the tomato slices on a deep platter or dish and season with salt and pepper. Set aside for 1 hour. The salt will leach some of the liquid from the tomatoes. Remove the tomatoes with a slotted spoon and arrange over the tart crust. Discard the liquid.

4 Preheat the broiler. Combine the olive oil, garlic, basil and parsley and sprinkle over the tomatoes. Add dollops of tapenade or scatter chopped olives about. Sprinkle the cheese evenly over top. Place the tart under the broiler until the cheese begins to bubble and brown. Cut the tart into squares and serve warm or at room temperature. Serves 6.

Gingery Carrot Soup

The Girl is into orange — the color of anti-aging antioxidants. This simple, low-fat carrot soup may be served hot or cold and it's more flavorful than you might imagine. Swirl in a little sour cream or plain yogurt to garnish (see page 100), and serve it to start any dinner in style.

2 Tbsp. (25 mL) butter or olive oil
1 onion, chopped
2 lbs. (1 kg) carrots, peeled and chopped
1 Tbsp. (25 mL) minced fresh ginger
3 Tbsp. (45 mL) all-purpose flour
6 cups (1.5 L) chicken or vegetable stock

1 bay leaf
1 tsp. (5 mL) granulated sugar
salt and white pepper
dash curry powder
sour cream or yogurt to garnish

1 Heat the butter or oil and sauté the onion, carrots and ginger, covered, until soft and starting to brown, about 10–15 minutes. Stir the flour into the vegetables and cook for 1 minute. Add the stock, bay leaf, sugar, salt and pepper. Simmer the soup until the vegetables are very soft, about 45 minutes.

2 Discard the bay leaf and purée the soup in a food processor or blender until smooth. Return to the soup pot and season with a little curry powder. Heat to boiling. Serve hot or cold, with a dollop of sour cream or yogurt. Serves 4–6.

Chicken Breasts Stuffed with Red Peppers and Goat Cheese

This is a main course that looks gorgeous fanned out on individual plates or sliced on a platter for buffet service. The chicken may be served warm or at room temperature but keep the herb sauce warm in a fondue pot or miniature chafing dish.

2 red or yellow bell peppers
6 boneless, skinless chicken breasts
1/2 lb. (250 g) creamy fresh goat cheese
1 Tbsp. (15 mL) olive oil
2 cups (500 mL) chicken broth, homemade or canned
1/2 cup (125 mL) dry white wine

1/3 cup (75 mL) heavy cream
2 Tbsp. (25 mL) chopped fresh herbs, like thyme, oregano and/or basil
2 green onions, chopped
salt and freshly ground black pepper
fresh herbs to garnish

1 To roast the peppers, grill or broil until blackened on all sides. Place the peppers in a paper bag to steam and cool, then peel off the charred skin and remove the stems, ribs and seeds. Slice the peppers into thin strips and set aside.

2 Lay the chicken breasts flat on a cutting board. Insert a small paring knife into the thickest part of the side of each chicken breast. Holding your palm over the breast, wiggle the knife back and forth to form a pocket, keeping the entry to the pocket small. Use your fingers to stuff the pockets with the goat cheese and roasted pepper.

3 Heat the olive oil in a heavy, nonstick skillet over high heat and brown the chicken quickly on both sides. This will take about 4 minutes. Add the broth and white wine to the pan. Bring to a boil, cover, reduce the heat and simmer for 6–7 minutes. Remove the chicken from the pan and keep it warm.

4 Boil the liquid in the pan hard until it has been reduced by half. Add the cream and cook until the sauce is thick enough to coat the back of a spoon. Stir in the fresh herbs and green onion and simmer 1 minute longer. If you want a smooth green sauce, purée it with a hand blender or transfer to a blender and process until smooth. Return to the pot and season with salt and pepper to taste. Keep warm over low heat.

5 Slice the chicken breasts and arrange on warmed, individual plates or on a platter for family-style service. Drizzle with some of the sauce and garnish with more fresh herbs. Heat the remaining sauce and pass separately. Serves 6.

Zucchini and Orzo

This is one of those simple combinations that results in a dish that transcends the sum of its parts. It's wonderful as a room-temperature salad or side dish in the summer, but just as good hot from the pan, alongside a piece of grilled fish or chicken. The Girl has recently discovered a multi-colored orzo at her local health food haunt (red, green and yellow, colored with spinach, beets and other healthy stuff), which makes this tiny pasta even prettier. And it's a great way to use up all of that zucchini that a gardening girlfriend so kindly donates every fall.

5 Tbsp. (60 mL) olive oil
1 medium onion, minced
2 cloves garlic, minced
2–3 lbs. (1–1.5 kg) summer squash (yellow,
   pale green koussa, dark green zucchini), unpeeled

3/4 cup (175 mL) toasted hazelnuts or pine nuts
1 1/2 cups (375 mL) orzo
1/3 cup (75 mL) chopped Italian parsley
1/3 cup (75 mL) chopped fresh basil
salt and freshly ground black pepper
2 Tbsp. (25 mL) fresh lemon juice

1 In a large nonstick sauté pan, heat the oil over medium-high heat. Add the onion and garlic and cook for 10 minutes, until the onion is very tender.

2 Wash the squash well and chop into tiny 1/4-inch (5–mm) cubes. Add the squash to the pan and sauté for 10 minutes longer, until tender.

3 To chop the hazelnuts, pulse briefly in a food processor or simply press them, a few at a time, under the blade of your chef's knife (this will instantly crush them into perfect pieces and you won't have nuts flying everywhere in the kitchen).

4 Meanwhile, cook the orzo in boiling salted water for 7–8 minutes until tender. Drain well and add to the sauté pan with the squash. Stir it around to combine. Remove from the heat and fold in the nuts, parsley and basil. Season with salt and pepper. Stir in the lemon juice. Serve hot or at room temperature. Serves 6–8.

Girl talk: Toasted hazelnuts are a wonderful thing to have in the freezer to add to salads, stuffings, pilafs and baking. To toast the hazelnuts, put them on a rimmed baking sheet in a 400°F (200°C) oven for 10 minutes, shaking the pan once or twice while they toast. Dump the hot nuts onto a clean kitchen towel, fold the towel over the nuts to enclose them, and scrub them together in the towel. This will remove most of the bitter brown skin (don't worry if it's not all gone).

You can toast any nut this way, although only hazelnuts need the scrubbing step. Every nut benefits from toasting, a chef's trick that brings out the best flavors. Once the nuts are cool, store them in a bag in the freezer — they keep best this way.

Ladies' Lunch Lemon Curd Tarts

Buy a package of frozen mini tart shells, then bake and fill with this lemony curd. A dollop of whipped cream and a baby violet from the garden — now that's Girly!

lemon curd

1/2 cup (125 mL) butter

1 Tbsp. (15 mL) lemon zest

1/2 cup (125 mL) fresh lemon juice

1 1/2 cups (375 mL) granulated sugar

3 whole eggs

3 egg yolks

tarts

1 box frozen mini tart shells

cream whipped with a touch of sugar until stiff

fresh or candied violets to garnish

1 Melt the butter in a double boiler over medium heat. Stir in the lemon zest, juice and sugar.

2 Using an electric mixer, beat the whole eggs and egg yolks until thick. Slowly add the beaten eggs to the lemon mixture in the double boiler. Whisk constantly until the mixture is hot and thick (don't boil it or the mixture will curdle). Remove the lemon curd from the heat and cool. Chill well. (Makes enough curd for 12 medium or 18 small shells.)

3 Bake the tart shells according to the package directions. Cool. Just before serving, fill each tart shell with lemon curd. Pipe a dot of whipped cream on top and garnish with a violet. Pretty! Makes 18 tiny tarts.

Girl talk: Using a double boiler makes cooking egg mixtures like this foolproof. Find a small metal bowl that fits inside one of your medium-sized pots. Fill the pan with about 4 inches (10 cm) of water, bring to a boil over medium-low heat and set the bowl over top. It should not be touching the water.

Easter Break

If you're not out spring skiing, you may get caught cooking the family meal for Easter. Ham is traditional, although a leg of lamb (page 236) might also be in the cards. For a raft of traditional meatless dishes to serve during Lent — the period leading up to Easter — see page 256.

Hard Cooked Eggs to Color (and consume)

Chocolate bunnies may multiply at Easter but you know what came first — the egg. The Girl comes from a long line of egg decorators. It's a tradition to color hard-boiled eggs and then have a little friendly competition to whet the appetite before Easter dinner. Everyone chooses one egg, then you go around the room "bouncing eggs" — tapping one egg against the other, fat end to fat end, pointy end to pointy end, until there's just one egg (or one end) left intact. Then you eat the eggs — a handy, healthy appetizer in a perfect package.

1 dozen free-range eggs
1 egg coloring kit (the color tablets you mix with
   vinegar and water)

1   To hard boil an egg perfectly, place several eggs in a saucepan. Add cold water to the pan, until the eggs are covered by about 1 inch (2.5 cm). If you start with eggs that are not perfectly fresh, they'll be easier to peel later. (Raw eggs are perfectly fine if they're refrigerated for up to a month, but don't leave them out — they will lose a week's freshness in a day at room temperature.) And do try to get some good-quality eggs to begin with — the flavor of true free-range eggs is the best and the yolks have a lovely natural orange tinge that comes from the plants the birds eat.

2   Put the pot on high heat and bring to a full rolling boil. Then put the lid on, remove the pan from the heat and let the eggs stand in the boiling water for 15 minutes. They will be perfectly hard cooked. Immediately drain and run under cold water. Don't color any eggs that have cracked in the cooking process (peel them under running water and use them for Deviled Eggs, page 275).

3   Color your eggs with a food-safe dye and put them back in the carton to drain excess dye. Store them in the refrigerator until Easter (they're okay for a week, but not longer).

Easter Ham

This recipe is delicious and foolproof for the kind of whole or halved cured hams you'll find at the supermarket. The classic side dish for baked ham is sweet potatoes or scalloped potatoes. The Girl likes to combine both in a colorful Potato Scallop (page 292). Or boil your white and sweet potatoes together and mash them up with a little cream and some onion and ginger that's been sautéed in butter. Then pass some steamed peas, seasoned with chopped fresh mint, for an incredible color contrast on your plate.

6– to 7–lb. (2.6– to 3.2–kg) cured or smoked
  ham half, skinned
2 cups (500 mL) orange juice, divided

2 Tbsp. (25 mL) Dijon mustard
1/2 cup (125 mL) brown sugar
1 Tbsp. (15 mL) soy sauce

1 Using a sharp knife, cut a shallow diamond pattern into the fatty surface of the ham. Set the ham in a shallow roasting pan, fat side up. Pour 1 cup (250 mL) of orange juice into the pan. (To save clean-up time later, think about lining your roasting pan with foil or using a disposable aluminum foil roasting pan — the glaze can be sticky.)

2 Place the ham in a preheated 300°F (150°C) oven and bake for about 1 hour.

3 Combine the remaining 1 cup (250 mL) of orange juice with the mustard, brown sugar and soy sauce in a small saucepan. Whisk together over medium heat until the sugar is dissolved and the mustard is incorporated. Pour this over the ham and continue to bake, uncovered, for another 2 hours, basting occasionally, until the fat and exposed meat is nicely glazed. At some point you will want to tip the ham up to expose its cut side, so you can properly baste and glaze the meat.

4 The entire baking process should take 25–30 minutes per lb. (55–65 minutes per kg). Use an instant-read meat thermometer to determine exactly when the ham is done — the internal temperature should be 140°–150°F (60°–65°C). Remove the ham from the pan and let it rest on a carving board for 15–20 minutes before carving. Save the bone for bean or lentil soup. Serves 8–10.

Girl talk: When the Girl says ham, she means the real kind – a smoked leg of pork, bone and all. Those other "rolled hams" are really nothing more than glorified luncheon meat, and although they don't have to be cooked, you'll never get the real flavor and texture of a perfect ham. If you bake a real ham like this from scratch, you will have amazing leftovers for sandwiches and breakfasts for a week.

Buy a fresh whole or halved ham, a leg or butt portion. Hams may be labeled uncooked or partially cooked, but both must be cooked before serving. A smoked ham just needs to be glazed and baked in a moist environment. A salted or country ham (usually only found in the South, like Virginia or Kentucky hams) needs to be soaked in cold water for up to 36 hours, then boiled for several hours before baking. But this kind of ham is the exception to the rule.

Potato Scallop

The Girl can't remember a ham supper that didn't include scalloped potatoes. But this combination of potatoes and cream ups the ante, adding bright orange sweet potatoes for a shot of color and healthy carotene. Use all yellow-fleshed or white potatoes if you like or be extra adventurous and add a layer of deep purple heirloom blue potatoes. Your guests will think you're a real gourmet.

1 medium orange-fleshed sweet potato, peeled
3 large yellow-fleshed potatoes, peeled
1 onion, thinly sliced, about 2 cups (500 mL)
salt and freshly ground black pepper

3–4 Tbsp. (45–50 mL) all-purpose flour
1 cup (250 mL) chicken broth
1 cup (250 mL) half-and-half cream or 2% milk
  (or a combination)

1 Slice the potatoes super thin, using a mandoline or the slicing blade of your food processor. You'll need about 4–5 cups of sliced potatoes.

2 Start with a large, shallow casserole dish and rub it lightly with oil or softened butter. Layer the orange and yellow potatoes with the onions, sprinkling each layer with salt and pepper, and dusting lightly with flour. Finish with a layer of potatoes.

3 Combine the broth and cream or milk in a saucepan and heat to boiling. Pour slowly over the casserole, making sure the liquid seeps into all the crevices. (Cream thickens this dish nicely, without flour, but milk makes it more virtuous. Take your pick.) You should just be able to see the liquid through the first layer of potatoes; add a little more cream or broth if needed.

4 Cover the casserole with foil and bake alongside the ham at 300°F (150°C) for about 1½ hours. Remove the foil during the last 20 minutes to brown the top of the dish. Serves 6.

Girl talk: This dish can be made in advance and reheated. If you want to get really fancy, bake the potato scallop in a square pan. When the scallop is cooked, cover it with foil, put a board over top of it and weigh it down as it cools. Chill. When cold, cut into diamond shapes or rounds using a biscuit cutter, and reheat on a baking sheet. The scallop makes a pretty side dish when you're plating anything from ham slices to grilled lamb chops or pork roasts.

Corn Pudding

Cook this dish in an 8–inch (20–cm) pan and you'll have a creamy pudding — or try a larger gratin dish for a firmer, crisper result.

½ cup (125 mL) cornmeal
½ cup (125 mL) minced onion
1 clove garlic, minced
1 Tbsp. (15 mL) granulated sugar
2 tsp. (10 mL) baking powder
½ tsp. (2 mL) salt
1 tsp. (5 mL) dry mustard

¼ tsp. (1 mL) dried thyme
2 cups (500 mL) buttermilk (or 1 cup [250 mL]
    skim milk and 1 cup [250 mL] plain low-fat yogurt)
2 cups (500 mL) fresh or frozen corn kernels
2 eggs, lightly beaten
few drops hot sauce
¼ cup (50 mL) Parmesan or aged Cheddar cheese

1 Preheat the oven to 375°F (190°C). In a bowl, combine the cornmeal, onion, garlic, sugar, baking powder, salt, mustard and thyme. Gradually add the buttermilk, whisking to remove lumps.

2 Whirl the corn, eggs and hot sauce together in a food processor to coarsely chop the kernels. Stir into the batter and beat to combine.

3 Pour the batter into a buttered 8–inch (20–cm) square baking dish or oval gratin dish. Bake for 20 minutes. Sprinkle with the cheese and bake 10 minutes longer, until the pudding is set and the cheese is lightly browned. Serves 6.

Roasted Beets

In the trendy new world of designer veggies, beets are gaining the kind of cachet once reserved for heirloom tomatoes. Look for yellow or striped pink and white Chioggia beets to add gourmet flair to this simple dish.

12 cylinder beets, scrubbed
1 Tbsp. (15 mL) olive oil
1 Tbsp. (15 mL) honey

1 Tbsp. (15 mL) balsamic vinegar
salt and white pepper

1 Wrap the beets in foil and roast alongside the meat in a 300°F (150°C) oven for 2 hours (alternately, roast for 45 minutes at 400°F/200°C).

2 When the beets are tender, cool them slightly and slip off the skins. Slice the beets into thick coins.

3 Heat the olive oil, honey and balsamic vinegar together, just until the honey is melted. Pour over the hot sliced beets and toss to coat. Serve warm, seasoned with salt and pepper. Serves 4–6.

The Big Birthday Bash

The big 2—o? 3—o? 4—o? Plan a party and invite everyone.
This is the perfect menu for a big backyard party — the Girl fed 40 at
girlfriend Alison's milestone birthday with this attractive, self-serve outdoor
meal. Create a fresh and colorful salsa bar for your buffet table, and add big
bowls of tortilla chips, chopped olives and shredded cheeses to help set the
scene. This menu is easy to increase for a larger crowd, or stretch it by
serving some spicy Mexican rice alongside. For the perfect finale, bake
up some Mexican Chocolate Cupcakes (page 300). Cue the salsa music,
pour the Margaritas or Mojitos (page 282) and dance!

Grilled Steak Fajitas

With a salsa bar on the side, this is a festive way to dine — interactive, self-serve food that's easy to make and fun to eat. Add some bowls of chopped black olives and shredded jalapeño Jack cheese for diners to add to their wraps at will.

marinade

3 Tbsp. (45 mL) canola oil
juice of 2 limes (about 1/4 cup/50 mL)
1 small hot pepper, minced
1 clove garlic, minced

1 green onion, minced
2 Tbsp. (25 mL) tequila
1/2 tsp. (2 mL) ground cumin
1/4 cup (50 mL) chopped cilantro

fajitas

2 red peppers, seeded and sliced into strips
1 green pepper, seeded and sliced into strips
1 yellow pepper, seeded and sliced into strips

1 white onion, peeled and cut into slivers
1 1/2 lbs. (750 g) round or flank steak

serve with

1/2 cup (125 mL) chopped black olives
chopped fresh tomatoes and avocados
2 cups (500 mL) shredded jalapeño Jack or
   Cheddar cheese

fresh salsas (page 296 to 297)
12 warm flour tortillas

1 Combine the marinade ingredients in a food processor and whirl until smooth. For the fajitas, place half the marinade in a bowl with the peppers and onion, and toss to coat. Put the remaining marinade in a resealable plastic bag with the steak. Set both aside at room temperature to marinate for 30 minutes.

2 Heat the barbecue grill to high. Using a grill wok (a perforated barbecue grill pan, see page 110), stir-fry the peppers and onions in batches on the grill until they begin to char. This will take 10–15 minutes. Grill the steak for 6–8 minutes per side, then set aside for 10 minutes to allow the juices to set.

3 Carve the steak into thin strips across the grain. Pile it in the center of a serving platter and surround with the grilled vegetables.

4 Serve with olives, tomatoes, avocados and shredded cheese on the side. Set out the salsas and warm tortillas. Let diners make their own fajitas, piling the tortillas with steak and vegetables, adding garnishes and salsas of choice, and rolling them up. Makes 12 fajitas, serves 6. Multiply at will.

Tomato Salsa

This is a simple salsa but it adds a burst of fresh flavor and spice to the fajita wraps. It's easy to make any time to scoop with tortilla chips for an instant appetizer.

1 cup (250 mL) fresh, ripe tomatoes, seeded and
  finely diced
1/3 cup (75 mL) minced onion
1 jalapeño or serrano chili, stemmed and minced
  (remove the seeds for milder salsa)

3 Tbsp. (45 mL) minced fresh cilantro
1 Tbsp. (15 mL) fresh lime or lemon juice
salt to taste

1 Combine all the ingredients in a bowl and set aside in the refrigerator for at least 30 minutes to allow the flavors to meld. Makes 1 1/4 cups (300 mL).

Salsa Verde

This spicy herbal mixture is based on a South American condiment called chimichurri, which is served with barbecued meats in Argentina, Chile and points south. Tomatillos look like green tomatoes with a papery husk. They are actually a type of ground cherry with a tart, fresh flavor. You'll find them in Latin markets or well-stocked supermarkets. Serve this tangy sauce with any grilled steak.

1 cup (250 mL) chopped green tomatoes or
  tomatillos
2 cloves garlic, minced
1/4 cup (50 mL) minced Italian parsley
1/4 cup (50 mL) minced cilantro
1/4 cup (50 mL) minced fresh oregano

1 jalapeño or serrano chili, seeded and minced
salt and freshly ground black pepper
1/4 cup (50 mL) extra virgin olive oil
2 Tbsp. (25 mL) lime juice
1 Tbsp. (15 mL) cold water

1 Combine all the ingredients in a food processor or blender and blend until smooth. Makes 2 cups (500 mL).

Corn, Avocado and Black Bean Salsa

This salsa can stand in as a salad or side dish — but it is equally good wrapped up with steak in a fajita.

3 ears fresh corn

1 large avocado

1 Tbsp. (15 mL) fresh lime juice

2 tomatoes, seeded and chopped

1 19–oz. (540–mL) can black beans,
  drained and rinsed

1 jalapeño pepper, seeded and minced

2 green onions, chopped

3 Tbsp. (45 mL) chopped cilantro

1 Tbsp. (15 mL) olive oil

1/2 tsp. (2 mL) cumin

salt

1 Remove the husks and silk from the corn and discard. Rinse the cobs well and cut the ends flat. Stand the cob on a cutting board and, using a sharp knife, start at the top and cut down to the base, removing a strip of kernels. Continue around the cob. Put the corn kernels into a bowl. You will have about 1 1/2 cups (375 mL).

2 Cut the avocado in half lengthwise, around the pit. Twist to break into two halves. Using your heavy chef's knife, whack the pit, embedding the knife, then twist to remove the pit (this is a chef's trick that will impress your audience). Cut the pitted avocado into strips, peel off the skin and cut into cubes. Add to the bowl with the lime juice and toss.

3 Add the tomatoes, black beans, jalapeño, green onions, cilantro, olive oil and cumin to the bowl and toss to combine. Season with a little salt. Cover the salsa and chill for several hours to meld the flavors. Makes 4 cups (1 L).

Celebration Cakes

When you're in charge of the birthday cake, here are a few tried and true recipes that will get you through any milestone.

Spicy Carrot Cake

This makes an impressive birthday cake, especially if you make it in four layers. Or make it into frosted carrot cupcakes for kids' birthday parties. (Line your muffin pans with colorful paper cups and get some sparklers, then dim the lights.) This is also the kind of cake you bake in a big sheet pan and take anywhere (from a church supper to a neighborhood potluck or a birthday at the office), and it looks impressive baked as a bundt. For a lower-fat cake, try substituting applesauce for half the oil in this recipe.

9– x 13–inch (23– x 32.5–cm) sheet cake pan, 10–inch (25–cm) bundt pan, two 9–inch (23–cm) cake pans or muffin tins

cake

½ cup (125 mL) raisins	2 cups (500 mL) dark brown sugar
2 Tbsp. (25 mL) Grand Marnier	¼ cup (50 mL) molasses
3 cups (750 mL) all-purpose flour	1 Tbsp. (15 mL) pure vanilla extract
1 tsp. (5 mL) baking soda	4 eggs
2 tsp. (10 mL) baking powder	1¼ cups (300 mL) canola oil
1 Tbsp. (15 mL) ground cinnamon	1 Tbsp. (15 mL) lemon juice
½ tsp. (2 mL) ground cloves	4 cups (1 L) finely grated carrots
½ tsp. (2 mL) ground nutmeg	½ cup (125 mL) chopped pecans

frosting

1 8–oz. (250–g) package cream cheese (low-fat is fine)	1 Tbsp. (15 mL) Grand Marnier or vanilla extract
2 Tbsp. (25 mL) softened unsalted butter	1 Tbsp. (15 mL) cream or milk
1 cup (250 mL) icing (powdered) sugar	finely chopped pecans (optional)

1 Preheat the oven to 375°F (190°C). Put the raisins in a bowl with the Grand Marnier and microwave on high for 1 minute, then set aside to allow the raisins to plump and soak up the liqueur.

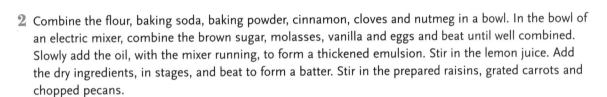

2 Combine the flour, baking soda, baking powder, cinnamon, cloves and nutmeg in a bowl. In the bowl of an electric mixer, combine the brown sugar, molasses, vanilla and eggs and beat until well combined. Slowly add the oil, with the mixer running, to form a thickened emulsion. Stir in the lemon juice. Add the dry ingredients, in stages, and beat to form a batter. Stir in the prepared raisins, grated carrots and chopped pecans.

3 Oil your baking pan(s). Dust with flour (put some flour in the greased pan, shake around to coat, then tip out the excess). Fill the pans $\frac{2}{3}$ full to allow for rising during baking. For round or sheet cakes bake for 50 minutes and a bundt cake 80 minutes, until a skewer inserted in the center of the cake comes out clean. (Cupcakes cook in 20–25 minutes.) Cool completely on a rack (this will take at least an hour).

4 To make the frosting, use an electric mixer to cream the cream cheese and butter together until smooth. Add the sugar and beat to combine. Beat in the Grand Marnier (vanilla if it's for kids) and enough cream or milk to make a spreadable frosting. Make a stiffer frosting (a little more icing sugar) if you're making a layer cake or cupcakes.

5 For a sheet cake, just frost the top of the cake evenly, sprinkle with ground pecans and serve it right out of the baking pan.

6 If you're making a layer cake, invert the cooled cake on a rack, then invert the cake again on a serving plate or a stiff piece of cardboard that's been covered in foil. Spread frosting over the cooled cake with a spatula. Place the second layer on top and frost the top and sides of the cake. (You can even cut each cake in half horizontally, using a long serrated bread knife, and make a four-layer cake, but you'll need to double the frosting recipe.) Press ground pecans around the outside of the cake to finish.

7 For a bundt cake, add a little more cream to the frosting so you can drizzle it over the top and sides of the cake and let it run down in decorative rivulets, then sprinkle the top with ground pecans. Serves 12.

Mexican Chocolate Cupcakes

Cupcakes are perfect for a big birthday party — set them on a large tray, a candle in each one, and let the birthday girl blow them out before passing them around to guests. No one needs a plate or a fork. A touch of spice intensifies the sinful dark chocolate, so don't omit the cayenne. It takes the rich chocolate flavor to new heights but you won't even taste it.

2 cups (500 mL) all-purpose flour
1½ tsp. (7 mL) baking soda
¼ tsp. (1 mL) salt
½ tsp. (2 mL) ground cinnamon
¼ tsp. (1 mL) cayenne pepper
½ cup (125 mL) unsalted butter at room temperature

1 cup (250 mL) granulated sugar
3 oz. (85 g) bittersweet dark chocolate
    (good-quality, like Callebaut or Valrhona)
2 large eggs
1 tsp. (5 mL) pure vanilla extract
1 cup (250 mL) buttermilk

frosting

3 oz. (85 g) good-quality bittersweet dark chocolate
2 cups (500 mL) icing (powdered) sugar
¼ cup (50 mL) unsalted butter

¼ cup (50 mL) buttermilk
1 tsp. (5 mL) pure vanilla extract
chocolate sprinkles (optional)

1 Before you start, make sure all the ingredients are at room temperature. Preheat the oven to 350°F (180°C).

2 Combine the flour, baking soda, salt, cinnamon and cayenne in one bowl and set aside.

3 In the bowl of an electric mixer, beat the butter with the sugar until fluffy and light. This will take about 2–3 minutes.

4 Melt the chocolate. The easiest way is to use the microwave, but be careful not to scorch the chocolate. Chop it, put it in a glass bowl and microwave in 30–second bursts, stirring each time. It will take a couple of minutes in total until the chocolate is completely smooth and melted. Set aside to cool.

5 Add the eggs, one at a time, to the mixer bowl and beat. Add the melted chocolate and vanilla and beat until smooth. Add the dry ingredients, a little at a time, alternately with the buttermilk, beating until smooth after each addition.

6 Line muffin cups with paper cups and fill nearly to the brim with batter. Bake for 20–25 minutes, until a toothpick inserted in the center comes out clean. Cool on a rack.

7 To make the frosting, first melt the chocolate (see previous page for method). Set aside to cool. Use an electric mixer to beat the sugar and butter together in a bowl. Add the buttermilk, melted chocolate and vanilla and beat until smooth. Adjust the consistency of the frosting with more sugar or buttermilk, 1 tsp. (5 mL) at a time, until it's a nice spreading consistency. Frost the cupcakes while still in the tins (these cupcakes are delicious and moist without frosting, too). Decorate with sprinkles, if using. Makes a dozen large cupcakes.

Girl talk: This amount of batter will also make two 9–inch (23–cm) layer cakes — when you're up for a more traditional birthday cake. Just use the frosting to ice between the layers and over the top of the cake. Remember to bake the cakes a little longer than the cupcakes — around 30–35 minutes. Test it with a skewer after 30 minutes. Overbaked cakes are dry.

Birthday Double Chocolate Cheesecake

The Girl developed this recipe to celebrate her girlfriend Anika's birthday. Cheesecake is great for birthdays — it feeds a ton of partiers, it's perfectly portable right in the pan and it's easy to make. Plus, what self-respecting woman (or man) doesn't love to celebrate with chocolate. Happy, happy.

crust

1 cup (250 mL) chocolate wafer crumbs

4 Tbsp. (50 mL) melted unsalted butter

3 Tbsp. (45 mL) granulated sugar

filling

1 lb. (500 g) cream cheese

1/2 cup (125 mL) granulated sugar

3 eggs

2 tsp. (10 mL) pure vanilla extract

pinch salt

1 cup (250 mL) sour cream

4 oz. (125 g) white chocolate

4 oz. (125 g) dark, semisweet chocolate

to garnish

fresh raspberries and chocolate curls (optional)

1 Preheat the oven to 325°F (160°C). Combine the crumbs, melted butter and sugar and mix well. Press evenly into the bottom and slightly up the sides of an 8– or 9–inch (20– or 23–cm) springform pan.

2 Use a large piece of foil to enclose the outside of the pan and press tightly to seal the base (this will keep any water out while you're baking the cheesecake in a water bath). Bake the crust for 8 minutes, until it's just set. Remove from the oven and allow to cool. Increase the oven temperature to 400°F (200°C).

3 Place the cream cheese in a food processor or large bowl and beat until soft. Add the sugar and beat for 2 minutes until smooth. Add the eggs, one at a time with the food processor running, and process until completely incorporated. Add the vanilla, salt and sour cream, and whirl to blend well.

4 Divide the batter in half — you will have 4 cups (1L) in total. Place the white and dark chocolate in separate microwavable bowls. Microwave each in 30–second bursts until melted, stirring until smooth between each burst. Cool slightly, then whisk the white chocolate into one half of the batter and the dark chocolate into the rest. The easiest way to do this is to add some of the batter to the chocolate and stir to lighten it, then pour the chocolate into the remaining batter.

5 Pour half the white chocolate batter into the crust. Top with half the dark chocolate batter, then add the remaining white and dark batter. Use a knife to cut through the mixture to create a swirled effect, being careful not to disturb the crust.

6 Fill a larger baking pan with about 1 inch (2.5 cm) of hot water and set the cheesecake into the pan. Baking in a water bath insures even cooking so your cheesecake won't crack.

7 Bake for 15 minutes. Reduce the heat to 275°F (140°C) and bake 1 hour longer, until the edge is set and the center still jiggles slightly. Turn off the oven and let the cheesecake cool for 1 hour in the oven before removing it and setting it on a rack to finish cooling.

8 Cover the cheesecake and refrigerate overnight, or for up to 2 days. Run a wet knife around the edge of the pan before releasing the sides. Set fresh raspberries around the edge and add a few chocolate curls for garnish. Serves 8–10.

Girl talk: No chocolate wafers left to crumble? Substitute 1 cup (250 mL) graham wafer crumbs mixed with 1/4 cup (50 mL) cocoa. To make chocolate curls, use your potato peeler to shave off slices of chocolate from a block of good-quality, semisweet chocolate.

Orange Honey Cake

Here's a great cake to end a special holiday meal — whether it's Ukrainian Christmas or Rosh Hashanah, this has traditional roots. Or just bake it and take it for any celebration. It's pretty and portable, and it keeps well.

4 eggs, separated
1 cup (250 mL) brown sugar
1/2 cup (125 mL) melted butter or canola oil
1 cup (250 mL) honey
1 tsp. (5 mL) pure vanilla extract
3 Tbsp. (45 mL) finely grated orange rind
3 cups (750 mL) all-purpose flour

2 tsp. (10 mL) baking powder
1 tsp. (5 mL) baking soda
1/2 tsp. (2 mL) ground cinnamon
1/4 tsp. (1 mL) ground nutmeg
1 cup (250 mL) chopped walnuts or pecans
3/4 cup (175 mL) strong coffee
1/2 cup (125 mL) fresh orange juice

to finish
icing (powdered) sugar to dust or melted honey to
   drizzle

1 Preheat the oven to 325°F (160°C). In a large bowl, beat the egg yolks with the brown sugar and butter or oil. Stir in the honey, vanilla and orange rind. In another bowl, combine the flour, baking powder, baking soda, cinnamon, nutmeg and nuts. Add the dry ingredients to the creamed mixture in three parts, alternating with the coffee and orange juice.

2 In another bowl, beat the egg whites until stiff. Pour on top of the batter, then use a spatula to fold them in, using a slicing motion down to the bottom of the bowl and lifting the batter over top. The egg whites should be combined but just barely. The idea is to lighten the mixture.

3 Pour the batter into a buttered and floured 10–inch (25–cm) tube or bundt pan. Bake for 60–80 minutes, or until the cake is a deep amber color and firm to the touch. A skewer inserted in the center should come out clean. This cake is best if it has a day or two to mature before slicing. Dust lightly with icing sugar or drizzle with warm honey before serving. Serves 12.

Baking for Fun, Profit and Emergency Sugar Fixes

Sometimes only sugar and chocolate can make it better. Whether someone's having a lousy week or there's a shortfall in the kid's school coffers, baking a cake or a batch of cookies can make a dent in almost any problem. Baking is a therapeutic exercise for the baker, too — a fun, creative pastime with an edible ending.

Oatmeal Coffee Cake with Crunchy Coconut Topping

This is an old-fashioned coffee cake with a layer of crunchy coconut topping baked right on top. Before there were cake mixes, there were easy everyday desserts like this. Pure comfort on a cold night.

cake

1¼ cups (300 mL) boiling water

1 cup (250 mL) quick-cooking rolled oats

1½ cups (375 mL) all-purpose flour

1 tsp. (5 mL) baking soda

1 tsp. (5 mL) baking powder

1 tsp. (5 mL) salt

2 tsp. (10 mL) cinnamon

½ cup (125 mL) butter

1 cup (250 mL) granulated sugar

1 cup (250 mL) brown sugar

2 large eggs

topping

1 cup (250 mL) unsweetened shredded coconut

¼ cup (50 mL) chopped pecans

½ cup (125 mL) firmly packed brown sugar

½ cup (125 mL) heavy cream or evaporated milk

1 tsp. (5 mL) pure vanilla extract

1 Preheat the oven to 375°F (190°C). Pour the boiling water over the oats and set aside to cool. Sift the flour, baking soda, baking powder, salt and cinnamon together and set aside.

2 Cream the butter with both sugars until light, using an electric mixer. Add the eggs, one at a time, beating until fluffy. Stir in the soaked oats, then gradually add the flour mixture and blend well.

3 Lightly butter a 9–inch (23–cm) square cake pan. Add 1 tsp. (5 mL) of flour and knock it around until the whole pan is lightly floured. Pour the batter into the pan.

4 Combine the topping ingredients and spread the mixture evenly over the batter. Bake for 55 minutes, until a cake tester comes out clean. Makes one cake.

Bake Sale Cheesecake Brownies

Want your brownies to stand out at the bake sale? Swirl in a cream cheese filling and you'll have a stylish square that combines the addictive decadence of two of the Girl's favorite desserts.

brownie part

2 oz. (60 g) unsweetened baking chocolate, chopped

1/2 cup (125 mL) butter

1 cup (250 mL) granulated sugar

1/2 tsp. (2 mL) pure vanilla extract

1 tsp. (5 mL) baking powder

2 eggs

1/2 cup (125 mL) all-purpose flour

cheesecake part

1 lb. (450 g) cream cheese

1/2 cup (125 mL) sugar

2 eggs

1 Tbsp. (15 mL) cornstarch

1 tsp. (5 mL) pure vanilla extract

1/2 cup (125 mL) sour cream

1 Preheat the oven to 350°F (180°C). For the brownie part, melt the chocolate with the butter in a medium-sized bowl in the microwave (a minute should do it). Stir to combine. Add the sugar, vanilla, baking powder, eggs and flour and beat with a whisk or electric mixer until smooth.

2 For the cheesecake part, beat the cream cheese and sugar until smooth. Beat in the eggs, one at a time. Add the cornstarch, vanilla and sour cream and mix well.

3 Grease an 9 x 12–inch (23 x 33–cm) rectangular cake pan with butter or cooking spray and pour in just enough of the cheesecake batter to cover the bottom of the pan. Dot with five spoonfuls of the brownie mixture and pour in half of the remaining cheesecake batter. Spoon in the rest of the brownie mixture, in the spaces, and top with the rest of the cheesecake batter. Swirl artfully with the tip of a knife.

4 Bake for 55–60 minutes. Cool to room temperature and refrigerate. Cut into 24 squares using a hot, wet knife to make slicing easier. Makes 2 dozen brownies.

Lemon Squares

These are the best things to take along to a baby shower — everyone loves them and they're dead easy to make. Don't forget to use freshly squeezed lemon juice.

1¼ cups (300 mL) all-purpose flour, divided
¼ cup (50 mL) icing (powdered) sugar
pinch salt
2 Tbsp. (25 mL) finely minced lemon zest, divided
½ cup (125 mL) unsalted butter, cubed

½ tsp. (2 mL) baking powder
3 large eggs
1½ cups (325 mL) granulated sugar
⅓ cup (75 mL) freshly squeezed lemon juice
icing (powdered) sugar for dusting

1 Preheat the oven to 350°C (180°C). Grease an 8–inch (20–cm) square baking pan. Combine 1 cup (250 mL) of the flour with the icing sugar, salt, half of the lemon zest and the butter. Using a pastry blender, cut the butter into the dry ingredients until the mixture is fine and crumbly. (Alternately, combine in a food processor and pulse until crumbly.) Press the mixture evenly into the baking pan. Bake for 20 minutes until light golden.

2 Combine the remaining ¼ cup (50 mL) of flour with the baking powder and set aside. Using an electric mixture, beat the eggs with the granulated sugar until they are doubled in volume. Slowly add the flour mixture, beating until just blended. Stir in the lemon juice and the remaining lemon zest. Pour the filling over the warm crust and bake for 20 minutes longer, until the filling is just set.

3 Cool on a wire rack. Lightly sift a layer of icing sugar over top, then cut into small squares to serve.
Makes 16.

Classic Lemon Loaf

Here's a recipe for that old standby that you can use under fresh strawberries and whipped cream for an impromptu shortcake or just add to your repertoire of grab and go family baking. Jazz it up with 3 Tbsp. (45 mL) of poppy seeds or a little minced fresh lemon thyme from the garden if you're feeling fanciful.

1³/4 cups (425 mL) all-purpose flour
1 tsp. (5 mL) baking powder
¹/2 tsp. (2 mL) salt
1 large lemon (preferably organic)
2 large eggs

1 cup (250 mL) granulated sugar
³/4 cup (175 mL) plain or vanilla yogurt
¹/4 cup (50 mL) canola oil (or
    any other neutral-flavored oil)
¹/4 cup (50 mL) icing (powdered) sugar

1 Preheat the oven to 350°F (180°C). Grease a large 9– x 5–inch (23– x 12–cm) loaf pan.

2 In a bowl, combine the flour, baking powder and salt. Scrub the lemon well. Remove the zest and mince it finely. Add to the flour mixture. Juice the lemon and set aside for the drizzle.

3 In a separate bowl, beat the eggs with the granulated sugar, yogurt and oil. Fold in the flour mixture and mix until the batter is smooth. (Add extras, such as poppy seeds, now.)

4 Pour the batter into the prepared pan and smooth the top. Bake for 50–60 minutes, or until a bamboo skewer inserted in the center of the loaf comes out clean.

5 Cool the loaf, in the pan, on a rack. Whisk the reserved lemon juice (about 3–4 Tbsp./50 mL) with the icing sugar to make a drizzle. Poke holes in the top with the skewer and drizzle the lemon mixture over the hot loaf. Let it cool completely before turning it out of the pan. Wrap tightly in foil to store or freeze.
Makes 1 loaf.

Chocolate Banana Bread

When the bananas turn black on the counter, recycle them. So easy, any girl can do it.

1/2 cup (125 mL) brown sugar
1/4 cup (50 mL) melted butter or canola oil
3 very ripe bananas (about 1 1/2 cups/
   375 mL mashed)
2 eggs
1/3 cup (150 mL) buttermilk or plain yogurt

2 cups (500 mL) all-purpose flour (or
   use half whole-wheat)
1 tsp. (5 mL) baking powder
1 tsp. (5 mL) baking soda
1/4 tsp. (1 mL) salt
3/4 cup (175 mL) chocolate chips

1 Butter a 9– x 5–inch (23– x 12–cm) loaf pan and preheat the oven to 350°F (180°C).

2 In the food processor, combine the sugar, butter or oil, bananas, eggs and buttermilk or yogurt. Process until smooth.

3 Combine the flour, baking powder, baking soda and salt. Add to the wet ingredients (pulse until just combined). Stir in the chocolate chips. Pour the batter into the pan and bake for 50–60 minutes, or until a toothpick inserted in the center comes out clean. Cool in the pan for 5 minutes, then transfer to a wire rack to continue cooling. Makes 1 large loaf.

Oatmeal Peanut Butter Cookies

The Girl has loved peanut butter cookies since she was a little girl (who hasn't?). Use crunchy natural peanut butter with no added sugars or fats, and sell them at the bake sale as power bars!

1 1/2 cups (375 mL) rolled oats
1 cup (250 mL) whole-wheat flour
1/2 tsp. (2 mL) baking powder
1/2 tsp. (2 mL) baking soda
1/2 tsp. (2 mL) salt
1/2 cup (125 mL) butter, softened

6 Tbsp. (100 mL) crunchy peanut butter
1 cup (250 mL) brown sugar
1/2 cup (125 mL) granulated sugar
1 egg
2 Tbsp. (25 mL) water
1/2 tsp. (2 mL) pure vanilla extract

1 Preheat the oven to 350°F (180°C).

2 Combine the oats, flour, baking powder, baking soda and salt. In a separate bowl, cream the butter with the peanut butter and sugars. Beat in the egg, water and vanilla. Gradually add the dry ingredients to the creamed mixture, stirring until well mixed. Drop by rounded tablespoons onto greased cookie sheets, about 2 inches (5 cm) apart. Bake for 12 minutes. Makes 3 dozen.

Ginger Cookies

Old-fashioned doesn't mean out of date — these classic ginger cookies, crackled and sugary on top, are just right to end a meal, along with a cappuccino. The candied ginger adds even more intense peppery ginger flavor, but they're just as good without it. Inspired by girlfriend Jane.

3/4 cup (175 mL) butter
1 cup (250 mL) granulated sugar
1 egg
1/2 cup (125 mL) molasses
2 cups (500 mL) all-purpose flour
1/2 tsp. (2 mL) salt
2 tsp. (10 mL) ground ginger

1 tsp. (5 mL) baking powder
1 tsp. (5 mL) baking soda
2 tsp. (10 mL) ground cinnamon
1/2 tsp. (2 mL) ground cloves
1/4 cup (50 mL) minced candied ginger (optional)
extra sugar for dipping

1 Preheat the oven to 350°F (180°C). Using an electric mixer, cream the butter with the sugar until fluffy, about 5 minutes. Add the egg and beat until smooth. Add the molasses and beat for several minutes longer.

2 In a separate bowl, combine the flour, salt, ground ginger, baking powder, baking soda, cinnamon and cloves. Gradually add the dry ingredients to the batter by hand, mixing with a wooden spoon until well combined. Stir in the candied ginger. Cover the batter and chill.

3 Roll the batter into small balls and dip one side in sugar. Set the balls, sugar side up, 1 1/2 inches (4 cm) apart on an ungreased cookie sheet and bake for 10 minutes. The cookies will crackle on top. Don't overbake or they will be hard — they should be chewy. Place the cookies on a rack to cool.

Makes 18–24 cookies.

Almond Biscotti

Biscotti — the stylish twice-baked cookie from Italy — is just the thing to end a meal with continental cachet. Serve these crisp, adult-style cookies alongside a frothy cappuccino or intense double shot of espresso after a Mediterranean meal. Feel free to alter the additions (try dried cranberries and orange rind instead of the nuts, chocolate chunks and cashews, or include chopped apricots or candied ginger, and sweet spices like cinnamon and nutmeg). This recipe makes a big batch — enough to package up in pretty jars for Christmas gifts.

cookies

1 cup (250 mL) whole almonds

4 large eggs, separated

1 cup (250 mL) sugar

finely grated zest of 1 large lemon or orange

2 Tbsp. (25 mL) orange liqueur or sambucca

2 tsp. (10 mL) pure vanilla extract

1 cup (250 mL) oil (a light-tasting olive oil works well)

2¹/₂–3 cups (625–750 mL) all-purpose flour

4 tsp. (20 mL) baking powder

topping

1 egg white beaten with 1 Tbsp. (15 mL) water (egg wash)

granulated sugar for sprinkling

1 Preheat the oven to 400°F (200°C). Roast the almonds on a baking sheet for 10 minutes. Cool. Put the almonds in a plastic bag and roll over them with a rolling pin to break them into large chunks. Set aside. Reduce the oven temperature to 375°F (190°C).

2 In a mixing bowl, combine the egg yolks with the sugar, citrus zest, liqueur and vanilla. Whisk in the oil, beating well. Combine 2¹/₂ cups (625 mL) of the flour with the baking powder. In another bowl, beat the egg whites until stiff. Stir the flour mixture into the wet ingredients alternately with the egg whites. Add the roasted almonds and stir.

3 Dump the batter onto a floured surface and knead the dough by hand — adding enough flour to allow you to roll the dough into long ropes, about 1–1¹/₂ inches (2.5–4 cm) in diameter and 12 inches (30 cm) long.

4 Oil a baking sheet lightly and line with parchment paper. Place the ropes about 3 inches (8 cm) apart on the baking sheet (they will spread into slightly flattened logs as they bake). Using a pastry brush, brush lightly with egg wash, then sprinkle with granulated sugar.

5 Bake for 20–30 minutes, until lightly browned. Remove from the oven and cool for 10 minutes. Place the logs on a cutting board and, using a serrated knife, carefully cut on the diagonal into biscotti, each about ³/₄ inch (2 cm) thick. Lay the pieces flat on the pan and return to the oven for 10 minutes to dry. Makes about 4–5 dozen.

Just Bring Dessert

If you think salad is stressful, what happens when you're in charge
of the grand finale? Yes, desserts can be grand, but what goes up, must
come down — the potential for disaster is always greatest with
dessert. Ergo, the Girl likes to keep it simple.

Herewith, some tried and true desserts. They may not be as spectacular
as some, but they're easy and foolproof. Or you can always let them
eat cake (see baking section page 298). Don't panic — just measure.

If all else fails, pristine, seasonal fresh fruit (strawberries, cherries,
tiny apricots, fresh figs) and a bottle of good dessert wine will
pull you through anything.

Cranberry Pecan Pie

A great dessert anytime — perfectly portable, impressive and especially lovely with holiday meals from Thanksgiving through Christmas. Like a big butter tart but with the added zing of dried cranberries. The fresh orange and cranberry sauce adds another dimension and balances the sweetness. Another perfect time to haul out that fancy tart pan with the removable bottom.

crust

1¼ cups (300 mL) all-purpose flour

2 Tbsp. (25 mL) brown sugar

pinch salt

½ cup (125 mL) butter

1 egg yolk

1 Tbsp. (15 mL) milk

filling

2 whole eggs

½ cup (125 mL) granulated sugar

1 cup (250 mL) corn syrup

½ cup (125 mL) melted butter

1 Tbsp. (15 mL) all-purpose flour

2 Tbsp. (25 mL) orange brandy or frozen orange juice concentrate

grated zest of 2 oranges

1 tsp. (5 mL) pure vanilla extract

pinch salt

2 cups (500 mL) chopped pecans

1½ cups (375 mL) dried cranberries

fruit sauce

4 oranges

1 cup fresh (250 mL) cranberries

½ cup (125 mL) granulated sugar

½ cup (125 mL) orange juice

1 Tbsp. (15 mL) orange brandy

1 To make the crust, combine the flour, sugar, salt and butter in the food processor and process until crumbly. Add the egg yolk and milk. Pulse until the dough forms a ball. Wrap in plastic and refrigerate for 1 hour to chill.

2 Preheat the oven to 350°F (180°C). Roll out the pastry and line a 10-inch (25-cm) tart pan. This pastry is totally forgiving, so don't panic — any rips or cracks can be repaired by pressing in extra bits of dough. Cover the pastry with foil and add some pie weights or dried beans (this helps the crust bake evenly) and bake for 20 minutes. Remove the foil and cool.

3 To make the filling, whisk the eggs, sugar, syrup, butter, flour, brandy, zest, vanilla and salt together in a bowl. Stir in the nuts and dried cranberries. Pour into the pie shell and bake for 35–40 minutes, until the filling is set.

4   To make the sauce, start by sectioning the oranges. Using a sharp, serrated knife, cut a slice from the top and the bottom of each orange, exposing the fruit. Then, working over a bowl to catch any juice, cut away the rind and white pith. Cut between the membranes and the orange segments will fall out into the bowl.

5   Meanwhile, in a small saucepan, cook the cranberries with the sugar and orange juice over medium heat. When the berries soften and begin to pop, they're done. Remove from the heat and stir in the orange sections and brandy. Chill.

6   Slice the pie into thin wedges and serve with the fruit sauce on the side. Serves 10–12.

Brûléed Apricots with Mascarpone

This is so easy and so decadent — but you must wait until midsummer when apricots are perfectly ripe. Great fruit = great dessert. Simple.

2 Tbsp. (25 mL) unsalted butter, melted
1 Tbsp. (25 mL) pure vanilla extract
2 Tbsp. (25 mL) grappa or brandy
12 ripe apricots, washed, halved and pitted
   (or substitute peaches or nectarines)

2 Tbsp. (25 mL) brown sugar
1/2 cup (125 mL) mascarpone or vanilla yogurt
crumbled amaretti cookies

1   Preheat the broiler. Combine the melted butter, vanilla and grappa or brandy.

2   Arrange the apricots, cut side up, in a shallow baking pan. Drizzle each with some of the butter mixture and sprinkle with sugar. Place on the middle rack, under the hot broiler, for 5 minutes or until they just start to brown and caramelize. Prepare 6 dessert plates.

3   Arrange four apricot halves on each dessert plate, adding a dab of mascarpone or yogurt to the center of each fruit. Sprinkle with amaretti cookie crumbs and serve warm (with more grappa and amaretti cookies on the side). Serves 6.

Pumpkin Custard

This is like pumpkin pie — but without the crust and all the extra work and calories. This is the Girl's preferred dessert for that other turkey-based holiday, Thanksgiving.

3/4 cup (175 mL) granulated sugar
3 Tbsp. (45 mL) water
1 cup (250 mL) half-and-half cream
1 cup (250 mL) evaporated skim milk
2 Tbsp. (25 mL) dark rum
pinch salt
3 large eggs
1 cup (250 mL) canned pumpkin purée
   (not pie filling)

1/3 cup (75 mL) brown sugar
1 tsp. (5 mL) cornstarch
1/2 tsp. (2 mL) cinnamon
1/2 tsp. (2 mL) ground ginger
1/2 tsp. (2 mL) mace
whipped cream to garnish

1 In a heavy skillet, melt the granulated sugar and water over medium heat, stirring until the sugar dissolves. Increase the heat and boil without stirring until the mixture turns golden brown, swirling the pan occasionally and using a wet pastry brush to rinse any sugar from the sides of the pot. This should take about 10 minutes.

2 Working quickly, pour the caramelized sugar into an 8–cup (2–L) round soufflé or baking dish, swirling to coat it well. Set aside to allow the sugar to harden. (You can also do this in 6 or 8 individual oven-proof soufflé molds, for individual desserts.)

3 Preheat the oven to 350°F (180°C). Bring the half-and-half, evaporated milk and rum to a boil in a heavy saucepan. Remove from the heat and stir in the salt.

4 Whisk the eggs, pumpkin, brown sugar, cornstarch and spices together in a large bowl to blend well. Gradually whisk in the hot milk mixture.

5 Pour the custard into the prepared baking dish. Place the dish in a larger baking pan filled with 2 inches (5 cm) of hot water. Bake the custard for about 1 hour, until set and puffed. If using individual molds, they should be set in 30–40 minutes. Remove from the water and cool. Cover with plastic wrap and chill overnight.

6 Before serving, run a knife around the edge of the dish and invert the custard onto a rimmed plate. The caramel sauce should form a pool around the custard. Cut into wedges and serve a little sauce spooned over each piece, with a dollop of whipped cream on the side. Serves 6–8.

Apple Berry Crisp

The Girl learned to make apple crisp — or Apple Betty as they called it at home — in grade school. This adult version has fresh berries and brandy for added zing, but you can leave them out for everyday dessert and it will be just as good (especially with a scoop of vanilla ice cream). Use tart apples, like Granny Smiths, for the best flavor. In the spring, substitute chopped strawberry rhubarb for the berries, and in the winter, use cranberries.

fruit

3/4 cup (175 mL) granulated sugar
2 Tbsp. (25 mL) honey
1/2 tsp. (2 mL) ground cinnamon
1/4 tsp. (1 mL) ground nutmeg

3 Tbsp. (45 mL) brandy, Calvados or Grand Marnier
2 cups (500 mL) blueberries
5 large Granny Smith apples, peeled and sliced
2 Tbsp. (25 mL) all-purpose flour

topping

1/4 cup (50 mL) whole-wheat flour
3 Tbsp. (45 mL) butter, softened
1/2 cup (125 mL) brown sugar

1/2 cup (125 mL) rolled oats or barley
pinch salt
1 tsp. (5 mL) ground cinnamon

serve with

tub of gourmet vanilla ice cream or lemon yogurt

1 Preheat the oven to 350–375°F (180–190°C). Combine the sugar, honey, cinnamon, nutmeg and brandy and mix well. Toss with the blueberries and apples and marinate for 1 hour until the fruit releases its juices. Sprinkle with flour and combine well. Pour into a greased shallow 8–cup (2–L) baking dish.

2 For the topping, combine the flour with the butter and brown sugar, mixing to form coarse crumbs. Stir in the rolled oats or barley, salt and cinnamon. Scatter the crumble over the fruit.

3 Set the baking dish on a baking sheet to catch any juice that may run over. Bake for about 45–55 minutes, until bubbling and golden brown. Serve the crisp warm with vanilla ice cream or lemon yogurt.
Serves 6–8.

Saucy Lemon Pudding Cake

The Girl is a sucker for mouth-puckering lemon desserts. Sure, she'll take to her bed with a box of chocolates, but life is usually more like a bushel of lemons, isn't it?

This is that classic childhood comfort — lemony cake batter that separates into a cake layer on top and a saucy lemon layer on the bottom. Simple enough for family suppers — or fancy, if made in individual molds (see below). You'll need to buy two medium lemons to get enough fresh juice for this recipe.

¼ cup (50 mL) butter, softened
1 cup (250 mL) granulated sugar, divided
2 Tbsp. (25 mL) minced lemon zest (about 1 lemon)
3 eggs, separated

¼ cup (50 mL) all-purpose flour
1 cup (250 mL) milk
⅓ cup (75 mL) fresh lemon juice

1 Preheat the oven to 350°F (180°C). Butter an 8-inch (20-cm) square glass or ceramic baking dish.

2 In a bowl, beat the butter and ¾ cup (175 mL) of the sugar with an electric mixer until fluffy. Beat in the lemon zest and add the egg yolks, one at a time, beating well after each addition. Add the flour, alternating with the milk and lemon juice, and beat until the batter is smooth.

3 Wash the beaters. In another bowl, beat the egg whites with the electric mixer until foamy, then add the remaining sugar, 1 Tbsp. (15 mL) at a time, while you continue to beat. When the egg whites are stiff, mix ⅓ of the whites into the lemon mixture, then carefully fold in the rest. The idea is to keep the batter fluffy, so don't overmix.

4 Pour the batter into the prepared baking dish and place the baking dish in a larger pan. Place in the oven and add boiling water to the larger pan, filling until it's about an inch (2.5 cm) deep. Bake for 35–45 minutes. The top should be slightly browned and set, which means it should be firm when you touch it.

5 Remove the pudding from the water bath and set it on a rack to cool. Cool for 20 minutes and serve warm, or chill. Scoop the pudding into dessert dishes to serve, making sure everyone gets some of the saucy stuff on the bottom of the baking dish. Serves 6.

Girl talk: If you want to make this simple comfort food into a fancy-pants dessert, bake the batter in six individual ramekins (they'll be done in about 20 minutes). Then call it Souffléed Lemon Pudding, dust it with icing sugar and garnish with fresh berries — très chic!

RAMEKIN

Real Chocolate Pudding (or Pots-de-Crème)

Sure you can just get a box at the store, add milk and stir, but this is so easy and you get a chocolate pudding that's as silky and creamy as any you've ever tasted. Yes, it's decadent, but worth every calorie. (Leave out the chocolate and you have the perfect vanilla custard filling for a fruit tart or for drizzling on any dessert.)

This chocolate pudding goes from family suppers to serious soirées with the slightest attention to presentation. Serve it in pretty espresso cups (or antique egg cups) with a dab of whipped cream and a pretty cookie on the side and call it pots-de-crème — easy elegance.

1/4 cup (50 mL) granulated sugar
2 Tbsp. (25 mL) cornstarch
1 cup (250 mL) milk
1 cup (250 mL) whipping cream
3 eggs, lightly beaten

2 oz. (60 g) good-quality bittersweet chocolate, finely chopped
1/2 tsp. (2 mL) pure vanilla extract
pinch salt

1 In a saucepan, combine the sugar and cornstarch. Whisk together the milk, cream and eggs and pour them over the sugar, whisking to combine. Stir in the chopped chocolate.

2 Heat the mixture over medium-low heat, whisking almost constantly until the pudding begins to thicken and the chocolate is melted into the mixture. Whisk in the vanilla and salt.

3 Divide the pudding among 4–6 small bowls (or use one large bowl for family-style serving). To prevent a skin from forming on the top of the pudding, cover with plastic wrap, letting the plastic film sit directly on the surface of the pudding. Refrigerate until cold (up to 24 hours).

4 For a firmer, baked chocolate pudding, divide the pudding among 4–6 small ovenproof ramekins, set in a pan filled with hot water, and bake at 350°F (180°C) for 30 minutes. Allow the puddings to cool in the water bath, then cover and chill. Serves 6.

Rum Raisin Spice Cake

This is one of those old-fashioned, comforting cakes that's perfect for a family potluck or to take to a friend in need. The raisins (soaked in rum) make this cake even more restorative. It doesn't need icing if you serve it warm with apple sauce or whipped cream, but it keeps better when iced.

cake

1 cup (250 mL) dark raisins

1/2 cup (50 mL) rum

1 cup (250 mL) light unsulfured molasses

1/2 cup (125 mL) granulated sugar

1/3 cup (75 mL) butter, softened

1 egg

1 tsp. (5 mL) baking soda

pinch of salt

2 tsp. (10 mL) ground ginger

1/2 tsp. (2 mL) ground cinnamon

1/2 tsp. (2 mL) ground cloves

2 1/4 cups (550 mL) all-purpose flour

1/2 cup (125 mL) hot tea or boiling water

icing

1 1/2 cups (375 mL) dark brown sugar

1/2 cup (125 mL) heavy cream

2 Tbsp. (25 mL) cold butter

1 Preheat the oven to 325°F (160°C). Grease an 8–inch (20–cm) square cake pan.

2 In a small bowl, combine the raisins with rum in a bowl and microwave for 1–2 minutes. Set aside to plump and cool.

3 In a large bowl, beat the molasses, sugar and butter together. Add the egg and beat to combine. In a separate bowl, combine the baking soda, salt, ginger, cinnamon, cloves and flour. Add the dry ingredients gradually to the batter, beating to combine. Add the hot tea or water, beating until smooth. Stir the plumped raisins into the batter.

4 Pour the batter into the prepared pan. Bake for 50–60 minutes. Set the cake on a rack to cool. To make the icing, combine the brown sugar and cream in a saucepan and bring to a boil over medium-high heat. Cook, stirring, for 10 minutes, then remove from the heat. Beat in the butter until the icing starts to thicken. Spread over the cooled cake. Chill before cutting into squares. Makes 1 cake.

Fruit Loaf Bread and Butter Pudding with Caramel Sauce

The Girl devised this decadent bread pudding when she found there was just too much panettone left over after the holidays. Panettone is an Italian sweet bread, filled with raisins, anise and peel, so look for one or something similar to make this simple and speedy dessert. Raisin bread will work, but panettone, with its brioche background, is far richer.

pudding

2 cups (500 mL) milk

2 cups (500 mL) whipping cream

1 tsp. (5 mL) pure vanilla extract

1/2 orange, chopped, including peel

1/2 tsp. (2 mL) fennel seeds

1 cup (250 mL) granulated sugar

4 eggs

4 egg yolks

1 loaf panettone fruit bread or raisin bread,
  a little dry

caramel sauce

1 can (300 mL) sweetened condensed milk

1/2 cup (250 mL) cream

1 Tbsp. (15 mL) Grand Marnier (optional)

1 In a saucepan, combine the milk, cream, vanilla, orange and fennel. Bring to a boil over medium heat. Remove from the heat and set aside to infuse for 20 minutes.

2 Preheat the oven to 350°F (180°C). In a bowl, whisk the sugar, eggs and egg yolks together until light and fluffy. Strain the infused warm milk into the bowl, whisking continually.

3 Slice the bread into 1/4–inch (5–mm) slices, then cut each slice on the diagonal. Arrange the slices, overlapping, in a shallow oval baking dish, making two or three rows. Pour the milk mixture evenly over top, pressing the bread into the custard so that it soaks up most of the liquid.

4 Place the pudding in a roasting pan, and fill the roasting pan with about 1 inch (2.5 cm) of hot water (this bain marie keeps the pudding moist and creamy as it bakes). Bake for about 30 minutes, until the pudding is just set in the middle. Let cool in the water bath.

5 Meanwhile, boil the sweetened condensed milk with the cream in a small saucepan over medium heat until it turns a caramel color. This will take about 15 minutes. Stir it regularly to make sure it doesn't burn. Remove from the heat and stir in the Grand Marnier, if using.

6 Serve the bread pudding warm or slightly chilled, drizzled with the warm caramel sauce. Serves 6.

Chocolate Banana Bread Pudding

This is one wicked kid-friendly dessert — the kind to haul along when you're playing auntie or doing dessert for a kid's party. It's basically a decadent double chocolate version of an old-fashioned trifle, loaded with the kind of yummy stuff kids love. Make your own chocolate pudding from scratch or use a mix if you're in a rush. Layer all of the gooey goodies in a clear, straight-sided bowl for the most dramatic presentation.

1 loaf Chocolate Banana Bread (page 310)
2 barely ripe bananas, sliced
3 cups Real Chocolate Pudding (page 319)
¹/₂ cup (125 mL) chocolate chips

¹/₂ cup (125 mL) toasted chopped pecans
sweetened whipped cream and chocolate shavings
   or syrup to garnish

1 Cut the banana bread into bite-sized cubes and spread half of them over the bottom of a deep glass serving bowl. Cover with the sliced bananas, pressing some of them against the glass, half of the chocolate pudding, the chocolate chips and the pecans. Top with the remaining banana bread cubes and chocolate pudding. Shake the bowl slightly to make sure the pudding oozes down between the layers and is fairly even on top. Cover with plastic wrap and refrigerate overnight.

2 Just before serving, spoon or pipe whipped cream around the edge of the bowl and sprinkle with shaved chocolate. Scoop the pudding in deep dishes — not pretty but pretty wild. Makes 8 servings.

TRIFLE BOWL

Plum Clafouti

The Girl makes this elegant dessert when beautiful red plums, brilliant deep ruby to the center, are ripe in July and August. This is so easy, it's ridiculous — but such a lovely way to eat plums, pitted sweet cherries or other summer fruit.

¼ cup (50 mL) unsalted butter, melted
3 large eggs
1 cup (250 mL) milk
½ cup (125 mL) all-purpose flour
⅔ cup (150 mL) granulated sugar
1 Tbsp. (15 mL) pure vanilla extract (or plum brandy,
   Grand Marnier or Amaretto)

pinch salt
2 lbs. (1 kg) sweet, ripe red plums, halved or
   quartered if large, pits discarded
icing (powdered) sugar for dusting

1 Preheat the oven to 400°F (200°C). In the blender, combine the melted butter, eggs, milk, flour, sugar and vanilla. Whirl until smooth. Add a pinch of salt.

2 Use a pretty, 12–inch (30–cm) round crockery casserole — the Girl has a special scalloped shallow tart dish for this dessert. Rub it all over with butter and arrange the plum halves, cut side down, in a single layer, covering the entire base of the dish. Pour the custard over the plums.

3 Bake for 45–50 minutes, until the clafouti is set and browned on top. Remove from the oven and cool slightly. Dust the warm clafouti with icing sugar (use a sifter, a fine mesh sieve or a shaker). Serve immediately. Serves 4–6.

Fruit Kuchen

Shortcake in a pan. This is another one of those incredibly versatile and comforting recipes that the Girl falls back on for casual parties and family dinners (even brunch) It's a big biscuit filled with sweet, oozy fruit that's lovely warm or cold and totally totable. Use whatever fruit is in season — plums and peaches in August, rhubarb and strawberries in the spring, or apples and pears all year round. No walnuts? Substitute chopped pecans or sliced almonds, which are especially tasty and pretty with peaches. Perfect for a fall harvest supper with a dollop of good vanilla ice cream or frozen yogurt on top.

kuchen

4–5 cups (1–1.25 L) sliced fruit (Granny Smith apples, pears, peaches, red plums)

1/4 cup (50 mL) maple syrup

1 tsp. (5 mL) lemon zest

2 1/2 cups (625 mL) all-purpose flour

2 tsp. (10 mL) baking powder

1/4 tsp. (1 mL) salt

1/4 cup (50 mL) softened butter

1/2 cup (125 mL) granulated sugar

1 large egg

2/3 cup (150 mL) buttermilk or plain yogurt

topping

1/2 cup (125 mL) granulated sugar

1 tsp. (5 mL) ground ginger

1/4 cup (50 mL) butter

1/2 cup (125 mL) chopped walnuts (or chopped pecans or sliced almonds)

1 Preheat the oven to 350°F (180°C). Butter a 10-inch (25-cm) springform pan.

2 Combine the fruit with the maple syrup and lemon zest in a bowl and toss to combine well. Set aside. (If you're using juicier fruits like peaches, strawberries or plums, toss in 1 Tbsp./15 mL of flour.)

3 In a separate bowl, mix the flour, baking powder and salt. Set aside.

4 With an electric mixer, beat the butter and sugar together until fluffy, then beat in the egg. Add the dry ingredients alternately with the buttermilk or yogurt, and blend well.

5 Spread 2/3 of the batter evenly in the prepared pan and arrange the fruit on top. Dot the remaining batter evenly over the fruit in spoonfuls, leaving spaces between the batter.

6 Mix the topping ingredients together, using your fingers to break the butter down into crumbs before adding the chopped nuts. Sprinkle the walnut topping evenly over the kuchen.

7 Bake for 45–55 minutes, until a toothpick inserted in the center comes out clean. Serve warm. Serves 8.

Zinful Poached Pears

The only thing really sinful about this simple dessert is the lemon mascarpone cream that's served along-side — but you can serve this pretty poached fruit naked and it's just as impressive. Make sure to get a hearty red Zinfandel from California or Australia for this dish (no wimpy white Zins). The redder the wine, the better the color in your poached pears. An easy, make-ahead finale.

4–6 pears (choose firm and slightly
   underripe pears like Bosc or Bartlett)
1 bottle (750 mL) red Zinfandel

1 cup (250 mL) granulated sugar
1 cinnamon stick

lemon mascarpone cream
1 lemon
1/2 cup (125 mL) mascarpone
   (Italian triple cream cheese)

1/2 cup (125 mL) whipping cream
1/4 cup (50 mL) icing (powdered) sugar
mint leaves to garnish

1 Peel the pears leaving the stem intact. Use a small melon baller or other small sharp spoon to remove the cores through the base of the fruit, leaving the pears whole.

2 In a tall, narrow pot (a small stock pot is ideal), combine the wine, sugar and cinnamon stick. Heat to boiling, then reduce the heat to medium and simmer for 5 minutes. Discard the cinnamon stick.

3 Add the pears to the pot, standing up if possible, and poach for 15 minutes. They should be cooked but still very firm. Use a sharp paring knife or skewer to poke the pears to make sure they're done.

4 Let the pears cool in the pan to room temperature, then carefully remove. Bring the poaching liquid back to a boil over medium-high heat and boil hard until it's reduced (at least half boiled away) and thickened. Pour over the fruit, cover and refrigerate overnight.

5 To make the lemon mascarpone cream, remove the zest from the lemon and mince. Press the lemon under your palm on the counter, rolling it to release the juices inside. Cut the lemon in half and use a reamer to remove the juice and pulp. Discard the seeds.

6 In a small bowl, whisk the mascarpone until smooth. Whisk in the lemon juice and zest.

7 Beat the whipping cream with the icing sugar until stiff, then fold into the mascarpone mixture to lighten it. Cover and chill.

8 To serve, arrange the pears upright in pretty individual dessert dishes (or slice and artfully fan on a plate). Drizzle with some of the sauce. Add a big dollop of lemon mascarpone cream and decorate with a sprig of mint. Serves 4–6.

Trucs

Dressings, sauces, condiments and other stuff to serve on the side.

Best Barbecue Sauce

Every girl has her own secret sauce for the barbie — this is one of my faves, torqued up with a touch of caffeine.

3/4 cup (175 mL) ketchup
1/4 cup (50 mL) espresso or strong black coffee
2 Tbsp. (25 mL) brown sugar
2 Tbsp. (25 mL) maple syrup
2 Tbsp. (25 mL) cider vinegar

1 Tbsp. (15 mL) Worcestershire sauce
1 Tbsp. (15 mL) olive oil
1 tsp. (5 mL) canned chipotle pepper in adobo or
   Asian chili paste, to taste
1 tsp. (5 mL) garlic powder

1 Whirl all the ingredients in a blender or food processor. Pour into a saucepan and simmer for 10 minutes, then cool. Adjust the heat with more chipotle pepper or chili paste, if desired. Refrigerate until ready to use (keeps several weeks). Makes 1 1/2 cups (375 mL).

Tapenade

This is one of those easy spreads that anyone can make. Buy a jar of air-cured black olives and soon you'll have something wonderful in the refrigerator to spread on toasts (page 216) for appetizers, to add to vinaigrettes and tomato sauces, to dollop on pizzas (page 121) or use to stuff a boned leg of lamb.

1 cup (250 mL) air-cured black olives (or
   green for green olive tapenade)
2 cloves garlic, pressed or minced
1 anchovy or 1 tsp. (5 mL) fish sauce (optional)
1 tsp. (5 mL) finely grated lemon zest

1 tsp. (5 mL) fresh lemon juice
1/4 cup (50 mL) good-quality olive oil
freshly ground black pepper
cayenne pepper

1 Put the olives on a cutting board. Place the flat side of your chef's knife over the olives and press down. This will split the olives so you can easily pick out the pits. Chop finely by hand, or use the food processor. Add the remaining ingredients and whirl them together, making sure your tapenade stays a little chunky. Put it in a jar and refrigerate. Makes 3/4 cup (175 mL).

Pesto

Good pesto comes in jars at any Italian grocery store, but you can easily make your own, in season, and save a bundle. The Girl likes to freeze her pesto in plastic ice cube trays, then she can pop out the cubes, store them in a zippered freezer bag and use them in soups or stews whenever a shot of fresh basil is in order and there's none at hand. Pesto is made simply — with fresh basil leaves, olive oil, toasted pine nuts or walnuts, Parmesan cheese and a touch of garlic. Use the best olive oil you can afford and real Parmigiano-Reggiano cheese. If you plan to freeze your pesto, leave the cheese out and add it later.

2 cups (500 mL) fresh basil leaves
1 large clove garlic
3 Tbsp. (45 mL) pine nuts, toasted

1/2 cup (125 mL) extra virgin olive oil
1/2 cup (125 mL) grated Parmigiano-Reggiano
 cheese

1 Wash the basil well and make sure it's dry before you start. If you blanch the herbs for a few seconds first (see page 332) the color of your pesto will be brighter.

2 Whirl all the ingredients together in a food processor until smooth. Add more oil if you want a thinner pesto. Pour the pesto into clean jars or ice cube trays and refrigerate or freeze (if the surface is covered with a skim of olive oil, pesto will keep in the refrigerator for several weeks). Makes 1 1/2 cups (375 mL).

Girl talk: While the classic Italian pesto sauce is made with basil, you can also make "pesto" (herb pastes) with cilantro, mint or parsley. Just leave out the cheese and season with a little lemon juice. Thai-style cilantro pesto can be made with ground peanuts, a green chili, a shot of lime juice and fish sauce. You can also vary the oils that you use — for Asian use peanut oil and a little sesame oil. Or try a pesto made with avocado or walnut oil.

Savory Rhubarb Sauce

I like to serve a bit of this savory sauce on liver pâté or foie gras, although it also tastes great with grilled chicken or fish. On melba toast, with some pâté from the deli, it makes a nice spring appetizer. Or take along a jar as a hostess gift.

1 lemon
1/4 cup (50 mL) balsamic vinegar
1/2 cup (125 mL) granulated sugar
1 clove garlic, minced

1/2 cup (125 mL) minced red onion
1 Tbsp. (15 mL) minced fresh ginger
3 cups (750 mL) young rhubarb, diced
   (the red parts)

1 Remove the zest from the lemon and mince. Juice the lemon. You should have about 3–4 Tbsp. (45–50 mL) of juice.

2 Combine the lemon juice and zest, vinegar, sugar, garlic, onion and ginger in a nonreactive saucepan and bring to a boil. Add the rhubarb, reduce the heat and simmer, uncovered, on low heat for 15 minutes, until the sauce is thick. Cool. Makes 2 cups (500 mL).

Port and Fig Preserves

When the Girl met chef Todd English she fell in love — with his pizza topped with prosciutto, Gorgonzola and his own savory fig paste. This recipe is inspired by that pizza and its addictive symbiosis of flavors. The secret is preserved figs, a sweet and sour concoction that the Girl makes at Christmas to give away in little jars. Even if you don't make pizza, a dab of this stuff with blue cheese on a cracker makes an amazing nosh.

1 cup (250 mL) ruby port
1/2 cup (125 mL) balsamic vinegar
1/4 cup (50 mL) water
3 Tbsp. (45 mL) honey
1 tsp. (5 mL) crushed juniper berries

2 cloves garlic, minced
1 cup (250 mL) finely chopped dried Mission figs
   (stems removed)
1/2 tsp. (2 mL) mixed peppercorns (pink, white,
   black), crushed

1 In a nonreactive saucepan, combine the port, vinegar, water, honey and juniper berries. Bring to a boil, stirring over high heat, and boil vigorously until reduced by half (that is, until half the liquid has boiled away).

2 Stir in the garlic, figs and peppercorns. Reduce the heat to low and simmer the mixture until it boils down to a thick, jam-like consistency, about 20–30 minutes. Put the preserves in small jars and refrigerate for up to 1 month. Makes about 1 cup (250 mL).

Salsa

While modern girls can get their canned tomatoes, raspberry jam and dill pickles at the supermarket, nothing beats the intense flavors of this homemade salsa, something you can proudly serve on its own as an appetizer with tortilla chips or pretty up for Christmas gifts. Make it in September, when the farmers' market is overflowing with ripe Roma tomatoes and multi-colored peppers.

8 cups (2 L) chopped plum tomatoes, about 3 lbs. (1.5 kg)

4 cups (1 L) chopped banana peppers (medium hot), seeds removed

1 cup (250 mL) chopped jalapeño or serrano peppers (hot), seeds removed

2 cups (500 mL) chopped onions

1 cup (250 mL) cider vinegar

1/2 cup (125 mL) chopped red bell pepper

1/2 cup (125 mL) chopped yellow bell pepper

4 cloves garlic, minced

1 5 1/2-oz. (156-mL) can tomato paste

2 Tbsp. (25 mL) granulated sugar

1 Tbsp. (15 mL) salt

2 tsp. (10 mL) Hungarian paprika

2 tsp. (10 mL) dried oregano

1/2 cup (125 mL) chopped cilantro

2 tsp. (10 mL) Asian chili paste, or to taste

1 Start with a large, nonreactive pot (stainless steel is the best). Chop all the ingredients into relatively uniform, 1/4-inch (5-mm) dice. Wear surgical gloves while chopping hot peppers and make sure you don't touch your face or eyes — these babies burn!

2 In the pot, combine the tomatoes, banana peppers, jalapeño or serrano peppers, onions, vinegar, bell peppers, garlic, tomato paste, sugar, salt, paprika and oregano. Bring to a boil over medium-high heat, stirring often. Then reduce the heat to medium-low. Simmer for 1–2 hours, until the salsa is thick.

3 Remove from the heat and stir in the chopped cilantro. Add enough Asian chili paste to make the salsa as hot as you like it. The Girl's recipe changes from year to year, as peppers have different levels of heat, depending on how they have been grown.

4 When you're satisfied with the flavor and texture, prepare the jars. Use the canning jars with two-part metal lids (the only kind that truly seal and preserve your efforts). Wash the jars and lids well and rinse in boiling water. Using a wide-mouthed funnel to guide you, ladle the salsa into 1–cup (250–mL) jars, leaving 1/4 inch (5 mm) of head space at the top to allow for expansion. Wipe the edges of the jars with a clean cloth, center the lids on top and tighten the screw bands. They should just be "finger tip" tight.

5 Place the filled jars in a canning kettle filled with boiling water. The water must be a couple of inches (5–10 cm) above the tops of the jars. Return the water to a rolling boil and process the salsa for 20 minutes.

6 Lift the jars from the water using tongs and cool on a folded kitchen towel on the counter. The lids should pop and snap down as the salsa cools, indicating that the jars are properly sealed and safe. Your salsa will keep in a cool dark place for a year or more. Refrigerate it after opening for up to a week.
Makes about 8 cups (2 L) of salsa. You can easily double or triple the recipe.

Herbal Oils

Any time you're making a dish with fresh herbs and want to torque the presentation up into gourmet territory, think about a drizzle of herbal oil (on the food or artfully around the plate). Basil and cilantro work particularly well, but you can also use Italian parsley, chives or a combination of other green stuff to create a brilliant green infusion.

1/4–1/3 cup (50–75 mL) herbs (basil or
   cilantro, Italian parsley, watercress, etc.)
3/4 cup (175 mL) olive oil

1/2 tsp. (2 mL) salt

1 Bring a pot of water to boil and quickly immerse the herbs to blanch for a second. Place in a bowl of ice water to chill. Drain well and dry.

2 Put everything into the blender or food processor and whirl until smooth. May be kept in a bottle in the fridge for a week or two, or strained for longer storage. Once strained, infused oils will keep for several months. Makes 3/4 cup (175 mL).

Roasted Peppers

Colorful red, orange and yellow bell peppers are expensive most of the year, but in the fall, when a bumper crop is available, you can buy big bags of fresh peppers for a song. Buy them, roast them and freeze them and you'll have wonderful appetizers all year long.

1 Start with thick-fleshed sweet bell peppers. Preheat the barbecue or broiler to high. Place the whole peppers directly on the grill, or under the broiler, and roast until all sides are browned and beginning to char. Make sure the peppers don't burn too badly, but don't worry if the skins begin to blacken. When the peppers are blackened on all sides, remove them to a bowl or a bag, cover and cool. This allows the peppers to steam. When cool enough to handle, peel off the charred skin and remove and discard the seeds and membranes.

2 The peppers can then be bagged in freezer bags and frozen, for use on pizzas, in pasta sauces, on sandwiches or marinated with garlic and basil for appetizers.

3 To serve marinated roasted peppers, thaw the peppers and tear into long thin strips. Mix 3–4 peppers with 3 Tbsp. (45 mL) extra virgin olive oil, a clove of pressed or minced garlic, a few teaspoons (10 mL) of balsamic vinegar, salt, freshly ground black pepper and a few fresh basil leaves, minced. Let the marinated peppers stand at least 1 hour to meld the flavors, or cover and refrigerate for up to 2 days.

Basic Vinaigrette

For all green salads. Vary the flavors by adding chopped fresh herbs like dill, oregano or basil, lemon zest, chopped sundried tomatoes or chopped roasted peppers.

½ cup (125 mL) extra virgin olive oil
2 Tbsp. (25 mL) balsamic vinegar or lemon juice
1 small clove garlic, minced

1 Tbsp. (15 mL) Dijon mustard
⅛ tsp. (.5 mL) salt
⅛ tsp. (.5 mL) freshly ground black pepper

1 Combine all ingredients in a blender, food processor or glass jar and whirl or shake until combined. Refrigerate for up to three days. Makes ¾ cup (175 mL).

Creamy Miso Dressing

Makes a funky Japanese-inspired coleslaw or a speedy sauce to dollop over grilled salmon.

½ cup (125 mL) mayonnaise
1 Tbsp. (15 mL) dark miso
1 tsp. (5 mL) minced ginger
1 tsp. (5 mL) garlic

1 tsp. (5 mL) granulated sugar
1 tsp. (5 mL) rice vinegar
1 tsp. (5 mL) sesame oil

1 Whirl together in a blender or food processor. Cover and refrigerate for up to three days. Makes ¾ cup (175 mL).

Buttermilk Salsa Salad Dressing

Try this creamy dressing drizzled over an old-fashioned summer garden salad of greens, cherry tomatoes, radishes and green onions. You'll never go back to bottled Thousand Island.

1 cup (250 mL) buttermilk or plain yogurt
1/2 cup (125 mL) bottled tomato salsa
1/3 cup (75 mL) mayonnaise
1/2 tsp. (2 mL) sugar

1/2 tsp. (2 mL) dill weed
1/2 tsp. (2 mL) dry mustard
salt and white pepper

1 Whirl all the ingredients together in a blender or food processor until smooth. Transfer to a covered container and refrigerate for up to 3 days. Makes 2 cups (500 mL).

Japanese Sushi Bar Dressing

This is the kind of dressing you'll find in Japanese restaurants, served over small crisp salads of chopped iceberg lettuce, purple cabbage and shredded carrot.

1/2 small apple, peeled and chopped
1/2 cup (125 mL) chopped onion
1/2 tsp. (2 mL) minced garlic
1 Tbsp. (15 mL) minced ginger
1 tsp. (5 mL) sugar
1 Tbsp. (15 mL) tomato paste or ketchup

pinch salt and pepper
1/2 cups (125 mL) sweet Japanese vinegar (mirin)
1/2 cup (125 mL) vegetable oil
2 Tbsp. (25 mL) Japanese soy sauce
2 Tbsp. (25 mL) fresh orange juice
1 Tbsp. (15 mL) fresh lemon juice

1 Combine all the ingredients in a blender and process until smooth. The dressing will be thick. Refrigerate in a covered container for up to three days. Makes about 2 cups (500 mL).

Big Blue Salad Dressing

The Girl is a sucker for blue cheese salad dressings — the best match for a glass of wine. Drizzle this big blue over a green salad, toss in some chunks of apple or pear and some toasted walnuts — brilliant!

1/4 cup (50 mL) red wine vinegar
3/4 cup (175 mL) olive oil
1 tsp. (5 mL) salt
1/4 tsp. (1 mL) freshly ground black pepper
1 tsp. (1 mL) Worcestershire sauce

1 tsp. (1 mL) dry mustard
1 tsp. (1 mL) dried basil
dash hot sauce
2 cloves garlic, minced
4 oz. (125 g) blue cheese, crumbled

1 Combine all the ingredients in the food processor and whirl until smooth. Keep in a jar in the refrigerator until serving. Serve over green salads or as a dip for dunking veggies like carrot sticks and cauliflower. Makes 1 1/2 cups (375 mL).

Red Curry Sauce

The Girl likes to drizzle this sauce over any piece of grilled chicken or fish for an instant exotic edge.

2 Tbsp. (25 mL) Thai red curry paste
1 cup (250 mL) coconut milk
1 tsp. (5 mL) fish sauce
1 tsp. (5 mL) brown sugar

1 cup (250 mL) chicken broth
2 Tbsp. (25 mL) lime juice
2 Tbsp. (25 mL) chopped cilantro

1 Combine all the ingredients, except the cilantro, in a saucepan and simmer over medium heat for 15 minutes until slightly thick. Stir in cilantro just before serving. Drizzle over grilled salmon, halibut or chicken. Makes 1 1/2 cups (375 mL).

Instant Pastry

The simplicity is stunning — mascarpone cheese (a super creamy Italian cheese available in tubs at the supermarket), flour and sugar — and you have tender pastry. This is the crust to make for fresh fruit tarts, the kind you bake in advance, fill with custard and top with sliced peaches, strawberries or blueberries in the summer. You can also use this pastry as the base for any single shell baked tart. Just arrange concentric circles of cinnamon-dusted apples or sliced red plums in the crust and bake. Or roll it out, cut it into squares and bake it, then layer with whipped cream and berries for a stylish "napoleon." Fashion is everything and the Girl is always *au courant*.

1¹/₂ cups (375 mL) mascarpone cheese   2 Tbsp. (25 mL) granulated sugar
1¹/₂ cups (375 mL) all-purpose flour

1   Put everything into the food processor and pulse until it comes together in a ball. Wrap in plastic. Chill for 1–2 hours.

2   Roll out on a floured surface and use to fill a shallow 10–11 inch (25–27.5 cm) tart pan with a removable bottom, pressing into the scalloped sides of the pan. Line with foil, fill with dried beans or pie weights, and bake at 425°F (220°C) for 8 minutes. Remove the foil and brown 5 minutes more.

3   If you're making napoleons, roll the pastry to ¹/₄ inch (5 mm) thickness, cut into equal-sized squares or rectangles (a size that would look nice in the middle of your favorite dessert plate, line a baking sheet with parchment and bake the squares at 425° F (220°C) for 10–12 minutes until golden. Makes enough pastry for one single-crust tart or eight 4–inch (10–cm) napolean squares.

Girl talk: Fill your baked tart shell with cold custard cream (use a mix) or the Crème Anglaise (page 339) and top with fresh fruit. A little apricot or red currant jelly (depending on the color of your fruit filling) can be melted in the microwave and brushed over the fruit for a shiny glaze.

For napoleons, start with a square of baked pastry, top with some sweet whipped cream and berries, then place another piece of pastry on top (make them even or offset, your choice). Put a little icing sugar in a sieve or shaker and dust the desserts. Voila!

Cheese Scones

When you're serving soup or stew for supper, a cheese scone or biscuit is the best thing to put on the side. You can even freeze them — perfect for breakfast on the run.

2$\frac{1}{2}$ cups (625 mL) all-purpose flour
2$\frac{1}{2}$ tsp. (12 mL) baking powder
2 Tbsp. (25 mL) granulated sugar
1$\frac{1}{2}$ tsp. (7 mL) salt
1 tsp. (5 mL) dry mustard
pinch cayenne pepper

$\frac{1}{2}$ cup (125 mL) butter
1 cup (250 mL) grated Cheddar cheese
$\frac{3}{4}$ cup (175 mL) milk
4 egg yolks
1 whole egg
1 egg beaten with 2 Tbsp. (25 mL) cold water

1 Preheat the oven to 350°F (180°C). Combine the flour, baking powder, sugar, salt, mustard and cayenne pepper in a large bowl. Using a pastry blender, cut in the butter to form coarse crumbs. Stir in the grated cheese.

2 Whisk the milk, egg yolks and whole egg together in another bowl. Add to the dry ingredients, stirring to combine. Gather the dough together in a ball but don't work it too much — the less you handle the dough, the flakier your scones will be.

3 Roll or pat the dough out on a floured surface, to about 1 inch (2.5 cm) thick. Cut into 3–inch (8–cm) scones using a cookie cutter or a floured glass. You can also pat the dough into a square, then cut the scones into squares, then triangles. Or make 1–inch mini scones (for stylish suppers or appetizers).

4 Place the scones slightly apart on a baking sheet. Brush the tops with the egg wash to glaze the scones and give them a nice shiny brown top. Bake for about 20 minutes or until golden. Makes about 15 large scones.

Buttermilk Biscuits

The Girl loves biscuits for breakfast. Eat them with ham and eggs, or, for an even more decadent treat, split them and fry them southern style in butter until golden and crisp. The trick to fluffy biscuits is a light hand. Don't overwork the dough and your biscuits will retain that ethereal quality.

2 cups (500 mL) all-purpose flour
1/2 tsp. (2 mL) salt
2 tsp. (10 mL) baking powder

6 Tbsp. (75 mL) cold butter, cut into cubes
3/4 cup (175 mL) buttermilk
light olive oil for brushing

1 Preheat oven to 425°F (220°C).

2 In a large bowl, combine the flour, salt and baking powder. Add the butter and, using a pastry blender or two knives, cut through the butter and flour repeatedly until the butter is chopped into small bits, no bigger than peas. Add the buttermilk and stir quickly with a fork until just combined. Turn the batter out onto a lightly floured surface, gather the dough lightly together, knead very gently and pat into a circle, about 3/4 inch (2 cm) thick.

3 Using a floured water glass or biscuit cutter, cut the dough into 2 1/2-inch (6–cm) rounds. Reshape any leftover pieces of dough and cut more biscuits.

4 Set the biscuits on an ungreased baking sheet, brush lightly with oil and bake until golden, about 15 minutes. Makes 1 dozen.

Girl talk: For savory herb biscuits, add 3–4 Tbsp. (45–50 mL) of chopped fresh herbs (like parsley, rosemary, basil, thyme) with the buttermilk.

For sweet biscuits to serve with strawberries for shortcake (or to use to top desserts like cobblers), make the biscuits with sweet cream instead of buttermilk and add 1/3 cup (75 mL) of granulated sugar to the dry ingredients. Brush the tops of the biscuits with melted butter and sprinkle with a little granulated sugar before baking.

To make the sweet biscuits into chocolate shortcakes (awesome with ice cream and hot caramelized banana and pineapple toppings), add 3/4 cup (175 mL) of Dutch process cocoa to the flour and toss in 1/2 cup (125 mL) of chocolate chips. The possibilities are endless!

Crème Anglaise

A.k.a. vanilla custard (that oh-so English sauce), this slick sauce drizzled over and around almost any dessert takes it up a notch. Great on plain pound cake, fruit, even pies and shortcakes. Learn to make it. Easy.

4 egg yolks, at room temperature
1/4 cup (50 mL) granulated sugar
1 tsp. (5 mL) cornstarch

1 1/2 cups (375 mL) milk
1/2 tsp. (2 mL) pure vanilla extract

1 Find a metal bowl that fits into one of your saucepans. Put a few inches (5–10 cm) of water in the saucepan, bring to a boil and reduce the heat to a simmer.

2 Put the egg yolks and sugar in the bowl and, using an electric mixer, beat until light, about 2–3 minutes.

3 Heat the milk in a separate bowl, but don't boil it. Gradually add the hot milk to the eggs, while beating with the mixer. Immediately set the bowl over the simmering water in the saucepan and continue to stir (with a spoon or wire whisk) until the custard thickens slightly. The usual test is running your finger down the back of the spoon — if the custard doesn't run quickly back together, it's thick enough.

4 To cool the custard quickly, set the bowl in a sink or bowl filled with a few inches of ice water and whisk. Stir in the vanilla, cover and refrigerate. Keeps for up to 2 days. Serve cold. Makes about 1 1/2 cups (375 mL).

Mix and Match Menus

In case I haven't given you enough ideas to put together a party,
here are some other great menu combinations, mixed and matched from
recipes in the book, to use when you're hosting an ethnic, seasonal or
otherwise themed affair. Eat, drink, cook — have fun!

Spring Fling

Lighten up and celebrate spring. Time for a return to Riesling.

Killer Crostini, p. 216
Farfalle with Salmon and Soybeans, p. 81
Lemon Soufflé Tart, p. 174
or Lemon Loaf, p. 309, with fresh strawberries
  and cream

Mardi Gras Menu

The last big blow-out before the fasting season of Lent (a good idea, even if you're only into it for the health and beauty benefits). Crank up the zydeco and party with this midwinter menu inspired by those hedonists in the *Big Easy*. Something sweetish but full-flavored, like a big Alsatian Gewurztraminer, will stand up to this spicy stew and will be fine with the bivalves, too. C'est si bon, girl!

Oysters on the Half Shell, p. 244
Chicken and Beer Stew, p. 168
Cornbread, p. 242
Maple Sugar Pie, p. 176

Summer Solstice

The longest day on the deck — need I say more? Find a fresh, crisp summer wine (can you say Champagne, Sauvignon Blanc or Pinot Gris?), put it on ice and enjoy the sunshine.

White Bean Slather with Caramelized Onions and
  Goat Cheese, p. 209
Chilled Tomato Soup with Tomato Tapenade, p. 132
Grilled Salmon Skewers on Mixed Greens with
  Lemon Basil Vinaigrette, p. 107
Plum Clafouti, p. 323

A Retro Schmooze

Thinking of those good ol' days — when everyone thought you could escape an international incident like, oh say a nuclear attack, by ducking under your desk? Why not revive those halcyon days with a little retro schmooze. Time to go shopping for a psychedelic thrift-store ensemble and some Sinatra. A big red Bordeaux pours perfectly.

Nuts and Bolts, p. 198
QDA, p. 208
Shrimp Cocktail from Scratch, p. 218
Wild Mushroom and Potato Bisque, p. 131
Green Goddess Caesar Salad, p. 253
Peppercorn Beef Tenderloin, p. 102
Pots-de-Crème, p. 319

Harvest Moon Dinner

The Germans celebrate the wine harvest with creamy onion tarts and carafes of sweet grape juice that's just beginning to ferment. It's apple season, too, so hard cider hits the stove in rich sauces and hearty fruit finales. Pick a dry cider to drink alongside this decadent fall menu. It's an October thing.

Onion Tart, p. 222
Pork in Apple Cider Sauce with Egg Noodles, p. 166
or Garlic Mashed Potatoes, p. 104
Roasted Heirloom Tomatoes, p. 105
Apple Berry Crisp, p. 317

Fall Colors Feast

Whether it's officially Thanksgiving or just time to celebrate the changing of the season, buy a big free-range chicken and get the family together for a feast. Pour something fruity and off-dry, with big flowery aromas (a ripe Riesling or Gewurz) and play in the leaves.

Gingery Carrot Soup, p. 285
Roast Chicken 101, p. 234
Roasted Beets, p. 293
Garlic Mashed Potatoes, p. 104
Pumpkin Custard, p. 316, and Ginger Cookies, p. 311

Fireside Winter Menu

After a day skiing, skating or just walking in the woods, it's nice to get cosy around a crackling fire with a hearty casual meal and a mug of steamy mulled wine. Don't even set the table — this dinner is easy to set out on the coffee table and eat in deep bowls on your lap while you watch the embers dance.

Warm Feta and Roasted Pepper Toasts
Spicy Marinated Olives, p. 213
Casserole of Lamb, Rosemary and White Beans
   with Creamy Polenta, p. 164
The Best Chocolate Fondue. p. 118
Smoking Bishop (a.k.a. mulled wine), p. 199

Chinese Buffet

Fire up the wok and create a stylish Chinese meal anytime. Start with the duck quesadillas (reminiscent of Peking duck pancakes) or get an order of pan-fried dumplings from the local Cantonese restaurant. Serve two stir-fries alongside steamy bowls of rice, and buy a bag of fortune cookies and some ice wine for dessert. Any off-dry white or sparkler will match this menu.

BBQ Duck Quesadillas, p. 226
East Meets Western Sandwich, p. 43

Beef and Baby Bok Choy, p. 56
Almond Chicken, p. 59
Steamed rice
Fortune cookies and ice wine

Viva Vietnam

Fresh, assertive and simple — the flavors of Southeast Asia are addictive and the Girl loves to surprise her guests with this easy and exotic menu that incorporates dishes from Vietnam, Thailand and points in between. Asian beer is the typical match but a fruity, off-dry white like a ripe Riesling will work, too.

Salad Rolls, p. 220
Solitary Saigon Satay Soup, p. 29
Panang Roast Chicken Curry, p. 57
Iced Coffee, p. 173

Tokyo Nights

Make this simple family-style meal and enjoy the fresh flavors of Japanese food. A plate of freshly made crab and cucumber rolls from the local sushi house makes a nice starter (it's sushi for the squeamish — no raw fish). Buy a good tropical fruit sorbet for dessert, or just pass some sliced mangoes or papaya with the cookies.

Big Bowl Miso Soup, p. 35
Green Salad with Japanese Sushi Bar Salad Dressing,
   p. 334
Tempura
Japanese Chicken Curry on rice, p. 62
Ginger Cookies, p. 311, with tropical fruit sorbet

Little Italy 1

Everyone loves the flavors of Italy, so pop the cork on a good Sangiovese, crank up the three tenors and eat, EAT!!

Pita Pizza, p. 44
Basic Risotto, p. 72
Baked Halibut with Tapenade Crust and Caponata, p. 247
Balsamic Strawberries Brûlée, p. 139

Little Italy 2 (a less formal feast)

Caponata, p. 274 on ciabatta bread
Almost Instant Spinach and Ricotta Lasagna, p. 82
or Pasta with Wilted Greens, Italian Sausage and Olives, p. 88
Tiramisu, p. 175

Athens by Night

The tavernas of Athens hold wonderful memories — casual places where you'll find lots of good food and fun. Make this menu when you want to celebrate summer or create a sunny getaway from the dull days of February. Greco de Tufo is a nice grape to explore with these Mediterranean flavors, or go full-on Greek with retsina and ouzo, then start breaking plates.

Tomato and Lentil Soup, p. 31
Saganaki on Chopped Tomato, Black Olive and Cucumber Salad, p. 24
Lamb Gyros Wraps, p. 109
or Chicken Souvlakia with Tzatziki, p. 52
Wilted Spinach with Rice, p. 259
Orange Honey Cake, p. 304

South of France Soirée

Imagine you're sitting in Provence, the heady aromas of wild lavender and thyme wafting through the air, an assertive salmon pink rosé in your glass. This is what you'd be eating.

Fresh Tomato Tart on Cornmeal Crust, p. 284
Mixed Greens with Goat Cheese Croutons, p. 130
Halibut Provençal, p. 154
or Bouillabaisse, p. 148
Chocolate Mocha Torte, p. 172

Middle Eastern Menu

Next time you're in a Middle Eastern grocery get a bottle of pomegranate molasses (syrup) and make this menu. A little mixed into a glass of sparkling wine makes a heady aperitif, too.

Mouhammara, p. 142
Hummus and Pita Crisps, p. 214
Room-Temperature Roasted Vegetable Couscous, p. 26
or Israeli Couscous Salad, p. 255
Persian Braised Lamb with Pomegranate, p. 169
Sliced oranges drizzled with wildflower honey

Southwestern Supper

Texas, Santa Fe, California or Baja, Mexico — a meal based on beans, corn and chilies, shot with fresh cilantro, always conjures up the sunny Southwest. This menu is perfect for a casual *al fresco* lunch or dinner, the way they eat all of the time down there. Serve the salad in summer, the Polenta Torte in cooler weather or when you want something more substantial. Uncork a creamy California Chardonnay or light fruity Zinfandel (even a mellow Merlot) — just make sure there are no tough tannins to fight with the spice.

Black Bean Dip, p. 238
Mexican-Style Chicken and Tortilla Soup, p. 30
Southwestern Polenta Torte, p. 278
or Grilled Steak Fajitas, p. 295
Corn, Avocado and Black Bean Salsa, p. 297
Mexican Chocolate Cupcakes, p. 300
or Espresso Flan, p. 177

A Kid-Friendly Affair

Go ahead, cover the place in plastic and invite the whole family for food at five. You'll become their favorite auntie — just make sure their parents take them home before their bedtime.

Nacho Cheese Dip, p. 238
Meatloaf, p. 96, with Honey Roasted Carrots, p. 185
or Kid-Friendly Fingers and Oven Fries, p. 50
or Cheese and Macaroni, p. 70
Chocolate Banana Bread Pudding, p. 322

The Big Family 'Que

Fire up the charcoal and barbecue, baby! Create this potluck menu and get your siblings to pony up with salads and desserts. Just copy the recipes and fax them out. A stress-free family gathering, perfect for a midsummer reunion of the clan. Buy beer and pop, and put it in an old wash tub filled with ice. Paper plates, of course.

Best Beef Burgers, p. 40
Vegetarian Burgers, p. 41
or Gooey Rack of Ribs with Killer Barbecue
    Sauce, p. 158
The Girl's Perfect Potato Salad, p. 251
Potluck Bean and Pasta Salad, p. 250
Green Goddess Caesar Salad, p. 253
Buttermilk Biscuits, p. 338
or Cornbread, p. 242
Chewy Chocolate Brownies, p. 281
Spicy Carrot Cake, p. 298
Real Lemonade, p. 282

The Big Breakfast Party

Sunday brunch can be a party with the right menu and a good group. Here's a start.

White Sangria, p. 112
Blueberry and Cornmeal Flapjacks, p. 262
Late Summer Garlic and Greens Pie, p. 263
Fresh Fruit Salad, p. 265, with lemon yogurt
Fruit Kuchen, p. 324, with coffee

She's a Vegetarian (casual)

No meat, no problem. For vegans, use The Mushroom Thing to start and the veggie burgers (no dairy). Lacto-ovo types will be fine with it all (just serve the sweetened mascarpone cheese on the side if she's sensitive). Red or white wine, or both, but nothing too heavy.

Spicy Whipped Feta, p. 257
or The Mushroom Thing, p. 212
Tomato and Lentil Soup (in small portions), p. 31
Vegetarian Burgers, p. 41
or Greek Pasta Toss with Chickpeas and Feta, p. 84
Brûléed Apricots with Mascarpone, p. 315

She's a Vegetarian (to impress her)

Use vegetable broth when making your soup and risotto and hold off on the mascarpone with the pears if she's a dairy-free type, too. Go with white wine — try something Spanish or Italian with enough crispness to cut through the richness of the risotto and the olive oil, and refresh your palate for the next big bite, or opt for a buttery, rich Chardonnay from Australia.

Roasted Parsnip Soup, p. 99
The Big Green, p. 252
Risotto and Roasted Heirloom Tomatoes, p. 105
or Artichokes and Potatoes Braised in Olive Oil, p. 260
Zinful Poached Pears, p. 325

More Stuff

Wanna know more?

Turn to this section — easily organized in alphabetical order — with all the details about unusual ingredients, basic equipment and techniques. When you aren't clear about something in the text, you can flip to the back of the book to learn everything you ever wanted, or needed, to know.

These are the secret weapons of chefs and foodies — the tricks that make cooking easy, the ingredients and prepared foods that every good cook uses to impress. It's not an exhaustive list, but it covers many of the FAQ bases. If the answer's not here, check the index for a full listing of Girl Talk tips. It doesn't hurt to read through this stuff once in awhile (great bedtime reading) to remind and inspire you.

Altitude

At high altitudes, the Girl's buns can be flat and unattractive. That's because altitude affects the way leavening agents like yeast, baking powder and baking soda work to make things rise. Know the tricks and adjust your recipes accordingly.

For cakes that rise and fall, try reducing the baking powder or soda by 1/8 tsp. per tsp. (.5 mL per 5 mL).

At high altitudes, moisture evaporates more quickly so adjust your recipes with a little more liquid.

The higher the altitude, the lower the temperature of the food. Don't crank the heat but plan to bake things a little longer than specified.

At higher altitudes reduce the amount of sugar called for by about 1 Tbsp. per cup (15 mL per 250 mL) since sugar can weaken the structure of baked goods.

Arborio Rice

This is the starchy, short grain rice you need to make creamy risotto. Don't try to use regular or converted rice for this dish — you won't get the right texture. And don't be tempted to add the liquid all at once. The trick to making risotto creamy is in the stirring, adding hot liquid, 1/2 cup (125 mL) at a time, then stirring until it's absorbed before adding more, resulting in a soft and creamy, but still slightly chewy grain. You'll need 3–4 cups (750 mL–1 L) of liquid for every cup (250 mL) of rice, and 30 minutes.

Arborio has lots of starch, so it makes a dense risotto (even gummy if improperly cooked). Vialone Nano is another type of risotto rice to buy. Grown in Veneto, it makes the looser style of risotto popular there, less starchy but firmer to the bite. Carnaroli (a cross of vialone and Japanese rice) is the most expensive rice for risotto — both firm and creamy when cooked.

Asian Chili Paste

An essential secret weapon in the Girl's arsenal, garlic chili paste (a.k.a. sambal oelek) is searingly hot, comes in jars at any Asian market and is far better than the usual liquid hot sauces for adding a jolt of tangy heat to almost anything without excess acidity. Of course, a dollop is appropriate in any Szechuan stir-fry sauce, but you'll also use this paste in barbecue sauces and rubs and to add heat to soups, salad dressings, chili or Italian puttanesca sauce. Use sparingly.

Balsamic Vinegar

Real balsamic vinegar (balsamico) is made in and around Modena, Italy. The cheapest versions are just red wine vinegar with caramel flavoring and sugar added. The best are aged for decades in tiny wooden barrels until they're sweet, complex and thick as molasses. You can pay anywhere from $5 for a quart (L) to $150 for 1/2 cup (125 mL) for balsamic vinegar. Try a few before you decide which to use on your salads. If you can't afford the real thing, see the Girl's Trilogy of Trucs (page 17) to see how to make a reasonable facsimile of aged balsamico at home using garden-variety balsamic vinegar.

Basmati Rice

This Indian rice has a perfumed, nutty flavor and delicate long grains. Buy a sack of top-quality basmati at an Indian grocery and use it for all rice dishes (except sushi and risotto).

Beans

There's nothing wrong with using canned beans, especially when you're using them in soups or purées like bean dip. Canned beans are fast, convenient and cheap. Just dump them into a colander and rinse them under the tap to remove the starchy broth (it's high in sodium). Chickpeas (garbanzo beans) are perfectly acceptable from the can, whether they're going into hummus (puréed) or to be used whole in salads and soups. But if you're planning a special dish where a nice, toothsome bean is important (chili, baked beans, cassoulet, etc.) start from scratch with dried beans.

To cook dried beans, wash them well and soak them overnight in water. If you don't have that much time, put the dried beans in a pot, cover them with lots of cold water and bring to a boil. Cover the pot, remove from the heat and let the beans soak for 1 hour before draining and starting your recipe.

Don't salt beans or try to cook them in an acidic sauce (like tomato sauce) or they will never soften properly. Cook them in lots of water first, then add your salty and acidic ingredients.

Remember, beans cook at different rates, depending on the type, size and how fresh they are, so don't combine a bunch of different dried beans and expect them to be done at the same time.

Blanch

This refers to quickly immersing food in boiling water to partially cook it. It's ideal for cooking tougher vegetables like broccoli or carrots before adding them to a stir-fry, or par-cooking green beans to a bright color for a salad. You can blanch your vegetables, chill them in ice water, drain and refrigerate before a dinner party, then reheat them by sautéeing them in butter just before serving. (This is what chefs do — the reheated veggies cook evenly and stay brightly colored this way.) Vegetables are usually blanched before freezing. And you can use blanching to help you peel tomatoes or peaches — cut an X in the skin, dump them into boiling water for a minute, then cool them in ice water and slip off the skins.

Bok Choy et al

Bok choy is one of the Girl's favorite Asian vegetables — especially the mild baby bok choy, less than 5 inches (13 cm) long, that can be split lengthwise and braised as a vegetable side to almost any meal. Bigger bok choy should be sliced and stir-fried — add the tougher ends to the pan first, and stir the more delicate leafy parts in at the end, so they're just wilted. See Greens 101 (page 351) for more.

Bowls

Pretty bowls are nice to display in the kitchen, but stainless steel bowls are the real work horses. Get a bunch in different sizes — a massive one for tossing big salads and making ice baths, and small ones that fit snugly into your saucepans like a double boiler, for cooking delicate sauces and custards.

Also handy are heatproof glass or crockery custard cups and individual straight-sided soufflé dishes — little bowls for making and serving puddings, poached eggs, soufflés, fruit napped in sabayon and crème caramel.

Braise

Braising is cooking something with liquid, usually with the lid on. You can braise in the oven or on top of the stove. You can braise with broth, wine, juice, cider, beer or water. Braised meats are usually seared first in a little fat over medium-high heat to brown the meat on all sides before braising — this adds more of that rich caramelized flavor to your braise. Then you lower the heat, add the liquid, clamp on the lid and cook slowly for a long time. Braising is a tenderizing step, for tougher cuts of meat. Braising is what makes beef stew, pot roast and daube of lamb so darned delicious.

Broth

Canned broth is fine but homemade is better. Save your scraps in the freezer (bones from chicken and pork, clean vegetable trimmings like leek and green onion tops, carrot peelings, etc.) and make stock from scratch, then freeze it in small containers. You can make stocks from chicken bones, meat bones and fish bones. All benefit by the inclusion of aromatic vegetables like sliced onions, celery, carrots, garlic and parsnips, and whole herbs and spices like black peppercorns, parsley and bay leaves.

Just place 4–5 lbs. (2–2.5 kg) of bones, vegetables and flavorings in a deep stock pot (the tallest pot you have) and cover with 12–16 cups (3–4 L) of cold water. Bring it to a boil over high heat, skim off any foam that rises to the top, then reduce the heat to medium-low and simmer the stock, uncovered, for 4 hours. Strain through a sieve that's been lined with cheesecloth. Discard the solids and chill the broth in the refrigerator or freeze it. Season the broth to taste with salt before using it in soups or other recipes.

Fish stock needs only about 30 minutes of simmering and benefits from the addition of some white wine. Use fish bones, heads and tails (avoid salmon as the flavor is too strong).

Beef stock is best if it's simmered for 5 hours or more.

For more intense broths, start by roasting the bones and vegetables in a 450°F (220°C) oven to brown for about 45 minutes before adding the water. This caramelizes the sugars and results in a broth with more color and flavor. Or use the already-roasted carcass of your Sunday chicken or holiday turkey. If your broth seems flat, boil it to reduce it further, or add a little salt.

Cheese

Real cheese is never processed, it is a natural product.

Try to buy good-quality, artisan cheese or at least authentic cheese made in countries like France and Italy where there are strict rules governing how cheeses are made. The industrial cheese we've created in North America usually isn't anything like real cheese.

Every refrigerator should have some good cheese for eating and cooking. Buy a chunk of Parmigiano-Reggiano for grating, a good artisan Brie or Camembert for serving with wine, a nice Gouda and aged Cheddar, and some fresh goat cheese and blue cheese. When you're making pizza, mozzarella or Friulano are good choices. Monterey Jack makes the best quesadillas. The next time you have a party, buy three or four interesting cheeses and offer a cheese tray with bread and crackers. Instant appetizer.

Make a trip to a proper cheese store and begin sampling good-quality cheeses — you'll never go back.

Chipotle Chilies

A chipotle is nothing more than a garden-variety jalapeño with a little experience — a pepper that's been smoked over a wood fire. Find them dried in the supermarket produce section (soak to rehydrate) or, even better, canned in adobo sauce (at a Latin market). Once you open a can of chipotles, you can store any leftovers in a sealed container in the refrigerator for several months. Chipotles add a wonderful smoky sweet heat to chilis, soups, stews, dips and rubs.

Chocolate

When the Girl goes for chocolate, she goes all out, for the real thing, because good chocolate is healthy and junk chocolate is not. Pick your battles, and your calories, she says.

Make sure the dark chocolate you buy — for eating or baking — is labeled "pure" and contains nothing more than chocolate solids (or chocolate liquor), cocoa butter, sugar and lethicin (an emulsifier). Milk chocolate will have some milk ingredients, too. But shy away from "chocolate" products that list sugar as the first ingredient and include unhealthy fats like hydrogenated oils. Good chocolate companies label their products with the amount of real chocolate solids — usually 60–70% for dark chocolate, 35% for milk chocolate. And while cocoa butter is high in fat — and is saturated — it's the kind of vegetable fat that can actually lower cholesterol. Really.

Coconut Milk

Coconut milk comes in a can and can be found in well-stocked supermarkets or Asian groceries. Look for the unsweetened kind (the sweet stuff is only for desserts). Buy fat-reduced coconut milk (often labeled "lite") as the full-fat stuff is a killer in the calorie department.

Couscous

Technically, couscous is a very small pasta, made by rubbing semolina flour into tiny balls with water. The easiest — and most commonly available — couscous to use is the instant variety. Look for it in the pasta sections of large supermarkets, Middle Eastern groceries and health food stores.

For every cup (250 mL) of couscous, you'll need about 1½ cups (375 mL) boiling water or broth. Simply mix the dry couscous into the boiling liquid, cover, remove from the heat and let stand for about 10 minutes while the couscous hydrates. Fluff it with a fork to separate the grains and serve. That's it.

Think of couscous as a blank slate — traditionally, the broth used to cook it is flavored with saffron and then bits like raisins and fried onions are added. But couscous takes to all kinds of creative additions, from roasted peppers and chili powder, to dried fruits, chickpeas and fresh herbs. Serve it hot with Moroccan stews or cold in potluck salads. A kind of tabouli can be made with couscous instead of bulgar (cracked and steamed whole wheat that cooks up about the same way — see page 351), by combining cooked couscous with lots of chopped parsley, olive oil, tomatoes and cumin. Play with it. Experiment.

Israeli couscous is an entirely different animal —

fat balls of semolina pasta with the look and texture of tapioca. Like the smaller version, Israeli couscous soaks up whatever flavor it's introduced to, and makes a substantial side dish or salad.

Cream

Whipping, or "heavy," cream is highest in fat and can be whipped. It also instantly thickens a sauce when it's added at the end and reduced. Half-and-half, or "cereal cream," is a combination of milk and cream — it won't whip but gives rich flavor to soups and sauces with fewer calories. For really low-fat cream soups, use condensed skim milk (canned) for a similar texture.

Crème Fraîche

This thickened sweet cream can go both ways — on a sweet dessert or swirled into a savory soup. Make it by mixing 2 cups (500 mL) of heavy (whipping) cream with ½ cup (125 mL) of sour cream. Whisk the mixture together in a bowl, cover with plastic wrap and set aside at room temperature for 12 hours. When the crème fraîche is nicely thickened, store it in the refrigerator for up to 2 weeks. Nice instead of sweetened cream on fruit desserts.

Curry Paste

This is another of the Girl's secret weapons. Indian curry pastes come in jars and are combinations of exotic spices like turmeric, coriander, fennel, cloves, chilies and cardamom with ginger, garlic and oil. There are mild and hot curry pastes for general cooking and pastes for specific Indian dishes like biryani, tandoori chicken or rogan josh, so look for them at Indian groceries and stock a few. Curry pastes replace the old-fashioned curry powders — they're more intense, fresher, more convenient to use, even shelf stable at room temperature.

Thai curry pastes are essential to Thai cooking and are completely different from the Indian versions. While serious Thai chefs would grind their own pastes by hand with a mortar and pestle, you can save time by buying prepared pastes. Thai curry pastes come in two basic varieties — red curry paste and green curry paste. Both contain classic southeast Asian flavorings like coriander seeds, lemon grass, galangal, shrimp

paste and kaffir lime zest; the red paste is colored and flavored with dried red chilies, while the slightly milder green curry paste has fresh Thai or serrano peppers, which give the paste its distinctive color. Find them in tubs or pouches in Asian markets. They should be refrigerated.

Stock both Indian and Thai curry pastes in your pantry for adding instant authentic flavor to stir-fries and other curry dishes, or for flavoring soups, dips and sauces. Thai pastes are traditionally combined with coconut milk in curries and soups. Use Indian pastes in rubs for grilling fish and chicken, to make a regular chicken and rice soup into an exotic mulligatawny, or to dress up side dishes of steamed potatoes and cauliflower.

Cuts (Chop, Dice, Mince, Cube, Chiffonade, Julienne)

Every recipe asks for a different cut, it seems. If you're not familiar with these terms it can seem like recipes are written in a foreign language. But it pays to get a good knife and hone your knife knowledge. The best chefs have the best knife skills and can cut those beautiful even little cubes of red pepper or cucumber by hand. It just takes practice.

Basic cuts range from coarse chopping and mincing to dicing, julienne, chiffonade and diagonal or rolled cuts. Coarse chopping is used for vegetables that are used for flavoring and will eventually be puréed or strained out of the dish.

A regular "chop" or dice is cutting into ¼– to ½–inch (.5– to 1–cm) even cubes; a finer dice might be pieces 1/16–1/8 inch (1–3 mm) in size. Mince means to chop very fine, almost purée. Julienne cuts are little sticks, batons or almost shreds — which may be 2 inches (5 cm) long or so, chunky or very fine (nice in pasta dishes or salads).

To chop an onion, peel it, cut it in half lengthwise, then lay it flat on a cutting board. Cut even horizontal and vertical slices through the onion, all the way up to, but not through, the root end. Then slice across the onion, from the stem to the root end, to evenly dice.

Garlic, ginger and herbs call for mincing. After the food is coarsely chopped, gather it into a pile. Hold the tip of the knife on the board and, using a rocking motion, continue to chop over the pile until everything is finely minced. To prepare both garlic and ginger for quick mincing, place the flat blade of the chef's knife over the peeled vegetable and give it a firm whack with your fist. You can also get both garlic and ginger even finer in an instant by using a fine grater or pressing it in a garlic press (but then you have to clean another tool, which the Girl hates to do).

To evenly dice vegetables like carrots and potatoes, peel them and trim them into blocks (save the trimmings in the freezer for stock). Cut the blocks into even strips (batonnets) or fine shreds (julienne). Stack the strips and cut crosswise for perfect dice. A mandoline (see page 354) makes this easiest but you can do it by hand if you're accurate.

To make a chiffonade, roll leafy vegetables or herbs into tight cylinders like cigars and slice thinly across the roll to form shreds.

The diagonal, or rolled, cut is used when you want to expose the most surface area to the heat and cook quickly — say in a stir-fry or stew. Cut even parallel cuts of celery, carrot or parsnips on a sharp diagonal or make one diagonal, turn the vegetable half a turn, then make a second diagonal cut and repeat. This gives you chunky pieces with two angled edges.

Edamame

These fresh green soybeans are the steamed, salty pods you get at the sushi bar. Buy them in bags from the freezer section of your local Asian grocery and simply steam them for 4 minutes in the microwave, douse with sea salt and serve for snacking like they do in Japan (just pull the pods through your teeth to remove the beans and toss away the pods). This may well be the coolest and easiest appetizer anywhere — and it's healthy, too.

The Girl also likes to buy the shelled soybeans at the market (same spot in the freezer department), steam and toss them with olive oil and garlic to serve as a side dish with almost anything. You'll see these electric green beans popping up on all of the best plates — they're rich tasting, incredibly easy to cook and beautiful to behold.

Eggs

Use large eggs in all of these recipes — free-range and farm-fresh, if possible. Bring eggs to room temperature before using them in baking.

Fish Sauce

You may think you will never use that big bottle of fish sauce (a.k.a. nam pla or nuoc nam), but it's essential flavoring for southeast Asian cooking. Don't smell or taste it straight — that strong, fermented fishy flavor will surely put you off — but use it when it's called for in an Asian recipe for authentic flavor.

Fish sauce, like soy sauce, has that elusive savory flavor that wine tasters call umami. It's a universally loved flavor sensation. So don't limit your fish sauce to Thai curries.

The Girl knows a chef who uses a dash of fish sauce to finish almost every soup and sauce he makes, whether it's French, Italian or Japanese. The fish sauce adds that *je ne sais quoi* that boosts the flavor of everything he cooks. Think of it as liquid anchovies. It could become your own secret weapon.

Food Processor

The Girl would never give up her chef's knife or her other essential mincing and puréeing tool, the food processor.

Cuisinart® is arguably the granddaddy of all food processors and buying a large, good-quality food processor will never let you down. Without it, you won't be able to make the simple dips, spreads, sauces, creamed soups, cheesecakes and other dishes that rely on the puréeing power of the food processor. And, although you can always do it by hand, a food processor lets you mince onions and garlic, and chop the carrots, mushrooms and celery that you need to start soups, sauces and stews almost instantly.

You can't do all of your mixing in a food processor (it's not great for whipping cream or beating egg whites, and it makes horribly gluey puréed potatoes) but you can make bread- or cracker crumbs, grate hard cheese and chop chocolate, grind nuts, purée whole tomatoes, chop spinach and mix bread and pizza dough. If a recipe calls for chopped or ground ingredients, pulse them in the food processor — using on and off bursts until the food is processed to your liking. Use the metal chopping blade for most jobs, the plastic blade for dough and special discs for shredding and slicing.

Always make sure the lid is securely in place before you turn the machine on (most models won't work unless the lid is attached) and always use the plastic pushing tool to feed foods into the shredding blades.

Garam Masala

This is a blend of Indian spices — a kind of chocolate brown curry powder that includes "hot" spices like cinnamon, cloves, black pepper, cardamom, fennel, mace, nutmeg, chilies and cumin. Buy it at Indian groceries.

Garlic Press

This is a nifty gadget that turns a clove of garlic or a chunk of fresh ginger into the perfect pulpy consistency you need in sauces and salad dressings. Not essential but handy — get a good name-brand version, the cheap ones are garage sale fodder.

Ginger

Ginger is a root with thin beige skin. The easiest way to peel a piece of ginger is by scraping away the skin with a teaspoon. Then you can lay the flat side of your chef's knife over the chunk of ginger and smash it with your fist — the result will be a pulpy mass that you can easily chop. Another good way to mince fresh ginger is to use your microplane grater or garlic press. You can even freeze fresh ginger and grate it when it's still frozen. Galangal is a type of mild Thai ginger — a pale yellow, pink-tinged relative.

Grains

Whole grains are healthier than processed white rice or flour. They come complete with all of the fiber, protein and vitamins that nature gave them.

Barley comes in two varieties — pearl barley or whole-grain barley. The latter is healthier but takes longer to cook. Cook 1 cup (250 mL) barley in 3 cups (750 mL) boiling water or stock for 45 minutes.

Bulgar wheat is whole wheat that's been steamed, dried and cracked. It cooks on its own (like couscous) in minutes. Just pour 2 cups (500 mL) of boiling liquid over 1 cup (250 mL) of bulgar, cover and let stand 30 minutes, or boil it like rice.

Kasha is toasted buckwheat — a triangular little grain with a unique smoky flavor. To keep the cooked grains separate, toast in a dry pan with a beaten egg for 5 minutes before adding 2$\frac{1}{2}$ cups (625 mL) of water or stock for every cup (250 mL) of kasha. Boil for 20 minutes.

Wild rice is not a rice but a long dark grain from a grass that grows wild and is cultivated in northern marshes and lakes. Cook 1 cup (250 mL) wild rice in 4 cups (1 L) broth for 45 minutes until the grains split.

Grater

For hard cheese like Parmesan the only grater to use is the microplane grater, a slim steel grater with rows of tiny square teeth. This tool is actually a type of wood rasp, borrowed from the woodworker's tool box, and the Girl acquired her inexpensive model at a hardware store. Nowadays, every culinary store has a tarted up version of this basic shop tool for the kitchen. Get one — it's the only way to get beautiful fluffy shreds of hard cheese and instantly minced garlic and ginger. Like a good knife, the microplane is an essential kitchen tool.

A box grater (the stainless steel kind with different sized holes on each side) is cheap and useful for grating Cheddar cheese, carrots and onions for coleslaw and other things. If you're grating a lot of stuff, get a grating blade for your food processor — makes shavings of carrots, cabbage and cheese in an instant.

Greens 101

Simple salads can be special when the green stuff in the bowl tastes fresh, crunchy and varied. Don't get stuck with limp lettuce or bland bowls of iceberg — experiment with new and eclectic greens for your salads and you'll be more likely to eat your greens.

You'll find an array of greens — from spinach and chard to gourmet salad mixes and kale — at most large supermarkets. For ethnic greens — bok choy, watercress and mustard greens — check Asian markets.

Italian markets often have fresh bunches of broccoli rabe, basil and tight heads of crisp radicchio. You can count on local farmers to bring ultra-fresh arugula, sorrel, dandelion and other fresh greens to market in the spring. Or toss some seeds in a pot for your own supply of quick-growing arugula and salad herbs.

Here's a primer on what you'll get from your greens.

Arugula: This peppery green is a member of the mustard family and flourishes in cool climates. Also known as rocket, spicy arugula will perk up salads or can be sautéed with spinach and garlic, tossed with hot pasta or stirred into a vegetable fritatta.

Basil: Technically, basil is a herb but the large-leaf varieties add a lovely sweet anise and mint flavor to salads. Fresh basil makes a savory base or topping for a fresh tomato salad and is good in pasta sauces, on pizza or stuffed into grilled vegetable sandwiches.

Sorrel: Sorrel looks like spinach but belongs to the buckwheat family and is a hardy perennial plant with a tart, lemony flavor. Shred some for a salad with a lemon vinaigrette, add chopped sorrel to lift a basic potato soup, purée it into mayonnaise or add it to butter sauces for fish.

Watercress: The Girl loves these small peppery leaves with their radish-like flavor. Look for watercress with the parsley in supermarkets — Asian groceries usually have the freshest watercress. Serve it in elegant composed salads with pears and blue cheese, or use it instead of lettuce in sandwiches or wraps.

Edible Flowers: Please don't eat the daisies from the florist (they're probably sprayed), but many blooms that grow in the home garden are edible and gorgeous as edible garnishes. Posies to pick for dinner include bachelor buttons, pansies, violets, blue borage, carnations, daisies, chive blossoms, fuchsias, marigolds, nasturtiums, roses and snap dragons.

Pea Shoots: With the fresh, crisp flavor of garden peas, pea shoots are wonderful greens to add to salads. Try a tangle of pea shoots atop a piece of fish as an edible green garnish, or chop pea shoots and stir them into your next risotto. Pea shoots are often cooked in Chinese stir-fries — look for a fresh supply at Asian markets.

Mustard Greens: Called baby gai choy at Chinese markets, this chard-like leaf is tangy and peppery and makes an excellent cooked green. Baby bok choy is another great candidate for stir-fries or to quickly grill or braise as a side dish.

Kale: Kale is a tough customer and needs to be cooked or braised for a long time, making it great for soups. But curly green, purple or ivory heads of flowering kale instantly decorate the buffet or salad station, and the leaves are perfect for lining salad bowls or adding color to winter plates.

Chicory: If you like bitter greens, chicory is the one for you. Also called curly endive and frisée, this green has sharply cut and curled leaves. The youngest leaves are generally sweetest, but all have a bitter tinge.

Radicchio: This Italian form of chicory has small purple and white heads. Radicchio adds color to mixed salads, and a bittersweet flavor.

Spinach: Spinach has medium-sized, arrow-shaped leaves and can be eaten raw or cooked. Blanch it quickly or sauté it just until bright green, but don't use an aluminum pan — your spinach will turn gray and take on a metallic taste.

Chard: Swiss chard is a sweet-flavored green for cooking that anyone can grow. Look for colorful rainbow chard with red, yellow and white stems. Substitute it for spinach or beet greens.

Nasturtium Leaves: The Girl always plants nasturtiums in her flower pots since they do double duty for entertaining. Not only are the plants and flowers beautiful — cascades of big round leaves and pretty red, orange and gold blooms — all parts of the plant are edible and add a unique peppery flavor to salads or garnishes.

Dandelion Greens: Keep the herbicides off your lawn, and harvest a spring crop of edible young dandelion greens for salads before the plants flower and go to seed. Dandelion greens are very nutritious. Eat them cooked or in salads.

Grill

Purists cook on charcoal (admittedly, it adds flavor), but speed demons go for gas (natural or propane). Instant on, instant off. When it's cold outside, fire up the broiler instead or get an indoor grill for similar results with most grilling recipes. The best things to grill are chicken, steaks, burgers, fish steaks — anything thin enough to be nicely browned on the outside and cooked through at the same time. For bigger pieces of meat, you'll need to brown it on the grill first, then turn off one of the burners, move the meat to the unlit side, cover the barbecue and roast until done.

While we often say "barbecue" we really mean "grill" — barbecue is slow cooking, indirectly over smoky heat, the kind of cooking that gives you pulled pork and the best brisket. Use the smoker.

Ground Beef

Not all ground beef (hamburger) is created equally and you want to choose the right ground beef for your recipe.

Regular: With the most fat, this is the ground beef to choose when you're making something like spaghetti sauce or tacos — recipes where the beef is browned first, and the excess fat can be drained off.

Medium: Less fat and better for meatballs or hamburgers, the kind of cooking that allows you to drain off at least some of the fat during cooking. Still enough fat to keep foods juicy.

Lean or Extra Lean: Choose this kind of ground beef for meat loaf, cabbage rolls and dumplings — recipes that don't let you drain off any of the excess fat.

Remember, always cook ground meat (beef, chicken, pork, lamb or any ground meat) until it's well done all the way through. The bacteria that is often found on the outer surfaces of raw meats is destroyed when that meat is seared on the outside, so a rare steak is fine. But when ground, that surface contamination can be mixed throughout the meat and you must get it all up to high temperatures to make sure it's safe.

Herbs

Use fresh herbs whenever possible. Do yourself a favor and plant some pots of basil, rosemary, mint, dill, cilantro and Italian parsley this spring. All of them are easy to grow. Then, when you need a bit of fresh herbal flavor, you can just snip off what you need. Some of the woodier herbs, like thyme and sage, are perennials and if you plunk a plant in a sheltered spot in the flower garden, it will come back year after year.

In most cases, you want to use just the leaves and discard the stems as they can be coarse or downright woody. If you end up with a bumper crop of herbs, try making pestos by puréeing the herbs with olive oil in the food processor and freezing the pesto in ice cube trays. Pop them out, put them back in the freezer in plastic bags and toss a cube into your next soup, stew or dip for instant fresh herb flavor.

If you must substitute dry herbs, remember that they are much stronger — use $1/3$ to $1/2$ the amount of dry herb when fresh herbs are called for in a recipe.

Hoisin, Black Bean, Oyster et al

Who knows exactly what it is about these assertive Asian sauces — suffice to say every Chinese restaurant kitchen uses them and you should, too. Dark, thick, sweet, spicy combinations of soybeans, chilies, sugar and other exotic notes, they add that authentic edge to every Asian dish. Don't use too much — a Tbsp. or two (15–25 mL) is always enough — but find a source of sauces and keep them in your refrigerator. Experiment when you're marinating chicken or pork for the grill, creating a new salad dressing or just stir-frying seasonal veggies.

Jicama

Ever seen a round, beige veggie in the market, like a flattened turnip with a tan skin the color of ginger? That's a jicama — a crisp, juicy Latin vegetable that makes a lovely addition to a vegetable tray and can be shredded with carrots into a refreshing slaw. You can also cube the sweet white flesh and use it in stir-fries instead of fresh water chestnuts.

Kitchen Shears

They may look just like hefty scissors but good kitchen shears (made by one of the European knife companies) are essential in the kitchen. Use them to cut up a whole chicken with ease, or just to remove the useless "back attached" bones from those inexpensive leg/thigh combos you find in the supermarket (save the trimmings in the freezer for soup).

Kitchen shears also make fast work of sticky stuff that's hard to chop, like dried apricots, pitted prunes, dates or sticky candies like jube-jubes. But be careful, and keep your fingers away from the sharp blades.

When a pot of cooked Chinese noodles or vermicelli binds up into a tangled ball when you try to toss it with the sauce, reach in with the shears and take several serious snips through the mass; the noodles will release into separated strands.

Knives

A couple of good knives are the only really essential kitchen tools you need to cook. The Girl's favorite knife is a big 12-inch (30-cm) chef's knife, which is used to chop and slice nearly everything she makes. She's had a German knife for years, but recently acquired a new fat-bladed Füri knife from Australia (a kind of hybrid chef's-knife-cum-cleaver) with an all-in-one stainless blade and handle. Very sharp, and sharp looking, too. The wide blade makes it easy to scoop up stuff from the cutting board to carry to the pan.

A good, short-bladed paring knife is also important and a serrated bread knife is necessary for slicing bread, tomatoes, cakes and similar stuff. If you plan to cook a lot of big things (roasts, turkeys, hams, etc.) invest in a long, narrow-bladed slicing knife.

Don't cheap out on your knives. Go to a good culinary store and buy good-quality knives. It's important that the tang (the extension of the blade) continues to the end of the handle and that the handle is riveted in place properly. The blade should be a high-carbon stainless steel alloy, a metal that is strong, keeps an edge and will not discolor or rust.

Good knives will last forever if you look after them. Get them professionally sharpened from time to time and don't put them in the dishwasher. A wooden cutting board is best for your knives — avoid cutting directly on glass or granite.

Leek Lore

Leeks are notoriously gritty. You can only use the bottom one-third of the leek (the white and pale green part) and the tough tops are really only good to save for the stock pot (freeze cleaned trimmings like this if you want to make your own stocks). Then you must cut the leek in half lengthwise and carefully rinse between the layers, under running water, to remove the sandy soil that somehow gets inside. Cut off the base, and slice in thin half-moons. Or you can slice them first, put them in a colander and give them a good soaking and rinsing under the tap. No leeks? Slivered white onions will do.

Lemon Grass

Spot this lemony herb in an Asian market and you'll think you've come across a big, tough, dried-out green onion. Use it in Thai cooking and curry pastes — but only the white bit at the bottom as the leaves are too chewy. And make sure to mince it or purée it in a blender. Add whole chunks of lemon grass to broths to add perfumed lemony flavor, but remove the chunks before serving.

Lemon Reamer

This simple hand tool is indispensable for removing the juice from citrus fruits like lemons, limes and oranges. The Girl's version is a plain wooden reamer with a handle attached at the base, although old-fashioned reamers were often incorporated into glass or metal dishes. Simply cut the lemon in half crosswise, insert the pointy end of the reamer into the center of the fruit and twist (or press down over the point of the dish). You'll soon have all of the juice and luscious pulp in your bowl.

Lentils

Brown lentils are the little, flat, disc-shaped ones that are most common. They keep their shape when cooked.

A similar and more rare lentil is the French green Puy lentil. Worth buying, if you can find them, for soups and lentil salads.

Tiny orange lentils disintegrate when cooked and turn a golden color — the basis for thick lentil soups and purées.

Mandoline

Not the musical variety, a cook's mandoline is a fancy slicer/dicer. It's a flat bed inset with an adjustable, ultra-sharp blade. You slide the food across to cut it into perfect, thin slices.

Use it to cut paper-thin potatoes or the finest julienne

of carrots and cucumbers. Professional mandolines are lovely, stainless steel affairs, but cost hundreds of dollars. You can find a very inexpensive and functional Japanese version at Asian houseware shops for about $40. Always use the plastic guard to hold the food while you're slicing — these babies are super sharp and dangerous in the wrong hands.

Measuring Cups/Devices

The Girl will say this again — in case you didn't read page 299. The glass measuring cups are for liquids, the individually sized metal or plastic cups (i.e. ¼ cup/50 mL, ½ cup/125 mL, etc.) are for dry ingredients. If you mix them up, your cakes and breads and cookies won't work out right. Dry measures and measuring spoons should never be heaped — fill them then use the back of a knife to scrape off any excess. Solid fats, like butter, shredded cheese or sour cream, are also measured in a dry measure.

Get down at eye level to see how much liquid you have in a glass measuring cup.

It's really handy to have some big, heatproof glass measuring cups, too — you can essentially mix batters right in the cup. A scale is also handy for weighing meats or following recipes that specify ingredients by weight.

Meats

The best way to learn about meat is from a butcher, and they're few and far between in our mega markets these days. If you have a local butcher, talk to him/her about the best cuts for grilling, roasting and braising. This is knowledge you need.

A lot of people get disappointing results because they buy the wrong meat — they try to grill or broil a tough cut, for example. The beef business is doing something to help, labeling different cuts with the appropriate cooking method. When you see something labeled "marinating steak" (like a round steak or sirloin tip) make sure to marinate it to tenderize it or it will be tough. On the other hand, meat labeled "grilling steak" (like t-bone, tenderloin, strip loin) can go right on the grill. Just make sure it's cut at least ¾ inch (2 cm) thick. (See page 232 for the skinny on beef roasts.)

The same goes for pork or lamb. Tenderloins and chops are tender and good for fast cooking. Shoulders need longer, slower cooking methods to render extra fat and tenderize.

Miso

This is a fermented Japanese soybean paste that adds salty flavor and substance to many Japanese dishes. The color ranges from a light golden color to a dark mahogany. Like wine, the lighter the color, the smoother and less complex the flavor. High in B vitamins and easy to digest, it's a very nutritious condiment. Use miso in soups, sauces, marinades, salad dressings and dips. It comes refrigerated, or frozen, in tubs in Asian markets, and keeps well for several months in the refrigerator.

Mushrooms

Morels, chanterelles, shiitake — you can't know your mushrooms without a program.

And you don't want to pick anything in the back forty and eat it unless you know exactly what you're getting into — tie into the wrong fungus and you're no longer among us.

But commercial mushrooms are a different story and there's an amazing selection of delicious mushrooms in the market.

Standard white and brown mushrooms are always available. Portobellos are massive versions of your basic brown mushroom (sometimes growing 8 inches/20 cm across) and take well to baking and grilling. Just brush them with a little olive oil, and sprinkle with some herbs and seasoning. They make great appetizers, topped with things like sundried tomatoes and Parmesan cheese, then baked and cut into wedges. A whole grilled portobello can also stand in for a meaty hamburger patty for vegetarians. **Morels** are wonderful earthy mushrooms that you get in springtime. The long, conical caps look like little black sponges and are perfect to add to pasta dishes or risotto, along with asparagus and other seasonal ingredients.

Chanterelles are available in the fall. They are elegant orange mushrooms, vase-shaped, with a beautiful aroma.

Porcini mushrooms are some of the Girl's favorites — a sweet, earthy brown mushroom that's perfect on all occasions. Porcini are from Italy and are most often sold dried. Cèpes are the same mushroom, usually from France.

Shiitake are Asian mushrooms, dark brown and meaty and rich in flavor. They are cultivated in North America so are sometimes found fresh, but are always sold dried in bags at Chinese grocery stores.

Speaking of dried mushrooms, this is the most convenient way to buy exotic mushrooms and the best way to make sure that you always have some interesting mushrooms on hand. Morels, chanterelles, shiitake and porcini — all are available dried for rehydrating on a whim. To rehydrate, soak them in warm water or simmer in a little white wine for added flavor. Asian mushrooms like shiitake can be simmered in water flavored with soy sauce and sugar to rehydrate.

Truffles — not exactly mushrooms but in the fungus family — are imported from France and Italy in the fall and winter, where they are routed out of the ground by trained pigs and dogs. There are black truffles and rare white truffles, but both of these luxuries are very expensive and used sparingly. The Girl actually owns a tool designed to shave paper-thin slices from a truffle, although she has never had an actual specimen in her kitchen.

If you really want to impress someone, buy a tiny bottle of good-quality truffle oil at a gourmet shop and drizzle a few drops over a dish just before you serve it. The aroma of truffles is heavenly and does magical things to scrambled eggs.

Mustard

Every culture enjoys the fiery flavor of good mustard. While most of the mustard seed that goes into the world's mustard is grown on the Canadian prairies, it's shipped around the globe to be ground and flavored for spicy English mustards, grainy German mustards, smooth Dijon, fiery Chinese mustard and oceans of American ballpark mustard for hot dogs. Buy a selection of different mustards for your pantry.

You can make your own mustards by combining dry mustard powder with cold water, vinegar and flavorings, then letting it cure for a few weeks in the refrigerator. You can even tailor mustard to your taste — using fruit juices and special vinegars, sweetening it with honey or maple syrup, or adding flavorings like chopped herbs and spices.

A spoon of mustard is the tie that binds a vinaigrette. Mustard adds zip and cuts the richness in a cheese sandwich. And cured meats like ham or sausages are always better with a dab of mustard.

Nuts

Nuts have a high oil content and can become rancid if not properly stored. Buy nuts in bulk from a busy natural foods store (where products turn over quickly) and use them up quickly. If you find yourself with too many nuts to use up quickly, bag them and freeze them — they won't go rancid like they do at room temperature.

To get the best flavor from nuts, especially if you're using them in salads or as a garnish, toast them first. Spread the nuts in a single layer on a cookie sheet and place in a 375°F (190°C) oven for about 10 minutes. Cool the nuts before using them.

The food processor is a great tool for chopping or grinding nuts. Use on/off pulses until the nuts are chopped to your liking. If the nuts are destined for a cake or other recipe that includes sugar or flour, add a little to the processor to prevent the nuts from turning into a paste. Or make your own nut butters and spreads — whole toasted almonds, puréed in a food processor, melt into beautiful crunchy spreads in just a couple of minutes.

Olive Oil

If you don't believe there's a significant difference between inexpensive olive oil and pricey extra virgin, take the Girl's advice and do a taste test at home.

Go to a supermarket and to a good Italian grocery, and buy three bottles of olive oil. Ask the grocer to recommend an especially tasty oil for salads or dipping. Buy one marked "light olive oil," one marked "virgin olive oil" and one marked "extra virgin olive oil." Then taste them side by side to see the difference.

There are regulations that govern these terms. It has to do with the natural acidity of the oil. The best extra virgin olive oil from the first cold pressing of the fruit has less than 1 per cent acidity, while virgin olive oil is of lesser quality and light olive oil is refined to remove much of the distinctive olive flavor and color (but none of the calories — it's exactly the same amount of fat). Make sure you see the words "cold pressed" on the label of your extra virgin olive oil, an indication of high-quality extraction methods.

Some olive oils are pale in color, some are deep golden and others are brilliant green. Color is not an indication of flavor, so you have to try different brands, from different countries, to see what you like. Good oils are produced in many countries, from Spain and Italy to Greece — find one you like that's in your price range.

Some olive oils are sweet and fruity, others have a distinct peppery flavor. Each works differently with different foods. Find an inexpensive virgin or light olive oil for everyday cooking and frying. Use a neutral-flavored olive oil in baking. Save the more expensive extra virgin olive oils for drizzling over salads and cooked vegetables or grilled fish.

Tasty extra virgin olive oil is also delicious served with good bread for dipping — serve two of your favorites drizzled on plates or shallow bowls to start a meal. It will stimulate both the appetite and the conversation.

Parchment Paper

This nonstick paper is a miracle when you're baking — cookies won't stick and you'll never have to scrub burned bits from your sheet pans. Use it to line baking pans whenever you make cookies or squares (easy release and cleanup), cake pans (ditto) or whenever you're baking chicken or fish. The paper is perfect for cooking lean meats like chicken breasts or fish fillets with vegetables and herbs in packets. They steam and brown at the same time. Just place the meat or fish on a piece of parchment, add the chopped veggies (bell peppers, pea pods, onions, green beans, etc.), a drizzle of olive oil or white wine, some herbs and seasoning, then fold over the paper and fold the edges over to seal, forming a neat square or oval.

Place the packets on a baking sheet and bake at 400°F (200°C) for 10 minutes. The packets will brown and puff up. Cut them open with kitchen shears to let the steamy aromas out — eat right from the paper packets. Very fast and delicious, especially for fish and seafood.

Pasta and Noodles

Good pasta has a nice bite when it's cooked, while bargain pasta can be soft and mushy. Make sure to look for a good semolina-based pasta — usually a brand imported from Italy is best. Whole-wheat or spinach pastas are interchangeable for most dishes, except those with delicate cream sauces. Look for multicolored pastas that are flavored naturally (with beets, spinach, carrots, etc.); they are pretty in cold pasta salads.

Make sure to buy a selection of pastas in different sizes and shapes. Long pastas, like spaghetti and linguine, work best with smooth and creamy sauces. Short pastas, like rotini and penne, are better for chunky sauces, as they grab and hold bits of vegetables, olives and meat. Orzo is a small pasta, shaped like grains of rice, and is good cold, in salads or room-temperature dishes. Small egg noodles (shaped like tiny diamonds) are also a staple in the Girl's kitchen. Dump them into chicken broth for instant chicken soup.

Asian noodles include Japanese soba (which are brown buckwheat-flour noodles, sold tied in bundles of 6–inch/75–cm sticks) or ramen (wheat-based egg noodles, including the deep-fried instant soup noodles), and Chinese noodles (nests of dried egg noodles, wonton noodles or other fresh noodles sold in the produce sections of many supermarkets). The Girl likes to serve the fresh steamed noodles beneath everyday stir-fries, instead of rice, or use them in Asian noodle soups and cold noodle salads. They need less than five minutes of cooking.

Rice noodles are another type of Asian noodle, usually from Thailand or Vietnam. They are translucent white noodles, sold dry or fresh, and used in salad rolls, soups and bowls of bûn. Rice noodles should be rehydrated by soaking for about 15 minutes in a bowl of warm water, then steamed or fried. Mung bean noodles (or cellophane noodles) are similar but are made with bean flour. They also require soaking before cooking.

Pesto

Pesto — purée of fresh herbs and oil — is always useful to have in the refrigerator, to add instant fresh flavor to your soups and sauces. Make your own classic pesto when basil is season and inexpensive (see page 329) or find a commercial brand that you like. Basil pesto is nice to slather over a thin crust pizza (instead of tomato sauce), to stir into chopped fresh tomatoes for bruschetta or to add to sour cream and mayo for a fast dip.

Sundried tomato pesto is another great pantry staple. Slather it on toasts for an appetizer, toss it with noodles for an instant pasta side dish, and mix it into dips and tomato sauces for a hit of tomato flavor.

Coriander chutney is an equally useful condiment (sort of an Indian version of pesto, using ground fresh coriander, a.k.a. cilantro). The Girl always has a jar in the fridge to stir into anything that calls for cilantro, from Mexican salsas to Thai curries.

Potatoes

The Girl is a sucker for almost any spud, but you should choose the right potato for the job. Some potatoes are perfect for mashing as they disintegrate and nearly mash themselves when cooked. Others are waxy in texture and retain their shape perfectly in dishes like potato salad and fried potatoes.

Red-skinned potatoes are usually waxy and best for boiling and roasting, while yellow-fleshed varieties like Yukon Gold have a lovely flavor and color for mashing. Large white potatoes, like Russets, are best for french fries and baked potatoes as they are low in moisture.

Gourmet potatoes add instant cachet to a special meal. Look for tiny yellow fingerling potatoes to boil in their skins and serve alongside grilled meats or fish. Blue potatoes, an heirloom variety from South America, are a deep purplish-blue all the way through, even when cooked, and make deliciously striking navy blue mashed potatoes.

New potatoes, freshly dug, can be scrubbed and boiled in their skins. Many chefs swear by boiling all potatoes in their skins, even potatoes destined for mashing — the skins come off quite easily and the flesh never gets waterlogged, keeping its true potato flavor.

When potatoes are new and skins are thin, try making rustic mashes of roasted garlic, caramelized onions and potatoes in their skins. You don't lose any of the healthy fiber and Vitamin C. Or try this delicious combo — regular potatoes and vivid orange sweet potatoes, mashed together with cooked carrots and/or parsnips, then seasoned with onions and ginger that have been fried until golden in butter. This amazing mash takes potatoes into a brand new realm — and makes a colorful statement on any plate!

Pots and Pans

Don't let the marketers convince you to buy a complete set of matching pots and pans. You'll end up with pans you don't need and will find some important ones are missing. The Girl's workhorse cooking vessels are industrial, heavy, spun aluminum frying pans, with a good non-stick coating. Chefs use small ones to cook individual portions *à la minute* (at the last minute) but you'll do best with a 12–inch (30–cm) model that will hold anything from pancakes to a batch of tomato sauce, and an 8– or 10–inch (20– or 25–cm) pan for crepes and omelets. Make sure they have lids and ovenproof handles (no plastic) so you can finish cooking something you sear on the stove (like a beef tenderloin or a chicken breast) in the oven.

You'll also need a covered Dutch oven, a good heavy wok, one small and one medium covered saucepan, a large, deep stock pot (with a pasta strainer insert), a heavy roasting pan for roasts and turkeys, two heavy rimmed baking sheets, a soufflé dish, a large covered baking dish, a shallow oval baking dish, and an assortment of loaf and cake pans, including a 9–inch (10–cup/2.5 L) springform pan, a square pan, a muffin tin and a tart pan with a removable bottom.

Prep

Cook like a chef. Always read the recipe through before you start and get everything out to make sure you have all the ingredients on hand. When you're cooking for a crowd, it's best to pre-chop, measure and portion ingredients for your recipes (in little bowls, plastic containers or resealable plastic bags) and label them, so you can cook quickly at the last minute when there are other pressures and distractions.

Always preheat the oven before baking or roasting.

Pressure Cookers

If you love to cook stews, soups and things that require long slow cooking (pot roast, beans, etc.) but don't have the time to make them, get a new generation pressure cooker — they are much improved over the pressure cookers our mothers used. These beautiful Italian-, Swiss- and French-made stainless steel pots are safe and super easy to use, and you can have beef stew or lamb korma on the table in half an hour. A blessing for girls who love to braise.

Salad Spinner

This is an important tool for whipping the water out of freshly washed salad greens. If you don't have one, loosely wrap your washed lettuce in a kitchen towel, gather it up like a sack, and go outside into the garden. Whip or whirl the towel around until all of the water is gone. Really, it works.

A salad spinner is also essential for drying fresh herbs, especially leafy ones like cilantro and parsley, after they're washed. Once washed and dried in a spinner, your greens can be kept in the fridge for several days, wrapped loosely in a paper towel to absorb excess moisture and sealed in a plastic bag.

Salt

With designer salts like sel gris, fleur de sel, kosher salt and rock salt vying with everyday table salt on the supermarket shelf, it may seem like there are too many salts in the sea these days. But sea salt is really the only kind to buy. Get rid of any iodized salt (the garden-variety table salt made from mined salts) and replace it with sea salt (made by evaporating sea water). Sea salts from different parts of the world even have different flavors. Some taste of minerals, some are actually sweet.

Kosher salt has large flakes and no additives, and dissolves more easily than regular salt. The hand-harvested sel gris and fleur de sel, gathered off the coasts of France, have a moist consistency. Both are nice for finishing dishes with a garnish of coarse salt.

Keep a small bowl of salt nearby when you're cooking, to add a pinch by hand. Salt should heighten the flavor of whatever you're cooking. If you can taste the salt, you've added too much. To absorb excess salt in a soup or stew, add a whole potato that you can remove later.

Sauté (Or Stir-Fry)

Don't we always say sauté when we really just mean fry? Well, sort of. When you sauté you heat food in a shallow pan (a sauté pan or a frying pan) over fairly high heat, usually with a little butter or olive oil, stirring it around until it's just starting to brown. This step is the basic beginning to every good sauce. Don't skip it.

You can also sauté meat and fish as a searing step, or cook thin, tender cuts like minute steaks, pork medallions or turkey cutlets in the sauté pan. Usually the best way is to season the protein with salt and pepper, dredge it in a little flour (shake, dip, dust), then brown in oil or butter. A mixture of olive oil and butter gives a nice flavor (from the butter) and it won't burn as quickly as butter alone, but olive or canola oil work well on their own.

Stir-frying is basically sautéing in a wok. It's faster, because you use higher heat, and the shape of the wok prevents the food from burning while you constantly move everything around. A traditional wok is round and sits on a wok ring over the burner, but an easier pan to handle at home has a small flattened bottom and a single long handle. You can't get the real flavor of restaurant stir-fries at home unless you have a professional gas stove (with big BTUs). The basic stir-fry drill is to heat the wok and oil on high until very hot; add the onion, ginger and garlic and cook for 20 seconds; add the small pieces of meat and veggies and stir-fry until almost tender; add the sauce ingredients and cover for 1 minute to steam; then thicken with cornstarch solution and serve.

Sesame Oil

Buy this nutty, amber oil at any well-stocked supermarket. Not only is it wonderful in Asian cooking, it makes a lovely addition to salad dressings. Use sesame oil at the end of cooking to flavor a dish like a stir-fry, not as a cooking oil. Refrigerate after opening (the oil will get cloudy and coagulate when cold, but will liquefy again as it warms to room temperature).

Silicon

No, not the valley or the implants — silicon is the latest high tech material in the kitchen. You may have heard of the Silpat, a rubbery looking silicon mat that you can use to line your baking sheets. Nothing sticks to this stuff — you will be making lacy tuile cookies, spectacular caramel decorations to crown your desserts and potato pavés just like the world's greatest chefs, on this miracle mat. A great, great toy.

But there's more. Now they're making spatulas out of silicon. They look just like the old rubber spatulas that are so handy for folding cake and cookie batters but these new units are heat proof, too — you can use them when you're sautéing or stirring stuff in your expensive nonstick cookware.

But the Girl's absolutely favorite silicon stuff is the bakeware. These Indian rubber–red cake pans go into the oven, and can withstand temperatures up to 450°F (230°C). You can literally turn them inside out to clean or to pop out that sticky carrot cake, like an ice cube. The bundt is brilliant — no more cakes that end up stuck in the pan. This is a lot more expensive than the usual metal cake tin, but you will never go back. And there are little tart pan molds for mini quiche, even miniature pyramids to shape little frozen desserts or make perfect tiny terrines and cakes. Girls love silicon!

Soy Sauce

Keep your wits about you in the soy sauce aisle of the grocery store. There are several kinds of soy, and they're not all created equally.

The Girl favors Japanese tamari, a naturally fermented soy sauce with lots of rich, dark flavor. But a light Chinese soy sauce is also handy to have on the counter. It's similar but lighter in color (like a white wine versus a red) and won't add an unwanted darkness to delicate sauces for vegetables or seafood.

Indonesian soy sauce (a.k.a. kecap manis) is a sweetened soy sauce, thick like molasses. If you don't have it, combine dark soy in equal parts with liquid honey or corn syrup.

Springform Pan

These are the round, straight-sided baking pans that come apart into two pieces — a flat bottom and an outer ring that springs open when you flip a latch on the side. This makes it easy to unmold cheesecakes, savory polenta tortes, layered and baked vegetable terrines, even carrot cakes. The Girl loves her nonstick springforms. A 9–inch (23–cm) is standard, but buy a few other sizes. A 10–inch (25–cm) pan is always useful, as is a deep tiny one that fits neatly inside a saucepan (or pressure cooker) to steam puddings or "pressure-bake" moist and tender cheesecakes.

Steamer Basket

This collapsible metal gizmo fits into any saucepan to hold potatoes, green beans, broccoli and other foods above simmering water for steaming. Cheap and useful. If you want to steam a whole fish or a batch of Chinese egg tarts, go to Chinatown and buy a bamboo steamer (looks like a flat basket with a tightly woven domed lid). This fits right into your wok, above steaming water and will hold a red snapper or a plate of steamed buns.

In a pinch, cut the bottom and top off a fish can to elevate any heatproof plate above the water in a wok or covered sauté pan for steaming.

Substitutions and Equivalents

Remember, most recipes are infinitely adaptable so you can be creative. Here are some simple substitutions that will work on most occasions.

1 Tbsp. (15 mL) Dijon = a tsp. (5 mL) dry mustard powder

large flake oats = quick-cooking oats (not instant)

1 cup (250 mL) white sugar = 1 cup (250 mL) brown sugar

ı cup (250 mL) cream cheese = ı cup (250 mL) puréed cottage cheese plus ¼ cup (50 mL) butter (for cheesecakes)

ı Tbsp. (15 mL) Worcestershire sauce = ı Tbsp. (15 mL) soy sauce + a dash of lemon, hot sauce and sugar

hoisin sauce = oyster sauce

ı cup (250 mL) self-rising flour = ı cup (250 mL) all-purpose flour + ı tsp. (5 mL) baking powder and a pinch of salt

ı teaspoon (5 mL) baking powder = ¼ tsp. (1 mL) baking soda + ½ tsp. (2 mL) cream of tartar

ı cup (250 mL) sour cream or buttermilk = ı cup (250 mL) plain yogurt

ı cup (250 mL) tomato sauce = ½ cup (125 mL) tomato paste and ½ cup (125 mL) water

ı Tbsp. (15 mL) chopped fresh herbs = ı tsp. (5 mL) dried herbs (not always a good substitute)

ı lemon = ¼ cup (50 mL) juice and ı Tbsp. (15 mL) grated zest

ı tsp. (5 mL) lemon juice = ½ tsp. (2 mL) vinegar

ı clove garlic = ¼ tsp. (1 mL) garlic powder

Sundried Tomatoes

In danger of becoming an '80s California cliché, sundried tomatoes nonetheless are delicious and great to have in the pantry. Keep a few small jars packed in oil (never discard the flavorful oil, add it to salad dressings) and some dried and ready for rehydrating. The oil-packed dried tomatoes are sweet and chewy, adding instant flavor to dips, salads and pizza. The dried versions can be kept in a dark, dry place for months, then rehydrated in hot water to use like oil-packed tomatoes, or simply crushed to a powder that adds intensive tomato flavor to sauces and dips.

Today's "fresh" alternative is the "oven-roasted tomato" — peeled tomatoes (even canned) that are cut in half, seeded, drizzled with olive oil and fresh herbs, and then roasted on a parchment-lined baking sheet for about 1½ hours in a 300°F (150°C) oven. Chewy, concentrated tomato flavor for soups, sauces and sandwiches. Keep them in the fridge.

Tahini

Tahini is a delicious paste made of ground sesame seeds — like peanut butter with intense sesame flavor.

It's essential for Middle Eastern foods like hummus. Find it in Middle Eastern groceries or most supermarkets. In a pinch, substitute natural peanut butter and a little sesame oil.

Tapenade

This condiment made with finely chopped black olives, olive oil, garlic and herbs is another pantry staple. Not only is tapenade an instant appetizer when smeared on toasts, it can be used on pizza, added to salad dressings and tomato sauces, tossed with pasta — anywhere you'd use olives, tapenade offers an instant jolt of flavor. Buy it in specialty stores or make your own (page 328).

Thaw

Thaw meats and poultry in the refrigerator overnight before cooking, on the bottom shelf, on a plate, so that raw juices don't drip down and contaminate other food. You'll need five hours to thaw every pound (500 g) of food, especially large cuts like roasts and turkeys.

You can use low power (or the defrost cycle) in your microwave to thaw, but you risk cooking the meat on the outside while the inside remains frozen (and then undercooking the final product).

Timing

Timing is everything, as they say, but it's never an exact science when it comes to cooking. You will learn to tell when a cake is done, how the cookies smell when they're ready to come out of the oven, when it's time to take a steak off the grill. There are always other issues that affect timing, too — the thickness of your pan, the calibration of your oven, whether you're cooking on a professional gas or aging electric stove, and if you're grilling in Alaska or Alabama. Even the food itself can have a bearing on its perfect preparation — some beans are older and drier than others and may take an extra hour in the pot, a really fresh cob of corn only needs a few minutes to heat it through. Don't cook by the clock. Taste and try things while you cook. They're done when you say they are.

Tomatoes

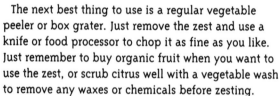

When the Girl says canned tomatoes in a recipe, she means plum or Roma tomatoes, which tend to be meatier, sweeter and less watery than other tomatoes. The best way to pick your favorite brand is to buy one of each, open the cans and taste them. Some canned tomatoes are more acidic than others, some can have a tinny taste. So you want to be brand savvy. You don't have to buy imported tomatoes to get good plum tomatoes — most domestically canned tomatoes are Romas, too. If you have the good fortune to come upon a case of beautiful, ripe plum tomatoes in the fall, buy them and can or freeze the lot. Canning tomatoes is a bit of work but the results are great — get a good canning book and make sure you process them properly so that they're well-sealed and safe. Or simply wash them, dry them, use a paring knife to cut out the cores and pop them whole into zippered plastic bags, then right into the freezer. When you need a tomato or two in the winter for a sauce, just run the rock-hard orbs under hot tap water. The skin will pop off and you can chop your Romas or plunk them directly into the sauce or stew where they'll disintegrate nicely.

In tomato season, search for fresh heirloom tomatoes at the farmers' markets for salads. These heirloom varieties are the old-fashioned flavorful tomatoes that people used to plant before some greedy guy decided it was more economical to ship tomatoes all over the planet and grow the cheap, watery ones that travel well but taste like nothing. Heirloom tomatoes are erratic, eclectic and beautiful. They come in different shapes, sizes and colors: little pear-shaped yellow tomatoes, electric green but sweet zebra tomatoes, tomatoes with black and purple stripes, and amazing-tasting big red beefsteaks. Buy them and try them — so you know what a real tomato is supposed to taste like.

Wasabi

Wasabi is the bright green horseradish paste that you get alongside your sushi at a Japanese restaurant. Buy it at Asian groceries in tubes (like toothpaste) that you can keep in the fridge, or in little tins (a dried wasabi powder that you mix with water). It's great for adding instant authentic flavor to Asian soups, salad dressings and sauces. No wasabi in the house? Substitute a touch of Dijon or hot dry mustard powder to taste for wasabi.

Whisk

A whisk is handy for keeping lumps out of your sauces. Get a medium-sized, fairly stiff version and whisk away.

Zest

This is the colored portion of a citrus fruit, whether it's a lemon, lime, orange or grapefruit. The best way to remove the zest (and not the bitter white pith) is with a zester, a little hand tool with a perforated, triangular metal end that strips the zest off any citrus fruit in long, thin strips. A microplane grater also makes fast work of citrus zest — making the finest, most delicate shreds.

The next best thing to use is a regular vegetable peeler or box grater. Just remove the zest and use a knife or food processor to chop it as fine as you like. Just remember to buy organic fruit when you want to use the zest, or scrub citrus well with a vegetable wash to remove any waxes or chemicals before zesting.

If you've got a lot of citrus zest, dry and pulverize it into a citrus "dust" to sprinkle over almost anything. Grated citrus zest may also be frozen.

Index

About the Author

After 20 years in the journalism trenches Cinda Chavich is sure of one thing — you can't beat the food and wine beat.

Writing about food is about more than regurgitating recipes or recommending a nice bottle to buy. It's about helping families and friends enjoy the communal experience of creating and sharing a wonderful meal together. It's about telling stories — stories about passionate people and unique places, culture and history, environmental and health issues related to food. And it's one of the warmest spots in the reporting world — because people who love food and wine, love life.

Cinda makes her living as a food and wine journalist, traveling the world and poking into kitchens wherever she goes. Every adventure is a new inspiration, a new chance to explore a regional cuisine, a unique ingredient, a particular chef or winemaker's passion. Dining with an extended family in the mountains of southern Greece, slurping spicy hot pots in Sichuan, following the southern barbecue trail in North Carolina or exploring the plight of the wild Pacific salmon, are topics that have taken Cinda around the globe.

Her food, wine and travel stories have appeared in newspapers and magazines across North America — from the *Globe and Mail* and *CBC Radio* to *Cooking Light, Wine Access, Health, Avenue, Wine Spectator* and *Chatelaine*. She has written several cookbooks — *High Plains*, which focuses on the regional cuisine from her home on the Canadian prairies, won two gold medals from Cuisine Canada, including the top Canadian Food and Culture Award.

Cinda loves to share food in her own home and created The Girl to speak to those who love good food, but haven't had the chances she has had to learn about this fascinating topic from the experts. After years of writing, traveling, creating recipes, food styling, broadcasting and hanging around in the world's best kitchens, she's developed a cooking style that's easy but eclectic, and filled with the tricks that the best cooks use to make fabulous food.

Her husband Delbert is one happy beneficiary of this cumulative knowledge. They spend quality time together hiking, cycling and relaxing at their cabin — and eating well!

About the Illustrator

Kirsten Horel is an illustrator and lettering artist. She uses her friendly art to help others decipher the world, working from her home studio, a small cozy room full of energy and treasures. The Girl started on her drawing board and then jumped into her computer for fine tuning. Kirsten spends more time making art than food, so her next challenge is to get The Girl to jump out of the computer and make some real meals! Kirsten lives with her husband and kids in Calgary, Alberta, and says to all her friends "OK, time to start cookin'!"